PARTIES, ELECTIONS,
and the FUTURE of
CANADIAN POLITICS

Y9

PARTIES, ELECTIONS,
and the FUTURE of
CANADIAN POLITICS

Edited by
Amanda Bittner and Royce Koop

UBCPress · Vancouver · Toronto

21 20 19 18 17 16 15 14 13   5 4 3 2 1

Printed in Canada on FSC-certified ancient-forest-free paper
(100% post-consumer recycled) that is processed chlorine- and acid-free.

Library and Archives Canada Cataloguing in Publication

  Parties, elections, and the future of Canadian politics / edited by Amanda
Bittner and Royce Koop.

Includes bibliographical references and index.
Also issued in electronic format.
ISBN 978-0-7748-2408-8 (bound); 978-0-7748-2409-5 (pbk.)

  1. Canada – Politics and government – 1993-2006. 2. Canada – Politics
and government – 2006-. 3. Political parties – Canada. 4. Elections – Canada.
I. Bittner, Amanda II. Koop, Royce, 1978-

FC635.P37 2013   971.064'8   C2012-906793-8

Canada

UBC Press gratefully acknowledges the financial support for our publishing program
of the Government of Canada (through the Canada Book Fund), the Canada Council
for the Arts, and the British Columbia Arts Council.

This book has been published with the help of a grant from the Canadian Federation
for the Humanities and Social Sciences, through the Awards to Scholarly Publications
Program, using funds provided by the Social Sciences and Humanities Research
Council of Canada.

UBC Press
The University of British Columbia
2029 West Mall
Vancouver, BC V6T 1Z2
www.ubcpress.ca

To all of our mentors
at the University of British Columbia.

Thank you.

Contents

Illustrations

Tables

Acknowledgments

This volume was conceived during Royce Koop's postdoctoral fellowship in the Department of Political Science at Memorial University of Newfoundland in 2010-11. The two of us had a number of conversations over the course of that year about parties and elections (both inside and outside of Canada), and early on we noted that there had not yet been a consolidated effort to unpack the tumultuous last two decades of electoral politics in Canada. Given our training at the University of British Columbia, where we had been doctoral students together, and the fact that our supervisors are the foremost experts in Canada on political parties (R. Kenneth Carty supervised Koop) and elections (Richard Johnston supervised Bittner), we thought it fitting to bring together scholars from these different subfields to talk about contemporary Canadian parties and elections in order to figure out what was going on.

The result of this planning was a Social Sciences and Humanities Research Council (SSHRC)–funded workshop at Memorial University in October 2010, focusing on parties, voters, and elections in Canada. Over two days, papers were presented by André Blais, Kelly Blidook, Ken Carty, Greg Clarke, Bill Cross, Munroe Eagles, Elizabeth Goodyear-Grant, Allison Harell, Harold Jansen, Chris Kam, Matthew Kerby, Georgia Kernell, Lisa Lambert, Peter Loewen, Alex Marland, Scott Matthews, Russell Williams,

Steven Wolinetz, and Lisa Young. Most travelled very long distances to be there, and we are grateful for the contributions of all the participants, which led to very lively and detailed discussions about the state of Canadian parties and elections and, ultimately, to this book. We have since discovered that editing a book is not easier than writing one, and we are very grateful to all our contributors for making this process as painless and enjoyable as it was. It has been a real pleasure working with you all, and your willingness to accommodate our editorial demands, revisions, and timelines is greatly appreciated.

Both of us have been supported throughout the process of compiling this book by our respective departments. Bittner thanks the Department of Political Science at Memorial University, while Koop is grateful to the Departments of Political Science at Memorial University and Political Studies at Queen's University and to the School of Public Policy at Simon Fraser University. We would also like to thank our excellent research assistants for their help with this project, including Susan Piercey, Xaiver Campbell, Shawn Kavanagh, and Erika Kirkpatrick.

The development and production of this book were made possible by considerable financial support. The book has been published with the help of a grant from the Canadian Federation for the Humanities and Social Sciences, through the Awards to Scholarly Publications Program, using funds provided by the Social Sciences and Humanities Research Council of Canada. In addition, we received funding support in the form of a scholarly workshops grant from SSHRC; workshop funding support from the Faculty of Arts and the Office of the President and Vice-Presidents (both Academic and Research) at Memorial University; funding from the Canadian Opinion Research Archive; and a book subvention grant from Memorial University. Koop acknowledges funding in the form of two post-doctoral fellowships, one from the Faculty of Arts at Memorial University and one from the Skelton-Clark Foundation at Queen's University. Needless to say, we are grateful for this financial support and could not have produced this volume without it.

We are also indebted to Emily Andrew at UBC Press for her enthusiasm for our ideas and for expertly shepherding this project from proposal to book manuscript. We would also like to acknowledge the excellent comments and suggestions from our anonymous reviewers and the Editorial Board at UBC Press, who made very thoughtful observations and recommendations and undoubtedly helped to make this book stronger.

Finally, we would like to thank Richard Johnston and R. Kenneth Carty. Thank you for giving us a solid foundation in and understanding of Canadian party and electoral politics, for helping us to ask and answer interesting questions, and for giving us the confidence to "go out into the world" unsupervised. We are so fortunate to count you as mentors and colleagues.

PARTIES, ELECTIONS, and the FUTURE of CANADIAN POLITICS

Introduction

Change and Continuity in Canadian Parties and Elections

AMANDA BITTNER AND ROYCE KOOP

Brian Mulroney's Progressive Conservative Party won a huge majority in the House of Commons in the 1988 national election, partly as a result of his "grand compromise" between the West and Quebec after the failure of the Meech Lake Accord. A few years later, following the multipurpose Charlottetown Accord and a failed referendum, Mulroney quit, leaving his successor, Kim Campbell, with a damaged party, a damaged nation, and a big job ahead of her. Canadians sent a message in the 1993 election: the party was devastated at the polls and its share of parliamentary seats fell from 169 in 1988 to 2 in 1993. The intraparty cooperation and compromise necessary to secure widespread support across Canada have not resurfaced since that election – Jean Chrétien's long period in power masked serious and enduring divisions within the Liberal Party itself – and, despite the fall of the Bloc Québécois in the 2011 federal election, seem unlikely to return anytime soon.

If we look back on the last eighteen years and seven elections in Canadian federal politics, on the surface it appears that a great deal has changed. The sovereigntist Bloc Québécois was a strong and solid presence in the House of Commons from 1993 until the 2011 election, even playing the role of Official Opposition for a single term. We have also seen the emergence and reshaping of a new party from the West, as Preston Manning's Reform Party first broke into the House in 1993 and then morphed into the Canadian Alliance in an effort to appeal to Canadians across the country.

We have also seen the demise of the Progressive Conservative Party as we knew it, followed by its merger with the Canadian Alliance to form the new Conservative Party of Canada in 2004. During this period, the Canadian public was governed by a succession of Liberal majority governments in the 1990s, followed by a string of minority governments (one Liberal followed by three Conservative) beginning with the 2004 election. The recent 2011 election has solidified Canada's transition to something different, with the formation of Stephen Harper's first Conservative majority government.

Although it may appear to the naked eye as though much has changed in Canadian politics, we do not really know whether this is in fact the case, since to date there has been no explicit, synthesized, in-depth analysis of the state of the Canadian political system dedicated to understanding the dynamics of electoral and party system evolution over the last two decades. Has there really been change in the nature of (1) party organizations, (2) party behaviour in the House of Commons, (3) voters' perceptions of national parties, (4) the institutions that shape the structures of parties and the actions of voters, and (5) patterns of competition – party systems – at the national level? This collection of essays provides an account of Canadian politics during this period, with contributors examining issues related to these different but interdependent aspects of national electoral politics.

A number of themes emerge throughout this volume, all related to what we nominally dub "continuity and change" in Canadian parties and elections. Longitudinal accounts of Canadian politics – such as those of Carty (1992), Johnston (1992), and Smith (1992) – have always grappled with issues of both continuity and change. Indeed, it is difficult to find examples of wholesale change in Canadian politics without also turning up corresponding signs of continuity. New parties have emerged, but the old parties have endured; the Canadian electorate has changed over the course of the twentieth century, but the single-member plurality system that translates the wishes of that electorate into representation has stayed the same; national campaigns have embraced new communication technologies such as television and the Internet to communicate with voters, but candidates in the ridings continue to campaign by shaking hands and kissing babies in much the same way as candidates running under the banners of Macdonald and Laurier did. By examining parties, voters, and the institutions within which these actors function, we are able to discern more clearly the dynamics of party politics over the last two decades: twenty years of both continuity and change.

The following sections briefly introduce and discuss the indicators of continuity and change that structure the presentation of chapters in this book, after which we briefly speculate on the future of Canadian politics in light of these contributions. This foreshadows our concluding chapter, which discusses the development of the Canadian party system in light of the results of the 2011 national election.

Parties in the Legislature

Mulroney's large Conservative majorities in the House of Commons in the 1980s were followed by a decade of strong Liberal majorities (although without quite the same level of voter support). These were followed by nearly a decade of successive minority governments, Liberal and then Conservative, until the 2011 election returned Canada to Conservative majority governance. Changes in the seating plan of the House of Commons aside, there are reasons to expect that differences in governments and the distribution of seats might have an impact on the nature of legislative activity. Indeed, as some of the essays in this book demonstrate, politics in Parliament in the last decade have been quite different from politics in years past. Some suggest that only small changes have taken place, whereas others point to fundamental differences in the ways that members of Parliament behave in the House of Commons. In Chapter 5, for example, Anthony Sayers observes that cabinet membership has, over time, come to favour urban areas. His story of change is one in which the distribution of leadership roles in the country has shifted in such a way that rural ridings are less likely to see one of their representatives sit at the decision-making table. This marks an important shift in the nature of representation in the House of Commons and reflects the urbanization of Canadian society over the course of the twentieth century.

In contrast, Chapter 6 paints a picture of both continuity and change. Elizabeth Goodyear-Grant argues that we have seen continuity in terms of women's presence as actual officeholders (the House of Commons has consisted of about 20 percent women for the past few decades) but that some change has taken place in relation to the parties' focus on women as voters. She points to more regressive policies directed towards women (but suggests that these changes are the result of a change in government rather than a change to the party system) and notes that recent electoral campaigns have been targeted more directly at women. Goodyear-Grant suggests that this is the result of increased electoral competition and constant election campaigning, a story similar to that told in Chapter 3 by Kelly Blidook and Matthew Byrne.

Minority governments, which both Canada's parties and its citizens endured from 2004 to 2011, operate differently from majority governments, regardless of the party at the helm. The instability associated with minority governments means that the ways that parties "work," both inside and outside of Parliament, change. Evidence suggests that minority governments lead parties to become more adversarial, as the scorekeeping required when they are "constantly campaigning" becomes more intense. This conflicts with notions of increased interparty cooperation that might be expected when clear majority governments do not form. Chapter 3 demonstrates that adversarialism in the House of Commons increased substantially as a result of the shift from majority to minority governments.

The risk of government defeat in minority parliaments is also likely to influence the policy positions articulated by MPs. Blidook and Byrne note that the tone of MPs' statements has changed over time and attribute this in part to the occurrence of minority parliaments. Chapter 4 supports this observation, as Munroe Eagles finds that MPs' policy positions are linked to the characteristics of their constituents. He suggests that MPs are concerned with presenting themselves as sensitive to the preferences of voters and will demonstrate responsiveness to constituents when provided with opportunities to do so. Minority governments and the frequent elections associated with them provide legislators with incentives to consistently demonstrate that they act on behalf of their constituents, in order to develop a local personal vote that will aid in their re-election.

We might have expected that the change in the nature and origins of the Conservative Party of Canada, combined with the regional strengths of the other national parties, would have caused policies and politics to become more regionalized since the 1980s. Chapter 8 suggests, however, that there is very little evidence to support this notion. Although policies emerging from Parliament may have become more conservative over the last three elections, especially in relation to gender, Blake Andrew, Patrick Fournier, and Stuart Soroka find no indication of an increase in the regionalization of politics as expressed through media coverage over the last twenty years. Similarly, William Cross and Lisa Young suggest in Chapter 2 that the methods used to select candidates have also exhibited continuity. They demonstrate that observations made in the early 1990s (e.g., Erickson 1993) about the role of political parties in recruiting candidates still hold: most candidates are recruited by either the local or national party organizations.

Cross and Young's findings about party recruitment of women and ethnic minorities are particularly interesting when placed alongside discussions of parties' appeals to both women and ethnic voters. Goodyear-Grant demonstrates that the parties changed their approaches over the course of the last two decades, especially in the elections punctuating Harper's Conservative minority governments. She points to the parties' targeted campaigns, including the Conservative approach of classifying women as "Zoe" and "Sheila" and aiming messages accordingly, as well as the Liberal Party's "pink book," developed prior to the 2008 election.

Parties in the Minds of Voters

While targeted appeals to specific groups of voters are not a new phenomenon, neither is the notion that certain groups will be more supportive of some parties than others. Indeed, it appears that although there may be substantial change in the ways that the parties have behaved in the House of Commons over the last two decades, not much has changed in the minds of voters. Three chapters very clearly make the case for continuity in voting behaviour: Allison Harell's discussion of the ethnic bases of party support (Chapter 7); Scott Matthews's assessment of how voters deal with partisan attacks (Chapter 11); and Amanda Bittner's evaluation of voters' abilities to engage with and process changes to the political landscape (Chapter 12).

For decades, the Liberal Party has benefited from the support of voters of non-European backgrounds. In response to observations in the popular news media about a shift in the support of ethnic minorities from the Liberals to the Conservatives, Harell examines the ethnic bases of support for parties at the federal level. She finds that the traditional linkages between voters of non-European ethnic background and the Liberal Party remain strong, which suggests strong continuity in the bases of party support despite the Liberals' lack of success in recent years. Although Harell's story is one of continuity, this may in fact be transformed into an account of change in light of the results of the 2011 national election.

The picture painted by Matthews is similar, in that he points to continuity from the point of view of voters. His findings suggest that partisans behave in the same way that they perhaps always have. We might expect the partisan bases of party support to have changed over the years, given changes in the menu of options available at the federal level. Furthermore, combining party system change with the increased adversarialism observed in the House of Commons during the recent string of minority parliaments, we might expect the commitment of partisans to their parties to wane when their parties are attacked. Increased negative evaluation of parties does not, however, appear to be linked with capitulation on the part of partisans. When their party is attacked, Canadian partisans will defend it fiercely, regardless of the level of negativity expressed towards the party in the legislature. Canadian politics in recent years has clearly not been for the faint of heart.

Since 1993, we have seen the demise of one of Confederation's founding political parties, the emergence of new (competitive) parties, and a series of minority governments. The notion that voters are not responding to those changes seems, on the surface, to be absurd. In Chapter 12, Bittner suggests that voters have difficulty coping with electoral flux. When parties and leaders change from election to election and a brand new menu of options appears on the scene, there is an associated impact on voters' ability to navigate through election campaigns. Changes in the party system make it difficult for voters to cope; the more stable things are and the more they know how they feel about leaders and parties, the better they are able to translate their evaluations into choices. Bittner suggests that new parties are at a disadvantage for being new: new parties and new leaders are penalized because voters are not familiar with them. This is not a function of changes in the party system: voters have not become less able to cope with change in recent years but have had this difficulty at least since Mulroney's second win in 1988.

Continuity also emerges as a theme in the media coverage of election campaigns in this period. Comparing the contemporary era to the 1980s shows that although new parties and new leaders emerged and received media attention in the 1990s, the system has stabilized once again to reflect earlier patterns of news coverage. Andrew, Fournier, and Soroka find that the emergence of new parties has not led to increased regionalization or ideological polarization, at least not in terms of media coverage (Chapter 8). They suggest that the rise and fall of Liberal and Conservative coverage reflects the parties' positions in government at the national level rather than regional patterns.

Parties Playing by the Rules of the Game

No discussion of Canadian electoral politics is complete without an assessment of the political institutions that structure how parties organize and compete with one another. For the most part, these institutions have remained stable over time. Despite many efforts at reform, single-member plurality continues to be the electoral system in place. Important institutional changes occurred and were again discussed in the 1980s and early 1990s, but changes in succeeding years were minuscule by comparison.

Nevertheless, small changes did take place, concerning the redistribution of seats in the House of Commons, boundary rules, and party financing laws. These changes were not inconsequential and may have fundamentally altered the nature of party competition for the future. In Chapter 10, Harold Jansen and Lisa Lambert examine the impact of changes to party financing laws, and tell a story of change as a result of institutional reforms. Based on their assessment of the decisions made by the Green Party over the last half-decade, they suggest that financing laws have had particularly important implications for new and emerging party organizations. They recognize, however, that the future remains unknown. The Green Party may be a lasting feature of the Canadian landscape, or it may be a reflection of recent short-term flux before the system heads towards a new period of continuity. Although the party secured a seat for its leader, Elizabeth May, in the 2011 election, its future remains unclear.

Uncertainty is a theme in this volume, as the status of a number of the features of the political landscape that have emerged over the last two decades is not entirely clear. In fact, some of this uncertainty may be the direct result of institutional reforms. Williams, for example, looks at the impact of changes to the political map through redistribution and boundary rules implemented in 1985 (Chapter 9). He suggests that the way electoral boundaries are drawn has contributed substantially to the string of minority governments in the first decade of the twenty-first century. He argues that the absence of a majority government made changes to electoral laws nearly impossible because of the way that apportionment has been politicized. Indeed, his earlier (pre-2011) predictions were confirmed when the election of a Conservative majority government led to the introduction of a new system of redistribution, with the passage of Bill C-20 in the House of Commons in December 2011.

Party Systems
Have things really changed in Canada, as pundits would have us believe? The most important way that Canadian politics might have changed is in the nature of the national party system. In Chapter 1, Kenneth Carty examines changes to Canadian electoral politics and argues that we are facing a major change in how we conceive of the federal parties. In particular, he suggests that the way that we think about the Liberal Party

must be fundamentally altered. No longer can it claim to be Canada's brokerage party, a party of the centre that seeks to appeal to voters of all stripes across all of Canada's regions. As a result, he suggests, the nature of party competition and organization has shifted, which has important implications for the future of Canadian party politics.

Although Richard Johnston, too, indicates the uncertain future of the Liberal Party, he also points out that flux is a recurrent theme in Canadian electoral politics (Chapter 13). He suggests that Canada stands out from other Westminster systems in terms of its electoral volatility, the number of parties competing in the system and sitting in the legislature, and the trajectory of changes to the system. In particular, he notes that when major electoral shifts take place in Canada, things often return back to "normal," in contrast to electoral earthquakes in other democracies, where permanent realignment is likely to result instead. One might argue, therefore, that the last twenty years have represented one of these periods, revolving around the fortunes of the Conservative Party (as Canada's electoral flux often does), and that a return to "normal" will take place in the near future. The question is whether the election of a Conservative majority government in the 2011 election is in fact the "new normal" in the Canadian party system. Only time will tell.

How Will Canada's Electoral Landscape Look in the Future?

Those of us who study parties and elections are usually loath to make predictions, and the 2011 Canadian election is a perfect example of why this is so. Going into the election, many thought that it was "business as usual": an election for an election's sake, and likely to lead to either another Conservative minority or perhaps a Conservative majority, depending on how Canadians felt about the parties. Instead, and nearly coinciding with the leaders' debates, polling numbers revealed a massive shift in party support, particularly a massive shift in support for the New Democratic Party.

To most Canadians, the 2011 election introduced enormous, unexpected changes. We think it quite possible, however, that 2011 really capped off a period of "electoral deviation" in which the parties struggled with non-traditional competitors and institutional changes that worked against the establishment of a stable pattern of competition of the sort that characterized Canadian politics prior to the 2004 national election. This book is about how parties and voters struggled to adapt to new challenges in the last two decades, and how their responses to these challenges ultimately led to the return of a national majority government in 2011. In some cases, these actors responded by adapting and changing; in other cases, they remained the same. The rest of this book charts both change and continuity throughout this period, and concludes with some reflections on the nature of the Canadian national party system during these years and what might lie in store for post-2011 Canada.

References
Carty, R.K. 1992. "Three Canadian Party Systems." In *Canadian Political Party Systems: A Reader,* edited by R.K. Carty, 563-86. Toronto: Broadview Press.

Erickson, Lynda. 1993. "Making Her Way In: Women, Parties, and Candidacies in Canada." In *Gender and Party Politics,* edited by Joni Lovenduski and Pippa Norris, 60-85. London: Sage Publications.

Johnston, Richard. 1992. "Political Generations and Electoral Change in Canada." *British Journal of Political Science* 22: 93-115.

Smith, David E. 1992. "Party Government in Canada." In *Canadian Political Party Systems: A Reader,* edited by R.K. Carty, 531-62. Toronto: Broadview Press.

1

Has Brokerage Politics Ended?

Canadian Parties in the New Century

R. KENNETH CARTY

"Canadian politics is brokerage politics." This claim is central to most accounts of the distinctive organizational and competitive dynamics of national party politics in Canada. It reflects a perception that the country's dominant political elites are forced to adopt unique mechanisms of sociopolitical brokerage in order to build winning coalitions capable of defining and defending a national interest. In his classic account, John Meisel (1963) argues that this stems from a fundamental incoherence in the body politic. He suggests that, in the absence of an "underlying social cohesion" and a "secular political culture," politicians are forced to act as accommodating brokers, continually reconciling the country's internal tensions.

In this interpretation, political parties are identified as the principal tools of these brokerage politicians. Meisel goes further and suggests that because they "are among the relatively few genuinely national forces in Canada," it is inevitable that "the chief and most important latent functions of the political parties and the party system are to foster and develop a sense of national unity and national being" (Meisel 1963, 370). Thus, the brokerage theory of Canadian politics is essentially an argument about the distinctive character of the Canadian party system, particularly about Canadian parties as *brokerage parties*.

Of course, the notions that successful democratic politicians need to be brokers and that their principal tools are political parties is hardly distinctively Canadian. Lowell (1913, 64) long ago pointed out that "if politicians are largely brokers, party is the chief instrument by which they work." Our question is whether Canada's so-called brokerage parties are a unique form of party organization, practising a distinctive kind of politics, or whether they are simply particular local manifestations of more general imperatives of party building.

The argument that brokerage parties are a distinctive form of political party is rooted in a conception that their approach to organization and competition is fundamentally different from that practised by other kinds of parties. In most democratic systems, the principal function of political parties is to articulate the distinctive interests of classes and of religious, ethnic, or other social groups, and to organize electoral competition designed to reflect the inherent conflicts among them. Thus "normal" institutionalized party systems mirror, but also perpetuate, the salience of particular lines of social cleavage and so provide a democratic mechanism for reconciling differences and balancing interests. Brokerage parties are held to turn this natural relationship on its head. Rather than articulating and defending the particular interests of distinctive constituencies, such parties are driven to obscure differences and to muffle conflicting interests in the name of social accommodation and the promotion of national community.

As consensus-seeking organizations, brokerage parties are characterized as determined to eschew ideological agendas and programmatic politics, embrace shifting and heterogeneous support bases, and establish often parochially structured organizations dominated by leaders ready to shift position in the interest of maximizing electoral support (cf. LeDuc et al. 2010, 33, 529). This portrait suggests that the brokerage party may be essentially just a version of the European catch-all party, whose theoretical and empirical physiology and development are well known to students of political parties. If, on the other hand, brokerage parties are unique organizational entities that differ in significant ways from catch-all parties, it is important to specify the differences in order to understand their consequences for the operation of a country's political life.

This leads first to a consideration of the recognizable characteristics of catch-all parties and then to an assessment of how brokerage parties do, or do not, differ. That will then allow us to apply the respective party models to Canadian experience in an analysis of the working of its party organizations and their competitive practices. At issue is the extent to which Meisel's conception of Canadian politics as brokerage politics holds true of the new party system emerging in the early decades of the twenty-first century.[1]

The Catch-All Party

Modern catch-all parties are portrayed as large, heterogeneous organizations engaged in a catholic, vote-seeking, pragmatic electoral competition that revolves around media-centred party leaders. These are organizations in which ideology has been deliberately abandoned in an attempt to operate as political consensus purveyors, and which do not offer ordinary members much opportunity to play a significant role in their affairs. Kirchheimer's classic analysis (1966) of catch-all parties recognizes their emergence in a number of competitive party systems of postwar Europe, and it is easy to identify many of the features he identifies as intrinsic to the character and behaviour of parties in most established party systems. This enables us to enumerate several essential features of catch-all parties and their politics.[2]

1 Despite the implications of the catch-all label, Kirchheimer is clear that such parties "cannot hope to catch all categories of voters," although they may reasonably expect to increase their support among voters "whose interests do not adamantly conflict" (186). This is because the inherent social cleavages of a political community put natural limits on the reach of any one party and its ability to make political bedfellows of those whose interests are intrinsically opposed. He illustrates this proposition by noting the inability of parties such as the German Social Democrats or British Labour to accommodate groups like agriculturalists, given those parties' history and natural base in urban populations. The important point to note is that the catch-all label is misleading: such parties do not even try to appeal to *all* voters.

2 Catch-all parties were not created *de novo*, as the mass parties had been by previous generations. Kirchheimer's analysis indicates that they evolved through a competitive dynamic as large parties sought to outdo their opponents in finding "a wider audience and more immediate electoral success" (184). Two aspects of that process command our attention. The first is that, having started with a clearly defined base, the catch-all party is never able to completely escape from its demands and the core support it provides. It is precisely this developmental history accounting for a party's structure and practice in the face of the continuing reality of politicized social divisions that inhibits the catch-all party from appealing to all members of the electorate.[3] Second, the competitive dynamic that drives the emergence of catch-all party competition suggests that a single catch-all party is unlikely to emerge on its own (188). This means that such parties exist in opposition to others of the same kind.

Thus, in Britain, both Labour and the Conservatives emerged as catch-all parties because of, and in response to, each other's presence and activity. With at least two major competitors, catch-all party systems ought not to be controlled by a single dominant party.

3 Kirchheimer is at some pains to discuss the contradictions visited upon the catch-all party, particularly with respect to the exercise of a party's traditional "expressive function," which he argues is left in "an ambiguous state" (189) with those parties' deliberate "de-ideologization" of political discourse (187). Transformed from an organization with a "vision of things to come" into a mere "vehicle for short-run choice" (195), the competitive catch-all party, with both ambitions to office and occasional responsibility for it, is forced to restrain its critical appeals as it seeks to broaden its electoral base.

4 In the traditional (cadre or mass) parties out of which catch-all institutions emerged, party loyalty was a central dimension of political life. It reflected the place that supporters naturally had in the wider political system and was a bulwark against the erosion of the party's organization. In Kirchheimer's catch-all organization, however, the attenuation of social roots that defines "the very character of the party makes membership loyalty far more difficult to expect" (193). As a consequence, the party is forced to depend on the technocrats of modern public relations to manage its electoral campaigns.[4]

5 Finally, catch-all orientations to political life involve more than a distinctive accommodative style, for, as Kirchheimer notes, these parties also transform both the role of leader and ordinary member in the life of the organization. (This is another version of Michels's 1915 observations about the natural oligarchic tendencies in large membership organizations like political parties.) The position of party leader in a catch-all party has heightened importance because that individual has the principal responsibility for first establishing and then carrying the party's electoral message. To do so successfully, leaders must be freed from "specific direction and supervision" (198). This leaves ordinary party members stripped of any significant ability to shape the agenda and direction of the party, a power Kirchheimer describes as "a historical relic" (190).

Taken together, these central features of a modern catch-all party would appear to constitute the key organizational ingredients required by democratic socio-political brokers. A consideration of each of them suggests, however, that a very different constellation comprises an organizational form more recognizable as a brokerage party.

The Brokerage Party

Whereas catch-all parties accept that it is unrealistic to assume they can win support from all groups and classes of voters, the raison d'être of the brokerage party is to do just that. It aims to reconcile, or at least accommodate, the full range of different perspectives and interests within the same single organization. Thus, in a fundamentally important way, the brokerage party, particularly one asserting a nation-building mission, claims to do precisely what the catch-all party cannot – that is, catch support from *all* categories of voters. This does not necessarily mean that it wants to catch all voters, for it may well be politically dysfunctional (i.e., electorally unstable) to build a party that catches too many.

Brokerage parties are not the product of an evolutionary dynamic in which mass-integration or bourgeois-cadre parties are transformed into catch-all organizations. Unlike the catch-all party, the brokerage party is not the product of a competitive evolutionary process. Such parties are the deliberate and independent creations of political leaders who wish to establish an autonomous organizational base. This frees these parties from historical structural linkages and allows them to act as a distinctive instrument of accommodation, reconciling the divergent interests and demands of a pluralistic electorate.

Brokerage parties are not restrained by a haunting ambivalence as to the limits of their expressive appeals. Indeed, quite the opposite is the case. Operating as an instrument of multi-interest accommodation, a brokerage party uses an exaggerated form of a party's normal expressive function – representing itself as the natural, national governing party – as one of its principal means of mobilizing support.

While the internal dynamics generated by the attenuation of traditional social roots means that party loyalty is not a critical feature of the catch-all party's organizational glue, the same cannot be said for brokerage parties. Indeed, in the absence of any social basis for membership, unquestioning organizational loyalty is the supreme virtue in brokerage parties. This requires that members commit to the party and accept its discipline whatever policy twists are required by the demands of electoral pragmatism.

The brokerage party's orientation to political competition engenders distinctive internal organizational relationships. While it is true that leaders

TABLE 1.1
Key differences between catch-all and brokerage parties

Characteristic	Catch-all parties	Brokerage parties
Target	Constrained by historic core	Entire electorate
Origins	Competition with other catch-all opponents	Created as original political instruments
Expressive function	Restrained to balance appeals to old supporters and new targets	Central message as articulation of national interest
Loyalty	Limited expectation	Supreme virtue
Leaders	Personification of message	Creator of message
Members	No significant role	Active participants

enjoy enhanced positions in virtually all modern political parties, a leader's place and authority in the brokerage party is unique. The leader is more than the public personification of the party message; the leader is the chief broker, the individual who determines both the style and content of the accommodative package the party represents. Responsible for creating the message, brokerage leaders are not especially constrained by past policies or any natural limits on the party's reach. This generates its own uncertainty for it means that the very thrust and direction of a brokerage party can be instantly changed by the simple process of changing the leader.

Determined to appeal to and represent all elements of society, the brokerage party accommodates them by enhancing the role that members of the party (the grassroots) play in internal party decision making (Mair 1994). This typically provides ordinary members significant power over personnel decisions, especially leadership selections and candidate nominations, but not over policy questions that would constrain the ability of party leaders to broker competing interests. Inevitably, intraparty competition may be a source of factionalism as elites and local activists seek to enrich their position at the expense of others. In such parties, ordinary members are the storm troops of vigorous intraparty democratic competition.

This brief comparison helps distinguish brokerage parties from otherwise apparently similar (in the sense of being non-ideological, electorally focused) catch-all parties. The key differences are summarized in Table 1.1.

The Politics of the Brokerage Party

As a unique party form, brokerage party organizations practise their own distinctive style of politics; they also shape the political dynamics of the party systems they inhabit.

Claiming the ability, and indeed defining their raison d'être as the accommodation of all significant interests in the political community, brokerage parties make electoral success and holding public office their central purpose and standard of success. Consequently, they are governed by no single principle but are the very embodiment of electoral pragmatism. Openness to shifts in policy and fluidity in their mobilization strategies force brokerage parties to depend on institutional loyalty as the primary organizational glue holding them together.

The need for creative responses to the electoral imperatives of the day gives the leader of a brokerage party a special position and responsibility. Unfettered by ideology or past commitments, the leader has comparatively greater latitude than leaders in other types of parties to set the direction and pace of the party. Indeed, the only effective check on this power is a direct attack on his or her leadership itself. The result is strong, but inherently fragile, leadership that is the ultimate focus of all intraparty division and conflict.

A party structure of this sort, supported by organizational practice and depending on electoral success rather than any social or ideological coherence, is bound to generate intraparty discord and competition. Some elements of the electorate that are being embraced within its bounds will inevitably prefer different means or divergent ends than others. The classic hierarchical structures of centralized mass parties are too inflexible to provide effective organizations. Thus brokerage parties thrive using a stratarchical structure that allows for the flexible incorporation of the wide range of supporters' and members' preferences and activities (Eldersveld 1964). This makes the "franchise" model the preferred organizational form. It is one that increases the opportunities for intraparty democracy, although at the cost of blurring organizational boundaries and increased internal competition articulated by personal factions (Carty 2004, 2013a).

This theoretical equilibrium of stratarchical form and brokerage function raises the question of whether function drives form or form shapes function. In any given case, this may well be a matter of the origins of the party (and party system) in question. It does suggest, however, that parties that seek to practise brokerage are not likely to be successful if they adopt a

tightly centralized organization, and that catch-all parties may be less efficient if they emulate the stratarchical forms of a brokerage competitor.

Presenting themselves as the system's "natural governing party" leaves
brokerage parties with a deep antipathy to coalition politics, for to accept
the principle or practice of coalition government would be to deny their
central identity. Thus brokerage parties would prefer to form a minority
government than enter a coalition with other political parties.

Successful brokerage parties have an insidious impact on the dynamics
of democratic party competition, for when one establishes itself as capable
of genuinely embracing the full range of interests in society, it leaves little
room for the emergence of similar competitors. Thus a party system is likely to have room for only one brokerage party at any time. Other parties are
left to adopt other representational strategies: some may adopt catch-all
forms, others may reject that approach and articulate more narrowly defined interests. This imbalance advantages the brokerage party and can
provide the structural basis for the party's long-term dominance of the
system.[5]

Recognizing dominant parties such as Ireland's Fianna Fáil, Japan's
Liberal Democrats, or India's Congress as brokerage parties would help us
understand their long-term success and the impact they have on the dynamics of their respective party systems.[6] We now turn our attention to the
Canadian case, often held up as the epitome of democratic brokerage.

Is Canadian Politics Brokerage Politics?
If the question is whether all Canadian political parties are brokerage parties, then the answer is obviously not. This seems theoretically impossible
as systems cannot successfully accommodate more than one. More to the
point, the historical record is filled with accounts of parties that explicitly
rejected any kind of either catch-all or brokerage appeal in favour of speaking for identifiable groups in the community. Some of these have had a
short life span (e.g., the Bloc Populaire, which contested the election of
1945 but was gone four years later), others persisted for decades (e.g., the
Co-operative Commonwealth Federation, which appeared in 1935 and lasted until it willingly transformed itself into the New Democratic Party in
the 1960s); most were rooted in either Quebec or the western provinces.
None were ever contenders for government office or accepted the idea that
the indiscriminate electoral appeals inherent in pragmatic accommodative
impulses represented an acceptable basis for representative politics.

This reduces the claim about Canadian electoral politics being structured by brokerage parties to an observation that its two large (significant) office-seeking parties have practised brokerage politics and that the minor parties were thus, by definition, a sideshow – interesting but relatively peripheral to the central dynamics of the party system. A closer consideration of the Conservative Party casts doubt even on this proposition, however.

For well over one hundred years the Conservatives cannot be said to have sought to accommodate the interests of all Canadians or incorporate them within the party. With the death of John A. Macdonald, the initial denial of the leadership to John Thompson and McCarthyite impulses at the grassroots signalled that Roman Catholics were not to be embraced as equal partners in the party; its subsequent estrangement from Quebec in 1917 crippled any capacity it might have had to act as a political bridge between the country's two dominant linguistic communities. This self-awareness and acceptance that the party could not, and should not, even attempt to act as a genuine national broker was perhaps best articulated in the famous (1954) Gordon Churchill memorandum that argued that the party "ought not to squander its resources on Quebec" but seek to build a majority by focusing on other regions (Beck 1968, 300). Since the party had "succeeded in alienating" (293) its own Quebec activists in choosing the individual least acceptable to the province as its leader, this may have simply reflected reality. This closed representational orientation was reinforced by the party's narrower, more ideological conception of Canada's essential nature, whether it was expressed as Arthur Meighen's support for British imperial adventures or John Diefenbaker's commitment to the Union Jack.

Although coalition politics has rarely been on the national political agenda, it is noteworthy that it was Robert Borden's Conservatives who, in 1917, formed the country's only coalition government. The Harper version of the party appears to have attempted to construct an anti-Liberal parliamentary coalition in 2005, suggesting that, despite its subsequent attempts to delegitimize the notion in the aftermath of the 2008 general election, it too was open to the possibility.

This all suggests that the Conservative Party can be best understood as a catch-all party wanting to expand beyond its traditional ideological and regional bases in an effort to fashion a majority government. Its inability to act as a genuine socio-political broker has meant that it has not often been successful, given the structure of the Canadian electorate. Three times during the twentieth century it constructed huge majorities – the three largest of the century – but each proved to be an oversized electoral coalition that imploded in the face of the party's inherent inability to encompass a large, disparate clientele.

It seems clear that the Conservative Party has been regularly disadvantaged by its attempts to marry a catch-all style of politics with an essentially stratarchical organizational form. This disjuncture has worked at cross-purposes, severely limiting the party's capacity to operate as a coherent, disciplined machine. The resulting tension has been manifested in recurring bouts of intraparty conflict, most of it centred on the party's leadership, which the stratarchical structure leaves open and vulnerable. By continually weakening the party's competitive capacity, this "Tory Syndrome" was at the heart of a century of political defeats (Perlin 1980).

On at least two occasions, the party abandoned the stratarchical principle to build a more appropriate hierarchically disciplined organization for its catch-all strategy, and in both cases the result was electoral success. Under Richard Bennett, however, the new structure did not outlive the leader, collapsing under the weight of the country's divergent localisms (Glassford 1992); it remains to be seen whether the current Conservative "garrison" party experiment (Flanagan 2010) will survive Stephen Harper's leadership.

If the minor parties have adopted classic group and interest representational strategies, and if the Conservatives have been (at best) a Canadian version of a catch-all party, then only the Liberals are left as a brokerage party candidate.

As early as 1906, André Siegfried pointed to features of Canadian parties that marked them as brokerage organizations: the special position of the leader (who is "the central organization" himself and whose "mere name is a program"), the critical place of loyalty in holding the party together (the party understood as a "sacred institution"), and the stratarchical character of organizational activity (the "shrewd working of the constituencies"). Although the Conservatives may have possessed these characteristics until Macdonald's death, by the time Siegfried was writing only the Liberals were capable of accommodating the interests of the two "races" (defined linguistically or religiously) that he recognized as one of the most central electoral tasks of a Canadian party. It was this capacity that led the Liberals to conceive of themselves as, and act as if they were, the country's natural governing party.[7]

This sense of themselves as the indispensable instrument of national unity has led the Liberals to resist forming coalitions on occasions when voters, and the electoral system, failed to deliver a parliamentary majority.

Thus King in the 1920s, Pearson in the 1960s, Trudeau in 1972, and Martin in 2004 established minority governments and sought a propitious moment to go back to the electorate in search of a majority. For the most part, however, the Liberals' monopoly of the national unity issue enabled it to control the political agenda and thus laid the foundation for its long-term dominance.

Recognizing the important roles leaders play in managing political brokerage, the Liberals have been careful to signal their commitment to the centrality of a French/English partnership through the party's leadership. Although some would argue that alternation is not a "rule," the reality is that for over a century the party's leadership has alternated between French and English native speakers – and the Liberal Party is the only party for which this has been true.

The Liberals' stratarchical structure, organized as a franchise system (Carty 2002), produced a succession of extraordinarily strong party leaders. Over the course of the twentieth century, the Liberals had four leaders who served as prime minister for over ten years; by comparison, all the parties in the four other Anglo-Celtic Westminster democracies managed to produce only three during the same period. The party was a pioneer in having its leaders chosen by party activists (Courtney 1973), a process that acknowledged the power and place of members in making key intraparty decisions. The fragility of this leadership pattern was exposed, however, when members and activists used their influence to drive Jean Chrétien from the party's leadership and the prime minister's office.

So dominant was the Liberal Party that its organizational framework became the norm to which other Canadian parties were drawn, despite its unsuitability to other representational modes. As we have seen, this proved to be dysfunctional for the Conservatives, thwarting their ability to effectively challenge Liberal pre-eminence. This left the Liberals perfectly positioned to lead in the reconstruction of electoral organization and competition on its own terms on each of the three occasions when the party system was reshaped during the twentieth century.

It is fair to ask, however, whether the Mulroney interlude, and the subsequent rise of the Bloc Québécois, finally eroded the essential basis for the Liberals' successful brokerage formula. The party has seen its national vote share drop to historically low levels and, importantly, it has not won a plurality of the Commons seats from Quebec since 1980. The most recent election, in 2011, has further eviscerated the party's parliamentary presence, not only in Quebec but also nationally. Targeting its appeals to identifiable social groups, largely in urban Canada, the Liberals now appear to have been reduced to a catch-all party not unlike their Conservative opponent. Although the party has not abandoned its nation-building calling, it is not obvious how, as long as Quebec continues to reject the party, it can re-emerge as a genuine brokerage party.

Brokerage Politics without Brokerage Parties?

Brokerage parties emerge as a distinctive organizational form where political elites manage to denigrate interparty division and celebrate intraparty accommodation as the most important feature of democratic electoral politics. A successful brokerage party's capacity to command the principal lines of division enables it to establish a dominant position in the party system and forces its opponents to adopt other modes of representation and organization. Thus, to say a country's party politics are brokerage politics is to highlight the style and form of the dominant party at the expense of the other parties, which are left with other party models and are engaged in different kinds (generally losing ones) of electoral politics. For a century, Canadian politics could be cast as brokerage politics because the Liberal Party – but only the Liberal Party – existed and operated as a brokerage party par excellence. Its opponents may have been driven to adopt its stratarchical form but they could not replicate its brokerage essence.

The collapse of the Liberals as a brokerage party leaves the contemporary party system one in which catch-all parties will compete for office. The continuing presence of more ideologically focused or regionally based parties will confound the possibilities of creating genuine national coalitions and make winning parliamentary majorities by any party more difficult. The continued absence of a brokerage party seems bound to fundamentally change the character of Canadian politics and end a century of brokerage politics.

Notes

1 Carty, Cross, and Young (2000) provide an account of the collapse of the third Canadian party system in the last years of the twentieth century.
2 It ought to be noted that Kirchheimer is not always as precise as one might like in his account of the distinctive features of the catch-all party. Here I have simply attempted to identify several key aspects that will allow us to contrast the catch-all party with a brokerage party. One can find elaborations and analyses of the Kirchheimer catch-all party in Wolinetz (2002) and Krouwel (2006).
3 On the importance of party origins, see Panebianco (1988).

4 Here is an important point at which Kirchheimer's analysis of "catch-all" party activity comes close to that of Panebianco's "electoral-professional" party.
5 This is not to say that all dominant parties are brokerage parties. As the case of the Swedish Social Democrats illustrates, it is possible for classic mass parties to become dominant parties.
6 For a sketch of such a comparison, see my "Brokerage Parties, Brokerage Politics" (2013b).
7 The classic statement of the Liberals as the "Government Party" is still that found in Whitaker (1977).

References

Beck, J.M. 1968. *Pendulum of Power: Canada's Federal Elections*. Scarborough, ON: Prentice Hall of Canada.

Carty, R.K. 2002. "The Politics of Tecumseh Corners: Canadian Political Parties as Franchise Organizations." *Canadian Journal of Political Science* 35 (4): 723-45.

–. 2004. "Parties as Franchise Systems: The Stratarchical Organizational Imperative." *Party Politics* 10 (1): 5-24.

–. 2013a. "Are Political Parties Meant to Be Internally Democratic?" In *The Challenges of Intraparty Democracy*, edited by W. Cross and R. Katz. Oxford: Oxford University Press.

–. 2013b. "Brokerage Parties, Brokerage Politics." In *Parties: Structure and Context*, edited by R. Johnston and C. Sharman. Vancouver: UBC Press.

Carty, R. Kenneth, William Cross, and Lisa Young. 2000. *Rebuilding Canadian Party Politics*. Vancouver: UBC Press.

Courtney, J. 1973. *The Selection of National Party Leaders in Canada*. Toronto: Macmillan of Canada.

Eldersveld, S. 1964. *Political Parties: A Behavioral Analysis*. Chicago: Rand-McNally.

Flanagan, T. 2010. "Something Blue ...: Conservative Organization in an Era of Permanent Campaign." Paper presented at the annual meeting of the Canadian Political Science Association, Montreal, June.

Glassford, L. 1992. *Reaction and Reform: The Politics of the Conservative Party under R.B. Bennett, 1927-1938*. Toronto: University of Toronto Press.

Kirchheimer, O. 1966. "The Transformation of the Western European Party Systems." In *Political Parties and Political Development*, edited by J. LaPalombara and M. Weiner, 177-200. Princeton, NJ: Princeton University Press.

Krouwel, A. 2006. "Party Models." In *Handbook of Party Politics*, edited by R. Katz and W. Crotty, 249-69. London: Sage Publications.

LeDuc, L., et al. 2010. *Dynasties and Interludes: Past and Present in Canadian Electoral Politics*. Toronto: Dundurn Press.

Lowell, A.L. 1913. *Public Opinion and Popular Government*. New York: Longman, Green.

Mair, P. 1994. "Party Organizations: From Civil Society to the State." In *How Parties Organize: Change and Adaptation in Party Organizations in Western Democracies*, edited by R. Katz and P. Mair, 1-22. London: Sage.

Meisel, J. 1963. "The Stalled Omnibus: Canadian Parties in the 1960s." *Social Research* 30 (3): 367-90.

Michels, R. 1915. *Political Parties.* Reprint, New York: Free Press, 1962.

Panebianco, A. 1988. *Political Parties: Organization and Power.* Cambridge: Cambridge University Press.

Perlin, G. 1980. *The Tory Syndrome: Leadership Politics in the Progressive Conservative Party.* Montreal and Kingston: McGill-Queen's University Press.

Siegfried, A. 1906. *The Race Question in Canada.* London: E. Nash.

Whitaker, R. 1977. *The Government Party: Organizing and Financing the Liberal Party of Canada, 1930-1958.* Toronto: University of Toronto Press.

Wolinetz, S. 2002. "Beyond the Catch-All Party: Approaches to the Study of Parties and Party Organization in Contemporary Democracies." In *The Future of Political Parties,* edited by J. Linz, J.R. Montero, and R. Gunther, 136-65. Oxford: Oxford University Press.

2

Candidate Recruitment in Canada

The Role of Political Parties

WILLIAM CROSS AND LISA YOUNG

One of the distinctive characteristics of Canadian political parties is the autonomy local party associations enjoy in the selection of candidates to stand for elected office. To say that the *selection* of candidates remains largely the prerogative of local associations does not, however, tell us a great deal about the *recruitment* of these candidates. Beginning in the 1980s, media coverage of intensely fought nomination battles involving candidates recruiting hundreds of new members to support their nomination bid created an impression that local associations are largely the arenas in which political entrepreneurs battle one another for their party's nomination. An alternative narrative is suggested by accounts of national parties recruiting and (in the case of the Liberal Party) appointing high-profile candidates or candidates from under-represented social groups. In both accounts, the local party association is portrayed as a largely passive and potentially irrelevant organization.

In this chapter, we explore the role of the local party association in candidate recruitment. Using data from a survey of Liberal and New Democratic Party (NDP) candidates in the 2008 federal election, we find evidence that the local association remains an active participant not only in selecting but also in recruiting candidates for elected office. Because there are no baseline data to compare this with, we cannot make strong claims about continuity. Nevertheless, the evidence we present suggests that older conceptions of active local associations playing a significant role in seeking out candidates rooted in their community remain valid in the contemporary era.

Political Parties and Candidate Recruitment

The most common function ascribed to political parties in democratic systems is the presentation of candidates for public office. Parties may fill many functions and emphasize different activities, both over time and in distinct party systems (King 1969). Thus, there are many models describing varying organizational patterns and focuses of political parties (Carty 2004; Katz and Mair 1995; Kirchheimer 1966; Panebianco 1988). Nonetheless, the one constant in any description of a political party is that it runs candidates in elections with the objective of having them elected and serving in the legislature.

In the Canadian case, parties not only fill this role of nominating candidates in general elections but essentially have become gatekeepers to public office. Election results indicate that it is virtually impossible to gain public office at the federal or provincial level without first being endorsed by one of the political parties. In the past seven federal elections, only one candidate – André Arthur (Portneuf–Jacques Cartier) – has been elected to the House of Commons in the first instance as an independent. It is increasingly rare for Canadians to even have the opportunity to vote for an independent candidate. In the 2008 election, of the 1,592 Canadians who stood for office, only 69 (or 1 in 25) were not affiliated with a political party. Thus, it is safe to say that Canadian general elections are contests among candidates put forward by the political parties.

Given this context, it is surprising that there is little attention paid to the role of parties in political recruitment in Canada beyond their role in recruiting candidates from under-represented social groups. Despite a growing literature relating to party nomination processes (Carty and Erickson 1991; Cross 2002; Sayers 1998) and how these influence the types of candidates chosen, the role of parties in recruiting candidates to stand for nomination has not been scrutinized closely. We are interested here in this first stage that precedes the nomination contest – the decision of a voter to stand for a party nomination.

Candidate selection in Canada is generally portrayed as largely a function of the local party organization, with this grant of authority being part of a stratarchical bargain between the national and local parties (Carty 2004; Carty and Cross 2006). At the same time, there is evidence that the national parties have increasingly been involving themselves in the candidate selection process through the appointment of candidates and general interference with these "local" processes (Cross 2006). What is less clear is the role that either level of the party organization, local or national, plays in encouraging individuals to stand for nomination – what we refer to in this chapter as candidate recruitment.

Traditionally, candidate recruitment has been a relatively informal process. As Patten (2010, 141) notes, "until the 1990s, a candidate search was often conducted quite informally by an unofficial committee that emerged from among members of the local political establishment." More recently, Canadian parties have adopted a variety of more formal mechanisms to conduct candidate searches. In some instances, these are entirely local, whereas in other cases (notably the Conservative Party), they include a representative of the national party (142). The move towards more formal candidate searches was driven in part by concerns about the demographic representativeness of the candidate pool, based on research suggesting that women were more likely to run for a nomination when the local party conducted a candidate search (Erickson 1991). More recently, however, questions have been raised about whether parties' informal and formal recruitment practices may serve to discourage candidacies from traditionally under-represented groups under some circumstances. This raises the question of whether recruitment efforts might reinforce traditional patterns of representation, as local constituency executives recruit people who resemble themselves. Supporting this, Cheng and Tavits (2009) find that female candidates are more likely to be nominated in constituencies where the local party president is female.

In this chapter, we address the following questions:

- Do local and national party associations actively recruit candidates for nomination, or do candidates tend to be political entrepreneurs who find their own motivation to seek office?
- When the parties are involved in recruiting candidates, are there observable differences in the types of candidates recruited by the local and national party organizations?
- Do candidates recruited by either branch of the party differ in meaningful ways from those who run for a nomination without a party "invitation"?

Analyzing the results of a survey of Liberal and NDP candidates in the 2008 federal election, we find evidence that parties, particularly local associations but also national parties, play a significant role in searching out and recruiting candidates. Most candidates surveyed reported having been encouraged to run by members of their local party organization, representatives of the national party, or both. The majority of candidates, including those who ran with no party encouragement, were long-time party members.

Like those in many Western democracies, Canada's political institutions are increasingly criticized on many fronts (Carty et al. 2000; Dalton and Wattenberg 2000). While the criticisms are many, two that are particularly relevant to this inquiry are that political parties are not sufficiently connected to civil society and that those elected to parliament are unrepresentative of the general populace – particularly of women and visible minorities (Cross 2009).

In relation to the question of gender and visible-minority representation in the House of Commons, the parties are generally criticized for not nominating sufficient numbers from these groups in constituencies where they are electorally competitive (see Bashevkin 1993; Black and Hicks 2006; Young 2009). The national parties routinely argue that while they would like to increase the number of women in both their candidate and MP pools, they are limited in their ability to do so because of the decentralization of candidate nomination. Thus, they have been unwilling to undertake reforms – such as all-female short lists and pairing ridings with a requirement that one of the constituencies nominate a female – that have been tried in other Westminster systems. It is true that the national parties have limited authority over nomination outcomes (unless they appoint candidates, which is always controversial), but they can play a role in encouraging members of under-represented groups to seek elected office. Thus, we are interested in ascertaining whether the national branches of the two centre-left parties are active in this regard. How frequently are prospective candidates approached by the national office and encouraged to stand, and is this activity targeted towards those groups that are under-represented in Parliament?

In terms of the parties' broader connection to civil society, we are interested in whether local associations continue to play an important role in encouraging would-be candidates to stand. There is some suggestion in the literature on candidate nomination that a significant number of candidates emerge from outside the local party apparatus and essentially use the local association as a way of winning the party's endorsement for the coming election (Carty et al. 2000, 158; Sayers 1998, 43). Thus, in every election we hear tales of candidates from outside the party emerging with hundreds of

their supporters to wage what amounts to a hostile takeover of the local
party association in order to win the nomination contest.

What is not clear is how widespread this phenomenon is. Is it the exception that makes the headlines or is it commonplace? We consider this
by examining the role of the local party association in the recruitment of
candidates and the depth of ties between candidates and the parties they
represent. We also consider how connected local candidates are to the
communities they seek to represent, whether parties encourage candidates
with deep community ties to seek public office, and whether these associational activities serve as an alternative route to seeking a nomination –
from outside the local party association.

To take a first look at some of these issues in the Canadian context, we
examine data from the 2008 Canadian federal election. Our data are derived from a post-election mail survey of local candidates in the Liberal
and New Democratic Parties.[1] With the assistance of letters of support
from the party offices and several reminder mailings, a response rate of
slightly greater than 55 percent was achieved, with 170 New Democrat and
168 Liberal respondents. Candidate surveys often suffer from attracting
few responses from winning candidates. Fortunately, the proportion of our
respondents who were elected in the 2008 election (19 percent) matches
the overall proportion of successful candidates from these parties.

Because this analysis relies on a survey of candidates, it is limited in
some ways. None of the individuals who ran unsuccessfully for party nominations are included in the study, nor are the even more elusive group of
individuals who considered running for a nomination but chose not to do
so. Consequently, we cannot address the role of party organizations in recruiting candidates among those other groups.

Recruitment to Candidacy

To what extent do Canadian political parties play an active role in recruiting
candidates? Respondents were asked "Which of the following first led you
to consider running for your party's nomination?" and could select more
than one possible response. Table 2.1 shows their responses to this question
and demonstrates that parties – particularly the local party branches –
continue to play a significant role in recruiting candidates to run for public
office. Six out of ten candidates indicated that their initial decision to run
for a party nomination was influenced, at least in part, by an approach from
the local party organization. The national party also appears to play a role

in recruitment, with one-third of respondents reporting that an approach from the national party encouraged them to first run, and 12 percent of respondents indicating that they had been approached by a representative of a party branch (usually the party's women's association).

Figure 2.1 shows that local and national party recruitment are not mutually exclusive. Fully 22 percent of candidates reported first being recruited

TABLE 2.1
Reasons given by Liberal and NDP candidates for initial decision to run

Reason	% indicating that this led them to consider running	N
Approached by a member of the local association executive	60	201
Concern about a particular public policy issue	46	155
Encouraged by family or friends	45	151
Approached by a representative of the national party organization	34	114
It seemed the next logical step in my political career	28	96
Encouraged by members of a group or association I belong to	21	72
Approached by a branch of the party organization (e.g., women, youth)	12	41

FIGURE 2.1
Candidate recruitment

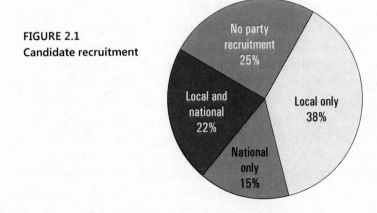

by representatives of *both* the local and the national party organization. Taken together, Table 2.1 and Figure 2.1 suggest that candidate recruitment remains predominantly a political party phenomenon. Political entrepreneurs who run without first being approached by the party, either local or national, are a minority among the candidates who responded to the survey, comprising only one-quarter of the group.

Although some candidates reported having been recruited by both the national and the local party, we will not separate out this group in the remainder of this chapter. Rather, for the purposes of our analysis, we will focus on three groups: (1) those who reported having been recruited by the local association, (2) those who reported recruitment by the national party, and (3) those who reported no party recruitment. The first two categories overlap to some extent, but there is no overlap between these two and the third (no party recruitment). Recruitment by the local party and recruitment by the national party are quite different phenomena. The local party is embedded in the constituency and is well placed to recruit individuals with strong constituency ties, whereas the national party is more likely to approach candidate recruitment with broader considerations in mind, including ensuring that the party's caucus will include individuals well equipped to assume cabinet appointments if the party wins, looking at the demographic representativeness of the national slate of candidates, and ensuring that the party runs a candidate in every electoral district across the country. Because the two types of party recruitment are conceptually different, it is important to examine each separately and not conflate the two into a measure of "party recruitment." It would be desirable to separate out those candidates who reported only local and only national recruitment, but the size of our sample does not facilitate this.

Differences in Recruitment Patterns
The literature regarding patterns in candidate recruitment gives us reason to expect gender differences in the patterns of party recruitment. Erickson (1991) concluded that women were more likely to be nominated by federal political parties when the local riding association had a candidate search committee. Other research, most notably the Lawless and Fox (2005) study in the United States, has produced compelling evidence that women even in occupations that often lead to political careers are less likely than their male counterparts to harbour political ambitions. Lawless and Fox conclude that parties' recruitment of women is an important means of increasing the number of women holding elected office. It follows from this that

female candidates are more likely than their male counterparts to report that they were recruited by the party, either local or national, and less likely to be found in the group of candidates who ran without being recruited by either arm of the party.

It is more difficult to predict whether visible-minority candidates might fall disproportionately among the recruited or non-recruited groups. On the one hand, minority candidates are relative outsiders to the political system and so might be similar to women in waiting to be invited. On the other hand, there is considerable anecdotal evidence that candidates from minority groups are able to mobilize supporters from their community in order to win party nominations. Our data do not include a good measure of visible-minority status. Instead, we are using candidates' self-reported membership in an ethnic association as a proxy for this measure. Certainly, this measure will pick up some candidates who are not visible minorities – they might, for instance, be active in a Scottish Canadians' organization – but it does tap into the candidates' self-identification as a member of an ethnic community.

Figure 2.2 shows that both women and members of ethnic organizations are more likely to report being recruited by representatives of their party, and are less likely to run without party recruitment. Fully two-thirds of

FIGURE 2.2

Candidate recruitment patterns based on gender and membership in ethnic associations

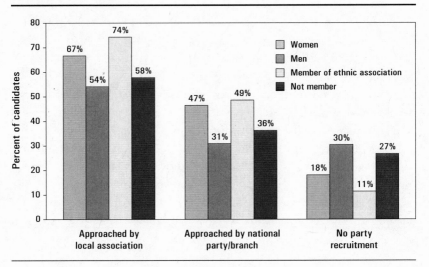

female candidates reported being recruited by their local association, compared with just over half of male candidates. Similarly, almost half of female candidates (47 percent) reported being recruited by the national party or its branch, compared with less than one-third of male candidates. In part, this reflects the role that the parties' women's associations continue to play in candidate recruitment: just under 10 percent of the female candidates responding to the survey reported having been approached by their party's women's association. A similar pattern of recruitment is found for candidates who belong to an ethnic association – three-quarters (compared with 58 percent) reported being recruited by their local party association, and half (compared with 36 percent) by their national party or its branch.[2]

Beyond these demographic variables, we expect that candidates' acquired characteristics – their place of residence, their prior party and community involvement, and any prior office holding – might affect their patterns of recruitment. It would be reasonable to assume that those candidates recruited by the party – either local or national – would have more extensive prior involvement in the party than those who ran without an invitation or encouragement by party officials. It is possible that involvement in civil society organizations, such as interest groups or unions, might have served as an alternative recruitment path for candidates who ran without party recruitment.

We find a significant pattern of difference with respect to the candidate's place of residence. Candidates who lived in the constituency were much more likely to report having been approached by the local party than those who did not (64 percent versus 47 percent, $p < .01$). Conversely, candidates who did not live in the constituency where they ran were significantly more likely to report having been approached by the national party than those who lived in the constituency (33 percent versus 48 percent, $p < .01$). There were no significant differences for candidates not recruited by the party. The proclivity of national party organizations to encourage non-resident candidates likely reflects both their recruitment of "stopgap" and "star" candidates, as discussed below.

Our hypotheses regarding the effect of prior party and community involvement prove to be entirely unsupported by our data. In terms of party involvement, we observe few differences between candidates recruited by party officials and those who self-selected. Most survey respondents reported extensive prior party involvement. On average, candidates recruited by the party had been members for 13.9 years, while those who ran without party recruitment had been members for 14.5 years. Similarly, prior office holding within the party (such as membership in the local association executive) did not affect recruitment patterns. It is noteworthy, however, that two-thirds of survey respondents had held some form of party office – at either the local, provincial, or national level – prior to winning a nomination. Taken together with the considerable length of prior party membership, this signifies that candidates are for the most part individuals deeply embedded in party life prior to running for office.

There is one exception to this. Candidates who joined the party in the year prior to the election were disproportionately likely to report having been recruited by the national party. This may reflect the national party's role in recruiting prominent candidates from other walks of life, and also its role in finding "stopgap" candidates in districts where the party is relatively weak.

Whereas differences in prior party involvement were modest, differences in prior community involvement were more noteworthy. Our measures of candidates' rootedness in civil society look at both the breadth of their involvement (the number of types of groups they belong to, selecting from a list of fourteen potential types of groups) and the intensity of this involvement (the number of hours of involvement in civil society associations). We find that the candidates who reported the highest number of civil society organizational memberships and those who reported devoting the most time to their civil society involvements were more likely to report party recruitment, particularly recruitment by the local party. Those candidates who reported relatively little prior civil society organization involvement were much more likely to be found in the group reporting no party recruitment (see Figures 2.3 and 2.4).

One might anticipate that prior office holding would make some individuals particularly attractive to party officials undertaking recruitment efforts. The survey included several measures of prior office holding (at the municipal, provincial, and federal levels), but we found no evidence that it affected the likelihood of party recruitment.

Differences in Context
In addition to differences in recruitment patterns based on candidates' personal characteristics, we also expect to find patterns based on the constituency context, in terms of both the party and the particulars of the local association. There is reason to expect distinctive patterns of recruitment

FIGURE 2.3
Recruitment of candidates based on membership in civil society organizations

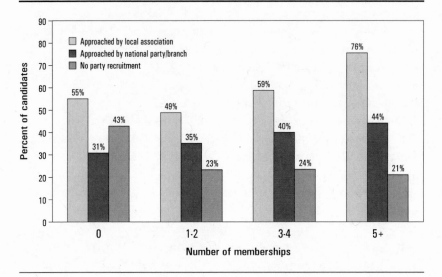

FIGURE 2.4
Recruitment of candidates based on involvement in civil society organizations

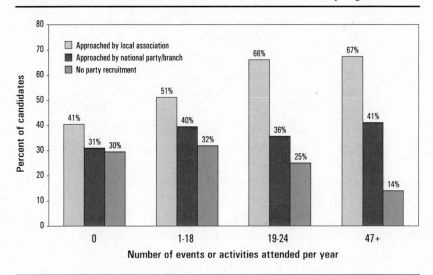

in the two parties in this study. The Liberal and New Democratic Parties each have their own cultures with regard to candidate recruitment, with the NDP emphasizing an internal affirmative action model designed to increase the representativeness of its candidate pool, and the Liberal Party appearing to have more high-profile competitive nomination contests. Despite these expectations, we do not find statistically significant patterns of difference between the two parties in terms of their candidates' recruitment or non-recruitment.

The party's anticipated competitiveness in the electoral district is also a likely determinant of patterns of candidate recruitment. We employ two measures of competitiveness: the respondent's party's place in the constituency in the 2006 election, and the candidate's sense, prior to the election, of his or her chances of winning. We find no patterns of difference among candidates in competitive versus non-competitive ridings with respect to their patterns of recruitment. Filtering out the sixty-five incumbents (because their initial recruitment predated 2008), we find a statistically insignificant but nonetheless noteworthy pattern in which candidates running in constituencies where their party placed first were more likely to report having been recruited by their local association than candidates running in constituencies where their party placed third or worse (71 percent versus 57 percent). In all probability, this reflects the relative strength of local associations with retiring members of Parliament, and the relative organizational weakness of associations in areas where the party is not electorally successful. An alternative way of approaching this might be to ask whether one level of the party plays a particular role in recruiting what Sayers (1998) refers to as stopgap candidates: those whose party is weak in the electoral district and who run for their nomination uncontested. When we identify a group of stopgap candidates (those whose party placed third in the electoral district in 2006 and who ran for their party's nomination uncontested), we find that this group is no more or less likely than other candidates to report having been encouraged to run by either the national or local association.

Although it is not statistically significant, we do see a clear pattern with respect to candidates' expectations of the outcome of the race (see Figure 2.5). We report these bivariate results because the expectation of losing is a statistically significant variable in the regression analysis reported later in this chapter. Among those who expected to lose, over six in ten had been approached by their local party association; the same was true of less than

FIGURE 2.5
**Recruitment of candidates based on candidate expectations
of electoral outcome**

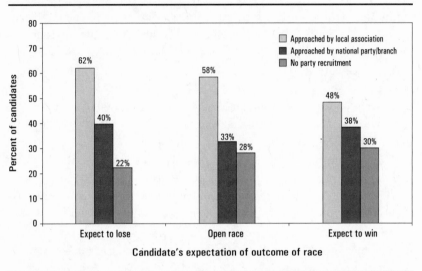

half the candidates who anticipated winning. The reverse pattern holds for those who did not report party recruitment. Of those who expected to lose, only two in ten ran without being approached by the local party; three in ten of the candidates who expected to win ran without being approached by the local party. The pattern for recruitment by the national party is somewhat different, as there appears to be greater likelihood of national party recruiting for constituencies that the party does not expect to win as well as for those that it thinks of as likely wins, but not for the constituencies where the party has placed second in the past. Besides finding stopgap candidates, the national party appears to be particularly interested in those ridings likely to produce an MP.

Another dimension of the constituency context is the geographic setting: candidates were asked to describe the riding where they ran as rural, small urban, primarily suburban, or urban. Once again, the bivariate results are not statistically significant but do follow an intriguing pattern. As Figure 2.6 illustrates, candidates in primarily rural ridings are more likely to report recruitment by their local association, with such recruitment becoming less likely as we move along the continuum to urban ridings. Conversely, recruitment by the national party is a more common phenomenon in urban and suburban ridings.

FIGURE 2.6
Recruitment of candidates based on geographic setting

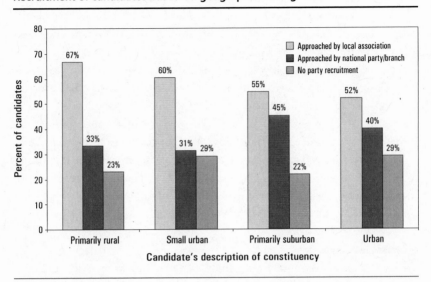

Alternative Paths of Recruitment

The candidate survey asked respondents to select all of the factors that affected their initial decision to run for office. The full list is found in Table 2.1. Besides recruitment by local or national party officials, respondents could indicate that support from family or friends, concern about a public policy issue, or other factors affected their initial decision to run. Because they could select more than one of these factors, we can examine the interplay between the non-party recruitment factors and party recruitment. We anticipated that encouragement from members of a group or association that the candidate belonged to might serve as an alternative source of recruitment for candidates who were not approached by the party, and also that political careerism might serve as an alternative for those political entrepreneurs who ran without being recruited by the party.

The data do not support this supposition. In fact, we find a positive association between encouragement from family, friends, or members of a group or association and being recruited by a party. This is consistent with the finding that greater community involvement was positively associated with recruitment by the local association. Those candidates who did not report being encouraged by family or by members of a group were more likely to run without party recruitment, leading us to suspect that these self-selected candidates were less concerned with external affirmations of support, and more driven by their own motivations.

We find additional support for our conception of the self-selected candidates as being more driven by their own internal reasons for running when we look at candidates who reported concern about a particular policy issue, or a perception that running was the logical next step in their political career. These candidates were significantly less likely to report party recruitment. Of candidates who identified concern about public policy as a reason for running, 32 percent ran without party recruitment, compared with only 19 percent of candidates who did not identify such a concern as a reason. The difference is even larger among candidates who indicated that running seemed like "the next logical stage in their political career": 37 percent ran without party recruitment, compared with only 21 percent of those who were recruited by some level of the party organization.

Multivariate Analysis

We conducted three multivariate analyses, using binary logistic regression (see Table 2.2 for results). The purpose of conducting these regressions was not to determine causation but rather to compare the three groups of candidates in terms of their demographic characteristics, constituency contexts, and other motivations for running. The dependent variables in the logistic regression were the same as those employed above: recruitment by local party, recruitment by national party, and no party recruitment. The multivariate analysis enables us to develop a profile of the types of candidates likely to be recruited by either level of the party, and of the self-selected group of candidates. The first analysis compares all candidates who reported local recruitment with those who did not report local recruitment. The "locally recruited group" includes candidates reporting recruitment only by the local party and those reporting recruitment by both local and national parties. The comparison group for this analysis comprises all the candidates recruited only by the national party and those who were not recruited by any party organization. Similarly, in the second analysis, the "nationally recruited group" includes candidates reporting recruitment only by the national party and those reporting recruitment by both local and national parties; this group is compared with all candidates reporting either local recruitment only or no recruitment. The third analysis compares respondents reporting no party recruitment with those reporting any type of party recruitment.

Locally Recruited Candidates

Candidates recruited by their local party executive were, above all else, deeply rooted in their electoral district. They were substantially more likely than other candidates to reside in the electoral district where they ran, and were encouraged by family and friends to run for political office. Compared with those candidates who were not approached by their local association executive, the locally recruited candidates reported a greater breadth of civil society association memberships as well as more intense involvement in these associations (as measured by the total number of hours devoted to them). When we think about parties as providing a link between civil society, or local communities, and the broader political system, one of the potential linkage mechanisms may well be the locally embedded candidates who run for party office, such as constituency association president. Certainly, the types of organizational involvement reported by locally recruited candidates suggest that local associations place some value on, or are inclined to reach out to, candidates with rich community ties. Although the relationship is not statistically significant, we note that candidates who identified the riding where they ran as predominantly rural were more likely to be recruited by the local association. This may be due to the greater localism of politics in predominantly rural parts of the country, where electoral districts may correspond more directly to genuine communities than is the case in larger urban and suburban areas.

In many respects, the locally recruited candidates appear to be political amateurs: individuals whose extensive party and community involvement made them look like attractive candidates, rather than individuals who have worked towards a political career. Table 2.2 shows that the locally recruited candidates were substantially less likely than other candidates to report that they ran because it seemed like the logical next step in their career, or because they were motivated by a particular public policy issue. Rather, they reported that they ran because they were asked, and because those around them encouraged them to do so.

It is difficult to draw firm conclusions from our data regarding the influence of competitiveness on the likelihood of candidates being recruited by local associations. It stands to reason that more vibrant local associations would be more active in recruiting potential candidates. While party competitiveness and the vibrancy of the local association would not be perfectly correlated, we would anticipate that local associations would be more active in areas where the party is competitive. It is not surprising, then, that locally

TABLE 2.2
Summary of logistic regression results

Explanatory variable	Recruitment by local association			Recruitment by national party			No party recruitment		
	B	Exp (B)	Significance	B	Exp (B)	Significance	B	Exp (B)	Significance
Woman	0.386	1.471	.145	0.676	1.965	.009	−0.475	0.622	.134
Member of ethnic association	0.532	1.703	.292	0.603	1.827	.177	−0.913	0.401	.194
Incumbent	−0.119	0.888	.810	−0.406	0.666	.410	−0.051	0.950	.926
Rural riding	0.371	1.450	.184	−0.361	0.697	.200	−0.151	0.859	.645
NDP	0.355	1.426	.235	−0.281	0.755	.338	−0.229	0.795	.517
Party's place in constituency, 2006	−0.686	0.503	.011	−0.080	0.923	.745	0.333	1.396	.266
Expected to lose	0.597	1.817	.083	0.659	1.934	.056	−0.584	0.558	.114
Expected to win	−0.695	0.499	.170	0.383	1.467	.445	0.653	1.922	.223
Nomination contested, 2008	0.394	1.483	.212	0.441	1.554	.175	−0.969	0.379	.008
Party member 1 year or less	0.418	1.519	.271	0.793	2.210	.027	−0.911	0.402	.070
Number of civil society memberships	0.132	1.142	.059	−0.039	0.962	.567	−0.102	0.903	.230
Total hours, civil society groups	0.006	1.006	.056	0.009	1.009	.005	−0.013	0.987	.023
Live in constituency	0.743	2.102	.011	−0.745	0.475	.009	0.226	1.253	.534
Encouraged by family and friends	0.964	2.622	.001	0.489	1.631	.077	−1.051	0.349	.002
Encouraged by group/association	−0.286	0.751	.400	0.336	1.400	.289	0.145	1.156	.714
Motivated by specific public policy issue	−0.485	0.617	.072	0.043	1.004	.869	1.128	3.088	.000
Seemed like next logical step in political career	−0.821	0.440	.006	0.212	1.237	.456	1.229	3.417	.000
Constant	−0.146	0.864	.852	−1.278	0.278	.102	−0.500	0.607	.580
Nagelkerke R^2	.231			.195			.289		

Note: Italic type indicates statistical significance at $p < .1$.

recruited candidates tended to be found in more competitive ridings (at least measured by the party's performance in the 2006 election). Paradoxically, however, once the party's place in the prior election was held constant, locally recruited candidates were also more likely to expect to lose the election.

Keeping in mind that locally recruited candidates constituted a majority of the candidates in our study, the profile that emerges from this analysis suggests that candidates remain an important linkage mechanism between local communities and national politics. Although the leader-focused national political campaign remains the staple of Canadian elections, and is the most important factor shaping Canadians' vote choices, the 308 campaigns on the ground also play a role in structuring vote choice. Local associations remain important players in recruiting candidates, and the candidates they look for appear to be modern-day "local notables": individuals with long-standing ties not only to their party but also with connections to their community, in terms of both their residence and their community involvement. In an era when observers worry about the disconnect between political parties and civil society, the ongoing role of local associations in recruiting candidates, and their preference for individuals with rich ties to the local community, should offer some reassurance about the mechanisms that connect national parties to the electorate at the local level.

Nationally Recruited Candidates

Candidates who reported being approached by the national party are quite different from those recruited by local associations, suggesting that the national party plays a very different role in its recruitment efforts. Although the patterns are not entirely clear, there is reason to think that in some of their recruitment efforts, the national parties are stepping in where local associations are relatively weak. Candidates recruited by the national party were more likely to report expecting to lose the election (although the party's place in the prior election was not a statistically significant predictor). This suggests that a substantial proportion of the nationally recruited candidates might have been recruited by the national party to run as what Sayers calls stopgap candidates in ridings where their party was relatively weak.

Nationally recruited candidates were also substantially less rooted in their local community and their party than other candidates. Conforming to the profile of candidates "parachuted in" by the national party, these individuals were significantly less likely to live in the constituency where they ran, and more likely to have joined the party in the past year. This profile could fit both stopgap candidates recruited to be a name on the ballot for a party in an area of weakness, but also high-profile candidates recruited from some other walk of life to run in a riding where the party was strong.

Finally, the profile of nationally recruited candidates suggests that, at least in the Liberal and New Democratic Parties, the national party (including its women's and other ancillary organizations) continues to play a lead role in working towards a more demographically representative candidate pool. The nationally recruited candidates were disproportionately female. In addition, it is noteworthy that there is a positive (although not statistically significant) relationship between being a member of an ethnic association and being recruited by the national party. Since the representativeness of the candidate pool became a salient issue in the 1970s, it has been predominantly the national parties that have encouraged candidacies from women and other under-represented groups, while local associations have for the most part been concerned with selecting the most electorally competitive candidate. In this respect, the ongoing role of the national relative to the local party organization in recruiting women represents an element of continuity.

Self-Selected Candidates

The candidates who ran without being recruited by a party present a very different profile from either the locally or nationally recruited candidates. Above all, these individuals fit the profile of political careerists: they tend to have lengthy party service but relatively little involvement in nonpartisan civil society organizations. Unlike candidates who were recruited by their party, these self-selected candidates were explicit in stating their political ambitions: they were more likely to report that they ran for their party's nomination because "it seemed like the next logical step in my political career," and also that they were motivated by a particular policy issue. Unlike the recruited candidates, they were less likely to report that the encouragement of family and friends was important to their decision to run. In short, these individuals presented themselves for political competition rather than being coaxed or encouraged by party, family, or other associates. Besides ambition, they exhibited considerable confidence: they were more likely than others to expect to win (although the relationship is not statistically significant).

In our bivariate analysis, we found that the self-selected candidates were disproportionately male, as would be predicted from the literature on gender and politics. In the multivariate analysis, gender is no longer a statistically significant predictor, but the sign of the coefficient remains in the expected direction.

Conclusion

The data presented in this chapter suggest that candidate recruitment remains largely a party-dominated phenomenon in Canada, confirming Mishler's observation in 1978. Most of the candidates who completed our survey reported being recruited by either their local association or the national party, and in some instances by both. Candidates, including those who ran without being recruited, were for the most part long-time party members. As suggested in much of the literature, the local party association remains the dominant player in recruiting candidates, although the national party's role is by no means trivial.

The two levels of the party organization appear to be recruiting different kinds of candidates for different contexts. Local parties tend to recruit local notables, individuals heavily involved in the community who live in the riding and have been active in party life. The national party, perhaps more concerned with the representativeness of the candidate pool, tends to play a role in recruiting female candidates as well as individuals without extensive prior involvement in either the community or the party. To some extent, this may reflect the national party's role in recruiting candidates where the party's local organizations and electoral support are relatively weak.

Although in the minority, some candidates ran for and won their party's nomination without first being recruited. These political entrepreneurs are disproportionately male, with some prior party involvement but relatively little prior community involvement. Unlike candidates who were recruited by the party, many of them reported that they decided to run in part because it seemed like the next step in their political career, and/or because they were concerned with a particular public policy issue.

Observers concerned about a decline of the party in Canadian politics should find these results reassuring. They suggest a degree of continuity in parties' recruitment functions, with local party associations taking the lead in recruiting candidates who are well connected to their electoral districts in a variety of ways. This apparent preference for such individuals highlights the importance of local associations and candidates in maintaining linkages between the electorate and the broader party apparatus, and in anchoring the party in local civil society. The traditional role of the local association has been supplemented, presumably for several decades, by national parties playing a more active role in recruiting candidates that reflect the diversity of the Canadian electorate, as well as in recruiting candidates as stopgaps in areas where the local association may be weak. Thus, in the important area of candidate recruitment, Canadian political parties remain robust and are attentive to the need to recruit candidates who combine party experience with other types of community involvement.

Notes

1 The Conservative Party of Canada was contacted on several occasions and invited to participate in this survey by providing contact information for its candidates. The party did not respond to these requests and was therefore not included in the study. The Bloc Québécois was similarly invited and declined to participate.
2 All differences (women versus men, and members of ethnic associations versus non-members) reported in Figure 2.2 are statistically significant at $p < .05$, except for recruitment by national party, for ethnic association membership.

References

Bashevkin, Sylvia. 1993. *Toeing the Lines: Women and Party Politics in English Canada.* Toronto: University of Toronto Press.

Black, Jerome, and Bruce Hicks. 2006. "Visible Minority Candidates in the 2004 Federal Election." *Canadian Parliamentary Review* (Summer): 15-20.

Carty, R. Kenneth. 2004. "Parties as Franchise Systems: The Stratarchical Organizational Imperative." *Party Politics* 10: 5-24.

Carty, R. Kenneth, and William Cross. 2006. "Can Stratarchically Organized Parties be Democratic? The Canadian Case." *Journal of Elections, Public Opinion and Parties* 16: 93-114.

Carty, R. Kenneth, William Cross, and Lisa Young. 2000. *Rebuilding Canadian Party Politics.* Vancouver: UBC Press.

Carty, R. Kenneth, and Lynda Erickson. 1991. "Candidate Nomination in Canada's National Political Parties." In *Canadian Political Parties: Leaders, Candidates and Organization*, edited by Herman Bakvis, 97-190. Toronto: Dundurn Press.

Cheng, Christine, and Margit Tavits. 2009. "Informal Influences in Selecting Female Political Candidates." *Political Research Quarterly* 64 (2): 460-71.

Cross, William. 2002. "Grassroots Participation and Candidate Nominations." In *Canadian Political Behaviour*, edited by Brenda O'Neill and Joanna Everitt, 373-85. Toronto: Oxford University Press.

–. 2006. "Candidate Nomination in Canada's Political Parties." In *The Canadian Federal Election of 2006*, edited by Jon Pammett and Christopher Dornan, 171-95. Toronto: Dundurn Press.

–. 2009. "Representation and Political Parties." In *Canadian Politics*, 5th ed., edited by James Bickerton and Alain-G. Gagnon, 249-64. Toronto: University of Toronto Press.

Dalton, Russell J., and Martin P. Wattenberg. 2000. *Parties without Partisans: Political Change in Advanced Industrial Democracies.* New York: Oxford University Press.

Erickson, Lynda. 1991. "Women and Candidacies for the House of Commons." In *Women in Canadian Politics: Toward Equity in Representation,* edited by Kathy Megyery, 101-26. Toronto: Dundurn.

Katz, Richard, and Peter Mair. 1995. "Changing Models of Party Organization and Party Democracy: The Emergence of the Cartel Party." *Party Politics* 1: 5-28.

King, Anthony. 1969. "Political Parties in Western Democracies." *Polity* 2: 111-41.

Kirchheimer, Otto. 1966. "The Transformation of the Western European Party Systems." In *Political Parties and Political Development,* edited by Joseph LaPalombara and Myron Weiner, 177-200. Princeton, NJ: Princeton University Press.

Lawless, Jennifer L., and Richard L. Fox. 2005. *It Takes a Candidate: Why Women Don't Run for Office.* New York: Cambridge University Press.

Mishler, William. 1978. "Nominating Attractive Candidates for Parliament: Recruitment to the Canadian House of Commons." *Legislative Studies Quarterly* 3 (4): 581-99.

Panebianco, Angelo. 1988. *Political Parties, Organization and Power.* Cambridge: Cambridge University Press.

Patten, Steve. 2010. "Democracy and the Candidate Selection Process in Canadian Elections." In *Election,* edited by Heather MacIvor, 135-54. Toronto: Emond Montgomery Publications.

Sayers, Anthony. 1998. *Parties, Candidates, and Constituency Campaigns in Canadian Elections.* Vancouver: UBC Press.

Young, Lisa. 2009. "Women (Not) in Politics: Women's Electoral Participation." In *Canadian Politics,* 5th ed., edited by James Bickerton and Alain-G. Gagnon, 283-300. Toronto: University of Toronto Press.

3

Constant Campaigning and Partisan Discourse in the House of Commons

KELLY BLIDOOK AND MATTHEW BYRNE

Over the past eight years, Canadians have witnessed their federal political parties engaging in what might be best described as a "constant campaign." The final months of 2003 and early months of 2004 saw the merger of two right-of-centre parties into the current Conservative Party of Canada and the beginning of the Liberal Party's succession of short-term leaders. Casual observers and the media have suggested that we have also seen an intensification in the adversarial nature of politics during this period – due to changes in political advertising, legislative tactics, and parliamentary behaviour. There is a risk that this increased adversarialism could lead to further decline in political trust, greater dissociation from political parties, and increased political disengagement, all of which are thought to decrease democratic participation (Clarke et al. 2000; Perlin 2007). Scholars have also pointed to increased party competition in recent years and the impact of the heightened adversarial environment on representation and policy outcomes (see Chapter 6 of this book, for example).

This chapter has two goals. First, we wish to determine whether minority parliaments are more adversarial than majority parliaments, or whether certain parties/leaders affect the extent to which the House of Commons is more or less adversarial. Second, against the backdrop of substantial changes in the seat distribution in Parliament, we seek to answer the broader question of whether change is occurring among Canada's political parties.

In particular, we test the popular assumption that there has been a notable change in parliamentary behaviour among legislators in the House of Commons. We look at behaviour in Parliament over the past fifteen years (1996-2010) in a single legislative arena where adversarial and partisan behaviour is generally thought to be minimal: Standing Order 31 Member Statements (SO31s). These are one-minute statements – with few restrictions on content – made by individual MPs during an allotted fifteen-minute period on each sitting day. By examining SO31 activity over these fifteen years, we are able not only to compare behaviour across periods of minority and majority governments but also to assess any variations between political parties to further explore whether specific parties drive certain forms of behaviour.

Our examination of one aspect of parliamentary activity (SO31s) suggests that Canadian parties in Parliament have become more adversarial since the 2004 election, and that this was an important new feature of Canadian politics during the study period. In addition, this increase in adversarial behaviour may be interfering with the ability of MPs to pursue individual actions. Although this evidence is uncovered through examination of a single venue within the House of Commons, our findings suggest a broader trend in how our politicians communicate with each other, which in turn affects how citizens perceive them and how political ends are accomplished.

Minority Parliaments
The potential impact of minority governments on parliamentary behaviour is not clear from the earlier literature or collected evidence. Some scholars have argued that minority parliaments force political parties to find compromises and to cooperate (Good 2004; Valeri 2005). Others suggest, however, that the constant threat of an election call causes parties to be constantly in electioneering mode and attacking their competitors (Cody 2008; Franks 1987; Strahl 2005). In Canada, the possibility of forming a majority government may also have an impact on the behaviour of parties, whereas in proportional or mixed-member systems such as Germany or New Zealand, where there is little hope of such an outcome, parties may require a more cooperative approach to form longer-term working relationships with legislative partners.

It is commonly assumed that majority governments are natural and proper in a Westminster parliamentary system. In theory, one of the key virtues of the Westminster system is that its first-past-the-post electoral process promotes decisive results by favouring larger parties, thereby creating single-party majority governments even when the largest party fails to obtain over 50 percent of the vote (Butler 1983). Through party discipline, a single-party majority can easily implement its agenda without concession to other parties, and in the event of unpopular choices, the electorate knows which party to blame in the next election and can replace it. Thus, a governing party holding a majority of seats in the parliament is believed to ensure efficiency, accountability, and responsibility (Franks 1987). Minority governments, often known as hung parliaments, are considered undesirable for lacking the advantages of majority government. Such electoral outcomes are becoming the norm in parliaments across Europe, and are even becoming a concern in Westminster systems despite the first-past-the-post electoral system (Butler 1983). Strom (1990) found that coalitions and single-party minority governments combined accounted for 87 percent of Western European and Commonwealth governments between 1945 and 1987. Scholars have focused their attention on coalition governments but have largely ignored single-party minority governments.

The assumption has been that if no party wins a majority of seats, the party with the most number of seats would form an alliance with smaller parties to create a majority between them. Riker (1962) influentially theorized that such a party would create minimum winning majority coalitions – coalitions that include the least number of members from other parties required to ensure a majority in the parliament. Empirical research has shown, however, that larger coalitions and even minority governments are also quite common (Laver and Schofield 1990; Russell 2008; Strom 1990). Because coalition theory and supporting empirical research have been the focus of research when elections fail to produce single-party majority governments, single-party minority governments have largely been viewed as the result of failure to negotiate an effective coalition.

Due to scholars' focus on coalition governments, there is a weak understanding, and considerable misunderstanding, of minority governments in general. They are wrongly assumed to be caused by instability, conflict, or malaise (Strom 1990), or by crisis or aberration (Russell 2008); in extreme cases, they are seen as a "faceless horror, the political fate that is worse than death" (Forsey 1964, 1). The result of such depictions is that minority governments are expected to be ineffective and short-lived. Strom (1990) demonstrates that single-party minority governments tend to produce better future election results for the governing party, and Russell (2008) demonstrates that they can effectively develop and implement large policy packages (such as those of Lester Pearson's minority governments). Of all these descriptions and predictions, the only one that has been demonstrated consistently is that minority governments are less durable than majority governments (Strom 1990).

A better understanding of single-party minority governments is of particular importance in the Canadian context because Canada has recently had three consecutive minority governments. Since the Conservative Party secured a majority in the 2011 election, it is even more essential to understand the behaviour of legislators in the House of Commons. If adversarialism has increased, is it because of the string of minority governments, or is it because "times have changed"? Of course, there will be much more to research as the dynamics of the new 41st Parliament become clear, but we believe this chapter will provide an important perspective on changes in the House up to this point.

The underlying question concerning the effectiveness and durability of minority governments is how they can pass confidence motions when most of the seats in Parliament are controlled by opposition MPs. The apparent answer is that parties must become more cooperative. There are academics and politicians who believe that single-party minority governments must act cooperatively to ensure the support of at least one opposition party in order to maintain a government. Good (2004) assumes that goodwill and cooperation among the leaders are necessary for Parliament to function. He also indicates that there are pressures that should promote more cooperation, from the standpoint of both opposition and governing parties. Opposition parties should display more prudence in their words and actions as they may be held accountable for them in an election that could occur at anytime. Consequently, their behaviour in Parliament, in committee, and in the media should be tempered and cautious. In turn, government ministers will come to depend on sustainable working relationships with opposition MPs. Speaking from his own experiences, Valeri (2005) agrees that cooperation is essential. He states that a minority government will work more effectively if it acts cooperatively. He notes that the Liberal government debated and compromised on two amendments to the Throne Speech in 2005, ensuring that confidence motions passed and that the government continued. He also suggests that the deliberative function of Parliament will strengthen through cooperation. Finally, he claims that when voters elect a minority government, they expect parties to cooperate; consequently, parties that ignore this expectation will pay electorally. This last point is crucial. The few scholars who specifically address the formation of minority governments place considerable importance on parties' planning for future elections. Most view this as a competitive pressure rather than a cooperative pressure, contrary to Valeri.

It may be more prudent to predict that single-party minority governments will make parties more competitive and partisan rather than co-operative. After all, by definition a single-party minority government has rejected the cooperative option of forming a majority coalition. The support that single-party minority governments receive from opposition parties in confidence motions often results from policy concessions. Rarely are these concessions even formalized agreements (Strom 1990). In the Canadian context, they have usually reflected backdoor bargaining between the Liberal government and the leader of the NDP, after the NDP threatens to precipitate an election if the Liberals do not provide policy for them (Russell 2008). This process more closely resembles extortion than cooperation. The lack of formalization allows each party to continue publically criticizing the other and to withdraw from the arrangement when it suits the party. The NDP withdrew support from the Liberals in 2006 to avoid tarnishing its image; in 1974 the Liberals, correctly predicting a Liberal majority if an election were called, intentionally produced a budget offensive to the NDP in order to lose the latter's support.

A minority government may also be more competitive in Canada than in other countries. This is due primarily to the value of small changes in public support and the likelihood that those small changes will occur. An estimated 44 percent of the electorate is apolitical – that is, voters with no strong affiliation with any party (Cody 2008). These voters are more likely to vote on short-term issues such as leader attributes, scandals, and other salient issues of the day. The fluctuations of support that can be expected from such an electorate, coupled with the amplifying effect of a first-past-the-post electoral system (Butler 1983), provides ample motivation to increase partisan competition. Changes in public support can be created by bringing potential scandal to light, so parties may try to take advantage of every such opportunity. Further, these changes in vote share can result in large swings in parliamentary seat allocation because of the electoral system. Thus, the reward for changing the balance of public support could easily be a change from minority to majority government status or a change in government.

The literature on electoral cycles can also be used to predict an increase in competitive behaviour in minority governments. The most accepted partisan models suggest that governing parties that are not at immediate risk of election will pass contentious legislation early in their mandate. They become more concerned with, and responsive to, public opinion as elections approach, or they time the benefits of earlier decisions to come to fruition at election time (Quandt 1986; Serletis and Afxentiou 1998). Minority parliaments should behave the same way, except that, since the early "safe years" do not exist for them, they should always focus on public opinion. Strahl (2005, 7) explains that this is indeed the case for the Canadian Parliament: "The last election never ended and the next has already begun." What he claims was always true for some is now a necessary lens for everyone in Ottawa because of minority governments. He also concludes that "since the next election can happen at any time, votes, policy decisions, press releases, statements, motions and Bills will frequently have both a policy and partisan *raison d'etre*" (7). The competitive incentives resulting from minority governments ought to have led to an increase in competitive partisan behaviour in the House of Commons in recent years.

We examine behaviour in the legislature to determine whether this prediction is borne out, and we also consider the possibility that if such an increase in adversarial behaviour exists, it could also be the result of a single political party or leader encouraging such behaviour, and possibly leading other parties to follow suit. Interviews with MPs conducted for separate research (Blidook 2011) revealed that many MPs in the current Parliament were pointing to the parliamentary tactics of the Conservative Party and its leader, Stephen Harper, suggesting that they were conducting themselves in a manner that was otherwise uncommon in the Canadian Parliament. MPs indicated that, in some cases, their parties had to follow suit in electioneering or competitive behaviour in order to keep pace with the Conservatives. Flanagan (2007) also suggests that the Conservative Party has learned that it has to do whatever it can within the realm of legality to continue to win elections and achieve a majority government. We therefore attempt to separate Conservative behaviour from that of other parties in order to assess the accuracy of such allegations and to avoid inaccurately assigning causality to minority status alone.

Methodology

Any attempt to measure whether an increase in partisan behaviour in Canada's Parliament has resulted from the existence of minority governments needs to consider the forum in which behaviour takes place – some forums are more effective for assessing change than others. First, it is widely accepted that partisan competition should be highly prevalent in new media spaces,. whether or not there are minority governments (Blumler and Kavanagh 1999; Norris 2002). Party websites and social media should simply be laden with partisan messages because they are easily and affordably maintained and are useful for that purpose. Second, venues such as Question Period have always been the locus of heavy partisan discourse (Penner et al. 2006). Thus, these two venues may not be the best places to look for increased partisan competitive behaviour related to minority government status. A more effective method would be to examine a parliamentary forum that does not have a tradition of fierce partisan competition – such as Standing Order 31 Member Statements – and that is not commonly considered in campaign literature (but see Sotiropoulos 2009 for an examination of personal attacks, and Speakers' rulings upon them, within this parliamentary venue). Further, since Strahl (2005) predicts that minority governments would promote more partisanship in these types of venues, SO31s will be explored to determine whether parties in minority parliaments have increased partisan competition, and in what form. The nature and rules of this forum are explained in greater detail below.

In order to ascertain the extent to which MPs are engaging in partisan behaviour, we collected the full text of SO31 statements for the last complete sitting week of April in each year from 1996 to 2010. We searched the text of each MP's statement for *total party mentions, mentions of own party,* and *mentions of other party.* We counted both total mentions of each party and the number of individual MPs making mentions. Variations of these counts are presented to determine whether there are trends in the nature of statements made, both over time and by party. We suggest that by examining what we call "partisanship" – based upon total mentions of all parties, including one's own – as well as what we call "negative partisanship" – based upon mentions of other parties only – we will be able to assess the impact of minority parliaments and/or a single-party instigator. We distinguish between minority and majority governments by looking at the time period in which the statement was made.

We aim to make a connection between quality and quantity of electoral behaviour in this chapter. We guide much of the quantitative analysis, which is quite simple in form, by text and examples to illustrate why the count of mentions of parties, and the party affiliation of the MP who mentions a party while giving a SO31 statement, tell us a great deal about the focus and tone of Parliament itself. Although one would need to read the statements in their entirety to understand the whole story, we hope to give an accurate representation of their meaning and implications as briefly as possible.

Standing Order 31 Member Statements

The procedures for SO31s are not complicated. According to O'Brien and Bosc (2009), "members who are not Ministers, when recognized by the Speaker, are permitted to address the House for up to one minute on virtually any matter of international, national, provincial or local concern." These may include (but are not limited to) recognizing an important accomplishment by a constituent or organization, calling attention to international persons or events, and requesting a moment of silence. Statements are made by individual MPs only, and statements have tended to be individual (as opposed to partisan or collective) in nature, although they may occasionally point out a partisan issue that the member feels requires attention, or call on the government to amend a policy. Statements are kept strictly to a maximum of one minute (the Speaker of the House cuts off the MP if necessary). There are some restrictions, at the discretion of the Speaker:

- All questions raised must be on matters of concern but do not necessarily have to be on matters of urgent necessity.
- Personal attacks are not permitted.[1]
- Congratulatory messages, recitations of poetry, and frivolous matters are out of order.

These guidelines are still in place today, although Speakers tend to turn a blind eye to the latter restriction (O'Brien and Bosc 2009).[2]

For the purposes of this chapter, what is important is that the statements historically have tended to be nonpartisan and normally focus on areas that are not usually the subject of partisan debate. SO31s are certainly a place in which representative action takes place, but the focus of representation by the MP may vary greatly – including, but not limited to, individuals, groups, localities, electoral constituencies, regions, or partisans. We do not claim that SO31s "matter" (i.e., have a tangible effect on outcomes) in terms of either electioneering or policy, but this does not preclude the possibility that they do. Rather, the primary importance of SO31s for the purpose of this study is as a measure of tone and focus in Parliament. That is, if the tone of SO31s has become increasingly partisan (and increasingly negative in partisanship), this tells us something about the broader behavioural trend in Parliament.

We use all SO31 statements from the last full sitting week (five days, Monday to Friday) in April (no overlap with May) over the fifteen years from 1996 to 2010. April was chosen because it is normally at least one month away (in both directions) from either a recess or an election campaign. The exceptions are 1997, when an election campaign began immediately following the week analyzed, and 2004, when an election campaign began twenty-three days following the week analyzed. These exceptions are useful in the analysis, as they provide examples of an "election-focused" parliament in a majority setting. All other periods prior to 2004 (1996, 1998-2003) were during majority parliaments with no elections expected in the near future; all periods after 2004 (2005-10) were during minority parliaments, where election campaigns are always far more likely in the short term than during majority parliaments.

The use of a consistent time period means that differences cannot be attributed to annual cycles. There are approximately 80 statements per week, with a minimum of 79 and a maximum of 87. The last four years appear to have seen a standardization on exactly 80 statements, whereas previously the number appeared to fluctuate depending on how many statements fit within the fifteen-minute time period each day. In most cases, we look at the relative frequencies of individuals as a portion of the total in that week, so that the difference in the actual number of statements does not affect results, although we also use raw frequencies (noted below) when useful for illustrative purposes concerning total mentions.

As an example (albeit one that breaches the abovementioned guidelines because it is poetry), Steve Mahoney (Liberal) delivered the following on 12 April 2000:

Mr. Speaker, today I have an ode to the Canadian Alliance and the former Reform Party:

C.A. so it seems
Are still living in dreams
As they continue to strive
To merely survive.
Changing their name

Still makes them the same
Changing their leader
Won't help them much either.
With Klees backing out, & Long jumping in
The battle within is about to begin.
So it's east versus west
To determine their best.
And so we must wonder
When we'll see their next blunder
'Cause as sure as the sun
More errors will come.
So it's back to the west
With pretensions of zest
After leaving in their wake
A political mistake.
Reform or C.A.
"What's the difference," you say
As Canadians all know,
They're the "same ole," "same ole."

In this statement, the MP mentions only the Reform Party/Canadian Alliance, of which he is not a member, and he does so five times. Table 3.1 demonstrates how this passage would be coded.

Because MPs from the Bloc Québécois tended to mention their own party much more often than members of other parties (there was a tendency to finish statements by referring to being "with one's colleagues in the BQ"), some analyses below show proportions for all parties as well as proportions with the BQ excluded.

TABLE 3.1

Demonstration of coding method using remarks by Stephen Mahoney (Liberal) on 12 April 2000

	Party mentions	Liberal (own-party mentions)	Reform/CA (other-party mentions)
Individual MP	1	0	1
Total mentions	5	0	5

FIGURE 3.1

Proportion of individual SO31 statements that mentioned a party name

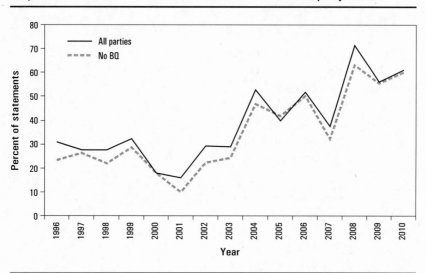

Results

We begin by looking at the fifteen-year trend in the proportion of MPs who refer to any parliamentary political party when delivering an SO31.

Figure 3.1 shows the proportion of all statements that included at least one mention of a political party name. During the Chrétien majority years, the proportion of statements remained less than about 32 percent, or one-third of statements. In 2004, at the time of the Martin majority when all parties were preparing for an election campaign, statements including party mentions increased to greater than 50 percent. This proportion fluctuated over the following years, and fell briefly below 40 percent in 2007. Nevertheless, mentions increased to well above 50 percent from 2008 onward. The average from 2004 onward is approximately double that of the years prior to 2004.

As a measure of overall partisanship in SO31s, these results show a reasonably consistent volume of partisan mentions in 1996-99, a slight drop in 2000-01, and then a moderate uptick in 2002-03 (notably, 2002 was the first year in which Stephen Harper was a political party leader). The most striking difference, however, is that between 1996-2003 and 2004-10, with the latter period showing a rather substantial increase in focus upon parties in SO31 statements compared with the former.

Although perhaps indicating a shift in focus, mentioning of party names is not indicative of tone. For example, consider the following two statements from 26 and 27 April 2004, respectively:

Ms. Sarmite Bulte (Parkdale – High Park, Lib.): Mr. Speaker, the government recognizes how vital women-owned businesses are to the Canadian economy. The fact is there are 821,000 women-owned businesses in Canada which contribute in excess of $18 billion every year to our economy, quite a significant sector of our economy.

The government has a proven track record in supporting the growth of small businesses. Our five year tax plan helps them retain more of their earnings and enhances opportunities and incentives for investors.

The report of the 2003 Liberal task force on women entrepreneurs contained recommendations that were in fact included in budget 2004: accelerated initiatives to provide more quality child care; working to update labour market programming to better reflect the realities of work in the 21st century; and announcing venture capital investment programs through the Business Development Bank of Canada and Farm Credit Canada, totalling $270 million.

The government is proud to help women business owners across Canada scale new heights.

Ms. Judy Wasylycia-Leis (Winnipeg North Centre, NDP): Mr. Speaker, the Prime Minister has been out on the election trail singing Liberal praises across the country. To Canadian listeners it sounds like an old, worn-out record, a broken record that no one wants to hear again.

Nowhere are the sour notes of the Liberal failure more pronounced than in gender equity.

A recent study by the Canadian Association of Social Workers takes stock of the Liberal decade: women's pre-tax income is still 62% of men's; 42% of unattached women aged 18 to 64 live in poverty; women's poverty has deepened; and lone-parent families headed by women remain on the bottom of the economic rung.

The study called for stronger transfers directed to women's needs, gender sensitive pension reform, progressive integration of tax and program spending, and flexible income benefits that foster equality.

Was any of this in the budget? Not a single note. When it came to women's equality, the silence was deafening. For women, Liberal budget day was indeed the day the music died.

FIGURE 3.2

Proportion of individual SO31 statements that mentioned the MP's own party

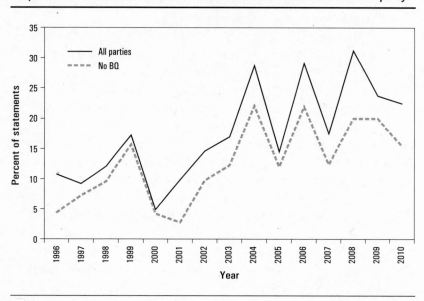

Both of these statements mention the Liberal Party, and both are on the topic of economic conditions affecting females. The one that contains a mention of the MP's own party is clearly positive with regard to the Liberal Party, whereas the other is not. This is true of almost all cases where parties are mentioned – MPs who mentioned other parties normally did so in a manner that portrayed that party negatively, with extremely few exceptions over the fifteen-year period. (No cases were found where MPs mentioned their own party in a negative manner.) Figure 3.2 shows trends in party mentions by a member of that same party; Figure 3.3 shows mentions by MPs of opposing parties, in order to better determine the trend in the tone of SO31s.

Is the increase in party mentions in SO31 statements due to MP's mention of their own party? In part, yes, but not consistently so. The average before 2004 is certainly smaller than that of 2004 and after, although the increase after 2003 fluctuates significantly, with 2005 and 2007 being virtually equal to 2003 and 1999, and 2009 and 2010 being only about 6-8 percentage points greater. In short, it seems unlikely that minority status led MPs to engage in "positive" partisanship more often than during the majority years, although there are certainly select years in which they did so at a higher rate during this period.

Figure 3.3, however, shows a much stronger and steadier increase in MPs' mention of parties other than their own in SO31s. Although the average in the first three years is close to 20 percent, the proportion falls off, then increases from under 15 percent between 2000 and 2003 to approximately 25 percent in 2004 and 2005, and up to 33-40 percent in 2008-10. The exception – although still a slight increase over the majority period – is 2007, with a proportion of just above 20 percent. This suggests that as minority governments led to election preparedness becoming a constant for these parties, MPs took opportunities to attack other parties. It is not that negative mentions necessarily outnumber positive mentions in all cases, but the increase in negative mentions is much starker. Figure 3.4 indicates which parties were the primary focus of this "negative" tone.

Not surprisingly, the parties that are mentioned by MPs from other parties are typically the governing parties. The vast majority of other-party mentions focused upon the Liberals up to 2006, at which point mentions of the Conservative Party increased significantly. In five years (2006-10) as the government party, however, the Conservatives surpassed the attention paid to the Liberals only once, in 2008. Others parties receive very little attention, with the least attention being paid to the BQ (generally less than 5 percent of statements).

As noted earlier, a separate question arose concerning what may cause change in the adversarial and partisan behaviour in Parliament – namely, whether specific parties contribute more than others to this change in tone. In this case, the expected link is based upon ongoing research rather than on assessments of previous parliamentary behaviour. Nevertheless, an alternative explanation was that the behaviour of Conservative MPs alone might provide some causal explanation. Figure 3.5 compares Conservative[3] SO31 statements with those of all other parties combined, with the focus of other parties being mentions of the governing party specifically (Liberal MPs are not included until 2006), while the Conservative trend line reflects mentions of the Liberal Party for the entire period.

Indeed, it appears that Conservative MPs do more than other MPs, on average, to affect focus and tone during SO31s. Despite a good deal of fluctuation over the entire fifteen-year period, there was an increase in the average proportion of Conservative MPs making such statements in the later years. It appears that in each year, a greater proportion of Conservative SO31 statements referred to the governing party (or the Opposition Liberals once the Conservatives formed the government) than statements from other parties. Apart from 1999, the proportion for Conservatives is significantly

FIGURE 3.3

Proportion of SO13 statements that mentioned another party

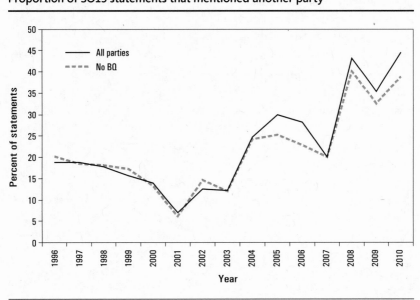

FIGURE 3.4

Proportion of SO31 statements that mentioned another party: specific parties

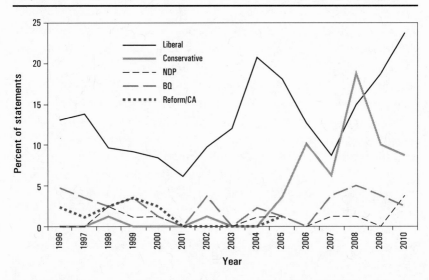

FIGURE 3.5

Comparison between Conservative and non-Conservative mentions of the governing party in individual SO31 statements

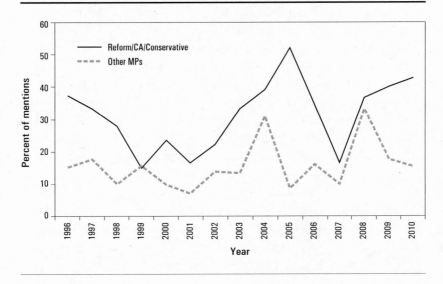

greater than that for the other parties. Nevertheless, the proportion for all other parties increased notably after 2003, except for 2005, with their average for 2004-10 being approximately double that for 1996-2003. The latter point suggests either some impact from minority status in parliament or emulation of Conservative behaviour. We cannot discount the apparent evidence that this particular political party has consistently had a much greater proportion of statements that mention an opposing political party, or that its behaviour might be traceable to its origins in the Reform Party/ Canadian Alliance. At the same time, we cannot ignore the evidence of an increase in the average for the remaining parties.

Other possible evidence of negative partisanship may be seen where MPs increasingly focus their statements on attacking a specific party and where they may refer to that party repeatedly. A case in point is opposition Conservative MP James Moore's statement in 2005:

> Mr. Speaker, in a recent survey, criminal justice issues ranked as the most important concern of my constituents and with this Liberal government, it is little wonder. Liberals have done nothing to fight marijuana grow ops.

Conservatives will shut them down. Liberals have done nothing to fight street racing. Conservatives will make it a crime. Liberals have done nothing to fight the rise in home invasions and auto theft. Conservatives will get tough on property crime. Liberals have done nothing to fight date rape drugs. Conservatives will protect women from those who abuse them. Liberals have done nothing to fight child pornography. Conservatives will raise the age of consent, have an effective sex offender registry and ban all forms of child pornography. Liberals have done nothing to fight violent criminals. Conservatives will impose consecutive, not concurrent, sentencing for violent thugs to hold them accountable. The Liberals have had 12 years to make Canada safer. They have failed. However, hope is around the corner when Canadians throw out these corrupt Liberals and elect a new Conservative government.

Mr. Moore's statement is an outlier with its sixteen mentions of party names, and nine mentions of a party other than his own, but it is suggestive of MP behaviour since parties do appear to have become the direct target (rather than something to be mentioned occasionally) in SO31 statements in recent years.

Figure 3.6 shows both the total number of MPs who mention parties and the total number of mentions overall. It is evident from the divergence of these lines that, after 2003, as the number of MPs mentioning political parties increased significantly (standardized here based on 80 MP statements per week), so did the number of party mentions per speaker. Before 2004, the total number of party mentions hovered slightly above the number of MPs mentioning parties, with an average of 1.7 mentions in statements that included at least one party mention. From 2004 onward, the average almost doubled, to 3.1. Not only are more MPs referring to political parties during their SO31 statements but they are referring to them more often (almost twice as many times) in each statement.

Conservative MPs, such as Mr. Moore, also appear most likely to be conducting themselves in this manner, however. Figure 3.7 shows the number of other-party mentions per statement that includes at least one other-party mention by the Conservatives, compared with all other parties. Until 2005, other parties appeared to keep pace with Reform/CA/Conservative MPs in terms of the number of mentions contained in statements (this is based only upon statements that include at least one mention, not an average of all statements). Beyond 2005, however, MPs from other parties averaged less

FIGURE 3.6

Total number of MPs mentioning parties in SO31 statements, and total number of mentions overall

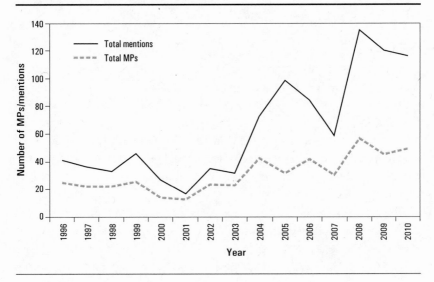

FIGURE 3.7

Number of other-party members in SO31 statements, per speaker

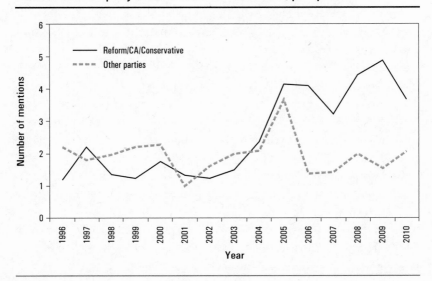

than two mentions in such statements, whereas Conservative MPs averaged approximately four mentions. Thus, while it appears that there has
certainly been a change in tone among MPs generally, these results suggest
that it is far more pronounced among Conservative MPs.

Discussion

We have suggested that minority parliaments should show a more combative than cooperative behavioural pattern primarily because parties are essentially in a state of constant election campaigning. The evidence presented
here indicates that the Canadian Parliament became more combative as a
whole in the period during which elections loomed constantly. A marked
difference in behaviour is evident across parties in this period, and the
trend was not only towards greater partisanship but also towards a negative
(or "attack") form of partisanship.

There is also evidence that one party – the Reform Party/Canadian
Alliance and later the Conservative Party – has played a notable role in this
change, exhibiting a much greater propensity than other parties for engaging in such behaviour. All parties increased their attacks on opposing
parties during the minority period, however, and it is unclear whether this
shift can be attributed to what appears to have been the Conservative lead;
it seems likely that both looming elections and Conservative behaviour
contributed to the shift. What *is* clear is that a change has occurred.

The results show that partisanship plays a greater role in this parliamentary arena, and this appears to have occurred around the same time
that elections were constantly on the horizon. Whether this behaviour is
adopted intentionally by political parties or simply by individual MPs
(the former appears more likely), the result is that the party plays a greater
role – likely to the detriment of the individual member – and parties are
increasingly in attack mode. This might be less striking in certain parliamentary venues, such as Question Period, but the fact that such behaviour
has overtaken SO31s should be regarded as significant. Canada's Parliament
has always provided venues for individual MPs to pursue individual initiatives and speak out on issues of personal interest, and parties appear to be
taking advantage of these opportunities for their own purposes.

All of this also suggests that the focus and tone of Parliament in general
has shifted in recent years. Of course, a more extensive study looking at a
larger number of statements and including other venues would certainly
shed more light on the nature and extent of this change, and provide more

conclusive evidence regarding the influence of both minority status and specific parties upon MP behaviour. The data from SO31 statements points to a Parliament that has changed significantly in recent years. It remains to be seen whether the adversarialism that now appears to be an entrenched feature of Canadian parliamentary politics continues into the current period of majority government.

Notes

1 The following is quoted verbatim from the footnote provided for the bullet point in O'Brien and Bosc (2009):

> In a 1990 ruling, Speaker John Fraser clarified that a statement about another Member's political position would be acceptable, but a personal attack against a Member would not be allowed (*Debates*, 26 November 1990, 15717). Speaker Parent further cautioned in a 1996 decision that "once they [the words] have been uttered, it is very difficult to retract them and the impression they leave is not always easily erased" (*Debates*, 29 November 1996, 6899). See also *Debates*, 22 September 1994, 6032-33; 3 December 1997, 2646; 23 November 2004, 1723; 20 October 2006, 4047-48.

2 It is debatable, when viewing the statements themselves, whether the restriction regarding personal attacks is enforced. One example (among several of a similar nature) is that of Gordon Brown (Conservative), who stated on 20 April 2009: "Dividing Canadians against one another is further proof that the Liberal leader is not in it for Canadians, he is just in it for himself."

3 For years prior to 2004, we include Reform Party/Canadian Alliance MPs as Conservative, and Progressive Conservative MPs as "Other."

References

Blidook, K. 2011. "Symbol vs. Substance: Theatre, Political Career Paths, and Parliamentary Behaviour in Canada." Canadian Study of Parliament Group. http://www.studyparliament.ca/English/pdf/KBlidookFinal-e.pdf.

Blumler, J.G., and D. Kavanagh. 1999. "The Third Age of Political Communication: Influences and Features." *Political Communication* 16: 209-30.

Butler, D. 1983. *Governing without a Majority: Dilemmas for Hung Parliaments in Britain*. London: Collins.

Clarke, H.D., A. Kornberg, and P. Wearing. 2000. *A Polity on the Edge*. Toronto: Broadview Press.

Cody, H. 2008. "Minority Government in Canada: The Stephen Harper Experience." *American Review of Canadian Studies* 38 (1): 27-42.

Flanagan, T. 2007. *Harper's Team: Behind the Scenes in the Conservative Rise to Power*. Montreal and Kingston: McGill-Queen's University Press.

Forsey, E. 1964. "The Problem of 'Minority' Government in Canada." *Canadian Journal of Economics and Political Science* 30 (1): 1-11.

Franks, C.E.S., 1987. *The Parliament of Canada.* Toronto: University of Toronto Press.

Good, D.A. 2004. "Minority Government and Public Servants." *Canadian Parliamentary Review* 27 (3): 9-15.

Laver, M., and N. Schofield. 1990. *Multiparty Government: The Politics of Coalition in Europe.* New York: Oxford University Press.

Norris, P. 2002. "Campaign Communications." In *Comparing Democracies 2: New Challenges in the Study of Elections and Voting,* edited by L. LeDuc, R.G. Niemi, and P. Norris, 127-47. London: Sage.

O'Brien, A., and M. Bosc. 2009. *House of Commons Procedure and Practice.* 2nd ed. Ottawa: House of Commons. http://www.parl.gc.ca/.

Penner, E., K. Blidook, and S. Soroka. 2006. "Legislative Priorities and Public Opinion: Representation of Partisan Agendas in the House of Commons." *Journal of European Public Policy* 13 (7): 1006-20.

Perlin, G. 2007. "The Malaise of Canadian Democracy: What Is It? How Is It to Be Explained? What Can We Do about It?" In *Political Leadership and Representation in Canada: Essays in Honour of John C. Courtney,* edited by H.J. Michelmann, D.C. Story, and J.S. Steeves, 154-75. Toronto: University of Toronto Press.

Quandt, W.B. 1986. "The Electoral Cycle and the Conduct of Foreign Policy." *Political Science Quarterly* 101 (5): 825-37.

Riker, W.H. 1962. *The Theory of Political Coalitions.* New Haven, CT: Yale University Press.

Russell, P.H. 2008. *Two Cheers for Minority Government: The Evolution of Canadian Parliamentary Democracy.* Toronto: Emond Montgomery.

Serletis, A., and P.C. Afxentiou. 1998. "Electoral and Partisan Cycle Regularities in Canada." *Canadian Journal of Economics* 31 (1): 28-46.

Sotiropoulos, E. 2009. "The Use and Misuse of Members' Statements." *Canadian Parliamentary Review* 32 (3): 10-14.

Strahl, C. 2005. "Politics and Procedure in a Minority Parliament." *Canadian Parliamentary Review* 27 (4): 7-9.

Strom, K. 1990. *Minority Government and Majority Rule.* New York: Cambridge University Press.

Valeri, T. 2005. "Collaboration or Confrontation in the 38th Parliament." *Canadian Parliamentary Review* 27 (4): 4-6.

4

Constituency and Personal Determinants of MPs' Positions on Social Conservative Issues in the 37th and 38th Canadian Parliaments

MUNROE EAGLES

André Siegfried (1906) once observed that Canada's distinctiveness stems from its being a North American society governed through European institutions. As a result, many Canadian political practices appear to be blends of elements of both European and American origin. One specific manifestation of this can be seen in the behaviour of members of Parliament, who despite being subject to the party discipline that is characteristic of parliamentary systems, are nonetheless strongly committed to advancing the interests of their constituents. The constituency focus of MPs is stronger in Canada than in Britain, and in this respect Canadian MPs may appear closer to American members of Congress than to their British parliamentary counterparts. The fact that there are relatively few career or senior MPs in the House – something that Norman Ward (1950, 137-43) noticed over sixty years ago – means that most legislators are necessarily concerned with cultivating their electorates and being responsive to their needs in order to secure re-election. Reconciling the tensions arising from the operation of responsible party government and the perceived need to be a good constituency representative is a central and enduring challenge facing Canadian MPs. Until recently, the strength of party discipline in Canada has deflected scholarly attention from the efforts of MPs to represent the views of their constituents in the policy process. Yet there are a number of ways in which tensions between the realities of party discipline and the imperatives of constituency representation can be reconciled, and these have evolved over time. In the postwar period, for example, there have been a number of "free votes," in which party discipline is suspended and MPs are given the opportunity to vote according to their conscience and/or their constituents (Franks 1997). In some cases, such as legislation regarding the death penalty in the 1960s and abortion in the 1980s and 1990s, free votes have been used to deal with morally contentious issues. More generally, the recent rise of legislation in such controversial areas has provided MPs with a distinctive opportunity to vote their constituents' positions. This chapter explores whether the public positions taken by Canadian MPs in the 37th and 38th Parliaments (specifically focusing on the 2003-05 period) on a variety of controversial issues that have been prominent in the social conservative movement in Canada are influenced by their personal characteristics and by the nature of their constituencies. The issues I examine are among a suite of controversial issues that, as Smith (2007, 77) notes, set up "a tension, deeply felt because the issues touch on moral values, between centre and constituency." Smith continues by arguing that because of the wide disparity in opinions on these moral issues, the "hand of the whip is heavier" on these matters.

While this may be true, moral issues are frequently also highly salient to at least an intensely mobilized minority of the general public, for many of whom they are closely related to an intensely held belief or value system. Compared with most issues involving legislative action, these issues are also essentially uncomplicated and therefore easily comprehended by most voters. As a result, any debate of these issues results in tremendous pressure being brought to bear on elected members. Accordingly, on moral issues such as these, there is relatively little opportunity for a politician to hide behind technical complexity or other potential sources of obfuscation. Moreover, such issues tend to embody a rural/urban cleavage, such that rural Canadians are more likely than city dwellers to hold traditional views about morality (Thomas 2001). This geographic structure renders it easier for many MPs to discern a majority preference among their constituents. For many MPs, it also likely produces less cross-pressuring of MPs from opposing sides of these issues. As a result of these various factors, there is an expectation of a correspondence between constituency opinion and legislator position (Mooney 2001, 10), and this may hold true even in parliamentary systems.

This chapter examines the extent to which this expectation is met in Canada by examining the strength of the relationship between selected personal and constituency characteristics and the positions taken by elected legislators, either in recorded parliamentary votes or in other public pronouncements. Specifically, I examine the role of these influences on MP positions on four iconic issues on which social conservatives have staked out intense positions and conducted highly public campaigns designed to influence legislative outcomes. Four separate measures of MP positions are available for the 37th Parliament, and three further ones come from the 38th Parliament. These include the issue of same-sex marriage (measured by parliamentary votes in 2003 and 2005, and by a measure of MPs' positions published in the media in advance of the latter vote in the spring and summer of 2005), the question of abortion (with two measures: voting on a motion asking for a study of the medical necessity of abortion in 2003, and a public listing of pro-life or pro-choice Liberal and Conservative MPs in the 38th Parliament), a bill adding sexual orientation to the list of protected groups under the hate crime legislation (2003), and finally an omnibus reproductive technologies bill (2003). For each parliament, MP positions are summed to form simple additive indices of social conservatism. These various dependent variables are described more fully in the Appendix. Analyzing the contribution of personal and constituency influences on these votes uncovers evidence of a sensitivity of MPs to the characteristics – and presumably the preferences – of their constituents. These findings contribute to a growing body of literature that underscores the strong but inadequately appreciated constituency foundations of Canada's system of parliamentary representation. The findings suggest that MPs are responsive to new opportunities to demonstrate their fidelity to their constituents' views.

Constituencies, Party Discipline, and Representation

Following the work of Heinz Eulau and colleagues (1959) and Warren Miller and Donald Stokes (1963), conventional approaches to representational behaviour identify three ideal/typical models: the delegate, the trustee, and the "politico" (the latter representing a hybrid version of the first two role types). Delegates are, as Edmund Burke famously put it, "local ambassadors" whose role it is to act on the basis of the preferences of their constituents. Smith (2007, 51-71) generalizes this view under the heading "electoral democracy" as one contending theoretical perspective for Canada's parliamentary system. Stephen Harper's Conservative government, like other recent governments before it, came to power in 2006 promising more free votes in Parliament, ostensibly to give greater scope for the representation of constituency-based interests in the policy process. Trustees, on the other hand, are less closely tied to the preferences of their electors. Rather, they are free to use their best judgment to act on behalf of the interests of their country or district. Politicos are those who "agree that constituents should have their views represented in Parliament but appreciate that this goal is easier done in principle than in practice" (Docherty 1997, 143-44).

In the happiest of circumstances, pressures on MPs from constituency, party, and conscience will be in close alignment. While we might expect the electoral process to normally result in the selection of representatives whose views are closest to many voters, obviously there are many reasons why electors and representatives may disagree on particular issues. The crux of the question of representational behaviour is what happens when their views conflict. There is considerable evidence that majorities of Canadian voters believe that MPs should be bound to follow constituency opinion in their voting behaviour (Carty et al. 2000, 112-17; Price and Mancuso 1991, 212). Surveys of MPs suggest that many elected representatives agree with this popular opinion. For example, in a mail survey of English Canadian MPs conducted in 1996, almost half of respondents agreed that consideration of constituents' wishes should be "very important" for MPs as they made their voting decisions in Parliament. Fully 57 percent mentioned that their greatest responsibility was to their constituents (mentioned almost three times as frequently as "Canadians as a whole," the second most popular response) (Eagles 1998). Similar research by Docherty also shows substantial support among MPs for the delegate model of representation. These results from the 1990s do not appear to have changed radically from those reported in Kornberg's survey of MPs in Canada's 25th Parliament, elected in 1962. Kornberg (1967, 108) found that almost half (49 percent) of MPs self-identified as "delegates" – surprisingly, a higher proportion than comparable studies suggest was true for American members of the House of Representatives or state legislators at the time. It should be noted, however, that Docherty's surveys show that experience in the job of MP enhances appreciation of the virtues of party discipline, and it sharpens an awareness of the very real challenges of determining and cleaving to constituency preferences (Docherty 1997, 143-44).

These findings, suggestive of the importance of the constituency connection in parliamentary representation, sit somewhat uncomfortably with what we know about the realities of life in Canada's House of Commons.

Whatever the disposition of MPs, there is precious little opportunity for them to express constituency views when they deviate from the positions staked out by the party leadership. Not only are their votes dictated by party leaders but open dissent or criticism of other party members is met with a variety of sanctions (e.g., Docherty 1997, 164-70). Consequently, the vast majority of votes in the House occasion no dissent (Malloy 2003, 117). For this reason, empirical studies of parliamentary voting behaviour in Canada are few and far between.[1] Even studies that focus explicitly on the constituency role of Canadian MPs, such as Franks' article (2007), do not explore for links between constituency opinion and House votes. The scholarly consensus appears to regard the question as closed. Moreover, studies of Canadian voters suggest that they do not seek to reward or punish good and faithful constituency representatives (Cross 2000, 9-10). Blais and colleagues (2003) estimate that only about 5 percent of all voters in the 2000 election based their vote decision on the local candidate, and this may reflect the presumed inattentiveness of the candidate to constituency service as much as their legislative voting record.

Thus, it might appear from our conventional understanding of the operation of the Canadian parliamentary system that neither the opportunity nor the incentive exists in Canada for MPs to base their parliamentary votes on the preferences or interests of their constituents. Accordingly, MPs have tended to seek out alternative means of representing constituents. Some MPs apparently seek to insulate themselves from potential electoral backlash against their support of locally unpopular decisions forced upon them by their party whips through dedicated and energetic service to the constituency. Such service is consistently rated the most important activity by MPs (Franks 2007). Other enterprising MPs deploy existing Commons mechanisms to advance the interests of their constituents. Although open to the public and the media, standing committees do not attract the attention of more high-profile debates on the House floor, and partisan posturing can therefore be relaxed somewhat. Skogstad's study (1985) of the House committees on Transport and Agriculture in the 32nd Parliament (1980-84) revealed that MPs were willing to push for changes in legislation that would benefit their constituents. Longley's analysis (2003) of House of Commons voting on the Canada-US Free Trade Agreement suggests that cross-pressured MPs are more likely than others to abstain from voting. More recently, Soroka and colleagues (2009) have produced compelling evidence of constituency influence in Question Period, that most visible of proceedings in the House of Commons. Similarly, Blidook (2007) has uncovered strong evidence of constituency influence on proposals introduced through Private Members' Business (Blidook 2012).

These findings suggest that constituencies factor in the representational practices of MPs in ways that the conventional scholarly focus on the strength of party discipline in the Canadian House of Commons obscures. While it may be that constituency preferences may not fully determine the voting behaviour of MPs, it seems plausible to expect that they have detectable effects on MP orientations and votes on some occasions. One likely opportunity for MPs to express constituency preferences in the legislative process arises when free votes are called. These are instances where party discipline is relaxed because of the morally or politically charged nature of the issue at hand. In free votes, MPs are able to vote either their conscience or their constituency. Yet even on these ostensibly unwhipped votes, party leaders feel free to lean on their front- and backbenchers. This may have convinced scholars that free votes will also largely be party affairs, and this is largely the conclusion of one empirical study of free votes in the Canadian House of Commons (Overby et al. 1998). This study focuses on fifteen recorded votes from all stages of parliamentary consideration of Bill C-43, a bill aiming to recriminalize abortion, between 23 and 29 May 1990. The authors found that party was by far the strongest predictor of MP behaviour on these "free" votes, and that the influence of party was strongest on the key votes that really mattered (where party unity averaged 90 percent) (Overby et al. 1998, 389). Evidence of constituency influences on MP voting was negligible in the early stages of consideration of Bill C-43, but emerged more strongly in later votes on amendments and in the final votes of record on the bill. In addition to MPs' partisanship, religious background, and cabinet membership, their results suggested that the presence of large numbers of Catholics actually disposed MPs to resist the various pro-life amendments that were considered during the legislative process. Yet, more in line with expectations, the presence of Catholics was also associated with MPs supporting the bill in the recorded votes after second and third reading.

Personal and Constituency Determinants of MPs' Public Profiles on "Social Conservatism Issues"

This chapter takes up the challenge of identifying personal and constituency factors associated with MPs' orientations to various indicators of social conservatism. Social conservatives have emerged as a significant social movement in contemporary Canadian politics. The movement emerged in the 1960s and 1970s as a reaction to the perception of moral decay of Canadian society and a desire to enlist the power of the state to return Canadians to traditional values. "For social conservatives, social order, stability, and cohesion are predicated on respect for and preservation of traditional values and beliefs – which means, simply, asserting in laws and public policy the paramount importance of traditional Judeo-Christian constructs of family, marriage, morality, and sexuality and the shared role and responsibility of both the church and the state in promoting and protecting these approaches to life" (Warner 2010, 24). In contrast to their counterparts in the United States, however, Canadian social conservatives tend to confine their political mobilization to moral issues and do not embrace conservative positions on economic or other issues (Hoover et al. 2002; Malloy 2009).

There are two ways to identify the stance that an MP takes on these moral issues. First, their recorded votes on the House floor can be examined. Second, an alternative to using the actual roll-call vote records is to turn to published sources that characterize MPs' overall positions on an issue. Often these are intended to inform voters about candidates' positions or inclinations on particular topics. In the case of the US Congress, a wide variety of characterizations and ratings of representative dispositions are available for this purpose and are frequently employed in academic analyses.[2] With the opportunity for MPs to express their personal or district interests so heavily constrained by party discipline, it is hardly surprising that Canadian voters and academics do not have a comparable variety of similar measures profiling their members of Parliament. In the case of highly contentious or deeply felt issues, however, particularly those involving moral values, the desire on the part of organized groups to mobilize and bring political pressure to bear on particular MPs, coupled with the possibility of free votes, makes it desirable to have some publicly available indication of MPs' dispositions.

Several of the issues championed by social conservatives are salient enough to merit mobilization efforts on the part of movement activists to exert political pressure on elected politicians. The issues of abortion rights and same-sex marriage are two such instances. Ever since the Supreme Court of Canada struck down Canada's existing abortion legislation in its landmark 1988 decision in *R. v. Morgentaler,* [1988] 1 S.C.R. 30, social conservatives have sought to introduce new regulatory legislation restricting

access to the procedure. The extreme position taken by social conservatives (against abortion under any circumstances) is not popular among
Canadians. Warner (2010, 25) notes that a 2008 survey showed only 5 percent holding the view that all abortions should be illegal. While the Bloc
Québécois (BQ) and the New Democratic Party (NDP) are officially pro-
choice, neither the Liberals nor the Conservatives have taken an official
position on the issue. Indeed, both major party caucuses are themselves
internally divided on the issue, but the Conservatives are generally more
pro-life and Liberals more pro-choice. Abortion emerged as an issue during
the 2004 leadership convention for the newly formed Conservative Party
of Canada (CPC) with the candidacy of pro-choice MP Belinda Stronach
alienating the more socially conservative former members of the Canadian
Alliance. Stephen Harper, the eventual winner of the CPC leadership, attempted to defuse the issue during the 2004 election campaign by saying
if elected his government would not introduce anti-abortion legislation
(though he didn't rule out this move for future Conservative governments).
So while no legislation dealing with abortion was considered by the 38th
Parliament, the issue was very much part of the political milieu. For a proxy
measure of the disposition of MPs towards the issue of abortion in the 37th
Parliament, I look at voting on the Private Member's Motion, M-83, introduced by Canadian Alliance MP Garry Breitkreuz (Yorkton-Melville) requesting a study of the medical necessity of abortion. For the subsequent
Parliament, I employ a simple dummy variable based on the listing of "anti-
choice" MPs who were elected in 2004 that was compiled by the Pro-Choice
Action Network of Canada (Arthur 2004). This list included the names of
eighty-nine pro-life MPs elected in 2004 and was used as the basis for a
dichotomous dummy variable (1 = pro-life) (see Appendix for further information on all dependent variables).[3]

If most Canadians are comfortable with some level of access to abortion
procedures, the same cannot be said for the issue of gay rights, particularly
the issue of same-sex marriage (SSM). A Canadian Broadcasting Corpora-
tion (CBC) poll taken in April 2005 suggested that 52 percent of Canadians
opposed the legalization of SSM, while 44 percent supported it (CBC News
2005). The rights of gay people have long been a target of social conservatives in Canada as elsewhere. In the 37th Parliament, the issue of same-sex
marriage was voted upon in 2003 as a motion introduced by the Canadian
Alliance opposing SSM. Introduced in February 2005 by Paul Martin's government, Bill C-38 promised to legalize SSM. The issue provoked widespread debate as well as discontent within the governing Liberal caucus.

The bill passed second reading on 4 May by a 164-137 vote, with 35 Liberal MPs voting "nay" (Deveau 2005). After the second reading vote, Liberal MP Pat O'Brien (London-Fanshawe) left the Liberal caucus to sit as an independent. Shortly afterwards, junior cabinet minister Joe Comuzzi (Thunder Bay–Superior North) resigned his cabinet post in order to be able to oppose the bill at third reading. Bill C-38 was passed by the House of Commons in June 2005 by a 158-133 vote, with support from the BQ and NDP caucuses.

A second type of measure of MP disposition concerns their general position on the issue of SSM as identified by the *Globe and Mail* (Toronto). This characterization of the MPs' stand on SSM appeared in a grid representing the floor of the House of Commons that was published by the newspaper on its website in the run-up to, and aftermath of, the period during which Bill C-38 was considered by the House of Commons. The grid showed the vote intentions of all MPs in 2005, coded as supporting (N = 140) or opposing (N = 118) SSM, or as being undecided (N = 48). The inclusion of the "undecided" category makes this a particularly useful measure for present purposes. This is because it might be assumed that MPs who are "undecided" about the issue are thus because of being subjected to significant cross-pressures, stemming from differences among positions staked out by their party, their district, or their conscience. In any event, it is plausible to argue that these waverers feel less strongly about the issue (for whatever reason) than either unabashed proponents or opponents. Having a third category between the extreme positions adds some welcome refinement to the SSM measure. A third measure of SSM attitudes is taken from the vote on the third reading of Bill C-38 itself in June 2005.

Two additional parliamentary votes in the 37th Parliament reflect other social conservative concerns. The first is an omnibus "reproductive technologies" bill that, among other things, banned cloning, facilitated assisted reproduction, and permitted research using embryonic stem cells that had been created in the course of fertility procedures (Bill C-13). A second gay rights issue was considered by the House of Commons in 2003, this one concerning a bid to add gays and lesbians to the list of groups (previously limited to those based on colour, race, religion, or ethnic origin) protected by the existing hate crimes laws (Bill C-250). Taken as a whole, these seven measures reflect the main themes of social conservative mobilization in recent Canadian political history. The available measures for each parliament are also combined to form simple additive indices (one for each parliament) of social conservatism. The empirical analysis that follows therefore assesses the relationship between individual and constituency factors and the level of support across MPs for a total of nine different indicators of social conservatism.

To explain variations in MP positions on social conservatism, I employ measures of their personal and political characteristics and various features of their constituency environments. Regarding the personal characteristics of MPs, I incorporate measures of party (where I expect Conservative, Alliance, and Independent MPs to be more socially conservative than other MPs) and cabinet membership (Liberals governed both parliaments, so a negative coefficient is expected for this measure), age and gender, marital status and whether they had children. Although Canadians from any background may be social conservatives, I expect this disposition to be strongest among older Canadians. Although I have no particular expectation about whether males or females will be more socially conservative, I include this variable to probe for any putative gender differences that may exist.[4] Similarly, I include measures of marital status and children in order to explore whether these are associated with social conservatism. Hoover and colleagues (2002, 362), for example, find that marital status is associated with "moralist priorities" and opposition to gay rights in the Canadian and US general populations. Similarly, Wilson and Lusztig (2004, 993) found that "married women in our study are much more supportive of Reform Party/Canadian Alliance candidates, and exhibit sharply more traditional social and moral views, than single women." I expect social conservatism to be negatively associated with Liberal/BQ/NDP membership (where the NDP and the BQ are included with the Liberals to serve as a reference category against which the Conservative/Alliance and Independent MPs can be compared), cabinet status, higher educational attainment, lower age, and being female.[5]

To capture the most relevant features of the riding context, I include measures drawn from the census for the 301 ridings in place for the 37th Parliament and for the 308 ridings in the 38th. Since social conservatives are active in organized religion (Malloy 2009; Warner 2010), I employ measures of the religious composition of ridings, specifically focusing on the concentration of Catholics and Protestants. My hypothesis is that concentrations of both religious groups in a riding will increase the pressure on MPs to embrace social conservative causes. For the 308 districts of the 38th Parliament, a more detailed religious breakdown is available. For the analysis of MPs in that parliament, I confine the Protestant indicator to fundamentalists (combining Pentecostals, Christian Reform, Evangelical

Missionary, Christian Missionary Alliance, and Jehovah's Witnesses). These groups are expected to be more socially conservative than more mainstream Protestant denominations. As Didi Herman has noted (1994, 273):

> For Christian moral activists, "gay rights" came to be synonymous with several things: anti-Christianity, dangerous morality, and government out of control. Foremost in fighting against such rights extension were the same type of activists as those leading the anti-abortion struggle – anti-secular conservative Christians for whom official recognition of lesbians and gay men was tantamount to the destruction of God-given family structure.

Because only cruder religious breakdowns are available for the 37th Parliament, I include a third measure capturing any effect stemming from concentrations of non-religious individuals (with the expectation that this will depress the likelihood that the MP will be a social conservative). In addition, the proportion of young people (under thirty-five years) is available for the ridings comprising the 38th Parliament, and this measure is included in those models in the expectation that younger riding populations will be less conservative on social issues than older ones (Hoover et al. 2002). The percentage of the riding's population who are university graduates and who are immigrants are available for analysis of both parliaments, as is a measure of population density (people per square kilometre). Higher educational attainment is expected to be associated with higher levels of tolerance of diversity (although Hoover et al. 2002, 362, uncover equivocal evidence of this in their survey analysis of Canadian and American respondents). Therefore, the guiding hypothesis is that high concentrations of university graduates will pressure MPs away from socially conservative positions. One might expect the well-known traditional support for the Liberal Party among immigrants to depress MP scores on social conservatism. However, over a quarter of recent migrants have come to Canada from socially conservative areas of the world (China, India, the Philippines, and Pakistan, which are not noted for their support for individual rights and where family values are strong), and this suggests that large segments of the immigrant community may support socially conservative goals (Ibbitson and Friesen 2010). In either case, it is important to include a measure of the concentration of immigrants to determine whether these communities exert pressure on MPs either for or against social conservatism. Immigrants typically settle in urban Canada, so any influence associated with this variable may embody the influences associated with a rural/urban cleavage. A substantial body of research suggests, however, that rural areas are more likely to be socially conservative than urban areas (see Cutler and Jenkins 2002; Wasko and O'Neill 2007), and these differences are not fully explained by the demographic characteristics of their residents. Thus, a measure of population density is included in every full model estimation to capture any residual rural/urban difference.

Identifying the influence of personal MP and constituency characteristics on MP disposition to social conservatism is neither a simple task nor one that leads to unequivocal results. In particular, since independent measures of MP disposition on the issues raised by social conservatives are not available (their demographic characteristics serve only as weak proxies for these), we cannot directly observe whether MPs modify their preferred behaviours to take account of constituency pressures. However, scholars studying such questions in a variety of countries have essentially relied upon a multiple regression framework in which measures of the personal characteristics of MPs and of the characteristics of their constituencies serve as key independent variables in an effort to explain variations in MP voting or attitude (for US, British, and Canadian examples, see Baughman 2004; Hogan 2008; Mughan and Scully 1997; Overby et al. 1998). In these studies, significant coefficients for constituency measures after the personal qualities of MPs are controlled are taken as evidence of the effects of constituency influence.[6] I adopt these accepted though imperfect practices in this analysis.

Results

I begin the examination of each measure of social conservatism by evaluating the contribution of personal MP characteristics solely at first, and then in combination with constituency characteristics, in the 37th Parliament.[7] Parallel analyses of the 38th Parliament follow. Table 4.1 reports binary logistic regression coefficients for the dummy dependent variable measures (2003 SSM vote, the vote on Bill C-250 dealing with hate crime, the M-83 vote on a study of the medical necessity of abortion, the vote on Bill C-13 dealing with reproductive technologies) and ordinal logistic regression coefficients for the summary five-point index (0-4) of social conservatism.

Looking first at the contribution of MPs' personal characteristics to their support for socially conservative measures, it is clear that an MP's political affiliations – with the Conservative/Alliance parties and the Liberal cabinet – are the most consistent and important influences on their positions on these issues. This accords with conventional wisdom about the strength of party in Canadian legislatures. It is also consistent with other research on free votes in Canada, where the party persists as a strong determinant of MP voting patterns (Overby et al. 1998) and in the United Kingdom (see Cowley and Stuart 2010). In fact, the impact of membership in the Conservative/Alliance caucus holds up robustly in every model – with individual and combined individual/constituency influences – in Table 4.1. The expected negative impact on social conservatism from membership in the Liberal cabinets did not materialize in the cases of the vote on adding homosexuality to the hate crimes laws or the vote on the reproductive technologies bill, but it was evident in the 2003 vote on the redefinition of marriage, the vote on studying the medical necessity of abortion, and the summary index of social conservatism.

As expected, male MPs appear to be somewhat more socially conservative, net of other personal qualities, than their female counterparts, but the effect is statistically significant only in two models (for the 2003 marriage vote and the index of social conservatism), and in both cases the effect fades when constituency characteristics are included in the full models (those including individual and constituency influences). Somewhat surprisingly, being married carries no implication for the level of social conservatism exhibited by MPs, but having children is associated with an MP's voting against gay marriage (in the full model only) and support for adding homosexuals to the groups protected by hate crimes (both models). Also surprisingly, it appears from these results that having children is more likely to result in socially conservative views on issues related to homosexuality than on right-to-life ones. There is no evidence to support the hypothesis that older MPs would be more socially conservative than younger ones, although the coefficient nears statistical significance with the expected positive sign on the issue of protecting homosexuals in the hate crime legislation.

Net of these personal factors, what happens when measures of the MPs' constituencies are included? The full models estimated for each of the dependent variables address this by adding the constituency measures to the characteristics of MPs. Several indicators of the constituency environment appear to be related to MPs' support for socially conservative measures. The presence of immigrants contributes to the social conservatism of MPs in the vote on gay marriage, in the vote requesting a study of the medical necessity of abortion, and in the summary index of social conservatism. These results appear to confirm the view expressed earlier that whereas traditional immigrants might have supported Liberal candidates (and liberal

TABLE 4.1

Personal and constituency determinants of MPs' social conservatism in the 37th Parliament

	Marriage vote, 2003[a]	Marriage vote, 2003[a]	C-250 vote, 2003[b]	C-250 vote, 2003[b]	M-83 vote, 2003[c]	M-83 vote, 2003[c]	C-13[d]	C-13[d]	SCI (0-4)[e]	SCI (0-4)[e]
Personal										
Male	0.93	0.94	0.68	0.49	0.74	0.73	0.11	-0.05	0.69	0.43
	(.03)	(.06)	(.22)	(.40)	(.11)	(.16)	(.77)	(.91)	(.03)	(.21)
Married	0.32	0.16	0.05	-0.26	0.87	0.58	-0.28	0.03	0.09	0.13
	(.58)	(.81)	(.95)	(.74)	(.20)	(.43)	(.60)	(.97)	(.84)	(.78)
Children	0.23	0.33	0.37	0.38	0.16	0.22	0.06	0.000	0.19	0.18
	(.09)	(.03)	(.02)	(.02)	(.26)	(.15)	(.65)	(.99)	(.06)	(.07)
Age	-0.003	-0.02	0.04	0.04	0.02	0.006	-0.01	0.005	0.003	0.001
	(.90)	(.44)	(.10)	(.08)	(.44)	(.81)	(.60)	(.97)	(.86)	.93
Conservative/Alliance	3.24	3.48	2.90	2.64	3.26	0.30	2.28	2.74	3.41	3.59
	(.000)	(.000)	(.000)	(.000)	(.000)	(.000)	(.000)	(.000)	(.000)	(.000)
Liberal cabinet member	-2.79	-3.73	-19.01	-19.03	-2.31	-2.78	-20.15	-19.9	-3.57	-3.68
	(.007)	(.001)	(.99)	(.99)	(.03)	(.01)	(.99)	(.99)	(.000)	(.000)
Riding										
% immigration		*0.15*		*0.02*		*0.10*		-0.05		*0.06*
		(.000)		*(.66)*		*(.02)*		(.21)		*(.03)*
% university degrees		-0.03		-0.06		*-0.11*		-0.07		-0.07
		(.34)		(.14)		*(.005)*		(.05)		(.01)

% Catholics	0.07 (.14)		−0.03 (.58)		0.02 (.64)		−0.05 (.32)		0.02 (.56)
% Protestants	0.09 (.06)		−0.014 (.79)		0.05 (.35)		−0.09 *(.05)*		0.01 (.74)
% no religion	0.04 (.43)		−0.05 (.39)		0.04 (.48)		−0.04 (.45)		0.004 (.92)
Population density (per km²)	*0.0001 (.001)*		0.0001 (.24)		*0.0001 (.025)*		0.0001 (.52)		*0.0001 (.000)*
Constant	−2.23 *(.045)*	−9.65 (.06)	−5.81 *(.000)*	−2.48 (.65)	−3.84 *(.001)*	−6.18 (.24)	−0.50 (.64)	5.73 (.24)		
−2 Log-likelihood	241.53	201.48	184.54	176.64	227.3	191.57	260.41	225.95	531.84	563.92
Cox and Snell pseudo R^2	.367	.456	.324	.344	.369	.448	.276	.364	.495	.537

Notes: Shown in the table cells are the binary/ordinal (for social conservatism index) logistic coefficients and *p* values (in parentheses). Personal MP characteristics are first analyzed singly and then in combination with constituency characteristics. Italic type indicates statistical significance at *p* < .05.

a Same-sex marriage vote (0 = yes; 1 = no).

b Bill C-250 on adding sexual orientation to hate crimes law (0 = no; 1 = yes).

c Motion M-83 on study of medical necessity of abortion (0 = yes; 1 = no).

d Bill C-13 on reproductive technologies (0 = yes; 1 = no).

e Social conservatism index (0 = most liberal; 4 = most socially conservative).

TABLE 4.2

Personal and constituency determinants of MPs' position on social conservatism issues in the 38th Parliament

	Pro-life?[a]	Pro-life?[a]	Same-sex marriage G&M[b]	Same-sex marriage G&M[b]	Same-sex marriage vote, 2005[c]	Same-sex marriage vote, 2005[c]	STI (0-3)[d]	STI (0-3)[d]
Personal								
Male	0.66	0.55	0.55	0.40	0.58	0.37	0.61	0.53
	(.19)	(.29)	(.17)	(.37)	(.24)	(.49)	(.09)	(.17)
Married	−0.17	−0.57	0.20	−0.25	−0.36	−0.74	0.20	−0.4
	(.85)	(.53)	(.82)	(.78)	(.75)	(.51)	(.78)	(.58)
Children	0.31	0.28	0.1	0.07	0.28	0.25	0.09	0.18
	(.04)	(.07)	(.45)	(.64)	(.09)	(.16)	(.10)	(.14)
Age (2005)	0.05	0.05	0.008	0.02	0.03	0.03	0.02	0.03
	(.03)	(.03)	(.68)	(.43)	(.31)	(.27)	(.18)	(.09)
Conservative	2.83	2.66	3.63	3.60	4.3	4.24	3.69	3.65
	(.000)	(.000)	(.000)	(.000)	(.000)	(.000)	(.000)	(.000)
Independent	1.99	1.71	21.6	21.2	−19.88	−21	3.48	3.14
	(.18)	(.26)	(n/a)	(n/a)	(.99)	(.99)	(.02)	(.03)
Cabinet member	−0.76	−0.54	−1.99	−1.79	−1.28	−0.96	−2.08	−1.89
	(.50)	(.64)	(.07)	(.12)	(.24)	(.40)	(.05)	(.08)
Riding								
% immigration		0.02	0.05	0.05	0.05	0.05	0.05	0.05
		(.24)	(.001)	(.001)	(.02)	(.02)	(.001)	(.001)

% university degrees		−0.04 (.26)		−0.05 (.08)		−0.03 (.32)		**−0.05** (.05)
% < 35 years		−0.06 (.41)		−0.12 (.07)		−0.10 (.21)		−0.08 (.12)
% Catholics		0.0001 (.99)		0.003 (.79)		0.003 (.85)		0.01 (.63)
% Fundamentalists[e]		0.11 (.48)		0.25 (.09)		0.17 (.28)		**0.24** (.04)
Population density (per km²)		0.0001 (.80)		0.0001 (.15)		0.0001 (.26)		0.0001 (.24)
Constant	**−5.42** (.000)	−3.76 (.07)			**3.27** (.03)	−1.17 (.65)		
−2 Log-likelihood	202.26	196.5	268.41	277.61	170.82	159.2	382.49	398.01
Cox and Snell pseudo R^2	.336	.353	.470	.536	.468	.497	.515	.575

Notes: Shown in the table cells are the binary/ordinal (for social conservatism index) logistic coefficients and p values (in parentheses).

Personal MP characteristics are first analyzed singly and then in combination with constituency characteristics. Bold type indicates statistical significance at $p < .05$.

a Pro-life dummy (0 = pro-choice; 1 = pro-life).

b Position on same-sex marriage, Globe and Mail (0 = for; 1 = undecided; 2 = against).

c Same-sex marriage vote (0 = yes; 1 = no).

d Social traditionalism index (0–3 additive index combining pro-choice and same-sex marriage Globe and Mail variables) (0 = socially liberal MP; 3 = socially conservative MP).

e Fundamentalists = Pentecostals, Christian Reform, Evangelical Missionary, Christian Missionary Alliance, and Jehovah's Witnesses.

causes), they may now be more inclined to press for socially conservative outcomes. High concentrations of university graduates in ridings were generally associated with lower MP support for socially conservative measures (the expected negative coefficient was found in all cases, and in three of the five full models it was statistically significant). Somewhat surprisingly, the religious composition of ridings bore no statistically significant relationship to MP positions – indeed, the only coefficient for religion that met the .05 threshold of statistical significance (% Protestant in the model for voting on the reproductive technologies bill) had a negative sign, which was the opposite of the hypothesis. Similarly, the rural/urban variable as measured by the population density of ridings also defies expectations. In three of the five models (the 2003 marriage vote; the vote on a study of the medical necessity of abortion, and the index of social conservatism), the coefficient for this measure is statistically significant, but in every case it carries a positive sign, indicating that social conservative support on the part of MPs is higher in more densely populated settings. This may reflect the fact that recent waves of immigration to Canada have come disproportionately from areas of the world where socially conservative values predominate.

The 37th Parliament featured a Liberal majority government led by Prime Ministers Jean Chrétien and, after December 2003, Paul Martin. The election of 28 June 2004 returned Martin to power for the 38th Parliament but with only a minority government, and he faced a united right in the Conservative Party under Stephen Harper. Were the personal and political characteristics of MPs important in influencing the levels of social conservative support on the part of MPs in the 2004-06 period? Did the increased uncertainty that accompanies a minority government mean that MPs seem to be more attuned to their constituents? Table 4.2 addresses these questions (albeit the second one only indirectly).

Looking first at the political factors, once again the affiliation of MPs with the now-united Conservative Party of Canada was the single most important and consistent factor influencing MP social conservatism, with a positive and statistically robust coefficient generated in every model. Independent MPs were also more conservative than the BQ, Liberals, and NDP, at least as captured by the composite index score. Surprisingly, and in contrast to the findings for the 37th Parliament, holding cabinet rank in Paul Martin's minority government was not generally associated with the MPs' diminished support for social conservative causes. Only in the case of the summary index of social conservatism was the expected negative coefficient statistically significant (although it approached the .05 level for the

Globe and Mail's SSM measure). Beyond this, the only other personal characteristic associated with a significant effect on MP social conservatism was an MP's age, in the case of being labelled "pro-life."

The full models, which incorporate constituency measures, do not generally add much more of general note to this story, and it seems clear from the large number of insignificant coefficients that the minority government situation did not render MPs any more likely than their counterparts in the 37th Parliament to stake out positions that might be in line with their constituencies. The one exception to this generalization is the concentration of immigrants in a riding. As with the analysis of the 37th Parliament, MPs from ridings with higher percentages of immigrants appear to be more socially conservative, although the coefficient does not reach significance in the case of the pro-life dummy. MPs representing ridings with higher concentrations of university graduates generally tend to be less socially conservative (negative coefficients in all four models), but only in the case of the summary index was the coefficient statistically significant. Contrary to expectations, the religious composition of a riding's population does not generally influence MP social conservatism, although higher index scores are associated (as expected) with higher percentages of fundamentalist Protestants. Once again, contrary to my hypothesis, there is no evidence of a rural/urban divide (with population density as proxy) in the 38th Parliament.

Conclusion

This chapter has presented evidence that party affiliation and cabinet membership are important determinants of MP voting and disposition on several social conservative issues in the 37th and 38th Parliaments (2000-06). This finding confirms the conventional wisdom that party politics dominates the House of Commons, even when controversial moral issues, which may cause extraordinarily high constituency pressure to be brought to bear on an MP, are at stake. The results also make it clear, however, that in this domain there is more to the representational story than these political factors. Other personal factors, such as MP gender, children, and age, also have an influence on their orientations towards socially conservative issues and legislation. No one personal demographic characteristic is significantly related to MP positions on every social conservative cause, but occasionally they do appear as significant determinants of MP positions, all other things being equal.

Similarly, the analyses provide evidence of a constituency connection in the representative process in the area of social conservatism. Although many of the hypothesized relationships between constituency settings and MP orientations did not materialize, the immigrant complexion of a riding and the presence of university graduates were two characteristics of the setting of MPs that appear to be influential in a number of cases. Given the relative bluntness of these measures of the constituency context, finding evidence of these relationships in a study of some of the most deeply controversial issues confronting contemporary Canadian parliamentarians underscores the significance of these results.

It appears that the practice of parliamentary representation is somewhat more complex and nuanced than conventionally depicted. Whereas MPs' desire for re-election has provided them with an incentive to vote in the House according to their constituents' views, the recent rise of "morality politics" provides them with an important new set of opportunities to do so. In these policy domains at least, and contrary to the scholarly consensus, it is not all about party discipline and responsible party government (although admittedly these are the dominant forces at work here, as in most policy domains). The findings reported here suggest that MPs respond to more than the party whip in voting and taking positions. Their personal characteristics also play a role, and so apparently do their constituents. Finding evidence of a constituency dimension to the social conservatism of MPs complements other recent work suggesting that there is more grounding of these processes in the constituency trenches than has heretofore been appreciated.

Important questions remain to be answered, however. In noting the relationship between MP orientations and riding characteristics, we cannot simply conclude that this correspondence results from a process whereby MPs subordinate their personal values on these issues to those of their constituents (i.e., a true exercise in "constituency control"). It is entirely possible that voters elect MPs because of the congruity of MPs' personal beliefs with their own, and therefore no yielding of MP preferences to constituency pressures is necessary to achieve effective constituency representation. This interesting question must be left to future research. For the moment, I simply suggest that answering this question should be an important priority if we are to advance our appreciation of how constituency interests and preferences continue to be reflected in the formal parliamentary policy process.

APPENDIX: Definition of Dependent Variables

Definition of Marriage Vote, 16 September 2003

This is the first of three measures reflecting MP orientations towards the issue of same-sex marriage. This issue has been on the public agenda of the gay and lesbian community since August 1989. This motion, submitted by the Canadian Alliance following the Chrétien government's request for a reference opinion from the Supreme Court of Canada on the text of legislation legalizing same-sex marriage on 17 July 2003, was defeated by one vote. Chrétien forced his cabinet ministers to oppose the motion, but fifty-two Liberal MPs supported it. A further 31 Liberal MPs abstained. Larocque (2006, 298) says that the motion was defeated by a vote of 137-132.

The text of the motion was as follows:

> That, in the opinion of this House, it is necessary, in light of public debate around recent court decisions, to reaffirm that marriage is and should remain the union of one man and one woman to the exclusion of all others, and that Parliament take all necessary steps within the jurisdiction of the Parliament of Canada to preserve this definition of marriage in Canada.

For accounts of this in the context of a full discussion of the same-sex marriage debates in Canada's parliament, see Larocque 2006; Hennigar 2009, 209-27; and Warner 2010, 146-87. Voting records of MPs were taken from the "LifeSiteNews.com Political Report – Oct. 30, 2003," available at http://www.campaignlifecoalition.com/fedvotes/mpvotingbyprovince.pdf.

Bill C-250, Adding Sexual Orientation to Hate Crime, 17 September 2003

This measure consists of the vote on the third reading of Bill C-250, introduced by Jean Chrétien's Liberal government. This bill followed an unsuccessful attempt in 2002 by New Democrat MP Svend Robinson to pass a Private Member's Bill to amend section 318 of the Criminal Code (regarding genocide) and section 319 (public incitement of hatred) to include sexual orientation within the listing of grounds to distinguish identifiable groups. Although Robinson's bill was not adopted, Bill C-250 added "sexual orientation" to the list of protected classes in the hate propaganda sections (318 and 319) of the Criminal Code. For an account of these legislative initiatives, and of the backlash they provoked among social conservatives, see Warner 2010, 139-45).

The text of the bill was as follows:

1. Subsection 318(4) of the Criminal Code is replaced by the following:

   Definition of "identifiable group"

   (4) In this section, "identifiable group" means any section of the public distinguished by colour, race, religion, ethnic origin or sexual
   orientation.

Voting records of MPs were taken from the "LifeSiteNews.com Political
Report – Oct. 30, 2003," available at http://www.campaignlifecoalition.
com/fedvotes/mpvotingbyprovince.pdf.

Private Member's Motion M-83, Request for a Study on the Medical Necessity of Abortion, 1 October 2003

Introduced by MP Garry Breitkreuz (Yorkton-Melville, Canadian Alliance),
the motion proposed:

That the Standing Committee on Health fully examine, study and report to
Parliament on: (a) whether or not abortions are medically necessary for the
purpose of maintaining health, preventing disease or diagnosing or treating an injury, illness or disability; and (b) the health risks for women under-
going abortions compared to women carrying their babies to full term.

Voting records of MPs were taken from the "LifeSiteNews.com Political
Report – Oct. 30, 2003," available at http://www.campaignlifecoalition.
com/fedvotes/mpvotingbyprovince.pdf.

Bill C-13, Reproductive Technologies Bill, 28 October 2003

This measure consists of the vote on third reading of an omnibus bill introduced by the Chrétien government in 2002 that would establish a legislative
and regulatory framework to address issues relating to assisted human reproduction and research involving the in vitro embryo. The legislation also
dealt with cloning, experimentation on embryonic humans, the buying
and selling of sperm and eggs, in vitro fertilization, the creation of animal/
human hybrids, and financial compensation for surrogates. On 28 October
2003, the House of Commons passed Bill C-13 (formerly Bill C-56) by a vote
of 149-109.

Voting records of MPs were taken from the "LifeSiteNews.com Political Report – Oct. 30, 2003," available at: http://www.campaignlifecoalition. com/fedvotes/mpvotingbyprovince.pdf.

MP Positions on the Same-Sex Marriage Issue, *Globe and Mail*, Spring-Summer 2005

In the run-up to the vote on Bill C-38, introduced by Paul Martin's Liberal government and passed by the House of Commons on 28 June 2005, the Toronto *Globe and Mail*'s website (http://www.theglobeandmail.com/) presented a floor plan of the House of Commons, indicating which MPs were on record as supporting or opposing the bill, or who were undecided. Given the high salience of this issue, my assumption is that those undecided MPs were most likely to have been experiencing significant cross-pressures on this measure.

Bill C-38, Civil Marriages Act, 28 June 2005

Introduced by Liberal Justice Minister Irwin Cotler on 1 February 2005, this bill aimed to change the legal definition of marriage from being the union of only one man and one woman by amending relevant federal legislation according to the following sentence: "Marriage, for civil purposes, is the lawful union of two persons to the exclusion of all others."

MP voting records were taken from "Third Reading Vote on Bill C-38 (Civil Marriage Act)" (http://www.campaignlifecoalition.com/fedvotes/C-38. htm). Since it was a government bill, cabinet members were bound to vote for it, but Liberal backbenchers and members of the Conservative Party, the NDP, and the Bloc Québécois had a free vote. In the run-up to the final House of Commons vote, at least a dozen Liberal MPs plotted to defeat the bill and Liberal MP Pat O'Brien (London-Fanshawe), resigned from the Liberal caucus over this vote (Taber 2005).

Liberal and Conservative Party MP Positions on Abortion, Pro-Choice Action Network, 2004

This measure is taken from a list of Liberal and Conservative MPs elected after 2004 who were considered anti-choice (i.e., "pro-life"), published by the Pro-Choice Action Network at http://www.prochoiceactionnetwork -canada.org/articles/discouraging-victory.shtml.

Acknowledgments

This is a revised and expanded version of a paper originally prepared (with Annika Hagley) for the annual conference of the Canadian Political Science Association held at Concordia University, Montreal, on 1-3 June 2010. I am grateful to David Docherty, Peter Loewen, and Kelly Blidook, among other participants at the conference, and to Amanda Bittner and Royce Koop, for their helpful suggestions. The standard disclaimer applies.

Notes

1 This is in significant contrast to the situation in the United Kingdom, where the generally lower level of discipline in House voting has prompted a number of empirical studies of the correlates and consequences of parliamentary dissent. See, for example, Cowley and Stuart (2005, 2010); Hibbing and Marsh (1987); Hoare (1996); Mughan and Scully (1997); Pattie et al. (1994); Read et al. (1994).

2 For example, Americans for Democratic Action (ADA) scores; Poole and Rosenthal's DW-Nominate scores; the American Conservative Union's ratings, etc. See, for example, McCarty et al. (2006).

3 In fact, the Abortion Rights Coalition of Canada has updated and extended this list of "anti-choice" MPs to account for subsequent elections. See http://www.arcc -cdac.ca/action/list-antichoice-mps-nov08.html. In addition to actual votes on relevant bills, this group sends questionnaires to candidates for elected federal office and makes responses available online.

4 Suggestive of this, for example, is the observation of Brooke Jeffrey that most Reform MPs elected in 1993 with strong links to social conservatives were "predominantly older, middle class, white males" (quoted in Warner 2010, 224). Similarly, Malloy (2010, 8) notes that nearly all the MPs who attend the weekly "prayer breakfasts" on Parliament Hill are male.

5 Biographical details on MPs from the 37th and 38th Parliaments were taken from a variety of reference sources. The primary source for both parliaments was the *Canadian Parliamentary Guide* (2001 and 2005 editions). When complete information was not available in this source, John Bejermi's *Canadian Parliamentary Handbook* was consulted. Finally, if questions persisted, the MP's web site and other available Internet sources were checked.

6 Christopher Kam's analysis (2001) of voting in the British and Canadian House of Commons attempts to advance on this by employing measures of MPs' orientations taken from their responses to candidate surveys in order to determine whether the high level of party voting observed in both chambers is the result of the exercise of party discipline or due to the tendency of like-minded MPs to be elected to each party. Unfortunately, comparable survey data are not available for the issues considered in this chapter.

7 Blidook (2007) shows that MP dyadic representational behaviour regarding PMB proposals varies according to the electoral context. Exploration for any sign that MPs elected by smaller margins of victory in the previous election was conducted for the 38th Parliament, but results are not included here because no evidence of any impact of competitiveness was uncovered.

References

Arthur, Joyce. 2004. "A Discouraging Victory: More Anti-Choice MPs Elected than Before." Pro-Choice Action Network. http://www.prochoiceactionnetwork -canada.org/.

Baughman, John. 2004. "Party, Constituency, and Representation: Votes on Abortion in the British House of Commons." *Public Choice* 120 (1-2): 63-85.

Blais, André, Elizabeth Gidengil, Agnieszka Dobrzynska, Neil Nevitte, and Richard Nadeau. 2003. "Does the Local Candidate Matter? Candidate Effects in the Canadian Election of 2000." *Canadian Journal of Political Science* 36 (3): 657-64.

Blidook, Kelly. 2007. "Dyadic Representation." PhD dissertation, McGill University.

–. 2012. *Constituency Influence in Parliament: Countering the Centre.* Vancouver: UBC Press.

Carty, R. Kenneth, William Cross, and Lisa Young. 2000. *Rebuilding Canadian Party Politics.* Vancouver: UBC Press.

CBC News. 2005. "Canadians Deeply Split on Same-Sex Marriage, Poll Suggests." CBC News. http://www.cbc.ca/.

Cowley, Philip, and Mark Stuart. 2005. "Being Policed? Or Just Pleasing Themselves? Electoral Rewards and Punishment for Legislative Behaviour in the UK in 2005." Paper presented at the Elections, Public Opinion and Parties Conference, University of Essex, Colchester, UK, September.

–. 2010. "Party Rules, OK: Voting in the House of Commons on the Human Fertilisation and Embryology Bill, Research Note." *Parliamentary Affairs* 63 (1): 173-81.

Cross, Bill. 2000. *Members of Parliament, Voters, and Democracy in the House of Commons.* Parliamentary Perspectives No. 3. Ottawa: Canadian Study of Parliament Group. http://www.studyparliament.ca/.

Cutler, Fred, and Richard Jenkins. 2002. "Where One Lives and What One Thinks: Implications of Rural-Urban Opinion Cleavages for Canadian Federalism." In *State of the Federation 2001 – Canadian Political Culture(s) in Transition,* edited by Harvey Lazar and Hamish Telford, 367-90. Montreal and Kingston: McGill-Queen's University Press.

Deveau, Scott. 2005. "O'Brien Leaves Liberals over Same-Sex Bill." *Globe and Mail,* 6 June. http://www.theglobeandmail.com/.

Docherty, David. 1997. *Mr. Smith Goes to Ottawa: Life in the House of Commons.* Vancouver: UBC Press.

Eagles, Munroe. 1998. "The Political Ecology of Representation in English Canada: MPs and Their Constituencies." *American Review of Canadian Studies* 28 (1-2): 53-79.

Eulau, Heinz, John C. Wahlke, William Buchanan, and Leroy C. Ferguson. 1959. "The Role of the Representative: Some Empirical Observations Based on the Theory of Edmund Burke." *American Political Science Review* 53 (3): 203-27.

Franks, C.E.S. 1997. "Free Votes in the House of Commons: A Problematic Reform." *Policy Options* (November): 33-36.

–. 2007. "Members and Constituency Roles in the Canadian Federal System." *Regional and Federal Studies* 17 (1): 23-45.

Hennigar, Matthew. 2009. *"Reference re Same-Sex Marriage:* Making Sense of the Government's Strategy." In *Contested Constitutionalism: Reflections on the Canadian Charter of Rights and Freedoms,* edited by James B. Kelly and Christopher P. Manfredi, 209-30. Vancouver: UBC Press.

Herman, Didi. 1994. "The Christian Right and the Politics of Morality in Canada." *Parliamentary Affairs* 47: 268-79.

Hibbing, John R., and David Marsh. 1987. "Accounting for the Voting Patterns of British MPs on Free Votes." *Legislative Studies Quarterly* 12 (2): 275-97.

Hoare, Anthony G. 1996. "Hunting for Votes: The Geography of Free Votes and Electoral Advantage in the British House of Commons." *Geoforum* 26 (4): 459-78.

Hogan, Robert E. 2008. "Sex and the Statehouse: The Effects of Gender on Legislative Roll-Call Voting." *Social Science Quarterly* 89 (4): 955-68.

Hoover, Dennis R., Michael D. Martinez, Samuel H. Reimer, and Kenneth D. Wald. 2002. "Evangelicalism Meets the Continental Divide: Moral and Economic Conservatism in the United States and Canada." *Political Research Quarterly* 55 (2): 351-74.

Ibbitson, John, and Joe Friesen. 2010. "Conservative Immigrants Boost Tory Fortunes." *Globe and Mail,* 4 October. http://www.theglobeandmail.com/.

Kam, Christopher. 2001. "Do Ideological Preferences Explain Parliamentary Behaviour? Evidence from Great Britain and Canada." *Journal of Legislative Studies* 7 (4): 89-126.

Kornberg, Allan. 1967. *Canadian Legislative Behavior: A Study of the 25th Parliament.* New York: Holt, Rinehart and Winston.

Larocque, Sylvain. 2006. *Gay Marriage: The Story of a Canadian Social Revolution.* Toronto: James Lorimer.

Longley, Neil. 2003. "Modeling the Legislator as an Agent for the Party: The Effects of Strict Party Discipline on Legislator Voting Behavior." *Contemporary Economic Policy* 21 (4): 490-99.

Malloy, Jonathan. 2003. "High Discipline, Low Cohesion? The Uncertain Patterns of Canadian Parliamentary Groups." *Journal of Legislative Studies* 9 (4): 116-29.

–. 2009. "Bush/Harper? Canadian and American Evangelical Politics Compared." *American Review of Canadian Studies* 39 (4): 352-63.

–. 2010. "The Private Faith and Public Lives of Evangelical MPs." Paper presented to the Canadian Political Science Association annual conference, Concordia University, Montreal, June.

McCarty, Nolan, Keith T. Poole, and Howard Rosenthal. 2006. *Polarized America: The Dance of Ideology and Unequal Riches.* Cambridge, MA: MIT Press.

Miller, Warren E., and Donald E. Stokes. 1963. "Constituency Influence in Congress." *American Political Science Review* 57 (1): 45-56.

Mooney, Christopher Z. 2001. "The Public Clash of Private Values." In *The Public Clash of Private Values: The Politics of Morality Policy,* edited by Christopher Z. Mooney, 3-20. Chatham, NJ: Chatham House.

Mughan, Anthony, and Roger M. Scully. 1997. "Accounting for Change in Free Vote Outcomes in the House of Commons." *British Journal of Political Science* 27 (4): 640-47.

Overby, L. Marvin, Raymond Tatalovich, and Donley T. Studlar. 1998. "Party and Free Votes in Canada: Abortion in the House of Commons." *Party Politics* 4 (3): 381-92.

Pattie, Charles, Edward Fieldhouse, and R.J. Johnston. 1994. "The Price of Conscience: The Electoral Correlates and Consequences of Free Votes and Rebellions in the British House of Commons, 1987-92." *British Journal of Political Science* 24: 359-80.

Price, Richard, and Maureen Mancuso. 1991. "Ties that Bind: Parliamentary Members and Their Constituents." In *Introductory Readings in Canadian Government*, edited by Robert M. Krause and R.H. Wagenberg, 211-35. Mississauga: Copp Clark Pitman.

Read, Melvyn, David Marsh, and David Richards. 1994. "Why Did They Do It? Voting on Homosexuality and Capital Punishment in the House of Commons." *Parliamentary Affairs* 47: 374-86.

Siegfried, André. [1906] 1966. *The Race Question in Canada*. Toronto: McClelland and Stewart.

Skogstad, Grace. 1985. "Interest Groups, Representation, and Conflict Management in the Standing Committees of the Canadian House of Commons." *Canadian Journal of Political Science* 17: 739-72.

Smith, David E. 2007. *The People's House of Commons: Theories of Democracy in Contention*. Toronto: University of Toronto Press.

Soroka, Stuart, Erin Penner, and Kelly Blidook. 2009. "Constituency Influence in Parliament." *Canadian Journal of Political Science* 42 (3): 563-91.

Taber, Jane. 2005. "Liberals Plot to Kill Same-Sex Marriage." *Globe and Mail,* 7 June. http://www.theglobeandmail.com/.

Thomas, Tim. 2001. "An Emerging Party Cleavage: Metropolis vs. the Rest." In *Party Politics in Canada*, 8th ed., edited by Hugh Thorburn and Alan Whitehorn, 431-44. Toronto: Prentice Hall.

Ward, Norman. 1950. *The Canadian House of Commons: Representation*. Toronto: University of Toronto Press.

Warner, Tom. 2010. *Losing Control: Canada's Social Conservatives in the Age of Rights*. Toronto: Between the Lines.

Wasko, Kevin, and Brenda O'Neill. 2007. "The Urban/Suburban/Rural Cleavage in Canadian Political Opinion." Paper presented to the Canadian Political Science Association annual conference, University of Saskatchewan, Saskatoon, June.

Wilson, J. Matthew, and Michael Lusztig. 2004. "The Spouse in the House: What Explains the Marriage Gap in Canada?" *Canadian Journal of Political Science* 37 (4): 979-95.

5

City Ministers
The Local Politics of Cabinet Selection
ANTHONY M. SAYERS

In a qualitative analysis of seven federal electoral districts in British Columbia during the 1988 election, I suggest that on the basis of the growing importance of the media, city contests play a key role in modern campaigns (Sayers 1999). Because of this, political parties have an interest in attracting candidates capable of suitably representing the party in these districts. One means of doing this is to offer potential candidates a position in cabinet. If true, we should see a tendency for city MPs to be over-represented in cabinet.

The driver of the relationship between city MPs and cabinet is the density of information networks – media outlets and the myriad organizations they use to help tell news stories – in city districts or ridings. Political parties see this as an opportunity to transmit party policy and images to the regional electorate – not just to the downtown area but also to related suburban constituencies and beyond – and to gauge the state of the regional campaign in return. These city campaigns act as critical nodes in national and regional campaigns, with high-profile local candidates personifying the party and its message.

To explore this question, the analysis in this chapter builds a model for distinguishing between city, suburban, and rural ridings and then, using data from the period 1984-2008, assesses whether there are significant differences in patterns of selection of city and non-city MPs to cabinet, both nationwide and by region.

The results suggest that parties and leaders do turn to cities to populate cabinet. Providing cabinet positions to MPs in these ridings helps to attract the high-profile candidates that political parties hope will carry their message in these districts. Parties have a resource in high-profile MPs, while in return city voters gain representation in government.

Cities are more heavily represented in federal cabinets than in governing party caucuses, although much more strongly in the case of the Liberal Party than for the Tories.[1] Conservative cabinets are in general less urban than Liberal cabinets.[2] The Progressive Conservative cabinets of the Mulroney era are relatively urban; this pattern is weaker but still true for Stephen Harper's Conservative cabinets of 2004 and 2006, but reversed in 2008 when the cabinet is very marginally less urban than the caucus. Given the Conservatives' success in 2011 and the potential for new alignments in the party system, it may take a couple of elections for any new pattern to emerge and stabilize.

The changing calculations of prime ministers with respect to building cabinets reflect changes in the character of campaigns and the growing importance of the media and cities in Canadian politics. To the degree that the media as currently structured remain central to election campaign strategies, so too will city ridings. Yet this changing calculus reflects continuity as well. Cabinet remains a key mechanism for balancing competing political forces and attracting and retaining competent politicians. As well, the manner in which this effect is manifested reflects continuing differences in the support bases and styles of the two parties that have held power, the Liberals and the Conservatives. As Siegfried noted over a century ago, Canadian politics is driven by two powerful logics: the importance of local impulses and the centrality of leaders (Siegfried [1906] 1966, 130, 136).

City Ridings

Industrialization, urbanization, and globalization have made cities hubs for both society and the economy; no political party can afford to ignore, or be seen to ignore, the major national metropolises. Yet the geography of single-member plurality electoral systems may fit uncomfortably with the demands of a modern election communication strategy; election strategists must find ways of addressing voters across a large number of city ridings. Selecting one or two of the local city campaigns as regional nodes in the national campaign is one solution to this challenge.

Positive media coverage is precious to any election campaign. Successfully managing relations with major metropolitan, provincial, and national

media as well as the social, political, and economic organizations head-
quartered in cities can have significant multiplier effects across the region
and beyond. Media reports of good relations between a party and major
business organizations housed in downtown Toronto play well with pro-
business voters not only in that metropolitan region but provincially and
even nationally. This is particularly true when national news organizations
are working feverishly to provide daily coverage of the election; stories close
to their city headquarters are much cheaper and easier to bring to air or
print, and are often read across the region or country (Sayers 1991).

Cities are socially and economically heterogeneous, with a politics
that relies more heavily on associational linkages among voters than the
communal ties found in traditional communities (Kasarda and Janowitz
1974, 328-29; Sayers 1999, 110). Voters experience sharply different levels
of economic well-being, are drawn from a range of ethnic backgrounds,
and exhibit a wide variety of lifestyles. High population densities and the
commercial character of cities attract large media outlets, while social
heterogeneity encourages smaller publications – such as ethnic and life-
style publications – that help sustain a complex local political environment
and agenda. The media play a central role in how residents and outsiders
understand the city, and reflect the increasingly dominant role of cities in
their regions and provinces in terms of population and economic and political clout (Hoffman and Eveland 2010; see Janowitz 1967).

Many of the groups with regional headquarters in cities have members
spread across the region and country. They see elections as opportunities to
force parties to address their concerns, priming the media to challenge politicians on these matters. Taken together, complex local agendas and good
media coverage have special appeal for political parties hoping to address
a wide range of issues and large number of voters not just downtown but
within the reach of city newscasts. Party strategists rely on this combination of associational politics and media and organizational density to transmit their election messages in what is a city-wide issue space that reaches
across several ridings and may be dominant over a larger region (Sayers
1991). To do so effectively, parties try to offer up candidates comfortable in
such an environment (Stipp 1991), which in turn makes these candidates
well suited to act as spokespersons for the party platform.

These pressures remain between elections. The social and political organizations in city ridings provide a convenient means for political parties
and governments to sustain their connections with civil society. Executive-

dominated Canadian governments rely heavily on such connections to provide them with critical information on the mood of the wider society and, in return, use these connections to help manage the relationship between government and society (Pal 1993). Again, media looking to make sense of a wide range of issues are likely to seek out nearby city MPs. If these MPs are competent media performers, this becomes a reinforcing cycle – the media seeking them out and the party providing them.

This underlying view of the special demands of city ridings influences how parties search for candidates (Sayers 1999, 32-33). Candidates and MPs must be comfortable in diverse social circumstances and able to make the most of the available media coverage. They must be able to confidently articulate the party's positions even when confronted with complex local and regional issues and agendas.

Attracting such candidates may require offering them a relatively free ride through the nomination process (Koop and Bittner 2011) and the promise of a ministerial appointment, the latter to encourage them to run for office and to offer back to the city the sorts of political connections and goods that may strengthen links between it and the government. For their part, city voters will come to expect representation in cabinet, and that their MP will be a powerful player in any government.

Methodology

The central claim to be tested here requires there to be identifiable, salient differences in the style of politics in city or urban ridings, which in turn relate to distinctive media profiles and social composition. While the distinct media profile of cities is clear (Janowitz 1967; Carrol and Hannan 1989), a dependable means of distinguishing the social composition of city ridings from others is required to test this claim. Conventional definitions of urban areas are too expansive to be useful for this analysis. Statistics Canada, for example, defines "urban" as an "area with a population of at least 1,000 and no fewer than 400 persons per square kilometre" (Statistics Canada 2001a). According to this definition, 78 percent of Canadians live in urban areas (Statistics Canada 2001b, 9). Moreover, this definition does not accurately capture the appropriate geographical unit of measurement, the electoral riding. For instance, one riding may encompass several urban areas, or one urban area may include several ridings.

For the purpose of this study, eight characteristics are used to better describe and identify urban districts. The first two – population density and land values – are geographic in character and associated with distance from the city centre. Several social features considered by sociologists and social geographers as indicators of urbanness (see Davies 1993; Kasarda and Janowitz 1974; Robinson 1991; Walks 2004) are combined with these geographic features in order to construct an index of urbanism for each federal riding, thus permitting easy comparison.[3]

Population Density

There are two limitations to using population density as an indicator of city ridings. First, it is a relatively crude indicator for identifying social change. Second, researchers have noted, "the most immediate physical characteristic of Canadian cities is their low density and extensive development pattern" (Thraves 1991, 271). In spite of its limitations, its capacity to make broad distinctions – density does increase as one moves from country to suburban and finally city ridings – makes it a widely used measure with the advantages of being both linear and simple to apply. So although it does not directly identify social features, it creates a continuum along which the three types of ridings are logically distributed and is a good initial indicator that ties in with other research on social change (Walks 2006; Wasko and O'Neill 2007).

Land Values

Analysis of the value of private dwellings is also useful, as research suggests that Canadian city centres can be distinguished "in terms of land values and bid rents" (Collins 1991, 156). In general, due to higher surrounding commercial prices, residential home prices and rents in city centres are higher than in surrounding areas.

Transience

A number of factors associated with housing and housing stock as well as mobility help us distinguish various types of ridings, particularly city constituencies. Kasarda and Janowitz suggest that transience is the primary characteristic of urban centres (1974, 328-29). As well, the mobility of urban voters indicated by "substantial numbers of voters living in high-rise apartments" (many of them renters) has shaped the organizational and campaigning behaviour of parties" (Sayers 1999, 115). The rental population and the number of individuals who have moved since the last year provide strong indicators of transience within different ridings and distinguish city ridings by their high levels of mobility.

Immigrants

City centres "tend to be occupied by more recent immigrant groups" than either suburban or rural centres (Collins 1991, 163). For example, in the 1990s, Citizenship and Immigration Canada reported that 94 percent of immigrants settled in urban areas. Moreover, 80 percent settled in the census metropolitan areas of Toronto, Vancouver, and Montreal (Citizenship and Immigration Canada 2003). The availability of rental housing in city downtowns encourages new immigrants to settle there. To capture this, a measure of the proportion of the population consisting of immigrants is included in the model.

Ethnic Heterogeneity

One result of increased immigration patterns to urban centres is the creation of "very different ethnic profiles in metropolitan centres, ensuring that there are considerable ethnic variations in the social balance of these centres" (Davies 1993, 112; see also Chapter 7 of this book). Put differently, country ridings are more socially homogeneous than city ridings, while suburban ridings vary greatly in this regard (Sayers 1999, 112). Although it does not always distinguish city ridings from the broader collection of ridings, as patterns of ethnic settlement are varied, the three categories of ridings cluster in a predictable pattern from country, to suburban, to city, with the last being the most ethnically diverse.

Occupation

Since the Second World War, occupation structures of urban centres have been characterized by specialization in the services/corporate sector (Davies 1993, 110). This suggests an increase in the proportion of individuals involved in managerial, financial, and/or administrative occupations. While this distinguishes city from suburban ridings, many country ridings require managerial staff to run primary sector industries. In order to clearly distinguish between city and country ridings, a measure for the percentage of the population employed in the primary sector is included. Together, these two variables provide a strong indication of the occupational and industrial structure of a riding and help distinguish city from suburban and country ridings.

Education

Country ridings are likely to have lower levels of postsecondary education, while suburban and city ridings are likely to have higher educational levels

(Sayers 1999, 112-16). Because high levels of education do not always translate into economic success for individuals in big cities, this measure, in
combination with economic indicators, helps distinguish well-educated
and economically homogeneous suburban from well-educated but economically heterogeneous city populations.

Age

Urban geographers note that "the elderly are usually over-concentrated in
core areas or older suburban locations" (Thraves 1991, 273). This is most
likely due to older settlement patterns coupled with city expansion. Again,
while not a robust measure in and of itself, as it does not help us distinguish
between city and some older suburban ridings, in combination with other
measures it strengthens the capacity of the model to identify different types
of ridings.

The following analysis uses these measures to build an index of urbanness (see Appendix 1). This index is then used to explore whether MPs from
city ridings are more likely to be appointed to cabinet than their suburban
or country colleagues.

Data

Data were collected from Statistics Canada, Elections Canada, and Eagles
and colleagues (1991) for the 1984, 1988, 1993, 1997, 2000, 2004, 2006,
and 2008 Canadian federal elections, matching census data and the relevant representation order. Table 5.1 outlines the data source for each election year.[4]

In terms of governments, these elections include both Liberal and
Progressive Conservative majorities as well as the Liberal minority of 2004
and Conservative Party minorities of 2006 and 2008. This enables us to test
whether the relationship holds regardless of party affiliation and government status. As noted by Cairns (1968), the present electoral system exacer-
bates regional tendencies and thus most federal majorities do not have
complete national representation. The inclusion of a range of elections increases the chances of including cases where each region has some representation within the government party and cabinet.

The city index is used to test the relationship between city ridings and
cabinet ministers in three ways. The initial comparison tests the extent to
which ridings represented by both cabinet ministers and backbench MPs
are city ridings. In each instance, ridings represented by non-government
parties are excluded, as these ridings cannot enjoy cabinet representation.

TABLE 5.1
Data sources for the analysis of Canadian federal elections
for the period 1984-2008

Election year	Representation order	Census
1984	1976	1981
1988[a]	1987	1987
1993	1987	1991
1997	1996	1996
2000	1996	2001
2004	2003	2001
2006	2003	2001
2008	2003	2001

a Data for the 1988 election are different from those for other elections due to a lack of readily available data at Statistics Canada. Data for this election have been drawn from Eagles et al. 1991.

Next, a binary logistic regression for the 2000 election enables us to differentiate between the social background of MPs and the characteristics of their ridings. This enables us to determine whether riding characteristics are in some way a proxy for personal characteristics that might be important in determining access to cabinet.

Finally, specific regions in different election years are analyzed to test whether the relationship holds when the government has robust representation within each region. Given Canada's pattern of regional representation (Carty et al. 2000), it is necessary to test each region separately to see whether the pattern holds across Canada. For this test, the government party must have at least twenty seats within a given region, guaranteeing that the prime minister has exercised a real choice rather than having to choose a regional minister from a very small group of MPs.

Riding Characteristics and Cabinet Membership
Applying the measures underlying the index for the 2000 election as a starting point, Table 5.2 provides preliminary evidence that the ridings from which cabinet ministers are drawn are indeed more likely to be in cities than those of backbench MPs. As these are population rather than sample data, significance is not strictly relevant. It is worth noting, however, that density, age distribution, transience, and ethnic makeup are distinctive enough to be statistically significant ($p < .05$). Table 5.2 confirms that the ridings from which cabinet ministers were drawn display characteristics consistent with the definition of city ridings used here. For example, they

TABLE 5.2
Comparison between backbench and cabinet MPs based on electoral district characteristics, 2000

Descriptors		Backbench MPs	Cabinet MPs
Geographic	Land value	$171,111.37	$186,681.35
	Density	1,342.60	2,650.74
Social	Elderly	11.87%	13.37%
	Transience	32.35%	43.81%
	Immigrants	19.58%	26.91%
	University education	18.22%	21.52%
	Minorities	13.88%	19.74%
	Ethnic homogeneity[a]	.7870	.6863
Economic	Primary sector employment	3.76%	2.63%
	Business sector employment	27.01%	29.25%

a   A lower score indicates greater *heterogeneity*. See Appendix 1 for an explanation.

exhibit, on average, higher land values, more immigrants, more minorities, more individuals with high education, and lower levels of primary sector employment.

This preliminary evidence from the 2000 election suggests that the proposed relationship between cabinet membership and urban-ness exists. An index based on these measures is used to test this across elections from 1984 to 2008. The results are displayed in Figure 5.1 (see Appendix 1 for an explanation of the index). It is worth noting that since the measure of urbanness is relative from one election to the next, these figures do not permit us to test any impact of variation in Canada's urban population on the selection of ministers.

Figure 5.1 suggests that the parliamentary average over time is relatively stable, although some decline may be associated with variation in the underlying measures used in the index across the elections (see Table 5.1) and the over-representation of rural regions in the Commons. A corollary of this is that city ridings have tended to become larger than average by population, reducing the expression of urban factors in the Commons over this period.

The data show that the seats from which cabinet members are drawn are more urban than those of the governing party caucus as a whole. In the early period of the dataset, the Mulroney Progressive Conservative cabinet was more urban than its caucus, although much less so than subsequent

FIGURE 5.1
Urban-ness of Parliament, government party, and cabinet, 1984-2008

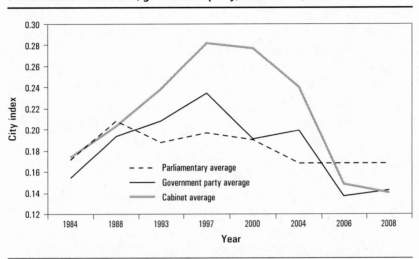

Notes: A higher score is associated with greater urban qualities. A continuous function is used here for illustrative purposes. The data are discrete, being the composition of each category immediately following the relevant election.

Liberal cabinets. The second Harper government, in 2008, is the only exception to the general rule that cabinet is more urban than caucus, being about as urban as the caucus. It is possible that the particular constellation of support for the Conservatives may help explain this 2008 outcome. The party's city seats are overwhelmingly western, and a desire to include representation in cabinet from outside the region may well have required greater reliance on non-urban ridings elsewhere in selecting ministers. The party caucus as a whole was marginally more urban in 2008 than in 2006, reflecting success in Ottawa and Quebec City.

The distinctiveness of cabinet in comparison with governing party caucus is most pronounced for the Liberals, for whom the cabinet is usually much more urban than the party caucus (1993-2004). The gap between caucus and cabinet is widest for the Liberals in 1997 and 2000, extraordinarily so in the latter case in the context of these data. The 2004 election produced a decline in the urban quality of Paul Martin's first post-election cabinet as Liberal leader. This, combined with an increase in the urban quality of the Liberal caucus as the Tories gained seats in the countryside at the expense of the governing party, leads to a sharply reduced difference for the 2004 Liberal minority government.

Partisan differences are also evident in the pattern of cabinet and parliamentary averages. The Progressive Conservative government of Brian Mulroney and the recent Tory governments of Stephen Harper are all below the parliamentary average. Their relative exclusion from urban centres is an example of just one of the many ways in which the PCs and the new Conservatives differ from the Liberals, seeming more like "outsider" parties. Put differently, the opposition parties were on average more urban than the PC party and about as urban as the PC cabinets of 1984 and 1988. This pattern is even more obvious under the post-2006 Conservative minority governments. The cabinet may be more urban than the party caucus, but both consist of MPs from seats that are on average much less urban than the average parliamentary riding. The Liberals, New Democrats, and Bloc Québécois are in general more urban than the post-2006 Tories.

With Liberal governments, the pattern is sharply reversed, with cabinet much more urban than parliament (Walks 2004). In 1997 and 2000, the gap between the governing Liberal Party and the parliamentary measure was at its widest, consistent with the very rural character of the Reform Party/ Canadian Alliance opposition in particular. The data do support the contention that cabinet seats are likely to be more urban on average than caucus seats, but with fairly distinctive patterns across Liberal and Conservative governments and caucuses.

Figure 5.2 provides another way of thinking about these data, displaying the ratio of the index for cabinet to the index for the governing party, for cabinet to Parliament, and for caucus to Parliament. Beginning with the first ratio, except for the 2008-11 Harper government, the data reveal that cabinet is always more urban than the governing party caucus (ratio > 1). It highlights the 2000 Liberal cabinet as being much more urban than its caucus. Considering the caucus/parliamentary ratio for this period (and also data in Figure 5.1) it is evident that this bump was produced not by the growing city character of cabinet but by a collapse in the average urbanness of the caucus, partly because the party broadened its appeal in Quebec and parts of Atlantic Canada. The electoral collapse of the party in 2004 left the caucus more like cabinet – more urban – as the party relied more heavily on its urban redoubts. This limited electoral appeal was more evident in the 2011 election.

These ratios bring into sharper relief several patterns in the relationship between cabinet and Parliament. For instance, the cabinet/Parliament ratio captures the loss of city seats by the Tories in 1988, resulting in the second

FIGURE 5.2
Relative urbanness of cabinet, government party, and Parliament

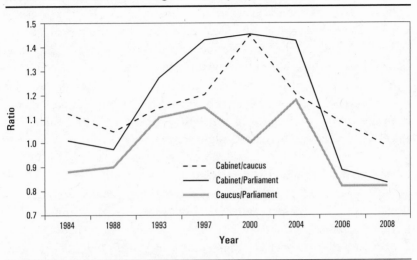

Notes: A score above 1 indicates greater urbanness, below 1 the reverse with respect to the comparator category. A continuous function is used here for illustrative purposes. The data are discrete, being the composition of each category immediately following the relevant election.

Mulroney-led government's being more reliant on the Tories' traditional non-urban base for its majority. The cabinet became less urban than Parliament (the ratio dropping below 1). This is in stark contrast to the massive differences between Liberal cabinets and Parliament between 1997 and 2004, the former being nearly 1.5 times as urban as the latter, and above about 1.3 for the entire decade of Liberal governments. The two end points clearly demonstrate that Progressive Conservative and Conservative cabinets tend to be less urban than Parliament on average, particularly in the case of the new Conservative Party. The Harper cabinet sends the ratio back below 1 for the first time since the Mulroney years, but it is even less urban than Parliament compared with its PC predecessor. It makes clear the challenges facing Mr. Harper as he tries to extend his party's reach into urban Canada. The caucus/Parliament ratio confirms the distinctive appeal of the Liberals and Conservatives in city and non-city ridings.

Across this time period, these data support the claim that cabinets are nearly always more urban than the caucus of the governing party. This is particularly so for the choices of Liberal prime ministers, who most strongly favour city MPs when choosing ministers. Liberal cabinets are much more urban than their caucus than is the case for PC and Conservative govern-ments. Liberal caucuses are more urban than Parliament, except after the 2000 election, when it was about as urban as Parliament; PC and Conserv-ative caucuses are less urban than Parliament. The traditional urban–versus–non-urban divide between the Liberal and Conservative Parties is quite evident (Blais et al. 2002, 93; Walks 2004, 419).

The analysis begs the question of whether the Liberals' penchant for over-representing city ridings in cabinet will have any effect on its long-term appeal outside cities, and brings into sharp relief its competition with the New Democratic Party, particularly for the votes of urban Canadians.

Factors that Determine Cabinet Selection

Given their distinctive and diverse character, it is possible that urban rid-ings act as a proxy for some other factor or factors that might influence se-lection to cabinet (Kerby 2009; Kam 2003; see Table 5.2) – that is, the city districts are disproportionately represented by certain types of MPs who have a greater chance of gaining cabinet selection. Logistic regression per-mits a direct comparison of a range of factors that might influence cabinet selection, including gender, minorities, occupation (lawyer), those with graduate-level education, and whether the MP represents one of the top thirty most urban ridings (approximately the number of cabinet members).

Each of these other variables was selected because it has been argued to have some effect on the likelihood that a particular MP might make it to cabinet. To be clear, the test here is not whether these characteristics have an effect, but whether city-ness is a proxy for these other factors; even if it is found not to be, this does not necessarily have a bearing on the relation-ship between these characteristics and the likelihood of cabinet member-ship. For the personal descriptors, each variable used is a dummy variable with data collected from the Library of Parliament or the *Canadian Par-liamentary Guide* (see Appendix 2).

In this instance, the city variable is modified to control for regional vari-ations in representation. It identifies the top thirty city ridings using a ratio of riding urbanness to regional urbanness. Given that representation is structured by province and region, it is important to identify these patterns at the subnational level. A national measure of urban-ness may well exclude some regions (the most urban ridings in some provinces may not register on such a list). For instance, if there are no Saskatchewan ridings in the mix, it is impossible to test for the effect in that province. This approach over-comes this problem.

TABLE 5.3
Characteristics that may affect selection to cabinet, based on the 2000 federal election results

Characteristic	Odds ratio	(Standard error)
City	3.911	(0.495)*
High education	1.038	(0.449)
Lawyer	0.735	(0.492)
Sex	0.952	(0.478)
Minority	1.344	(0.631)
N	301	
–2 Log-likelihood	160.878	
Cox and Snell R^2	.156	
Nagelkerke R^2	.307	

* $p < .01$

This ratio then enables us to control for regional disparities in partisan representation that Docherty (2002, 350) notes decrease and increase the likelihood of cabinet representation among certain regions. Because of variation in partisan representation by region, a prime minister may be choosing from a limited number of city MPs or even the reverse, a limited number of rural MPs, the latter biasing any measures in favour of the hypothesis. For example, in the case of the 2000 election, after which the Liberals' western representation was highly urban, this measure enables us to identify whether the *most* urban of the ridings held by the Liberals in the west gained cabinet representation. This ratio is therefore a rigorous test for any relationship between urbanness and cabinet selection.

Table 5.3 reveals that in 2000, of this set of characteristics that might affect cabinet selection (see Kerby 2009), only being from a city district had a statistically significant impact on the chances of selection. This does not mean that cabinet ministers are uneducated and/or unqualified, only that there are just as many highly educated and qualified individuals in the backbench as there are in cabinet. Being from a city riding increases the odds of an MP's being in cabinet by about four times (3.91) that of his or her non-city colleague. That is, the city effect is independent of personal characteristics. It may still be the case that personal characteristics shape selection to cabinet, but these effects are under-theorized.

TABLE 5.4

Ratio of average cabinet-seat city index by region to average
government-seat city index by region

	1984	1988	1993	1997	2000	2004	2006	2008
Atlantic	●	✳[b]	✕	✳[b]	✕[a]	●	✳[b]	✳[b]
Quebec	●	✕	✳[b]	●	●	●	✳	✳
Ontario	●	●	●	●	●	●	●	●
West	●	●	●	✳[b]	✳[b]	●	●	●

Notes: ● = ministers' seats on average more urban than the average for the region; ✕ = ministers' seats less urban than average; ✳ = insufficient choice. Only regions where the government party has at least twenty seats from which to select cabinet ministers, with one exception (noted below).

a In 2000, the Liberals won nineteen seats in Atlantic Canada, but it is included as a borderline case.

b Although choice was limited (< 20) in these regions, in these cases ministers were drawn from seats with a higher city index on average than the average for the government party in the region.

Regional Variation in Cabinet Selection

Given regional patterns of partisan representation and the dilemma posed in the logistic regression regarding access to seats in Parliament, it is worth exploring whether the relationship between city-ness and cabinet holds across each region when there are sufficient numbers of regional MPs to allow for such an effect. To guarantee choice, the analysis includes each region where the governing party has at least twenty seats following an election, to determine whether, given reasonable choice, prime ministers are more likely to select an MP from a city constituency.

Table 5.4 compares the average city-ness of the seats of cabinet ministers in a region with the average for all government seats in that region. Solid bullets indicate cases where the seats of ministers are overall more urban than the average for government seats in the region; ✕'s indicate where they are less so. Excluded are those cases where there was no adequate choice (fewer than twenty seats, with one noted exception). As Table 5.4 illustrates, when given adequate choice, prime ministers select cabinet members disproportionately from city ridings in all regions of the country. Only in Atlantic Canada is there any serious challenge to this pattern, partly due to lack of choice.

City Ministers and the Power of Party Leaders and Prime Ministers

The debate over the role of regional ministers as power brokers in cabinet is central to the nature of modern cabinets (Sayers 2002, 310). According to some authors, the growth of the administrative state leaves senior ministers with relatively few discretionary powers (Cairns 1979, 6; Smiley 1980, 134). Others argue that ministers have taken advantage of project funding opportunities to carve out a role in directing resources (Bakvis 1991, 287-89). Both sides agree, however, that the centralization of the federal executive and replacement of regional party organizations with assertive provincial ones have altered the nature of regional representation (Sayers 2002, 310).

This analysis suggests that the selection of cabinet is shaped by the growing importance of cities both broadly and with respect to election campaigns. Offering ministerial appointments to high-profile city MPs increases the likelihood that regional ministers will be from such districts. Given the manner in which they are nominated and join cabinet, these MPs are likely to see themselves as having a particular allegiance to the socially complex cities they represent and to the prime minister, another manifestation of the central role of localism and party leadership in Canadian political parties and politics (Siegfried [1906] 1966). The particular constellation of skills required to meet the challenges of being a party spokesperson, to deal with the media, and to interact with powerful political and economic groups may well result in a new type of regional power broker (note, for example, the story of David Emerson, discussed later). It is perhaps the novelty of this new form of regional representation that prevents traditional accounts of cabinet politics from explaining changing patterns of cabinet composition. A sound understanding of local conditions is critical to a comprehensive account of cabinet politics.

The power of the party leader to shape nominations and of the prime minister to control access to cabinet are the critical mechanisms that permit this pattern to emerge. The veto over nominations is a formalization of the central role of leaders in Canadian parties and politics (Siegfried [1906] 1966, 118 and 136; Whitaker 2001, 16). It reveals the continued reliance of Canadian parties on a clientelistic organizing principle centred on the leader balancing local political forces rather than the ideological or institutional incentives common in political parties elsewhere. It has remained perhaps the defining feature of successful Canadian parties even as their form has changed from cadre to stratarchical over the last century (Carty 2004). These two features indicate the distinctive trajectory of Canadian parties within the broader pattern of increasing electoral professionalism among parties throughout the democratic world (Panebianco 1988).

That the major parties retain the imprint of nineteenth-century cadre-style organization says much about the continuity in this trajectory across one and a half centuries. There has been a lack of historical breaks such as domestic war or revolution to disrupt party development. Coupled with high levels of social mobility, Canadian parties have not experienced the pressures that led to the development of mass parties elsewhere (Sayers 2008). Canada's relatively slow rate of urbanization and uneven industrialization over that period (Gibson 1973) also spared parties the disruptions that attend these processes. As in the United States, the growing importance of urban and suburban Canada in recent decades (Walks 2004) is re-shaping the way parties operate. Even the rising NDP, perhaps the closest to a mass party of all the Canadian parties, has had to adopt many of the forms found to be effective by its older counterparts. The importance of Jack Layton's leadership to its success in Quebec in the 2011 election highlights this continuity.

Prime ministers have long had to balance regional, linguistic, gender, ethnic, and other factors in building their cabinets (Bakvis 1991; Kerby 2009). To these must be added the particular appeal of urban representation in cabinet as a factor in shaping its final composition. This appeal is driven by deep changes in Canadian society associated with increased urbanization and the growing centrality of cities – including fast-growing suburbs – to the economy and politics over the twentieth century (Walks 2005, 2006; Wasko and O'Neill 2007). Yet it is mediated by traditional forms found in Canadian politics, particularly the unusual importance of party leaders, the power of localism, and long-standing differences in the appeal of Liberals and Conservatives to urban, rural, and suburban Canada. The importance of cities in the formation of cabinet also suggests that concern over rural over-representation in the Commons should be kept in perspective: cities may indeed have a great deal of influence in the core decision-making body of government.

Conclusion

Canadian cabinets are generally disproportionately urban compared with the party caucuses and parliaments from which they are drawn. As one MP has noted, "you have to have a minister from PEI, you have to make sure you have a minister from the big cities ... then you have 100 other factors, demography, ethnicity" (Kam 2003). It seems that the selection of cabinet ministers reflects the interaction of local conditions, organizational incentives, and strategic electoral and legislative considerations. This suggests that local riding factors have a powerful effect on national politics.

City ridings hold special appeal for party strategists, one that rests on a range of factors that distinguish them from their suburban and rural counterparts. They are densely populated, socially heterogeneous, and economically important. These ridings are home to, or adjacent to, the headquarters of major media organizations as well as myriad smaller organizations and publications aimed at niche audiences. These media give form to the local political agenda, and broadcast throughout the suburbs and regions adjacent to cities. Parties have a vested interest in attracting competent, high-profile candidates in such ridings who go on to lead nodal regional campaigns. Party leaders hope that the offer of a cabinet position is enough to attract such candidates to run for the party.

There is support for this conclusion in a comparison of the composition of federal and Ontario provincial cabinets (Walks 2004). It suggests that urbanness has an impact on the formation of federal cabinets but not on their Ontario counterparts. This is consistent with the notion that a particular set of forces, such as the need to wage federal campaigns in distinctive regions centred on major cities across a large and diverse country, helps drive the salience of local conditions in the selection of cabinet members.

The link between cities and cabinet reveals a number of important features of Canadian parties and the national party system. The centrality and power of the party leader formalized in the leader's veto over candidates and the power to select the cabinet as prime minister are the mechanisms that permit the effect. The effect is also modulated by traditional differences between the major parties, particularly the Liberals' greater success in urban areas and the Tories' appeal in the suburbs and rural Canada.

The synergy between finding good candidates to run in important, complex city ridings so that the party looks good and performs well, and the appeal of adding known supporters to cabinet, is a strong inducement for party leaders to become involved in some local nomination contests. At the same time, Canadian parties rely on members of riding associations to fulfill important functions, such as candidate selection and campaigning. In using their veto – or suasion – to shape the selection of candidates, party leaders must consider whether interference will repel these local activists who are critical to electoral success.

This study also suggests that to the degree that cabinet membership is important to career advancement, ambitious candidates or MPs are likely to seek out city ridings. An example is seen in Liberal MP Tony Valeri's willingness to change ridings to fight Sheila Copps for the nomination in Hamilton–Stoney Creek in 2004, and his subsequent appointment as Liberal House Leader. As well, prime ministers seeking high-profile candidates to represent important ridings or fulfill particular roles in cabinet are likely to be open to appointing candidates, bypassing the normal nomination processes. Liberals Glenn Murray in Winnipeg and Bev Longstaff in Calgary are examples from 2004; Jean Chrétien made use of this approach throughout his tenure as prime minister from 1993 to 2004.

Stephen Harper's successful post-election wooing of Vancouver Liberal David Emerson, which led Emerson to cross the floor to join the Tory government, and his appointment of Montreal native Pierre Fortier to the Senate so that both could sit in cabinet after the 2006 federal election are also consistent with this view. There is also evidence that MPs appointed by the party leader are more likely to fill high-profile roles – such as membership in cabinet – than those who undergo the standard riding-based nomination process (Koop and Bittner 2011). The link between being appointed as a candidate and being rewarded with a cabinet position is consistent with the story told here.

A close examination of the role of local politics in cabinet formation may help explain the composition of cabinets and policy outcomes. The cabinet calculus is becoming increasingly complex as urban representation is added to traditional regional and linguistic concerns and more recent gender and ethnicity considerations when prime ministers select cabinet colleagues. To the degree that these considerations have displaced or modified the traditional regional calculus in the formation of cabinet, there should be a decline in the salience of models that rely on the latter to explain cabinet membership. A city minister may see his or her core tasks – representing the government to the region and the interests of the region to the government – in a manner that is distinct from ministers in previous eras, who were appointed directly on the strength of their regional connections.

It is quite possible that the over-representation of rural Canada in the House of Commons may be less important to political outcomes than the degree of urban representation in cabinet. Consideration of the impact of urban, suburban, and rural concerns on policy making should take account of the representation of these interests within the various branches of government. There are, for instance, predictable differences in the opinions of urban, suburban, and rural Canadians (Walks 2005, 2006; Wasko and O'Neill 2007). The pattern of representation of these Canadians in the key executive body is likely to have important implications for government and public policy.

APPENDIX 1: Operationalization of the City Index

The city index results from the addition of the normalized scores on the following measures and has a hypothetical range of 0 to 1. Given the structure of the variables, however, the index typically ranged from .15 to .50.

Riding Density. Each riding's basic density was calculated as "population/ km^2" using Elections Canada data, after which the density of each riding was divided by the value of the most densely populated riding.

Residential Land Value. Each riding's average land value, as determined by Statistics Canada, was divided by the value of the riding with the highest land value.

Proportion Immigrants. As determined by Statistics Canada, the total number of immigrants as a percentage of the total population.

Proportion Minorities. As determined by Statistics Canada, the total number of visible minorities as a percentage of the total population.

Ethnic Homogeneity. Using the ethnic groups reported by Statistics Canada, a value of 0 to 1 was created using the Herfindahl index, as defined by:

$$EDI = \Sigma^n_{i=1} (E_i)^2$$

where E_i is ethnic group i's proportion of the total population in the district and $n = x$ ethnic groups. If all x ethnic groups are of equal size in a riding, then the *EDI* would be equal to $1/x$. Ridings dominated by one ethnic group will be associated with *EDI* measures approximating 1. (Description based on Eagles et al. 1995.)

Proportion High Education. As determined by Statistics Canada, the number of individuals with university education as a percentage of the total population.

Proportion Elderly. As determined by Statistics Canada, the number of elderly individuals over sixty-five years of age as a percentage of the total population.

Proportion Movers. As determined by Statistics Canada, the number of individuals who moved residence in the past year as a percentage of the total population.

Proportion Renters. As determined by Statistics Canada, the number of individuals who rented as a percentage of the total population.

Proportion Business Industry Classification. As determined by Statistics
Canada, the number of individuals in industries related to finance, in-
surance, and business services as a percentage of the total population.

Proportion Business Occupation Classification. As determined by Statistics
Canada, the number of individuals employed in occupations related to
management, business, finance, and/or administration as a percentage
of the total population.

TABLE 5.5
Variables used in determining the city index

	Election Years					
Variable	2004-08	2000	1997	1993	1988	1984
Geographic descriptor						
Riding density	•	•	•	•	•	•
Residential land value	•	•	•	•	•	
Social descriptors						
Proportion immigrants	•	•	•	•	•	•
Proportion minorities	•	•	•			
Ethnic homogeneity	•	•	•			
Proportion high education	•	•	•	•	•	•
Proportion elderly	•	•	•	•	•	•
Proportion transience						
Movers			•	•	•	
Renters	•	•	•	•	•	•
Economic descriptors[a]						
Proportion business						
Industry classification			•	•	•	•
Occupation classification	•	•	•			
Proportion primary sector						
Industry classification			•	•	•	•
Occupation classification	•	•	•			
Cronbach's alpha	.792	.892	.890	.851	.839	.806

a In 1997, Statistics Canada used both occupation and industry to measure primary, secondary, and tertiary
employment. As a result, for this year the two variables have been averaged to avoid duplication.

Proportion Primary Sector Industry Classification. As determined by Statistics Canada, the number of individuals in industries related to agriculture, fishing, trapping, logging, forestry, mining, and quarrying as a percentage of the total population.

Proportion Primary Sector Occupation Classification. As determined by Statistics Canada, the number of individuals employed in occupations unique to the primary sector as a percentage of the total population.

Due to differences in measurement over time, not all the variables selected were available for each election year. At a minimum, seven variables were used, and at a maximum all thirteen were used. This information is outlined in Table 5.5. Despite the differences in measures used, the inter-reliability of the variables in each election year illustrates that the variables are reliable indicators of city ridings.

APPENDIX 2: Operationalization for the Binary Logistic Regression

For the binary logistic regression, the following dummy variables were created:

City. Since only districts representing the government party were selected, each district's city index was divided by the average value of the index for each region (Atlantic, Quebec, Ontario, West) to control for regional discrepancies in partisan representation. In this manner, Liberal representation in western Canada was not washed out by their urban domination in this region. Following the creation of this index, the top thirty districts were selected as being "city ridings," and given a value of 1.

Sex. Using data provided by the Library of Parliament, any female MP was given a value of 1.

Minorities. Using data provided by the Library of Parliament, any MP born outside of Canada (excluding the United States and the United Kingdom) was given a value of 1.

High Education. Using the *Canadian Parliamentary Guide* for the 2000 election, any MP with graduate education (MA, MS, MSW, MDiv, LLM, MBA) was given a value of 1.

Lawyer. Using the *Canadian Parliamentary Guide* for the 2000 election, any MP whose occupation was listed as "lawyer" was given a value of 1.

Acknowledgments

Thanks to David de Groot and Paul Fairie for their excellent research assistance.

Notes

1 The Tory name is given to both the Progressive Conservative Party and the Conservative Party of Canada, which was created in 2003 by the merger of the Canadian Alliance and the Progressive Conservative Party.
2 Unless otherwise noted, the terms "urban" and "city" are used interchangeably in the text.
3 An initial attempt to use a categorical measure to separate city districts from others foundered on the apparent arbitrariness of the distinction both within individual cities and across provinces and regions.
4 Semi-Custom Census Profiles were applied by Statistics Canada to the 1976, 1987, 1996, and 2003 Representation Orders that define the electoral district boundaries used in federal elections, available at http://www5.statcan.gc.ca/bsolc/olc-cel/ olc-cel?lang=eng&catno=97C0002.

References

Bakvis, Herman. 1991. *Regional Ministers: Power and Influence in the Canadian Cabinet.* Toronto: University of Toronto Press.

Blais, André, Elisabeth Gidengil, Richard Nadeau, and Neil Nevitte. 2002. *Anatomy of a Liberal Victory: Making Sense of the Vote in the 2000 Canadian Election.* Peterborough, ON: Broadview Press.

Cairns, Alan C. 1968. "The Electoral System and the Party System in Canada, 1921-1965." *Canadian Journal of Political Science* 1 (1): 55-80.

–. 1979. *From Interstate to Intrastate Federalism in Canada.* Kingston, ON: Queen's University, Institute for Intergovernmental Relations.

Carrol, Glenn R., and Michael T. Hannan. 1989. "Density Dependence in the Evolution of Populations of Newspaper Organizations." *American Sociological Review* 54 (4): 524-41.

Carty, R. Kenneth. 2004. "Parties as Franchise Systems: The Stratarchical Organizational Imperative." *Party Politics* 10 (1): 5-24.

Carty, R. Kenneth, William Cross, and Lisa Young. 2000. *Rebuilding Canadian Party Politics.* Vancouver: UBC Press.

Citizenship and Immigration Canada. 2003. "Immigrants in Canada: Census 2001 Highlights." *The Monitor* (Summer): 6.

Collins, Lyndhurst. 1991. "Canadian Cities: Recent Developments and the Changing Image." In *A Social Geography of Canada,* edited by Guy M. Robinson, 154-69. Toronto: Dundurn Press.

Davies, W.K.D. 1993. "Metropolitan Dominance and Differentiation." In *Canadian Transformations: Perspectives on a Changing Human Geography,* edited by W.K.D. Davies, 96-117. Swansea, UK: University of Wales Canadian Studies Group.

Docherty, David. 2002. "Political Careers in Canada." In *Citizen Politics: Research and Theory in Canadian Political Behaviour,* edited by Joanna Everitt and Brenda O'Neill, 338-54. Toronto: Oxford University Press.

Eagles, M., J. Bickerton, A. Gagnon, and P. Smith. 1991. *The Almanac of Canadian Politics.* Peterborough, ON: Broadview Press.

–. 1995. *The Almanac of Canadian Politics.* 2nd ed. Toronto: Oxford University Press.

Gibson, Campbell. 1973. "Urbanization in New Zealand: A Comparative Analysis." *Demography* 10 (1): 71-84.

Hoffman, Lindsay H., and William P. Eveland Jr. 2010. "Assessing Causality in the Relationship between Community Attachment and Local News Media Use." *Mass Communication and Society* 13: 174-95.

Janowitz, M. 1967. *The Community Press in an Urban Setting: The Social Elements of Urbanism.* Chicago: University of Chicago Press.

Kam, Christopher (Liberal MP). 2003. Interview by author. Ottawa.

Kasarda, John D., and Morris Janowitz. 1974. "Community Attachment in Mass Society." *American Sociological Review* 39: 328-39.

Kerby, Matthew. 2009. "Worth the Wait: Determinants of Ministerial Appointment in Canada, 1935-2008." *Canadian Journal of Political Science* 42 (3): 593-611.

Koop, Royce, and Amanda Bittner. 2011. "Parachuted into Parliament: Candidate Nomination, Appointed Candidates, and Legislative Roles in Canada." *Journal of Elections, Public Opinion, and Parties* 21 (4): 431-52.

Pal, Leslie. 1993. *Interest of State: The Politics of Language, Multiculturalism and Feminism in Canada.* Montreal and Kingston: McGill-Queen's University Press.

Panebianco, Angelo. 1988. *Political Parties: Organization and Power.* Cambridge: Cambridge University Press.

Robinson, Guy M., ed. 1991. *A Social Geography of Canada.* Toronto: Dundurn Press.

Sayers, Anthony M. 1991. "Local Issues Space in National Elections: Kootenay West–Revelstoke and Vancouver Centre." In *Reaching the Voter: Constituency Campaigning in Canada,* edited by Frederick J. Fletcher and David V.J. Bell, 15-48. Toronto: Dundurn Press.

–. 1999. *Parties, Candidates, and Constituency Campaigns in Canadian Elections.* Vancouver: UBC Press.

–. 2002. "The Study of Political Leaders and Activists." In *Citizen Politics: Research and Theory in Canadian Political Behaviour,* edited by Joanna Everitt and Brenda O'Neill, 301-20. Toronto: Oxford University Press.

–. 2008. "The End of Brokerage? The Canadian Party System in the 21st Century." In *Canadian Politics in the 21st Century,* edited by Michael S. Whittington and Glen Williams, 137-52. Peterborough, ON: Broadview Press.

Siegfried, André. [1906] 1966. *The Race Question in Canada.* Toronto: McClelland and Stewart.

Smiley, Donald. 1980. *Canada in Question: Federalism in the Eighties.* Toronto: McGraw-Hill Ryerson.

Statistics Canada. 2001a. *Geography, 2001 Census Dictionary.* Ottawa: Minister of Supply and Services Canada.

–. 2001b. *Rural and Small Town Canada Analysis Bulletin* 3.3: 14. Ottawa: Minister of Supply and Services Canada.

Stipp, Ron (campaign manager for Johanna den Hertog, NDP candidate for Vancouver Centre, 1988). 1991. Interview by author, 10 October, Vancouver.

Thraves, Bernard D. 1991. "Urban Canada 2001." In *A Social Geography of Canada,* 2nd ed., edited by Guy M. Robinson, 267-82. Toronto: Dundurn Press.

Walks, R. Alan. 2004. "Suburbanization, the Vote, and Changes in Federal and Provincial Political Representation and Influence between Inner Cities and Suburbs in Large Canadian Urban Regions, 1945-1999." *Urban Affairs Review* 39 (4): 411-40.

–. 2005. "The City-Suburban Cleavage in Canadian Federal Politics." *Canadian Journal of Political Science* 38 (2): 383-413.

–. 2006. "The Causes of City-Suburban Political Polarization? A Canadian Case Study." *Annals of the Association of American Geographers* 96 (2): 390-414.

Wasko, Kevin, and Brenda O'Neill. 2007. "The Urban/Suburban/Rural Cleavage in Canadian Political Opinion." Paper presented at the Annual Meeting of the Canadian Political Science Association, University of Saskatchewan, Saskatoon, May-June.

Whitaker, Reg. 2001. "Virtual Parties and the Decline of Democracy." *Policy Options* (June): 16-22.

6

Women Voters, Candidates, and Legislators

A Gender Perspective on Recent Party and Electoral Politics

ELIZABETH GOODYEAR-GRANT

Without making 2004 seem like a break from the past – a transition into some fundamentally altered political era – it is fair to say that the last three electoral cycles have witnessed important changes in Canadian electoral and party politics. The focus in this chapter is on women voters, candidates, and legislators and how these have been affected by two particular forces brought about since the 2004 federal election: the intensification of party competition and the return to power of a conservative party. This chapter offers a selective examination of these two forces in order to identify their consequences for the representation of women within the political system. I argue that the party in power and the nature of competition between the major parties in the system affect women's representation, both as political actors as well as within policy related to the distinct interests of women.

Critically, these two forces have produced what Dobrowolsky (2008) calls the "invisibilization" and "instrumentalization" of women. This is a dual process in which women and gender equality are nudged to the margins of politics at the same time that women are used strategically by political actors for instrumental gain. What follows is an empirical examination, principally, of how the intensification of party competition and return of conservative governments have affected women's representation (as legislators and within policy); however, I also make use of a distinctly evaluative perspective in considering events over the time period.

The Intensification of Party Competition

Between 2004 and 2011, there were three consecutive minority govern-ments in Ottawa. Connected to this change in electoral outcomes was an intensification of party competition compared with the preceding decade of one-party Liberal dominance; in Chapter 3, Kelly Blidook and Matthew Byrne point to increased partisan adversarialism in the legislature, and this heightened competition can also be seen outside of the House of Commons. The intensification of party competition has resulted at times in greater attention being paid to women and gender, which may counteract to some extent the invisibilization of women and gender associated with the Con-servative Party's control of government, examined below. All the same, pol-itical parties' strategic uses of women and gender have been motivated by electoral and political gain, and have relied heavily on gender stereotypes and shallow electoral appeals, resulting in negative outcomes on various fronts.

Women Voters

What did increased party competition mean for women voters in the 2004-11 period? To begin with, there were gender gaps in vote choice. Across many countries of the developed West, women have veered left of men, and men have veered right of women, over the past few decades (e.g., Box-Steffensmeier et al. 2004; Erickson and O'Neill 2002; Gidengil 1995; Gidengil et al. 2003, 2005; Gilens 1988; Inglehart and Norris 2003; Studlar et al. 1998). Over the last two decades, the Canadian gender gap has been largest on the right. The 2000 Canadian federal election, for example, saw an eleven-point gap in support for the Canadian Alliance, and the gap fa-voured men. Its "lack of appeal to women was a prime reason why the Alliance had failed to achieve its hoped-for electoral breakthrough in cen-tral Canada in the 2000 election" (Gidengil et al. 2006, 3). When the two right-of-centre parties (the Canadian Alliance and the Progressive Con-servative Party) merged to form the Conservative Party of Canada (CPC), the gender gap diminished, "making it seem as if the new Conservative Party of Canada had succeeded in shedding the Alliance's radical right-wing baggage and overcoming one of its key electoral liabilities" (3). Gender gaps on the right and left re-emerged in the 2006 and 2008 elections, how-ever. The six-point gap on the right in 2006 was consequential for the CPC, for "if the Conservatives had held as much appeal for women as they did for men in the 2006 election, they would not have ended up forming a minority government with the smallest share of seats in Canada's history" (4).

Women voters have become a battleground for parties, particularly in 2008, an election that saw the CPC push hard for a majority. In such an electoral climate, the importance of each seat is elevated beyond its usual perceived value, and the electorate is combed for potential opportunities. During the 2008 campaign, polls showed women moving away from the Liberals on account of Stéphane Dion (Agrell 2008a, 2008b), and suggested that more women were willing to consider voting Conservative (MacCharles 2008a). At the same time, Conservative support among women shifted over the course of the campaign – falling about 6 percent from early to mid-campaign (MacCharles 2008a). There were reports that third parties were picking up the female support that was being lost by the Liberals and Conservatives, and so on. All of this is to say that there was a sense among parties that women's loyalties were more flexible than in the past, suggesting the possibility of significant inroads among women voters.

Women voters became targets for the Liberals and Conservatives in particular. There are general dangers associated with the treatment of women voters as a cohesive bloc. It suggests that women have a monolithic set of political concerns. It encourages parties and candidates to look for women's voting blocs, and diverts their attention away from the idea that "women do not have to vote as a cohesive bloc for their values and policy preferences to have political relevance (Gidengil 2007, 820). Obviously, there are also good outcomes associated with attention to "the women's vote," such as increasing the visibility of women voters, sending the message that women are electorally powerful, and encouraging responsiveness to women's political concerns. Analyses of the Liberal and Conservative strategies to woo women voters must be viewed from the same balanced perspective, identifying both positive and negative consequences. At times, the Liberal and Conservative campaigns treated women voters as a fairly undifferentiated bloc. Parties assumed, in various cases, that women voters would respond favourably to campaign gestures that were superficial and image-based, or that appeared to focus on women while offering little to advance substantive gender equality. When women voters were differentiated, it tended to be along stereotypical lines, as seen most clearly in the Conservatives' strategies around the female characters Zoe and Sheila.

Facing intense electoral competition from their Liberal rivals, and knowing that women voters might give them the numbers they needed to move into majority government territory, the Conservatives used various strategies to woo women in the 2008 campaign. At the most superficial level, the campaign team attempted to remodel Stephen Harper's image to enhance his appeal to women voters. The most visible symbol of this was the sweater vest Harper donned in televised advertisements (*Daily News* 2008). The sweater was worn to make Harper appear more approachable, softer, and more relaxed. In the ads, Harper buttressed this softer, family-man image by talking about his children to an unidentified blonde woman. Essentially, the ad depicted Harper having a close conversation with the woman about family and fatherhood.

It was obvious from the start that Conservative advances could not be made among all female voters. Certain segments of the female electorate were targeted by the campaign, and these were represented by the female characters Zoe and Sheila, which were constructed for internal use in the campaign to identify likely pockets of female support for the party. Zoe was an urban-dwelling, unmarried, childless, twenty-something with a sociology degree who "eats organic food, does yoga, and lives in a downtown apartment" (Kidd 2008, ID1). Zoe was quite similar to the so-called *Sex and the City* voter – symbolic of young, unmarried women voters – who garnered significant attention in recent US presidential elections (e.g., Anderson and Stewart 2005). As Anderson and Stewart note, "political operatives and party strategists constructed the image of the unmarried woman voter as a rich, white, sexually appealing consumer" (2005, 610). In 2008, the CPC decided it had very little hope of attracting the "Zoe women," and focused instead on Sheila, "a suburban mother of two who drives a minivan" (Proudfoot 2008, B5). Sheila bore remarkable resemblance to the "security moms" that the Republicans have focused on over the past few electoral cycles in the United States (e.g., Burrell 2005). Like Sheila, "security moms" are married with children under the age of eighteen, and live largely in suburban communities.

The Conservative campaign avoided treating women as an undifferentiated bloc. The "microtargeting" of particular segments of women voters has become commonplace in the United States (MacManus 2006), and represents a positive development in thinking about such voters. Microtargeting recognizes that women's political preferences are affected by other factors, such as age, education, and occupation. On the other hand, the Conservative segmentation of the female electorate relied heavily on differences in marital and parental status among women, and viewed these as key determinants of women's vote choice. This was also true of campaign strategies in the 2004 US presidential election, for example (e.g., Anderson and Stewart 2005; Carroll 2006). The danger here is that women voters become defined primarily by their relation to spouses and children, an electoral strategy Carroll calls "*mom*ipulation" (2006, 366).

There is potentially a greater danger. As Carroll notes about the US context, women voters have been subject to what she calls "electoral manipulation," which "involves the creation of a socially constructed target group of voters (whether Reagan Democrats, NASCAR dads, or security moms) who do not consciously identify with one another and who are not represented by any existing organization or interest group" (Carroll 2006, 366). A candidate can target electoral appeals to such a group safe from repercussions if promises are neglected. The key is the lack of organizational structure representing the group: "Since there is no organized entity to articulate the political interests of this social construction, to lobby the candidate or his or her staff once elected, or to call attention to the victorious candidate's failure to be responsive to the social construction's political interests ... [a] candidate can appear to be responsive to the voters who are supposedly most critical to the outcome of an election, while promising little or nothing to "real" organized groups that could actually hold the victorious candidate accountable" (ibid.).

This is not to say that Conservatives have failed to deliver on their campaign promises or that they have failed to represent "Sheila" once in office, claims that are outside the scope of this chapter. Rather, the point here is to identify the considerable scope for instrumentalization of women voters – or, to use Carroll's language, "electoral manipulation" – that exists in the Conservatives' microtargeting strategies in recent elections.

The CPC is not the only culprit in the instrumentalization of women voters in 2008. The Liberals realized some time before that campaign that the party had run into trouble with these voters. The intensification of electoral competition, particularly the spectre of a Conservative majority, encouraged Liberal strategists to make use of women voters to build vote share. This did enhance the visibility of women in the party's campaign efforts, particularly in relation to the leader's promise to field a greater number of women candidates and the party's focus on women's issues in the campaign. At the same time, however, it was clear that the Liberals used gender-based appeals in order to *draw* women. Like Harper, Dion engaged in superficial tactics directed towards gaining the support of women voters, such as his media appearance in late September to celebrate women in politics as part of his birthday festivities. Photos from the appearance showed Dion surrounded by prominent women Liberal candidates, such as incumbents Carolyn Bennett, Maria Minna, and Ruby Dhalla, as well as his wife, Janine Krieber (Blanchfield and O'Neill 2008; MacCharles 2008b), as if to remind women voters that Dion was well loved by his women candidates as well as his wife. The strategic deployment of women candidates, which was also a tactic used by the Conservative campaign, will be discussed in greater detail in the next section.

The centrepiece of the Liberal Party's efforts to attract women's votes was *Pink Book II*, a document intended to draw attention to the party's policies on women's issues. *Pink Book II* was drafted by the National Liberal Women's Caucus, chaired then by Belinda Stronach. *Pink Book II* focused on violence against women, housing and homelessness, rural women, Aboriginal women, and immigrant women, and it is clear that the policies discussed in the document are rooted in an understanding that poverty and other structural barriers are leading causes of women's inequality. Unlike the Harper government's rhetoric around women and gender, *Pink Book II* does not shy away from the word "equality" and does not discuss women primarily in terms of their roles as mothers. Nowhere in the text of *Pink Book II* are the terms "feminism" or "justice" used, however.[1]

While *Pink Book II* demonstrated understanding of the causes of gender inequality, its format can be criticized. First, policy related to women's issues and gender equality was separated from the party's primary campaign platform, *Richer, Fairer, Greener: An Action Plan for the 21st Century*. In fact, *Richer, Fairer, Greener*, a seventy-six-page document, had only a single page on "women's equality," and the only other mentions of women were in discussions of domestic violence and Aboriginal women's vulnerability to violence.[2] The scant attention paid to women and gender equality in the party's primary platform document does not suggest that the party prioritized women's issues in the 2008 campaign. Not only were women's issues segregated, but *Pink Book II* also played into traditional gender stereotypes in its style and format. It is called "Pink," and its pages and much of its font were also pink, the colour associated with girls and "girlieness." The front cover of the document had a rose on it, as did every second page throughout. Finally, one also wonders about the timing of the document's arrival on the political scene, for it was in 2006 that the first *Pink Book* made its debut, the very year that the Liberals lost power and initially realized that its advantage among women voters had shrunk (Bryden 2006). The segregation of the women's issues platform from the "regular" platform continued under Michael Ignatieff, with the release of *Pink Book III* in 2009.

Women Candidates, Legislators, and Cabinet Members

An "electoral contagion" framework can be used to understand changes in women's representation as candidates and legislators from 2004 to 2011. Electoral pressure encourages parties to emulate their rivals' strategies, a classic idea within the literature on parties (e.g., Duverger 1954; Epstein 1967; Kirchheimer 1966). Pivotal to the idea of electoral contagion is the assumption that parties are goal-directed organizations whose chief aim is to maximize political power in the form of seats and votes. The framework functions well to explain the Conservatives' and Liberals' greater attention to nominating women as electoral competition has increased over the past half-decade. Indeed, the parties' seat shares have been very close, they appear to be competing for similar constituencies, and they respond to each other's actions – in this case, nominating more women – in a predictable way: by following suit.

Yet the feminization of candidacies has been, in part, another manifestation of the instrumentalization of women within the current system, particularly in the 2008 campaign. Women as a voting bloc have become a battleground for the parties, as discussed above, and one way in which the female vote was courted was through the growth in women's candidacies. In 2008, for the first time in Canada's federal electoral history, the Liberals had the highest number of female candidates (see Figure 6.1), a distinction typically claimed by the New Democratic Party. Dion pledged early on to have at least one-third female candidates, and this was motivated in part by the desire to enhance the party's appeal to women. Indeed, Dion even considered holding women-only nominations in a small number of ridings. Trumpeting the Liberal Party's record number of women candidates in the 2008 Canadian federal election, a campaign co-chair expressed the view that in British Columbia, "by having 44 per cent women candidates in the province we'll be better able to attract female voters" (Luba 2008, A14). Dion and his campaign team were not the first to use female candidates in this way. Former Prime Minister Jean Chrétien's appointment of female candidates in selected constituencies in 1993 and 1997 was "part of the Liberals' largely successful bid to claim large parts of the female vote in Canada" (Delacourt 2000, A1).

The Conservatives felt even greater pressure to nominate women in 2008. In 2006, the party had a dismal proportion of women candidates (see Figure 6.1), and this was reflected in its caucus and Harper's first cabinet, issues that will be taken up again later in this chapter. While the Reform

FIGURE 6.1
Women candidates and MPs, by election year and party

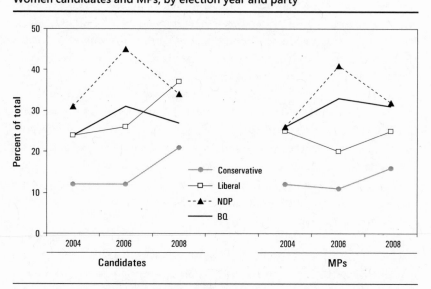

Source: Parliament of Canada, "History of Federal Ridings since 1867. Women Candidates in General Elections – 1921 to Date," http://www.parl.gc.ca/.

Party/Canadian Alliance did not worry about the representation of women in the party, this has been a concern for the Conservatives, primarily because the party has not kept pace with its rivals and also because it has been within striking distance of a substantial breakthrough with women voters, which would put it in a better position to form a majority government. Put differently, the CPC has been more sensitive to criticism of its record on women's numerical representation because of changes in its competitive position since the mid-2000s. While the instrumentalization of women has created political opportunities for women office seekers as a result of the intensification of electoral competition, this has been done in order to draw women voters and to silence criticisms from the media and other observers about the under-representation of women, particularly in the first Conservative minority government.

With regard to women MPs and cabinet members, the intensification of party competition has affected the Conservatives' treatment of women in various ways. Among the more obvious is the government's strategic use of its women members to present policy that either has a gender angle or that is anticipated to generate controversy. This has been done by a government that until 2011 did not enjoy a majority, and has been very much influenced by the intensification of partisan competition in the past several years. Consider the fact that it was Bev Oda who was responsible for acting as spokesperson for the cuts to Status of Women Canada (SWC) and changes to the agency's mandate in 2006. It was Bev Oda again who became the key spokesperson for the government's maternal health initiative in 2010, particularly in emphasizing the fact that the initiative does not include funding for safe abortion services. Regarding the changes to SWC, part of the reason for Oda's prominent role on the issue was the fact that she was minister for status of women in the fall of 2006, so she directly oversaw the alterations that were made. Even keeping this in mind, however, Harper said virtually nothing publicly about the cuts or the removal of the word "equality" from the agency's mandate. Similarly, Oda's current position as minister of international cooperation is part of the reason why she is involved in the maternal health initiative, although it is not clear why she has emerged as the chief spokesperson for the policy.

Looking at some other examples, however, suggests that women MPs may have been utilized at times to "soften" controversial issues or to appeal to women voters. An example of the former may be Candice Hoeppner's Private Member's Bill (PMB) on eliminating the long-gun registry, an initiative that was seen by various observers as a government bill in disguise. There is insufficient evidence about the "true" sponsor of the bill and, if anything, it might be safer to assume that the bill is Hoeppner's own, as PMBs do tend to originate with their sponsors (e.g., Blidook 2010, 39). An example of the latter – using women MPs to enhance the appeal of policy for women voters – may be found in Rona Ambrose's emergence as a key champion of the Universal Child Care Benefit (UCCB) during the 2008 campaign. In the fall of 2008, Ambrose's responsibilities in cabinet had little connection to child care. She was in charge of Intergovernmental Affairs and Western Economic Diversification, and was Queen's Privy Council president. She does not herself have children, which is not to say that this is a requirement for interest in child care policy. All the same, she made various campaign stops, including at a children's toy and clothing consignment shop, to publicize the virtues of the Conservative policies relating to child care (McGregor 2008). Presumably, part of the reason why she was given this role in the 2008 campaign was her exchange with Ken Dryden in the House in 2005 over the Liberal child care plan, when she told him "working women want to make their own choices; we don't need old white guys telling us what to do" (Ivison 2005, A6).

A Phoenix Rises: Conservatives Return to Office

The nature of competition *between* parties is essential for understanding the representation of women as voters, candidates, and legislators within the system, and indeed this force has resulted in less direct or readily apparent effects on that representation. This is only half the story, however. The second change requiring analysis is turnover in government.

Women as Voters: The Policy Agenda

In the 2006 federal election, the Conservatives took office with a narrow plurality of seats. Government had been controlled by the Liberals since 1993. A shift in the political agenda and its accompanying discourse occurred, both reflecting the CPC's core values and policy priorities. Gender equality was demoted as a policy goal and as a component of the government's larger vision. Advanced democracies have persistently shifted rightward over the past few decades (Esping-Andersen 1996), and the Conservative government has moved the policy agenda and political discourse further along in Canada, with important consequences for the representation of women and their policy needs. Analyzing Conservative initiatives in three domains – child care, the "women's state," and global initiatives on women and gender – the following paragraphs illustrate this claim.

Access to affordable high-quality child care is essential for gender equality. Norms and behaviours are changing in terms of care for children, with many modern fathers assuming equitable portions of child-rearing work and sometimes acting as primary caregivers. Inequalities in the division of labour remain, however, and the rate of change has not been all that rapid (Marshall 2006). Moreover, women head the bulk of lone-parent families – 80 percent in 2006, a proportion representing 1.1 million single mothers.[3] Demands for universal publicly funded child care have persisted since the 1970s, when the report of the Royal Commission on the Status of Women called for such a program. Governments have experimented with different approaches to supporting child care, and Paul Martin's government (2004-06) seemed close to building a national program. Martin negotiated bilateral Early Learning and Child Care agreements with all the provinces, and the Liberals' 2006 election platform pledged to spend $5 billion on registered care programs (Collier and Mahon 2008).

The Conservatives' two-pronged Universal Child Care Plan is dramatically different. It consists of the Universal Child Care Benefit, a cash transfer to parents worth $1,200 per year per child under the age of six, and the Child Care Spaces Initiative (CCSI), which offers tax incentives to the private sector to create child care spaces. The Conservative government pledged $250 million per year for the CCSI, and has claimed that it is creating 25,000 new care spaces per year.

The first criticism of the plan is that the investment is too thin. The sum of $1,200 per year taxable is a small amount in relation to the cost of child care, and 25,000 new spaces per year does not meet current needs. Looking at discourse and framing, the Conservatives have promoted the UCCB using gender-neutral language that emphasizes "families" and "choice." The "UCCB is designed to help Canadian families,"[4] says a government website, and another states that "the Government of Canada recognizes that each family has its own circumstances and needs, and parents must be able to choose the child care that is best for their children."[5] There is no mention of women as caregivers or gender equality as a motivator of government support for child care. The focus is on families, not women, and the emphasis on individual choice suggests that a national, public program would hinder choice. While the language of choice may be appealing, it also assumes that parents have the resources to make meaningful choices. As Collier and Mahon note (2008), with the focus on families rather than on women and gender equality, and emphasis on market provision of care spaces, the government's plan reflects its blend of social conservatism and neoliberalism.

The year 2006 also saw the government turn its attention to Status of Women Canada, an essential component of the women's state. It cut SWC's $13 million annual operating budget by $5 million – a decrease of nearly 40 percent, nearly identical to the cuts imposed on Australia's Office of the Status of Women by the conservative Howard government (Sawer and Laycock 2009). Moreover, the Harper government altered SWC's grant rules to disallow funding for advocacy or research, it excised the word "equality" from SWC's mandate, and it closed twelve of SWC's sixteen regional offices. These changes resulted in negative substantive and symbolic effects for the agency. SWC is an interdepartmental agency responsible for the promotion of gender equality and women's full participation in politics, society, and the economy. It was created after the report of the Royal Commission on the Status of Women and is one of the few remaining components of the women's state in Canada. The government is resistant to the idea that gender is a legitimate category of political analysis; in fact, in response to the closing of most of SWC's regional offices in 2006, Conservative Minister Bev Oda noted: "We don't need to separate the men from the women in this country" (CBC News 2006). In 2008, the Harper government reinserted the word "equality" into SWC's mandate, and increased its funding to record levels, perhaps in an effort to appeal to women voters, as discussed below.

The third initiative is the government's maternal health plan – formally called the Muskoka Initiative for Maternal, Newborn and Child Health – which was unveiled at the 2010 G8 summit in Huntsville, Ontario. This is part of a G8 initiative on maternal and child health in the developing world, and Canada's pledge of $1.1 billion makes it a leader in this project. Simply put, the plan encourages policy makers, aid agencies, and others to view women as mothers and nurturers, as well as to equate the broad topic of women's health with their reproductive roles. Thus, the policy encourages a traditional view of women's roles in the public and private spheres. Initially, it appeared as though Canada's funding was not to be spent on contraception or abortion services. Later, the government changed its position to allow contraception, but not abortion services. All this despite the fact that the Canadian Supreme Court has affirmed freedom of choice as a *Charter* right in *R. v. Morgentaler*, [1988] 1 S.C.R. 30, and despite the number of deaths that occur in developing countries because of unsafe abortions. Forty-two million women seek abortions worldwide every year, and 20 million of these are unsafe, with 68,000 women dying each year as a result (Haddad 2009).

Important components of the maternal health plan are out of step with Canadian women's views. A survey conducted by Nanos Research and the *Globe and Mail* in early 2010 demonstrates that nearly 70 percent of Canadians support government funding for safe abortions in the developing world, and there is no real gender gap in opinion (Moore 2010). The same survey asked Canadians which activities should be prioritized in Canada's overseas aid programs,[6] and 23 percent of women respondents, compared with 13 percent of men, chose maternal and family health, indicating a gender gap on the salience of this issue. Given that the issue is particularly important to women and that the majority of women believe that women in developing countries should have access to safe abortions, the maternal health plan does not represent the views of women in the electorate.

There is evidence of a similar mismatch between Canadians' views and the Conservative government's actions on the child care issue. For example, a 2006 poll reported that a majority supported the 2004 Martin plan briefly outlined above (Environics Research Group 2006). Three-quarters of respondents viewed the lack of affordable child care as a serious problem. The 2008 Canadian Election Study (CES) asked respondents: "What should the government do: fund public daycare or give the money directly to parents?"

Sixty-three percent of respondents chose the first option, so support is generally high for government activism on the issue. Disaggregating by gender, women were more likely than men to prioritize government funding to daycare rather than cash to parents (66 versus 61 percent).

Thus far, the analysis reminds us that the party in power plays a fundamental role in whether and how women's views are represented, and, more importantly, whether a gender equality agenda is pursued, ignored, or even assailed. That right-of-centre parties tend to present barriers to women's representation and to a feminist agenda are well known (Bashevkin 1998; Chappell 2002). The damage to gender equality over the Conservatives' time in office is reflected in recent data. A report prepared for a United Nations session on the fifteenth anniversary of the Beijing conference on women concluded that "during the period of 2004-2009, Canadian women's achievements in all twelve areas of critical concern outlined in the Beijing Platform for Action have slowed or been turned back" (Canadian Feminist Alliance for International Action and Canadian Labour Congress 2010, 2). Slippage over time is evident in Canada's ranking on gender indices. Canada was 7th in the 2004 World Economic Forum Gender Gap Index, 25th in the 2009 Gender Gap Index, and 73rd in the 2009 UN Gender Disparity Index.

Women Candidates

The numerical presence of women in federal politics has not changed for some time. From 1993 to 2008, there was a meagre 5 percent increase in women's share of House of Commons seats, from 18 percent in 1993 to 22 percent in 2008. In fact, this represents an element of continuity over the past two decades, when changes in women's share of House seats have typically been in the direction of gradual growth. The Conservative rise to power in 2006, however, coincided with a decrease from 21.1 percent to 20.8 percent, the first decline since 1968, when women's representation went from four seats to one.

The 2006 decline in women's seats was due to the turnover in government. The CPC had only thirty-eight women candidates in 2006, or 12 percent of the party's slate (see Figure 6.1). The NDP led with 45 percent women candidates, the Bloc Québécois had nearly 31 percent, and the Liberals had 26 percent. The Conservative caucus was only 11 percent female following the 2006 vote, compared with 41 percent for the NDP, 33 percent for the Bloc, and 20 percent for the Liberals. In 2008, the Conservatives had a greater female presence on their slate – 20.5 percent – but the party still trailed its rivals. Women accounted for 37 percent of Liberal candidacies in

2008, for example – growth spurred in large measure by the desire to capture more female votes.

Why the Conservatives lag on women's numerical representation is an important question, although a detailed examination is beyond the scope of this chapter. A critical difference appears to lie in recruitment policies and practices across the major parties, with the Conservatives doing the least to identify, encourage, and nominate women candidates (e.g., Cross 2004). The NDP has a multi-stage recruitment procedure designed to increase the number of candidates from marginalized groups. Liberal leaders have exercised their prerogatives to handpick women candidates – Jean Chrétien appointed eleven in 1993 and four in 1997. Stéphane Dion delivered a slate in 2008 that was one-third female; to achieve this, the party even flirted with the idea of women-only nomination contests (Bryden 2007).

While the party may periodically endeavour to enhance the presence of women in its ranks – as it did from 2006 to 2008 – the CPC's relatively poor record on the recruitment of women candidates is a consequence of its core values. Looking at the two parties that came together to form the Conservative Party of Canada, the Progressive Conservatives had supports for women candidates, such as the Ellen Fairclough Fund, and the CPC has kept the fund. The Reform Party/Canadian Alliance, however, rejected affirmative action measures for candidates as "special treatment." In Young's view (2000), the fact that the Reform Party/Canadian Alliance replaced the NDP as the dynamic element of the Canadian party system post-1993 had dismal consequences for women's representation. These negative consequences continue, arguably, as a result of the influence of the Reform Party/Canadian Alliance contingent within the CPC. The CPC has no internal affirmative action instruments for the recruitment of candidates from marginalized groups, and is openly critical of the idea. Three-quarters of Conservative candidates in the 2004 federal election reported that women's under-representation was not a problem, "an individualistic view of representation that is predominant in the party, particularly in the larger premerger Canadian Alliance component" (Black and Hicks 2006, 26). By comparison, the majority of NDP, Liberal, Bloc, and Green candidates in the study reported the opposite view.

Women Legislators and Cabinet Members
While still trailing the other major parties, the Conservative Party saw its women's presence grow substantially from fourteen MPs in 2006 to twenty-three in 2008. Looking at the roles played by women legislators, however,

provides evidence of further invisibilization of women in politics as a result of Conservative governments. Harper appointed only six women to cabinet in 2006, and none to the most influential posts. During the party's first term, the number of women in cabinet declined to five at one point, and two of these (Diane Ablonczy and Helena Guergis) were in less important secretary of state positions. Part of the problem facing Harper was the small group of women MPs from which to select cabinet members in 2006, a situation directly related to the small number of Conservative women candidates in that election.

Worldwide, research has demonstrated that women's representation in political executives tends to be inadequate, and their appointment to cabinets tends to be disproportionately in low-power, low-prestige positions, often in "feminine" portfolios such as health, education, and culture (e.g., Bashevkin 1993; Davis 1997; Escobar-Lemmon and Taylor-Robinson 2005; Krook and O'Brien 2010; Moon and Fountain 1997; Reynolds 1999; Studlar and Moncrief 1999). There has been upward movement in women's success at "cracking the inner circle" over time (e.g., Escobar-Lemmon and Taylor-Robinson 2005, 838; see also Bashevkin 1993; Davis 1997; Erickson 1997; Krook and O'Brien 2010; Moon and Fountain 1997), but in Canada, the election of the Conservatives has diminished women's cabinet power, not only numerically but also in terms of their positions. Federal governments of the past two decades have tended to appoint at least one woman to a key position in each cabinet. Anne McLellan was deputy prime minister in Paul Martin's government. Jean Chrétien appointed McLellan minister of justice and Sheila Copps deputy prime minister. Brian Mulroney gave External Affairs (now Foreign Affairs) to Barbara McDougall and Justice and Defence to Kim Campbell. In fact, on all indicators – proportion of women candidates, number of women in cabinet, and portfolios assigned to women ministers – "the PCs in 1988 were slightly ahead of where their successors in the merged Conservative organization would be 20 years later" (Bashevkin 2009, 131).

After the 2008 federal election, and following criticism about the dearth of women in his first cabinet (e.g., Ditchburn 2008), Harper increased women's cabinet presence (eleven of thirty-eight, or 28.9 percent), resulting in record female representation in cabinet. Again, however, women have tended not to hold the most important cabinet positions. No woman in any of the three Conservative governments has held the defence, foreign affairs, finance, or deputy prime minister portfolios. In the cabinet chosen after the 2008 federal election, a news article on the subject noted that, "apart from Human Resources Minister Diane Finley, women are not in charge of the departments the Conservative government considers a priority" (Delacourt 2010, A1).

Conclusion

The chapter has examined how the intensification of party competition and the return to power of a conservative government has affected women's representation in the Parliament of Canada. While the rise of the Conservative Party of Canada in the mid-2000s represents an important change to the political system, and one that has had measurable impacts on women's descriptive and substantive representation, much is familiar too. The pattern in Canadian federal politics tends to be one of long periods of Liberal dominance punctuated by shorter, conservative interregnums (as demonstrated quite clearly in Chapter 13). Because of the established pattern, therefore, questions about the effect of a conservative government on women's representation in the political system have been addressed in the past when conservative governments have been elected (e.g., Bashevkin 1998; Dobrowolsky 2009; Young 2000), providing current observers with a familiar framework for interpretation.

Similar to past conservative governments, the CPC's core values – from mild anti-statism, to individualism, to fiscal conservatism – undermine serious work on gender equality in the political agenda or in women's representation as parliamentarians. At the same time, the Harper governments have been different in important ways from their conservative predecessors, which represents a current of "change" in this story. Earlier counterparts were Progressive Conservative governments, with the Mulroney and Mulroney/Campbell administrations (1984-88, 1988-93) being the obvious comparators. The Harper CPC has been dominated by a contingent from the West, with roots in the populist, more "New Right" Reform Party/Canadian Alliance, the numerically and organizationally stronger of the CPC's two predecessors. As such, Harper's Conservatives govern to the right of previous conservative administrations, particularly on social issues, if not on fiscal and foreign affairs/defence issues. This is an important consideration because much of the invisibilization of women and of gender equality that has occurred over the past few years has been in the context of shifting policy and discourse on social issues. The Mulroney Conservatives, for example, made every attempt to avoid divisive social issues – such as abortion – and Mulroney's government avoided taking a stance on that particular matter (Bashevkin 1998). To be fair, Harper's government has repeatedly stated that it has no intention of reopening the abortion debate in Canada and has made no moves to suggest otherwise. Yet it has prohibited funding for safe abortion services in its maternal health initiative, and its framing of the issue casts women as mothers – for whom childbearing is the raison d'être – not as autonomous individuals with control over their bodies. Different variants of conservatism, then, must be considered when analyzing the effects of the party in power on women's representation. In the end, one of the conclusions that must be drawn here is that Young's observations (2000, 2002) about the Reform Party/Canadian Alliance in the post-1993 party system must be treated even more seriously now, because the anti-feminist Reform/Alliance contingent is the dominant faction in the CPC. This is a very consequential change indeed.

The second major development is the intensification of party competition since 2004. Since competitiveness has increased, parties appear to have become more responsive, at least on the surface, to women's representational demands, and this is in no small measure because women voters have become a battleground. Since neither the Liberals nor the Conservatives has secured the "women's vote," they have incentives to make further representational advances in electoral cycles to come. So far, both major parties have engaged in similar strategies to court women: "feminize" the party leader's image; get more women on the party's slate; and adopt policies, or at least policy rhetoric, geared towards women. In many cases, however, such as the CPC's policies on child care and global maternal health, and the Liberal *Pink Book II*, the electoral overtures towards women have important drawbacks in that they stereotype women, ghettoize their policy interests, or offer less than what is necessary for gender equality. Taking a pessimistic view of the situation, instrumentalization may have even larger, more negative consequences, even if these are not intended by the parties. The superficial attention given to women voters and politicians, particularly during election periods, may give the misleading impression that parties are doing substantive policy work that puts women and gender equality on par with other goals. Certainly, the Liberals' *Pink Book* series encourages such a view. As such, parties may encourage further invisibilization of women in policy and political discourse as a result, because the superficial attention paid to women and gender-based policy concerns will suggest that all is well.

Notes

1 National Liberal Women's Caucus, *The Pink Book: A Policy Framework for Canada's Future*, vol. 2, 2007. http://www.liberal.ca/pdf/docs/071205_pinkbook_2_en.pdf.
2 Liberal Party of Canada, *Richer, Fairer, Greener: An Action Plan for the 21st Century*, 2008. http://www.llbc.leg.bc.ca/public/pubdocs/docs/446629/2008_liberal_action_plan.pdf.
3 See Statistics Canada, "Census Snapshot of Canada – Families," http://www.statcan.gc.ca/pub/11-008-x/2007006/article/10380-eng.htm.
4 See Canada Revenue Agency, "Universal Child Care Benefit (UCCB)," http://www.cra-arc.gc.ca/bnfts/uccb-puge/menu-eng.html.
5 See http://www.hrsdc.gc.ca/eng/family/uccp/index.shtml.
6 See Nanos Research, "Stat Sheet – Globe and Mail – Abortion Tabulation," http://www.nanosresearch.com/library/polls/POLNAT-W10-T428.pdf.

References

Agrell, Siri. 2008a. "Liberals Failing to Draw Female Voters." *Globe and Mail*, 25 September, A8.

–. 2008b. "Polls Show Women Drifting Away from Liberal Party over Leader." *Winnipeg Free Press*, 26 September, A13.

Anderson, Karrin Vasby, and Jessie Stewart. 2005. "Politics and the Single Woman: The 'Sex and the City Voter' in Campaign 2004." *Rhetoric and Public Affairs* 8 (4): 595-616.

Bashevkin, Sylvia. 1993. *Toeing the Lines: Women and Party Politics in English Canada*. 2nd ed. Toronto: University of Toronto Press.

–. 1998. *Women on the Defensive: Living through Conservative Times*. Chicago: University of Chicago Press.

–. 2009. *Women, Power, Politics: The Hidden Story of Canada's Unfinished Democracy*. Don Mills, ON: Oxford University Press.

Black, Jerome H., and Bruce M. Hicks. 2006. "Strengthening Canadian Democracy: The Views of Parliamentary Candidates." *Policy Matters* 7 (2): 1-44.

Blanchfield, Mike, and Juliet O'Neill. 2008. "Liberals, NDP Fight for Official Opposition Status; Harper to Take Cautious Approach in Leaders' Debates." *Calgary Herald*, 29 September, A5.

Blidook, Kelly. 2010. "Exploring the Role of 'Legislators' in Canada: Do Members of Parliament Influence Policy?" *Journal of Legislative Studies* 16 (1): 32-56.

Box-Steffensmeier, Janet M., Suzanna De Boef, and Tse-Min Lin. 2004. "The Dynamics of the Partisan Gender Gap." *American Political Science Review* 98: 515-28.

Bryden, Joan. 2006. "New Poll Suggests Tories Nine Points Up on Liberals." St. John *Telegraph-Journal*, 10 January, A1.

–. 2007. "Liberals Set to Bar Men in Some Ridings in Bid to Boost Female Candidates." Canadian Press, 8 February.

Burrell, Barbara C. 2005. "Gender, Presidential Elections and Public Policy: Making Women's Votes Matter." *Journal of Women, Politics and Policy* 27 (1): 31-50.

Canadian Feminist Alliance for International Action and Canadian Labour Congress. 2010. "Reality Check: Women in Canada and the Beijing Declaration and Platform for Action Fifteen Years On: A Canadian Civil Society Response." Canadian Labour Congress. http://www.canadianlabour.ca/.

Carroll, Susan J. 2006. "Moms Who Swing, or Why the Promise of the Gender Gap Remains Unfulfilled." *Politics and Gender* 2 (3): 362-74.

CBC News. 2006. "Tories Shutting Status of Women Offices." CBC News, 30 November. http://www.cbc.ca/.

Chappell, Louise A. 2002. *Gendering Government: Feminist Engagement with the State in Australia and Canada.* Vancouver: UBC Press.

Collier, Cheryl, and Rianne Mahon. 2008. "One Step Forward, Two Steps Back: Child Care Policy from Martin to Harper." In *How Ottawa Spends 2008-2009: A More Orderly Federalism?* edited by Allan M. Maslove, 110-13. Montreal and Kingston: McGill-Queen's University Press.

Cross, William. 2004. *Political Parties.* Vancouver: UBC Press.

Daily News. 2008. "Harper Ads Aim to Snag Women's Vote." Nanaimo *Daily News,* 9 September. http://www.canada.com/.

Davis, Rebecca Howard. 1997. *Women and Power in Parliamentary Democracies: Cabinet Appointments in Western Europe, 1968-1992.* Lincoln: University of Nebraska Press.

Delacourt, Susan. 2000. "Grits Hunt for Female Candidates: Party Nowhere Near Goal of Fielding Women in 25 Per Cent of Ridings." *Ottawa Citizen,* 31 October.

–. 2010. "Analysis: More Woman Trouble for Stephen Harper and His Cabinet." *Toronto Star,* 10 April, 1.

Ditchburn, Jennifer. 2008. "Women in Power Not a Priority for Tories: Ex PM Campbell." Canadian Press, 10 January.

Dobrowolsky, Alexandra. 2008. "Interrogating 'Invisibilization' and 'Instrumentalization': Women and Current Citizenship Trends in Canada." *Citizenship Studies* 12 (5): 465-79.

–, ed. 2009. *Women and Public Policy in Canada: Neoliberalism and After?* Don Mills, ON: Oxford University Press.

Duverger, Maurice. 1954. *Political Parties: Their Organization and Activity in the Modern State.* London: Methuen.

Environics Research Group. 2006. "Canadians' Attitudes Toward National Child Care Policy." Child Care Advocacy Association of Canada. http://www.ccaac.ca/resources/research.php.

Epstein, Leon. 1967. *Political Parties in Western Democracies.* New York: Praeger.

Erickson, Lynda. 1997. "Parties, Ideology, and Feminist Action: Women and Political Representation in British Columbia Politics." In *In the Presence of Women: Representation in Canadian Governments,* edited by Jane Arscott and Linda Trimble, 106-27. Toronto: Harcourt Brace.

Erickson, Lynda, and Brenda O'Neill. 2002. "The Gender Gap and the Changing Woman Voter in Canada." *International Political Science Review* 23 (4): 373-93.

Escobar-Lemmon, Maria, and Michelle M. Taylor-Robinson. 2005. "Women Ministers in Latin American Government: When, Where, and Why?" *American Journal of Political Science* 49 (4): 829-44.

Esping-Andersen, Gøsta, ed. 1996. *Welfare States in Transition: National Adaptations in Global Economies.* London: Sage.

Gidengil, Elisabeth. 1995. "Economic Man–Social Woman? The Case of the Gender Gap in Support for the Canada-US Free Trade Agreement." *Comparative Political Studies* 28 (3): 384-408.

–. 2007. "Beyond the Gender Gap: Presidential Address to the Canadian Political Science Association, Saskatoon, 2007." *Canadian Journal of Political Science* 40 (4): 815-31.

Gidengil, Elisabeth, André Blais, Richard Nadeau, and Neil Nevitte. 2003. "Women to the Left? Gender Differences in Political Beliefs and Policy Preferences." In *Gender and Electoral Representation in Canada,* edited by Manon Tremblay and Linda Trimble, 140-59. Don Mills, ON: Oxford University Press.

Gidengil, Elisabeth, Joanna Everitt, André Blais, Patrick Fournier, and Neil Nevitte. 2006. "Gender and Vote Choice in the 2006 Canadian Election." Paper presented at the annual meeting of the American Political Science Association, Philadelphia, 30 August–3 September.

Gidengil, Elisabeth, Matthew Hennigar, André Blais, and Neil Nevitte. 2005. "Explaining the Gender Gap in Support for the New Right: The Case of Canada." *Comparative Political Studies* 38 (10): 1171-95.

Gilens, M. 1988. "Gender and Support for Reagan: A Comprehensive Model of Presidential Support." *American Journal of Political Science* 32: 19-49.

Haddad, Lisa B. 2009. "Unsafe Abortion: Unnecessary Maternal Mortality." *Review of Obstetrics and Gynecology* 2 (2): 122-26.

Inglehart, Ronald, and Pippa Norris. 2003. *Rising Tide: Gender Equality and Cultural Change around the World.* New York: Cambridge University Press.

Ivison, John. 2005. "'Old White Guy' Takes the High Road: Ex-NHLer Seen as Potential Contender for Leadership." *National Post,* 18 February, A6.

Kidd, Kenneth. 2008. "How Harper Let It Slip Away." *Toronto Star,* 18 October, 1.

Kirchheimer, Otto. 1966. "The Transformation of Western European Party Systems." In *Political Parties and Political Development,* edited by Joseph LaPalombara and Myron Weiner, 177-200. Princeton, NJ: Princeton University Press.

Krook, Mona Lena, and Diana Z. O'Brien. 2010. "All the President's Men? Numbers and Portfolio Allocations of Female Cabinet Ministers." Paper presented at the Midwest Political Science Association national conference, Chicago, 22- 25 April.

Luba, Frank. 2008. "Liberals, NDP Duke out Gender Race: 'Best Candidates in the Riding' Is Policy, Says Official." Vancouver *Province,* 12 September, A14.

MacCharles, Tonda. 2008a. "PM Reaching Women, Urban Voters: Boost in Support from Females Due to Female-Friendly Platform, Conservatives Suggest." *Toronto Star,* 29 September, A17.

–. 2008b. "Dion Moves to Shore Up Support among Women." *Toronto Star,* 29 September, A17.

MacManus, Susan A. 2006. "Targeting [Specific Slices of] Female Voters: A Key Strategy of Democrats and Republicans Alike in 2004 ... and Most Assuredly So in 2008." *Politics and Gender* 2 (3): 374-87.

Marshall, Katherine. 2006. "Converging Gender Roles." *Perspectives on Labour and Income* 7 (7): 5-17.

McGregor, Glen. 2008. "Stroller Moms Drawn Unwittingly into Child Care Debate." *Ottawa Citizen,* 11 September, A5.

Moon, Jeremy, and Imogen Fountain. 1997. "Keeping the Gates? Women and Ministers in Australia, 1970-1996." *Australian Journal of Political Science* 32: 455-66.

Moore, Oliver. 2010. "Most Canadians Support International Access to Safe Abortions: Poll." *Globe and Mail,* 21 June, A3.

Proudfoot, Shannon. 2008. "Parties Courting Female Vote." *Leader-Post,* 6 October, B5.

Reynolds, Andrew. 1999. "Women in the Legislatures and Executives of the World: Knocking at the Highest Glass Ceiling." *World Politics* 51 (4): 547-72.

Sawer, Marian, and David Laycock. 2009. "Down with Elites and Up with Inequality: Market Populism in Australia and Canada." *Commonwealth and Comparative Politics* 47 (2): 133-50.

Studlar, Donley T., Ian McAllister, and Bernadette C. Hayes. 1998. "Explaining the Gender Gap in Voting: A Cross-National Analysis." *Social Science Quarterly* 79: 779-98.

Studlar, Donley T., and Gary F. Moncrief. 1999. "Women's Work? The Distribution and Prestige of Portfolios in the Canadian Provinces." *Governance: An International Journal of Policy and Administration* 12 (4): 379-95.

Young, Lisa. 2000. *Feminists and Party Politics.* Vancouver: UBC Press.

–. 2002. "Representation of Women in the New Canadian Party System." In *Political Parties, Representation, and Electoral Democracy in Canada,* edited by William Cross, 181-200. Don Mills, ON: Oxford University Press.

7

Revisiting the "Ethnic" Vote
Liberal Allegiance and Vote Choice among Racialized Minorities

ALLISON HARELL

Until recently, the Liberal Party of Canada (LPC) has been what some consider to be Canada's "natural governing party." In the federal election of 2004, however, Paul Martin and his party managed to secure only a minority of seats in Parliament. In the three subsequent elections, Stephen Harper and his Conservative Party secured enough seats to form governments, two minorities followed by a majority in 2011. The rise of the Conservative Party of Canada (CPC), as well as the Liberals' apparent inability to attract voters in recent elections, raises serious questions about the changing bases of party support in Canada.

This chapter explores Liberal Party success outside Quebec, and the party's recent fall from electoral grace. As Blais (2005) argues, Liberal Party success results in part from the existence of three important cleavages in Canadian society: region, religion, and ethnicity. The Canadian party system is highly regionalized (Gidengil et al. 1999; Simeon and Elkins 1974), and Liberal support has been strongest in vote-rich Ontario and Atlantic Canada.[1] Along with its regional base, Liberal Party dominance is due in large part to the support the party has among Catholics and, to a lesser extent, voters from non-European backgrounds (Blais 2005; Lijphart 1966; Meisel 1956).

Since 2004, however, the newly formed CPC has had increasing success outside of its regional base in the West. In the 2000 election, the Reform

Party and the Progressive Conservatives garnered only two seats in Ontario. After merging to form the CPC, they experienced increasing success in Ontario, garnering twenty-four, forty, and fifty-one seats in the next three elections. This Conservative success in Ontario is a major reason why the Liberals have been unable to form a majority government since 2000.

In this chapter, we re-examine the link between Canadians of non-European origin and Liberal vote choice. Although Blais (2005, 825) argues that they have not traditionally been a large enough group to change electoral outcomes, voters of non-European origin are poised to make up an increasingly electorally salient group of voters in the twenty-first century. According to the 2006 Census of Canada (Statistics Canada 2008a), Canada's total visible minority population is currently 16.2 percent, an increase of 5 percentage points in ten years, making it one of the fastest-growing populations in Canada. Especially important from an electoral perspective is the regional concentration of these communities. Over half of the visible minority population in Canada lives in Ontario, and almost 80 percent of these live in the Toronto census metropolitan area.

Given their demographic growth in Ontario, combined with Conservative success in that province in recent years, this chapter examines whether those of non-European origin continue to disproportionately support the Liberals, or whether we are seeing a fundamental alteration to the social bases of Liberal support in Canada. In other words, is Liberal support among visible minorities a case of continuity in Canadian politics, or can the recent success of the Conservatives be linked to a more profound change in a traditional base of Liberal support? Drawing on Canadian Election Study data collected since 1993, this chapter shows that, despite the creation and success of the new Conservative Party of Canada, Liberal support among visible minority voters remains strong.

The "Ethnic" Vote in Canada

Much of the work on ethnic and racial voting has been conducted in the United States. Early work on immigrant integration suggested that new immigrant groups from Europe would vote as a bloc because of shared socioeconomic status or a shared sense of identity (see, for example, Dahl 1961, 434-45; Wolfinger 1965). This literature was largely eclipsed in the 1980s and 1990s by a focus on racial, specifically African American, voting patterns in light of controversies surrounding minority representation and its relationship to electoral rules, the so-called "minority vote dilution" problem (for an overview, see Grofman et al. 1992).

At the individual level, there is evidence that racial and ethnic identities do matter for vote choice (Rea et al. 2010; Stokes-Brown 2006), and that this sometimes even overrides partisan identification (Hill et al. 2003). The 2008 election in the United States, where Barack Obama became the first black president of the United States, provides a telling example. According to the US Census Bureau, turnout increased by about 4 percentage points among blacks, Hispanics, and Asians (Edwards 2009). Obama's support among black voters was nearly universal: 99 percent of them voted for him, according to Gallup exit polls (Saad 2008) and post-election surveys (American National Election Studies 2008). Both the mobilization of black voters and their choice at the ballot box arguably were motivated in large part by the presence of a (viable) black candidate.[2]

In Canada, there has been substantial work that looks at minority candidates. Visible minority MPs have become more common in the House of Commons over time, although such minorities are still under-represented relative to their population size (Black and Hicks 2006, 27). While the evidence is mixed about the causes of this under-representation, it does not appear to be due to discrimination against visible minority candidates on the part of voters (Black and Erickson 2006).[3]

When it comes to minority voters, one thing is clear: regardless of who is running for office, voters from non-European backgrounds tend to overwhelmingly support the Liberal Party. According to Blais (2005, 831), such voters were about 28 percent more likely to vote for the Liberals after 1990 than voters of European descent, after controlling for region and religion. Since minority voters make up a smaller portion of the population, an effect of this size is striking. At the same time, little is known about what causes this gap.

Blais explores several possible explanations, including incumbency effects at time of immigration and ideological considerations. He finds no support for the argument that the Liberals' hold on office has been self-perpetuating (i.e., that immigrants vote Liberal because Liberals were in office when they immigrated to Canada), and only small support for ideological considerations (i.e., that visible minorities' greater support for minority issues explains their Liberal vote choice).

Clearly, however, Liberals have historically been the party of choice among voters of non-European origin. What is it about the party that attracts these voters? We explore three sets of possible explanations. The first set relates to voters' socio-demographic characteristics. Along with religion and regional differences, Blais and colleagues (2002) have shown that

Liberal supporters are more likely to be university-educated and to live in urban areas. As noted earlier, the vast majority of visible minorities in Canada live in urban centres. It is possible that living in urban areas (rather than minority status) is pushing voters towards the Liberal Party.

The educational status of non-Europeans at the aggregate level might also push them towards the Liberal Party. Compared with the general Canadian population, about 20 percent of whom hold university degrees, about one-third of immigrants do. If we consider just the most recent wave of immigration, this figure goes up to 51 percent (Statistics Canada 2008b, 17). The ethno-cultural portrait is even more telling. While 10.5 percent of non-visible minorities have bachelor's degrees, three of the four most populous visible minority communities (Chinese, South Asian, and Filipinos) have substantially higher proportions (22, 17, and 27 percent, respectively).[4] In other words, part of Liberal support may be explained by the different socio-demographic characteristics of visible minorities.

A second explanation revolves around ideological considerations. In Blais's original analysis (2005), ideological differences were found between those of European and non-European descent. Non-Europeans, not surprisingly, were more supportive of minority issues, which should predispose them to voting Liberal. This was in fact the case, although this explained only a small portion of the gap. Given the recent increase in number of Conservative seats in Ontario, it is also important to note that those of non-European backgrounds tend to be more socially conservative (Blais 2005; Hyder 2005). In other words, although some ideological considerations may incline non-Europeans towards the Liberal Party, there are certainly ideological tendencies that would also draw them towards the Conservatives.

A third explanation may be found in the mobilization of the ethnic vote. This is a subject that has received scant attention, although it is perhaps one of the most promising avenues for explaining the tendency of non-Europeans to vote for the Liberal Party (Bird 2005). There are two interconnected avenues through which mobilization may take place. On the one hand, parties may make special outreach efforts to specific communities. Evidence for the effect of outreach activities on vote choice in the general population is limited (Campbell et al. 1960; Lazarsfeld et al. 1948; Nickerson 2005; but see Gerber and Green 2000), but research has provided evidence of partisan mobilization in ethnic communities. For example, Nuño (2007) has shown that in the 2000 US presidential election, outreach by Latino party members had a significant impact on vote choice.

On the other hand, members of different ethnocultural communities may also be motivated by co-ethnics to rally around a party that is perceived to be in those groups' interest. Bloc-voting theories assume that various communities have more in common with each other than with people from other communities. Indeed, the earliest voting studies focused on how shared socio-demographic characteristics were important predictors of vote choice (Berelson et al. 1954; Lazarsfeld et al. 1948). Living in milieus and interacting with those who share things in common can facilitate awareness of shared interests (Huckfeldt and Sprague 1987, 1992; Huckfeldt et al. 2000). When it comes to ethnic and racial communities, comparative evidence suggests that ethnic, racial, and religious organizations can play an important role in mobilizing voters (Fennema and Tillie 1999; Tate 1991, 1993) and that social context is important in this respect (Leighley 2001; McKenzie 2008).

The extent to which the Liberal Party is disproportionately successful at targeting voters of non-European descent, and the extent to which ethnic organizations and social networks are acting as partisan mobilizers, are unclear. Research has shown that contextual characteristics are related to voting Liberal. In one of the few studies of the effect of ethnic concentration on vote choice, Gerber (2006) shows that ridings with greater percentages of immigrant and visible minority voters are more likely to vote Liberal, even after controlling for socio-economic status. Importantly, she showed that Conservative inroads in the Greater Toronto Area (GTA) base of the Liberals most likely occurred in less diverse ridings (113).

From the party side, we know that political parties are more likely to field visible minority candidates in ridings with more visible minority voters (Black and Hicks 2006; Dhillion 2005), and that party outreach efforts to promote ethnic participation in party affairs are tied to efforts to mobilize ethnic voters more generally (Carty 1991). There is at least a perception that Liberals have been particularly good at ethnic-minority outreach, but in recent elections more parties have made concerted efforts to mobilize ethnic voters (Dhillion 2005).

In her examination of ethnic representation in France, Denmark, and Canada, Bird (2005) notes several features of the Canadian electoral system that have a direct bearing on the mobilization of visible minority voters. First, she notes that the strong incumbency rate in Canada has promoted a "clientelistic" relationship between ethnic community leaders and the Liberal Party (453).[5] Despite the attempts of other parties to lure voters away from the Liberals by nominating visible minority candidates, she notes that incumbent Liberals do surprisingly well in the GTA. Second, when nomination contests are open, the local nomination process also leads to mass partisan mobilization efforts of ethnic voters. Bird (2005) notes that party membership levels are highest in ridings with high levels of visible minorities, and that new party members signed up by nominees are overwhelmingly from visible minorities (452).[6]

Both Liberal Party outreach and partisan mobilization by ethnic community leaders and organizations may help explain Liberal vote choice among voters of non-European descent. Other parties have clearly begun to target ethnic voters as well (Bird 2005; Dhillion 2005; Hyder 2005). For example, Hyder (2005) notes that the Conservatives made explicit appeals to ethnic communities on the issue of same-sex marriage (see also Black and Hicks 2006, 29). One of the Conservative election promises during the 2006 election (which they kept) was to cut the cost for many immigrant applications in half (for example, fees for permanent residency applications were reduced from $975 to $475). And in 2004, the Conservatives ran the highest number of visible minority candidates (twenty-nine) of any party (Bird 2005, 464n69; Black and Hicks 2006). Party and ethnic mobilization may be a source of Liberal support, but other parties are capable of similarly organizing. Indeed, the Conservative Party has made concerted efforts to mobilize the so-called ethnic vote (Ibbitson and Friesen 2010).

Data and Methods

The data for this analysis are drawn from the 1993-2008 Canadian Election Studies (CES).[7] Each election campaign includes a nationally representative sample of Canadians, usually in three waves: a pre-election, a post-election, and a mail-back survey.[8] The 1993-2000 CES data are used for descriptive purposes, to demonstrate the level of Liberal Party support prior to the last three elections.

This chapter then focuses more specifically on the three elections held between 2004 and 2008. In order to ensure a sufficient number of visible minority voters to make statistical inferences, the 2004, 2006, and 2008 data have been pooled for the analysis.[9] The analysis is based on reported vote choice in the post-election survey for respondents outside Quebec.[10] A total of 2,669 respondents across those three elections reported voting in the election and provided a valid vote choice response and ethnic background information.[11] Of these, approximately 7 percent ($N = 172$) were coded as being of non-European descent.[12] I will use the terms "non-European descent" and "visible minorities" interchangeably. Four other groups were created: Anglo (including British Isles, North America, Australia, and New Zealand), French (French, Québécois, and Acadian), Other European, and Aboriginal.[13]

This chapter has two goals. First, we establish the extent of Liberal voting among visible minority voters between 1993 and 2008. Has the level of support decreased, remained the same, or increased? Second, we explore whether we can "explain away" any propensity to vote Liberal among visible minorities by controlling for three sets of explanatory factors: demographic differences between visible minorities and non-visible minorities, ideological gaps, and higher identification with the Liberal Party. The analysis proceeds in three steps. First, vote choice in the period is examined to ascertain whether the Liberal advantage in vote choice among visible minority voters is present (1993-2008). In a second step, Blais's analysis (2005) is reproduced, controlling for region and religion. Finally, in a third step, multinomial logistic regression models are created to examine whether three sets of factors (demographics, ideology, and mobilization) reduce the predictive power of non-European ancestry with regard to Liberal vote choice.[14]

Discussion

Figure 7.1 examines the changing fortunes of the Liberal Party by ancestry since 1993. As a reference, the percentage of the vote garnered by the Liberal Party, as reported by Elections Canada, is also included in the figure.[15] Liberal support has decreased steadily from 1993, when the party garnered 41 percent of the popular vote. By 2008, Liberal support had fallen 15 percentage points, to 26 percent. The breakdown by ethnic ancestry is instructive on two levels. First, Liberal support appears to have fallen among all ancestry groups, suggesting that the Liberal Party during this period has become less appealing to voters across the board. Second, the ordering of support among ancestry groups is consistent with past research. Liberal support is least strong among those of Anglo and other European backgrounds, and stronger among those of French and non-European backgrounds. Indeed, in every year except 1993, Liberal support among those of non-European origin has been highest.

Some caution is warranted in interpreting the precise level of support among those of non-European background, given that they make up a relatively small percentage of each election year sample.[16] Small shifts in support can result simply from random sampling. The overall trend from 1993

FIGURE 7.1
Liberal Party vote share by ethnic background across Canada outside Quebec

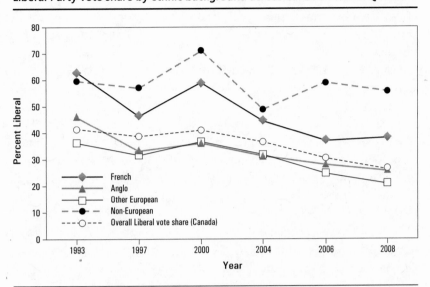

Notes: Data are unweighted and exclude respondents in Quebec, panel respondents, and those whose ethnic background was "other." Overall Liberal vote share reflects Elections Canada official results for all of Canada.
Sources: Canadian Election Studies (1993-2008).

to 2008 is slightly downward, however. If we pool the first three elections, where the Liberals won majorities, and the second three elections, which resulted in consecutive minority governments, the Liberal vote share average falls from 61 percent to 55 percent, a drop of about 6 percentage points. The average overall Liberal vote share (country-wide) averaged 40 percent prior to 2004, and fell to 31 percent in elections held since then. In other words, although Liberal support dropped among visible minorities, this drop was relatively small and did not outpace by any means the larger drop in Liberal support more generally.

The Liberal Party has traditionally had strong support among visible minority communities and, in the aggregate during this period, this support appears to remain rather strong. The slide in Liberal support in recent elections and concerted efforts on the part of Conservatives to mobilize visible minority voters have led some to argue that visible minority voters may now be more aligned with the latter party (Hyder 2005). Indeed, popular news accounts in the past few years have highlighted Conservative tendencies among immigrant voters. For example, a 2010 *Globe and Mail* article titled "Conservative Immigrants Boost Tory Fortunes" argues that "a tectonic shift is reshaping Canada's political landscape" (Ibbitson and Friesen 2010). Noting a significant drop in Liberal support among immigrant voters since 2000 (for which they rely on CES data), the authors point to Conservative efforts, especially those of Jason Kenney, minister of citizenship, immigration and multiculturalism, to target visible minority voters. Figure 7.1 suggests no such "tectonic shift," however.

It is indeed true that support for the Liberal Party has fallen among immigrant voters. And it is also true that visible minorities make up a greater and greater segment of the immigrant community in Canada.[17] The immigrant community is not synonymous with visible minority status, however. Indeed, only about one-half of immigrants in Canada are visible minorities, and about a third of the visible minority population are not Canadians by birth (Statistics Canada 2008a). In other words, Tory success may indeed be linked to increased support among immigrant voters, but this support seems to be primarily drawn from older immigrant communities from Europe. Figure 7.1 shows that support for Liberals among those of "other European" descent dropped from 36 percent in 2000 to 21 percent in 2008. Such a drop is significant, considering that those of other European origins make up almost a quarter of the sample, whereas non-Europeans comprise only 8 percent. In other words, a drop in support among respondents of other European origins would be felt more strongly at the ballot box, and, combined with declining support among voters of Anglo and French origin, paints a very different picture of the success of the Tories' courtship of the "ethnic vote."

Indeed, since the creation of the new Conservative Party in 2004, the Liberal vote among visible minorities has, if anything, increased. In 2004, about 49 percent of voters of non-European descent reported voting for the Liberal Party, compared with 58 percent and 55 percent in 2006 and 2008, respectively. These differences could result from small sample sizes, but there is clearly no evidence that support for the Liberals among visible minority voters is declining. If support for the Liberals has fallen in recent years, the drop has occurred among the two historical linguistic communities and subsequent waves of European immigrants.

The general pattern is therefore not consistent with recent musings that the Conservative Party is making inroads into visible minority communities. One possibility is that, given the regional nature of Canadian party politics, the inroads are region-specific. If we consider just Ontario voters, where the CPC has shown increasing success in recent elections, we again find little evidence of a shift to the party. If anything, support for the Liberal Party is stronger among visible minorities in Ontario than in the full sample, with nearly two out of every three voters of non-European origin voting for the Liberals.

In addition, this high level of support does not appear to be declining. The increasing success of the Conservative Party in Ontario appears to be concentrated among European immigrant groups other than those of Anglo or French backgrounds, such as those of Italian, Polish, or German descent. In 2004, 30 percent of those of other European backgrounds voted Conservative in Ontario. This number increased to 40 percent in 2006 and 45 percent in 2008. Importantly, those of other European (non-Anglo, non-French) descent make up the second-largest group of voters outside of Quebec. A 15-percentage-point shift in their party allegiance can translate into a substantial shift in a party's electoral fortunes.

Clearly, voters of non-European descent continue to support the Liberal Party at levels beyond the reach of other groups, despite the instability in the party system that has led to three consecutive minority governments and the increased electoral viability of the Conservative Party. At the same time, the mainly European immigrant communities that settled in Canada over the past century do appear to be shifting their allegiance to the Conservatives. What explains these ethno-racial bases of vote choice?

In Table 7.1, I predict vote choice using a binary logistic regression model, where Liberal vote is 1, and all other votes (CPC, NDP, Green) are 0. Table 7.1 presents odds ratios for ancestry on voting for each party, controlling for region and religion to mirror the largest salient social cleavages in Canadian politics (Blais 2005), as well as election year to control for the pooled nature of the data and to capture over-time effects in the vote shares of parties.[18] This model reproduces the models presented by Blais (2005) with pooled data from the 1965-2000 period, except for the election year controls.

The results largely replicate those found in earlier work. Being of non-European descent has a positive and significant effect on one's propensity to vote for the Liberal Party, compared with being of Anglo background. Those of French and other European backgrounds do not show a significantly greater likelihood of voting Liberal than Anglos.[19] Table 7.1 also confirms the expected regional and religious support for the Liberals. Liberal voters are more likely to come from Ontario than from the West, and there was a small positive effect for being from Atlantic Canada as opposed to Ontario. Liberals also continue to have a strong base among Catholics. As expected, the odds of voting Liberal decreased steadily after 2004.

TABLE 7.1

Predicting vote choice by ancestry, region, and religion in the 2004, 2006, and 2008 Canadian federal elections (outside of Quebec)

		Odds ratio
Ancestry	Anglo (reference)	
	French	1.28
	Other European	0.95
	Non-European	3.30***
Region	Ontario (reference)	
	Atlantic	1.25*
	West	0.44***
Religion	Not Catholic (reference)	
	Catholic	1.45***
Election year	2004 (reference)	
	2006	0.79**
	2008	0.65***
N		2,593
Pseudo R^2		0.0602

Notes: The table reports odds ratios for a binary logistic regression where Liberal vote is 1 and all other votes (Conservative, NDP, and Green) are 0. Unweighted.

* $p < .1$, ** $p < .05$, *** $p < .01$

Source: Canadian Election Studies, 2004-08, excluding Quebec.

In other words, being from a non-European background continues to be linked with Liberal voting. Why might this be? In Table 7.2, three sets of explanatory factors are added to the base model from Table 7.1: demographics controls, ideological controls, and party identification. If the effect of being of non-European descent is reduced when adding these controls, this would provide evidence that the source of Liberal support among voters of non-European descent may be based more in the aggregate demographic or ideological differences between visible minorities and other voters in Canada. The odds ratios for each variable are presented for voting Liberal, as in Table 7.1.

In Model 1, the demographic controls are added for gender, marital status, and education, which have been shown to influence vote choice in Canada (Blais et al. 2002). Immigrant status is also included in the model. The growth in the visible minority population in Canada has been largely driven by immigration (although, as noted, not all visible minorities are

TABLE 7.2

Exploration of Liberal vote choice outside of Quebec in the 2004, 2006, and 2008 Canadian federal elections

		Model 1	Model 2	Model 3
Base model	Ancestry			
	Anglo (reference)			
	French	1.32*	1.12	0.94
	Other European	0.92	1.00	1.08
	Non-European	2.84***	2.80***	2.56***
	Region			
	Ontario (reference)			
	Atlantic	1.30*	1.23	1.52**
	West	0.45***	0.47***	0.56***
	Religion			
	Not Catholic (reference)			
	Catholic	1.48***	1.45***	1.07
	Election year			
	2004 (reference)			
	2006	0.77**	0.65***	0.68**
	2008	0.63***	0.55***	0.59***
Demographics	Female	1.02	0.89	1.04
	Married	0.97	1.05	1.05
	Education			
	High school or less (reference)			
	Some postsecondary	1.18	0.78	0.71
	Completed BA or higher	1.64*	0.88	0.74
	Born in Canada	0.87	0.84	0.91
Ideology	Personal retrospective economic evaluation			
	Worse (reference)			
	Same		1.09	1.09
	Better		0.96	1.04
	Agree: gay marriage		1.69***	1.05
	Agree: better if women stay home		0.88	0.93
	Level of immigration			
	Less (reference)			
	Same		1.34**	1.04
	More		1.47**	1.27
	Level of welfare spending			
	Less (reference)			
	Same		1.52***	1.40**
	More		1.91***	1.92***

▶

◄ **TABLE 7.2**

		Model 1	Model 2	Model 3
Party	None/other (reference)			
identification	Liberal			7.44***
	Conservative			0.13***
	NDP			0.52***
N		2,568	2,145	2,142
Pseudo R^2		0.0642	0.0795	0.35

$^*p < .1,$ $^{**}p < .05,$ $^{***}p < .01$

immigrants). Although Model 1 slightly improves the fit of the model, there is no discernible impact on the effect of non-European ancestry.

In Model 2, ideological questions are included. As noted previously, the ideological tendencies among visible minorities move in two directions: although there is greater support for immigration and issues related to minority issues in Canada (which should lead them to parties on the left), visible minorities tend to be more socially conservative. Indeed, Conservative efforts to court such voters have often focused on the latter types of issues (Ibbitson and Friesen 2010; Hyder 2005). Five sets of ideological items are included. The first is a retrospective economic question (which serves primarily as a control, given its importance in explaining vote choice). Two questions related to social conservatism are included: whether the respondent agrees with gays and lesbians having the right to marry, and whether it would be better if women stayed at home. A question about the desired level of immigration and support for welfare spending is also included. The former captures an important issue that disproportionately affects visible minorities, and the welfare spending question taps respondents' views on the size of government.[20]

The effect of ideological considerations is largely as expected. More socially liberal voters (i.e., those who agree with gay marriage) are more likely to vote for the Liberal Party, and those who support increased immigration and increased welfare spending are more likely to vote Liberal. And, again, the fit of this model improves. There is little evidence, however, that these ideological differences in and of themselves explain Liberal support among voters of non-European descent. If we move from the base model presented in Table 7.1 to this model (i.e., controlling for demographics and ideological considerations), the predicted probability of visible minorities voting Liberal drops from .55 to .51. Even after controlling for a host of demographic and ideological considerations, the effect of being of non-European descent is positive, significant, and almost as great as before.

In Model 3, one additional set of controls is added, namely, partisan identification. Citizens who report attachment to a particular party are more likely to vote for that party, and here the Liberals have traditionally had an advantage (Blais et al. 2002, 116-17). Blais and colleagues report that fully 85 percent of those who expressed a partisan identification voted for "their" party in the 2000 election (120).

One reason why non-Europeans may vote Liberal disproportionately is Liberal attachment. During the critical elections of 2004-08, Liberal Party identification is greatest among those of non-European descent (41 percent), followed closely by those with French ancestry outside Quebec (38 percent). This is in stark contrast with Conservative Party identification among visible minorities, yielding a gap of 26 percentage points between the two major parties. The gap between Liberal and Conservative identification is not that large between any other group. In fact, among the two largest groups of voters outside Quebec (Anglo and other European), Conservative Party identification is actually highest (31 percent and 26 percent, respectively).

Does partisan identification explain why voters of non-European descent vote so heavily Liberal? In Table 7.2, Model 3 lends some support to this claim. Being a Liberal Party identifier strongly affects voting for the Liberal Party, and the inclusion of this variable reduces the odds ratio for voting Liberal from 2.84 to 2.56 for those of non-European descent compared with Anglos. This drop is further highlighted if we consider the marginal effect of voting Liberal for non-Europeans: from Model 1 to Model 3, the marginal effect is halved from .23 to .11. In other words, strong Liberal partisan identification partly explains strong Liberal voting among voters of non-European origin. That said, being of non-European descent continues to be significant.

Like Liberal voting, there is no evidence that Liberal Party attachment is weakening over time among visible minorities either. Between 39 and 44 percent of visible minority voters identified with the party during the 2004-08 period. On the contrary, as with vote choice, Conservative Party identification appeared to be rising among other European voters. In 2004, only 24 percent of voters of European descent identified as Conservatives. This increased to 33 percent in 2006, and to 41 percent in 2008. In other words, Conservative success *does* appear to hinge on immigrant communities, but contrary to popular commentary, it is the older immigrant communities in Canada that appear to be flocking to this party's banner.

Of course, partisan identification is a poor proxy for party mobilization. Although partisan identification is part of the answer, it begs the question of why voters of non-European origin identify with the Liberal Party in the first place. Equally important is trying to understand why voters of European origin have increasingly shifted to the Conservatives.

This is where the third possible explanation (party mobilization) appears to be the most plausible explanation. As Bird (2005) has noted elsewhere, the Liberal Party has been particularly adept at mobilizing ethnic minority voters in local party politics. This is partly because of the residential concentrations of visible minority communities within urban centres in Canada (Fong and Wilkes 2003). Residential concentration in cities like Toronto does not necessarily correspond to poverty either, as is often the case in European and American cities. Qadeer (2004, 4) notes that ethnic enclaves in Toronto exhibit a variety of socio-economic diversity, and that above and beyond their available socio-economic resources, they are also "rich in social capital, mutual support networks, and community organizations."

Given the first-past-the-post electoral system and decentralized candidate nomination processes in Canada, parties clearly have incentives to mobilize geographically concentrated voters. The residential patterns of visible minority communities combined with the resources within them that bind people along ethnic, cultural, and religious lines provide fertile ground for such mobilization. The Liberal Party may be particularly adept at tapping into these networks. Although evidence of this is limited (but see Bird 2005), high levels of Liberal identification may be a self-reinforcing phenomenon in closely knit communities.

A strong test of this hypothesis is not possible with the data at hand, but several pieces of evidence point in this direction. First is the qualitative data provided by Bird (2005) into the disproportionate mobilization of visible minorities in nomination contests in urban centres in Canada. This is complemented by research in the Greater Toronto Area into the unprecedented success of visible minority candidates in the largely visible minority (especially South Asian) suburbs, where ethnic concentration is combined with higher levels of socio-economic status (Matheson 2006). A second piece of evidence from Gerber (2006) demonstrates that ridings that are heavily visible minority or immigrant are more likely to vote heavily Liberal. Finally, the evidence of the high levels of Liberal partisanship among visible minorities and its corresponding relationship to vote choice in Table 7.2 suggests that there is a strong correspondence at the level of voters.

Can we discern direct evidence of partisan mobilization of visible minority communities? Although this chapter provides only a first attempt, a final round of analyses provides a limited test of ethnic mobilization. One of the primary mediators in mobilizing ethnic communities (especially those that are residentially concentrated) consists of the ethnic, cultural, and religious organizations that connect community members together and provide elite cues on how to vote. The mail-back survey in 2004 and 2008 included an indicator for involvement in either an ethnic organization or a religious organization.[21] Not surprisingly, Anglo respondents are least likely to be involved in an ethnic organization (2 percent), with levels increasing to 6 percent among those of French background, 9 percent among those of other European background, and 18 percent among those of non-European background. Involvement in religious organizations is more evenly distributed, with around 28 percent reporting participation, except for those of other European backgrounds (37 percent).

Involvement in any association has been shown to increase political participation (Putnam 2000; Verba et al. 1995), but the ethnic mobilization argument here is slightly different: it has to do with whether involvement promotes a particular vote preference. If evidence were found that involvement in such organizations promoted voting Liberal, it would provide further support for the contention that the disproportionate number of Liberal votes among voters of non-European origin is partly driven by targeted mobilization efforts.

Unfortunately, the analysis provides little evidence of ethnic mobilization. Neither a cross-tabular analysis ($N = 1,102$) nor a simplified vote choice model ($N = 968$) provided evidence that Liberal vote choice was affected by membership in a religious or ethnic association. Furthermore, in the multivariate model, the effect of having non-European ancestry remains positive and significant. Because of the smaller sample sizes, a comparison of the size of this effect with that found in previous models is inappropriate. In other words, little support for ethnic mobilization was found in this (admittedly limited) test of the hypothesis. In order to tease out such effects, it is essential that an oversample of visible minorities be included in future surveys. Associational involvement, social network, and campaign contact variables are regularly included in the CES and provide a rich source of data, but the small numbers of visible minority respondents make it very difficult to tease out unique effects among them.

Conclusion

Liberal support among visible minority voters remains strong, despite the success of the Conservative Party in recent elections and the party's targeted efforts to attract the ethnic vote. Given the changing demographic realities in Canada, this support may begin to exercise a significant effect on the electoral fortunes of the Liberal Party. The sources of this link remain a mystery, however: analysis of demographic, ideological, and partisanship factors have failed to dent the strong direct effect of ancestry on vote choice. The only notable effect is for partisan identification, which simply reframes the question of what leads voters of non-European ancestry to disproportionately identify with, and in turn vote for, the Liberal Party. The most promising area of research appears to be ethnic mobilization by both political parties and community organizations. Although the analysis described here failed to find a direct effect for ethnic and religious organizational involvement, better measures may be able to capture the ways in which social networks can inform and transform people's preferences, and especially the ways in which a political party's machinery is able to tap into such networks.

If there has been a significant change in party politics in the past three elections, it centres on the increase in Conservative partisanship and Conservative votes among those of European origin other than Anglo or French. During the two minority parliaments from 2004 to the present, the Conservative Party broke the Liberals' stranglehold on power. Part of this success may lie in shifting allegiances not among visible minorities but rather among longer-standing immigrant communities such as the Italian, Polish, and Ukrainian communities. Their support for the Conservatives, which appears to be increasing, is an under-researched phenomenon of recent elections. Given the size of this community in Canada, future research needs to lead to a better understanding of not only why visible minorities are so attached to the Liberal Party but also why primarily white immigrant communities are increasingly supporting the Conservatives. What is clear from this analysis, however, is that the social bases of party support in Canada are remarkably robust. Despite an erosion in support for the Liberals since 1993, social cleavages continue to be powerful explanatory factors in understanding vote choice in Canada.

Notes

1 The Liberal Party also relies on seats in Quebec, although they have not won a majority of seats there since the electoral success of the Bloc Québécois in 1993.

2 But see Tate (1991) for less clear results in the candidacy of Jesse Jackson.

3 Whether parties tend to run visible-minority candidates in less viable ridings remains disputed. Tossutti and Najem (2003) found no evidence that visible minorities run in less competitive ridings, but Black and Erickson (2006) did find some evidence to the contrary. See Black and Hicks (2006) for a breakdown by party.

4 The other group in the top four most populous categories comprises blacks, who have bachelor's degrees at levels similar to non-visible minorities (9 percent).

5 Whereas she notes that Liberal incumbency is an impediment to visible-minority representation, Black and Hicks (2006) note that visible minorities were more likely to run in the safest ridings for the Liberals.

6 She estimates that as many as 75 percent of new party members in the GTA were visible minorities, based on interviews with candidates and campaign managers (Bird 2005, fn67).

7 Data were provided by the Institute for Social Research, York University. The surveys were funded by Elections Canada and the Social Sciences and Humanities Research Council of Canada (SSHRC), and were completed for the Canadian Election Team, including André Blais (Université de Montréal), Joanna Everitt (University of New Brunswick), Patrick Fournier (Université de Montréal), Elisabeth Gidengil (McGill University), and Neil Nevitte (University of Toronto).

8 There was no mail-back survey in 2006.

9 The 2004, 2006, and 2008 CES included a panel of respondents from the 2004 election that was reinterviewed in the subsequent elections to create a panel. In order to maximize cases, panel respondents were included unless they responded in multiple waves. The inclusion of multiple-wave respondents would violate the independence assumption of the models presented. The choice to include any panel respondents who failed to participate in multiple waves enables us to maximize the number of minority voters.

10 Quebec has been excluded from the analysis because of the overwhelming importance of issues around sovereignty for vote choice in Quebec (Blais et al. 2002), but see Lavoie and Serré (2002), who have shown that among immigrants in Quebec, sovereignty is becoming less salient.

11 All results are presented in unweighted form. A decision was made to maximize visible-minority respondents (see note 9 above) by including any single-election panel respondents. Their inclusion means that regular sampling weights are not appropriate. While this limits the generalizability of the point estimates to the general population, it has minimal effect on the ability to tease out relationships between variables. When possible, sample results are verified against population data, as in Figure 7.1.

12 Only the first reported ethnic background is used to construct ancestry categories.

13 Due to their small numbers in the survey, Aboriginal respondents are included in descriptive tables only.

14 The mobilization factors available in the survey are limited to questions asked in the mail-back survey, so these analyses are restricted to a smaller number of respondents.

15 As noted, the unweighted data may raise questions about the relationship of the point estimates to the population. The Elections Canada data reinforce the fact that the trends in voting captured by the CES data, even in unweighted form, reflect the real trend.

16 The number of non-Europeans in each CES election year sample varies from 45 to 125.

17 According to the 2006 Canadian census, visible minorities made up 54 percent of the immigrant population. Although the CES under-represents the visible-minority immigrant population in its sample, the trend in the data reflects actual population trends.

18 Note that alternative models were estimated using multinomial logistic regression. Non-European voters are significantly more likely to vote Liberal than either Conservative or NDP, even when estimated separately (not shown).

19 But note that when estimated using a multinomial logistic regression, French voters are less likely to vote Conservative. All other results are identical in terms of direction and significance, whether estimated using a logistic regression for Liberal vote or a multinomial model that distinguishes among non-Liberal voters.

20 Support for social assistance is often considered a key ideological dividing line between the left and the right, and as such, serves as a good proxy for ideological orientation.

21 Because I have to rely on the mail-back survey and only two waves, the sample sizes for these variables are reduced substantially (to about 1,250 respondents, of whom only 65 are from non-European backgrounds).

References

American National Election Studies. 2008. *The ANES Guide to Public Opinion and Electoral Behavior.* Ann Arbor: University of Michigan, Center for Political Studies. http://www.electionstudies.org.

Berelson, Bernard, Paul Lazarsfeld, and William McPhee. 1954. *Voting: A Study of Opinion Formation in a Presidential Campaign.* Chicago: University of Chicago Press.

Bird, Karen. 2005. "The Political Representation of Visible Minorities in Electoral Democracies: A Comparison of France, Denmark and Canada." *Nationalism and Ethnic Politics* 11 (4): 425-65.

Black, Jerome, and Lynda Erickson. 2006. "The Ethnoracial Origins of Candidates and Electoral Performance: Evidence from Canada." *Party Politics* 12 (4): 541-61.

Black, Jerome, and Bruce Hicks. 2006. "Visible Minority Candidates in the 2004 Federal Election." *Canadian Parliamentary Review* (Summer): 26-31.

Blais, André. 2005. "Accounting for the Electoral Success of the Liberal Party in Canada." *Canadian Journal of Political Science* 38 (4): 821-40.

Blais, André, Elisabeth Gidengil, Richard Nadeau, and Neil Nevitte. 2002. *Anatomy of a Liberal Victory: Making Sense of the 2000 Canadian Election.* Toronto: University of Toronto Press.

Campbell, Agnes, Philip E. Converse, Warren E. Miller, and Donald Stokes. 1960. *The American Voter*. New York: John Wiley and Sons.

Carty, R.K. 1991. *Canadian Political Parties in the Constituencies*. Toronto: Dundurn Press.

Dahl, Robert. 1961. *Who Governs*. New Haven, CT: Yale University Press.

Dhillion, Sheila. 2005. "Political Parties and Ethnic Participation: A Question of Access." *Canadian Issues* (Summer): 85-88.

Edwards, Tom. 2009. "Voter Turnout Increases by 5 Million in 2008 Presidential Election, U.S. Census Bureau Reports." US Census Bureau News Release. Report #CB09-110. http://www.census.gov/.

Fennema, Meindert, and Jean Tillie. 1999. "Political Participation and Political Trust in Amsterdam: Civic Communities and Ethnic Networks." *Journal of Ethnic and Migration Studies* 25 (4): 703-26.

Fong, Eric, and Rima Wilkes. 2003. "Racial and Ethnic Residential Patterns in Canada." *Sociological Forum* 18 (4): 577-602.

Gerber, Alan, and Donald Green. 2000. "The Effects of Canvassing, Telephone Calls, and Direct Mail on Voter Turnout: A Field Experiment." *American Political Science Review* 94: 653-63.

Gerber, Linda. 2006. "Urban Diversity: Riding Composition and Party Support in the Canadian Federal Election of 2004." *Canadian Journal of Urban Research* 15 (2): 105-18.

Gidengil, Elisabeth, André Blais, Richard Nadeau, and Neil Nevitte. 1999. "Making Sense of the Regional Vote in the 1997 Federal Election: Liberal and Reform Support Outside Quebec." *Canadian Journal of Political Science* 32: 247-72.

Grofman, Bernard, Lisa Handley, and Richard Niemi. 1992. *Minority Representation and the Quest for Voting Equality*. Cambridge: Cambridge University Press.

Hill, Kevin, Dario Moreno, and Lourdes Cue. 2003. "Racial and Partisan Voting in a Tri-Ethnic City: The 1996 Dade County Mayoral Election." *Journal of Urban Affairs* 23 (3): 291-307.

Huckfeldt, Robert, and John Sprague. 1987. "Networks in Context: The Social Flow of Political Information." *American Political Science Review* 81 (4): 1197-1216.

–. 1992. "Political Parties and Electoral Mobilization: Political Structure, Social Structure, and the Party Canvass." *American Political Science Review* 86 (1): 70-86.

Huckfeldt, Robert, John Sprague, and Jeffrey Levine. 2000. "The Dynamics of Collective Deliberation in the 1996 Election: Campaign Effects on Accessibility, Certainty, and Accuracy." *American Political Science Review* 94 (3): 641-51.

Hyder, Goldy. 2005. "Gaining the Political Support of Minorities in Canada." *Canadian Issues* (Summer): 46-48.

Ibbitson, John, and Joe Friesen. 2010. "Conservative Immigrants Boost Tory Fortunes." *Globe and Mail*, 4 October. http://www.theglobeandmail.com/.

Lavoie, Nathalie, and Pierre Serré. 2002. "Du vote bloc au vote social: Le cas des citoyens issus de l'immigration de Montreal, 1995-1996." *Canadian Journal of Political Science* 35 (1): 49-74.

Lazarsfeld, Paul, Bernard Berelson, and Hazel Gaudet. 1948. *The People's Choice*. New York: Columbia University Press.

Leighley, Jan. 2001. *Strength in Numbers? The Political Mobilization of Racial and Ethnic Minorities.* Princeton, NJ: Princeton University Press.

Lijphart, Arend. 1966. "Religious vs. Linguistic vs. Class Voting: The 'Crucial Experiment' of Comparing Belgium, Canada, South Africa and Switzerland." *American Political Science Review* 73 (2): 442-58.

Matheson, Andrew. 2006. "Political Representation in Suburban Canada." *Electoral Insight* 8 (2): 24-29.

McKenzie, Brian. 2008. "Reconsidering the Effects of Bonding Social Capital: A Closer Look at Black Civil Society Institutions in America." *Political Behavior* 30: 25-45.

Meisel, John. 1956. "Religious Affiliation and Electoral Behaviour: A Case Study." *Canadian Journal of Economics and Political Science* 22: 481-96.

Nickerson, David. 2005. "Partisan Mobilization Using Volunteer Phone Banks and Door Hangers." *Annals of American Academy of Political and Social Science* 601: 10-27.

Nuño, Stephen. 2007. "Latino Mobilization and Vote Choice in the 2000 Presidential Election." *American Politics Research* 35 (2): 273-93.

Putnam, Robert. 2000. *Bowling Alone: The Collapse and Revival of American Community.* New York: Simon and Schuster.

Qadeer, Mohammad. 2004. "Ethnic Segregation in a Multicultural City: The Case of Toronto, Canada." *Policy Matters,* CERIS Bulletin no. 6, 1-7.

Rea, Andrea, Dirk Jacobs, Celine Teney, and Pascal Delwit. 2010. "Les comportements électoraux des minorités ethniques à Bruxelles." *Revue Française de Science Politique* 60 (4): 1-26.

Saad, Lydia. 2008. "Blacks, Postgrads, Young Adults Help Obama Prevail." http://www.gallup.com/.

Simeon, Richard, and David Elkins. 1974. "Regional Political Cultures in Canada." *Canadian Journal of Political Science* 7 (3): 397-437.

Statistics Canada. 2008a. *Canada's Ethnocultural Mosaic, 2006 Census.* Catalogue no. 97-562-X. Ottawa: Industry Canada.

–. 2008b. *Educational Portrait of Canada, 2006 Census.* Catalogue no. 97-560-X. Ottawa: Industry Canada.

Stokes-Brown, Atiya Kay. 2006. "Racial Identity and Latino Vote Choice." *American Politics Research* 34 (5): 627-52.

Tate, Katherine. 1991. "Black Political Participation in the 1984 and 1988 Presidential Elections." *American Political Science Review* 85 (4): 1159-76.

–. 1993. *From Protest to Politics: The New Black Voters in American Elections.* Cambridge, MA: Harvard University Press.

Tossutti, Livianna, and Tom Pierre Najem. 2003. "Minorities and Elections in Canada's Fourth Party System: Macro and Micro Constraints and Opportunities." *Canadian Ethnic Studies* 34: 85-112.

Verba, Sidney, Kay Lehman Schlozman, and Henry Brady. 1995. *Voice and Equality.* Cambridge, MA : Harvard University Press.

Wolfinger, Raymond. 1965. "The Development and Persistence of Ethnic Voting." *American Political Science Review* 59: 896-908.

8

The Canadian Party System

Trends in Election Campaign Reporting, 1980-2008

BLAKE ANDREW, PATRICK FOURNIER, AND STUART SOROKA

There is little doubt that there have been significant changes in the Canadian party system over the last twenty years. The 1993 election saw the collapse of the Progressive Conservative (PC) Party, in seats if not also in votes, and the rise of a right populist party that has in one form or another – Reform Party or Canadian Alliance – replaced the PCs as the main party of the right. In 2004, the right reunited under the banner of the Conservative Party of Canada, an entity significantly dissimilar from the PCs. The Liberals suffered a string of failures during the last decade, falling from a majority government in 2000, to a minority government in 2004, to opposition in 2006, to even more losses in 2008, and finally to the most devastating defeat of its entire history in 2011. While the New Democratic Party (NDP) vote share climbed steadily between 1993 and 2008 (from 7 percent to 18 percent), its breakthrough in terms of seats and votes occurred in 2011. NDP success in that election coincided with the collapse of the Bloc Québécois (BQ), a party that had maintained strong regional support in the province of Quebec between 1993 and 2008. In 2011, Canada experienced a sea change in the distribution of seats in the House of Commons, as the Conservative Party formed a majority government with the NDP as official opposition, while the Liberal Party and the Bloc Québécois were nearly decimated. Clearly, the Canadian party system in place today is fundamentally different from the one that existed throughout the 1960s, '70s, and '80s.

That the distribution of party support has shifted is beyond doubt – both within constituencies and across regions. The Trudeau and Mulroney majorities garnered votes from across the country. Indeed, this pan-Canadian support is the defining feature of what scholars have labelled the "third party system" (Carty 1988; Carty et al. 2000; Johnston et al. 1992). This system collapsed in 1993, however, when two regionally based and predominantly ideological parties broke through in both public support and seats. In short, 1993 saw the end of pan-Canadian politics. The newly minted "fourth party system" – one that Carty and colleagues (2000) defined in terms of regionalization of party support and campaigning, as well as growing ideological polarization across parties – has been in place ever since. Arguably, the electoral upset of 2011 has continued this trend.

With regard to seat and vote shares, the regional dimension of contemporary Canadian politics is fairly obvious. The largest parties all rely heavily on regional strongholds. Since 1993, the West has been dominated by the Reform Party/Canadian Alliance/Conservative Party of Canada, Ontario has tended to be a secure realm for the Liberals, and the BQ has systematically collected the plurality of seats in Quebec. But the regionalization picture is not static. Most notably, the Conservative Party has begun gaining support east of the Prairies, particularly in Ontario, where in 2008 it surpassed the Liberal Party in both seats won and vote share, marking the first time in two decades that this province has slipped out of the hands of Canada's "natural governing party." The 2011 election consolidated this change in the base of Conservative support, while Quebec swung dramatically from supporting the BQ to supporting the NDP.

Until the dramatic shift in the distribution of seats in the House of Commons after the 2011 election, ideological polarization across parties had been less evident in election results. It has nevertheless been a popular thesis among many political pundits, who liken trends in Canada to the polarization that has occurred between the Republicans and Democrats in the United States during the same time frame. Recent studies of Canadian voting behaviour do find some evidence of growing ideological differentiation (Blais et al. 2002; Gidengil et al. 2012; Nevitte et al. 2000). Values and fundamental outlooks have played an increasingly important role in explaining voters' preferences under the fourth party system.

These two trends – regionalization and ideological polarization – can be analyzed in various ways. Generally, they have been examined with evidence relating to voting behaviour or party organizations. We believe that campaign-period political communication may also offer useful means of capturing – and perhaps even explaining – these shifts. In this chapter, we first ask whether evidence of regionalization is found in news coverage of elections. Is newspaper coverage of parties increasingly divergent across Canadian regions? We then ask whether polarization is evident in newspaper coverage. We explore the possibility that more polarized party politics is reflected in the relationship between parties and issues in campaign-period news content.

This chapter represents a first attempt to use news content from recent election campaigns to explore the relationships between parties, issues, coverage, and voters, and to examine the ways in which party competition and the party system have changed during the last three decades. We analyze all campaign stories published in five major Canadian newspapers over the course of the six federal elections held between 1993 and 2008, as well as all stories from the *Globe and Mail*'s coverage of federal campaigns during the 1980s. We explore differing coverage of parties and leaders across regions, and trends in the reporting of issues. Whether this type of analysis tells a story of continuity or change about the fourth party system is the focus of the work described in this chapter. Our evidence points towards continuity.

Background

Regionalization
Regional protest parties have been a staple in Canadian politics (Johnston et al. 1992), and include the agrarian Progressives during the 1920s, Social Credit during the middle third of the twentieth century, and the western Reform Party of the 1990s, to name just a few. There have also been some durable regional divides in the traditional support bases of the major parties throughout Canadian history (Johnston et al. 1992). For instance, from Confederation until the 1960s, the Liberals – the party of Catholics and those less adamant about the connection to Britain – were generally stronger in Quebec and the Maritimes than in other parts of Canada. Indeed, the forty-year period from the 1920s to the 1950s was defined largely by regional parties and regional support. As Carty and colleagues (2000, 19) put it, "regional brokerage seemed so much the essence of Canadian politics that it was difficult to imagine that this party system might end." But that is exactly what happened. Compared with the second party system, both the Progressive Conservatives and the New Democrats broadened their support base during the period that began in the 1960s. The Liberals, though, actually exhibited the reverse pattern: they contracted

geographically in relation to the previous system, in which they had dominated nationally (Johnston et al. 1992). Nonetheless, the third system was marked by nation building and pan-Canadian politics. This was most notably the nature of the Trudeau governments, and it culminated with the Mulroney majorities of the 1980s.

With the explosion of the third party system – and the birth of a fourth one – in 1993, regionalization of party support again became the norm. The Reform Party, the Canadian Alliance, and the Bloc Québécois all depended heavily on geographic pockets of support. The major, formerly pan-Canadian parties do so as well, with the Conservatives based strongly in the West and the Liberals relying on Ontario and Atlantic Canada. It is also important to note that regional divides are not simply the result of differing population profiles (Gidengil et al. 1999). Even after controlling for a myriad of socio-demographic characteristics, the significance of region as a predictor of vote choice remains very strong (Nevitte et al. 2000; Blais et al. 2002; Gidengil et al. 2012). Indeed, the regional cleavages in Canada have been noted as the greatest in all Western democracies except Belgium (Dalton 1996, 325).

Regionalization is not limited to the basis of party support. It also extends to the patterns of campaigning (Cross 2004). More and more, Canadian political parties are running regionally targeted campaigns. Based on internal polling and analysis of past election trends, campaign organizers are highly informed about where their support base resides (and where it does not). This knowledge has meant that electoral strategies, directions, and communications are becoming increasingly regionalized.

In the analyses that follow, our goal is to further test the regionalization hypothesis through the lens of media coverage. That voting is regionalized is indisputable. Whether media representations of party competition are too is another matter, however, and one that has been barely explored thus far. We aim to determine whether or not the media's treatment of the 1993-2008 campaigns reflects growing regional divides and perspectives.

Parties, Issues, and Polarization

Why does support for each political party fluctuate across elections? Clearly, many factors could be at play – notably socio-demographic characteristics, fundamental beliefs, partisan identification, leader evaluations, economic perceptions, government performance, and strategic considerations – either because the values of these factors or their effects on vote choice change from one election to another. Policy issues are another potential cause.

Dynamics of party support could be a consequence of some combination of (1) the shifting priorities and policy preferences of Canadian voters, and (2) the shifting priorities and policies of Canadian parties. The movements in vote shares of Canadian parties have received a good deal of attention, much more than the extent to which either voters or parties have changed in terms of policy objectives and priorities.

Where voters are concerned, we can glean some information from research on public opinion. Two strands of the literature are useful in this regard. First, there are studies of agenda setting. They have documented that the ebb and flow of the importance attached by the public to different issues stems from the amount of media attention and government activity devoted to the topics (Iyengar and Kinder 1987; McCombs and Shaw 1972; Soroka 2002). Second, there is work on issue ownership. Political parties are perceived to be more competent than others in certain policy domains (Budge and Farlie 1983; Petrocik 1996; Bélanger 2003). While issue ownership is generally quite stable over time, reversals do occur. Fluctuations in issue competence can be explained by variations in party popularity and government performance, as well as by party system change – namely, the appearance of new parties (Bélanger 2003).

Surveys can only go so far, however. Election questionnaires typically include a small number of policy attitudes. Also, issues come up unexpectedly during campaigns, and they are not always captured by survey instruments. Even with a perfectly policy-focused questionnaire, the link between issues and parties cannot be adequately explored using survey data alone. Surveys measure those issues that are most important to voters, but insofar as these issues do not mirror exactly parties' priorities, they miss part of the story. Party system change, where party policy is concerned, is reflected partly by shifts in what citizens want to buy, and also by shifts in what parties want to sell.

Media coverage can inform us about the variations in the overall salience of policy issues. The main advantage of news content is that it will likely reflect some combination of voters' (and journalists') interests and parties' campaign foci. The main disadvantage is that the two cannot be easily disentangled. In short, the methods we use below cannot distinguish between content that reflects what voters might think about when they think about the Liberals, and what the Liberals want voters to think about when they think about the Liberals. Nevertheless, campaign media content tells us what elections were about and what they are remembered for. These are the stories told during the campaign.

The analyses below explore the connections between policy issues and political parties as they are captured in news content. Results provide information not only on the shifting attentiveness to issues over time but also on the varying links between parties and issues, both within a given election and from one election to the next. Results may also speak to the potential polarization of party politics in Canada. Are parties increasingly linked to different policy domains? More specifically, are Conservatives now more clearly linked to issues on the right, while other parties are more clearly linked to issues on the left? Ultimately, we are interested in whether the post-1993 period should be viewed as a watershed moment in terms of party polarization in Canada.

A Note: A Changing Media Environment?

Our data reflect not just changes in party politics and election campaigns but also changes in the media environment. Indeed, the dynamics outlined above could be strengthened, or weakened, by transformations in the media industry.

During the period under study, most mainstream media, particularly newspapers, faced a rapid and sizable decrease in both audiences and revenues. This may have influenced the quantity and perhaps quality of campaign coverage. Both newspapers and television news outlets (public and private) had fewer reporters on the campaign trail, and many turned more and more to newswire services as a source of information. As a result, variation across newspapers may be limited, and/or media coverage may increasingly focus on topics that are easier to treat: horserace and polls, party leaders, regional heavyweights, and long-standing issue reputations. Indeed, consumer demand may also be pushing for this type of coverage (Iyengar et al. 2004). There is already ample evidence of a large focus on horserace coverage in recent Canadian elections (Soroka and Andrew 2010), but there is no empirical research focusing more broadly on the ways in which the nature of the news industry has affected news content in Canada. The latter will not be our focus either, though we should not discount the possibility that some of what we find (or do not find) is a consequence not just of shifts in electoral competition and party politics but also of the nature of the media industry.[1]

Methods

Our analysis is based on an automated content analysis of a database containing over twenty-seven thousand stories from the 1980 to 2008 election campaigns. The database includes all stories on the last six federal elections published in five English-language newspapers: *Globe and Mail, Calgary Herald, Montreal Gazette, Toronto Star,* and *Vancouver Sun.* The database also includes *Globe and Mail* election coverage of the 1980, 1984, and 1988 federal campaigns. Stories were extracted from a combination of the Nexis and Factiva full-text news indices.

For the sake of simplicity, particularly in terms of automated content analysis but also where the discussion of the party system is concerned, we focus here on English-language print media content. With that (significant) limitation in mind, the selection of newspapers was intended to capture some regional variation. The *Globe and Mail* is the largest nationally circulated newspaper in Canada, while the *Herald, Gazette, Star,* and *Sun* are widely distributed dailies in Canada's four most populated regional markets. All papers produced exclusive daily reports from the campaign trail during each of the campaigns included in the analysis.

The reason for the decision to use newspapers rather than television is partly substantive and partly pragmatic. Substantively speaking, although television was undoubtedly the main source of campaign information for many Canadians during these campaigns, about 80 percent of Canadian voters typically pay some attention to print media during campaigns, and newspapers tend to be the main source of news for about 30 percent of voters on average (Gidengil et al. 2004), so newspapers are a significant source of campaign news. They also serve an agenda-setting function for television, and recent analyses find few significant differences in content, at least in terms of subject focus, between newspapers and television (Soroka 2002). More pragmatically, television transcripts are not available for the entire twenty-eight-year period surveyed here, and when they are, they capture only the audio content. Video content is obviously a critical component of television news and has a strong influence on the way audiences process the audio component of a given TV news story (Graber 2001). Even when it is available, video content is notoriously difficult to code, and, because much of the story information is communicated through video, television content tends to have far fewer words than newspaper content.

The volume of words in news stories is especially important to our research here, since words are the unit of analysis for our automated content analysis. Computer automation has become a mainstay of empirical research in the study of political communication. Since the 1950s, scholars have been developing computer-assisted methods to analyze textual information in new and interesting ways. Given the ever-increasing volume of political information, automation enables the processing of enormous bodies of data efficiently and effectively. Reliability – the degree to which all stories are coded using exactly the same decision rules – is a key advantage of computer-automated content analysis. And validity – the extent to which automated analyses produce results that are in line with what we would find with trained human coders – is typically much better for text-oriented newspaper stories than for video-oriented television reports.

There are of course numerous approaches to automation. The dictionary-based approach used here to identify parties and leaders and to assign topics is the oldest and simplest type of computer automation, and has been widely used in the social sciences. The method, often referred to as frequency analysis, involves calculating a simple word count of definitive keywords in a predefined categorical dictionary. The relative frequency of words from dictionary categories can then be analyzed to classify various texts. With a well-defined dictionary, a basic word count provides a surprisingly powerful analysis of the topical composition of a text. There are many different programs available to implement computer automation. Here we use Lexicoder, our own Java-based multi-platform software that implements frequency analysis. (The program, available at http://www.lexicoder.com, can be adapted for any number of categorical dictionaries.)

Of course, the validity of frequency analysis depends on the quality of the coding dictionary. The real challenge is to develop a conceptually sound, comprehensive lexicon that is valid over time and across diverse corpora. Numerous machine-readable dictionaries are available for automation. Many of the most well-established content-analytic lexicons focus on psychological or cognitive categories (Martindale 1975, 1990; Namenwirth and Weber 1987; Stone et al. 1966). There are a number of sentiment and affect lexicons to automate the tone of texts, but far fewer to automate topics.

The first dictionary used here is very straightforward: a list of all major party and major party leader names at the time of each federal campaign between 1993 and 2008. The full list includes party names (and derivatives) of the following major party labels during the twenty-eight-year period: Liberals, Progressive Conservatives, Conservatives, Reform, Canadian Alliance, NDP, and Bloc Québécois. The dictionary also includes all party leaders in each of the six campaigns: (1980) Pierre Trudeau, Joe Clark, and Ed Broadbent; (1984 and 1988) John Turner, Brian Mulroney, and Ed Broadbent; (1993) Jean Chrétien, Lucien Bouchard, Preston Manning,

Audrey McLaughlin, and Kim Campbell; (1997) Jean Chrétien, Preston Manning, Gilles Duceppe, Alexa McDonough, and Jean Charest; (2000) Jean Chrétien, Stockwell Day, Gilles Duceppe, Alexa McDonough, and Joe Clark; (2004) Paul Martin, Stephen Harper, Gilles Duceppe, and Jack Layton; (2006) Stephen Harper, Paul Martin, Gilles Duceppe, and Jack Layton; (2008) Stephen Harper, Stéphane Dion, Gilles Duceppe, and Jack Layton. In most cases, the last name of the party leader alone captures leader mentions; this is more difficult for Stockwell Day, for instance, although even here we can use a capital "D" to distinguish leader mentions using last names only.

The topic dictionary used here is the most recent version of the Lexicoder Topic Dictionary (LTD). It is based on a "seed list" of five to fifteen paradigmatic words for each topic, reflecting the core policy focus for that domain, and generated manually by expert coders with reference to comprehensive policy indexes, particularly the Policy Agendas Project coding scheme (see http://www.policyagendas.org). The seed list is then expanded using WordNet, a comprehensive lexical database of the English language (Miller et al. 1990; see http://wordnet.princeton.edu). The topic dictionary used here is freely available at http://www.lexicoder.com. It is worth stressing that the number of keywords varies by topic, and therefore cross-topic comparisons for a single campaign should be viewed with caution. (Simply put, topics with greater numbers of identifiable keywords will tend to show greater frequencies.) We will make some cross-sectional inferences below, but will focus on longitudinal analyses, for which our data are better suited.

For the time being, the important point is that, with such a dictionary, frequency scores can be generated for parties, leaders, and policy domains. For our cross-analysis of parties and issues, we rely on a new proximity feature in Lexicoder – namely, we look at the co-occurrence of topic keywords and party/leader names within a single story and also within the same sentence. These co-occurrences can be easily and reliably (indeed, as reliability is defined above, perfectly reliably) tracked across news content from the past six federal election campaigns.

For the first set of tests regarding regionalization, analyses are very straightforward comparisons of the relative frequency of party names. Basic dataset descriptives are shown in Table 8.1, which indicates the number of stories collected from each newspaper in the sample. All stories published in the respective papers during the official campaign period

TABLE 8.1

Dataset descriptives, number of stories collected from newspapers during national election campaigns

Newspaper	1980	1984	1988	1993	1997	2000	2004	2006	2008
Calgary Herald				908	516	653	656	940	611
Globe and Mail	1,053	1,390	1,061	506	672	785	968	1,455	828
Montreal Gazette				941	612	672	632	833	635
Toronto Star				1,443	841	921	945	1,152	1,040
Vancouver Sun				904	507	563	595	737	354
Total	1,053	1,390	1,061	4,702	3,148	3,594	3,796	5,117	3,468

have been included. Note that campaigns varied somewhat in length during the period of our study. The longest campaign occurred in 2006, while the shortest occurred in 1997, 2000, and 2004.

Results

Tables 8.2 and 8.3 present some initial trends in party coverage over time. Table 8.2 shows how frequently each party's name (or its leader's name) occurred across all of the newspapers included in the analysis, during each campaign. Party/leader mentions for each party are expressed as a percentage of all party/leader mentions in that campaign. For instance, in 1980 the Liberal Party's share of coverage (47.4 percent) is calculated by dividing the number of times that party was mentioned by the total mentions of all main parties/leaders during that campaign period.

TABLE 8.2

Party mentions in different newspapers, by election

Party	1980[a]	1984[a]	1988[a]	1993	1997	2000	2004	2006	2008
Liberal	47.4	47.2	40.0	30.0	31.4	42.7	44.1	41.3	34.5
PC/Conservative	40.5	39.4	41.2	33.8	25.9	18.9	37.6	40.9	49.3
Reform/CA	–	–	–	17.7	23.7	23.9	–	–	–
NDP	12.1	13.4	18.8	10.1	8.7	8.6	14.0	13.2	12.8
BQ	–	–	–	8.4	10.2	5.9	4.2	4.7	3.4
N	11,153	18,319	15,093	60,384	44,994	44,559	52,597	62,815	34,252

Note: Cells contain party mentions as a percentage of all party and leader mentions in an election.
a *Globe and Mail* only.

Two key points are illustrated in Table 8.2. First, 1993 was clearly a watershed for party visibility. All parties holding seats in the House of Commons during the 1980s suffered a significant decline in commentary directed towards them during the 1993 campaign. In particular, Liberal and NDP share of mentions dropped by 33 percent or more from their respective 1988 levels.[2] The 1990s (including the 2000 election) marked a significant period of decline in relative visibility for the popular parties of the 1980s, a trend clearly precipitated by the arrival of the Reform Party/Canadian Alliance and the Bloc Québécois.

That being said, viewed in the context of the almost thirty-year span of our dataset, it is also clear that more recent elections (2004, 2006, and 2008) bear a much stronger resemblance to campaigns of the 1980s than to those of the 1990s. Indeed, by 2004 all of the major players in Canada's political party landscape were, for the most part, fully restored to 1980s standards in terms of media coverage. This return to pre-1993 levels fits with the restorative patterns identified by Richard Johnston in Chapter 13: periods of flux and volatility followed by a return to earlier, more stable patterns.

Table 8.3 reinforces these points, showing coverage of "main" parties by article, where "main" is the party/leader name mentioned most in an article. Whereas Table 8.2 treats all party/leader mentions equally and ignores articles as a unit of analysis entirely, Table 8.3 focuses on articles and assigns each a main party. There are some advantages to thinking about articles that focus most on one party or the other: the main party as measured here is very likely the party a typical newspaper reader would recall if asked to explain what a given story was about; it is the party name he or she would

TABLE 8.3
Main party mentions in different newspapers, by election

Party	1980[a]	1984[a]	1988[a]	1993	1997	2000	2004	2006	2008
Liberal	46.6	55.2	40.6	29.5	38.9	50.6	49.1	46.3	26.4
PC/Conservative	44.1	36.5	48.1	40.0	21.9	14.7	38.2	42.2	64.1
Reform/CA	–	–	–	16.5	21.9	24.1	–	–	–
NDP	9.3	8.3	11.3	7.1	7.6	6.2	10.6	8.5	8.1
BQ	–	–	–	7.0	9.8	4.4	2.2	3.1	1.4
N	850	1,092	833	3,671	2,458	2,820	2,978	3,962	2,399

Note: Cells contain "main" party mentions as a percentage of all articles mentioning at least one party or one leader.
a *Globe and Mail* only.

come across first and be reminded about most frequently in the course of reading through the full story.

That said, the results in Table 8.3 are very similar to those in Table 8.2. Our measure of main party points to major changes during the 1990s, but also to a pattern, in recent years, of continuity with campaigns of the 1980s. The most striking indication of continuity is media coverage allotments for the Liberal and Conservative parties. During the 1980s, the combined share of Conservative and Liberal main party coverage was about nine articles out of ten. Comparatively, for the three elections since 2000, the combined main party share for those two parties has been 8.9 out of 10. Clearly the party merger on the right prior to the 2004 election is the significant driver of this result. But it is also noteworthy that since 1997 the Bloc Québécois has virtually disappeared from English-language media coverage insofar as its being the main party of election news stories.[3]

Tables 8.2 and 8.3 suggest that, when viewed in the aggregate, recent media coverage of Canadian politics shares much in common with coverage patterns of the 1980s. The key outlier is the Conservative advantage in main party mentions in 2008. Nearly two-thirds of stories about the 2008 campaign featured the incumbent Conservatives. The next closest party was featured in about one of every four stories (26 percent). Where main party mentions are concerned, 2008 clearly stands alone – not just from campaigns of the 1980s and '90s but also from the campaigns of 2004 and 2006. The gap between incumbent and main rival was much wider (38 percent) and the intensity of focus on the incumbent party (64 percent of stories) was never stronger than in 2008.

What about regionalization in Canadian media coverage of election campaigns? The prominence of party coverage should correspond with that party's regional support base; it should also, relatedly, mirror to some degree the attention each party pays to a given region. Most importantly, we expect to find evidence of growing regionalization since 1993. Have consumers of regionally based newspapers been exposed to increasingly distinct narratives of Canadian party politics over the past fifteen years? Four of the five papers in our analysis are regionally based, and not widely distributed outside their respective markets. We explore cross-sectional differences between these papers – the *Sun, Herald, Star,* and *Gazette* – here.

Table 8.4 shows, above all, that variance in party coverage is driven more by party strength in national elections than by party strength in regions. When a party's prominence in one regional newspaper went up (or down), it also tended to go up (or down) in other regional newspapers at the same

TABLE 8.4
Main party mentions, by regional newspaper

Election	Party	Vancouver Sun	Calgary Herald	Toronto Star	Montreal Gazette
1993	Liberal	25.6	24.3	29.8	32.5
	PC	42.3	36.1	44.0	37.3
	NDP	9.7	3.6	8.8	5.5
	Reform	17.9	31.3	13.1	8.5
	BQ	4.4	4.8	4.4	16.1
1997	Liberal	41.5	36.3	43.5	41.8
	PC	20.7	20.8	21.8	17.7
	NDP	9.9	6.0	8.4	4.9
	Reform	24.7	31.5	19.0	14.0
	BQ	3.2	5.5	7.4	21.6
2000	Liberal	62.2	53.3	52.3	54.8
	PC	11.2	15.4	13.7	12.8
	NDP	5.5	4.2	6.9	5.3
	Canadian Alliance	20.1	25.9	24.8	14.2
	BQ	1.0	1.1	2.3	12.9
2004	Liberal	46.1	49.9	49.4	52.6
	PC	38.2	42.2	39.4	30.5
	NDP	14.9	7.0	9.7	10.5
	BQ	0.9	1.0	1.6	6.3
2006	Liberal	45.9	45.2	50.2	47.6
	PC	41.8	46.4	38.1	36.9
	NDP	10.1	7.0	10.1	6.8
	BQ	2.2	1.4	1.6	8.7
2008	Liberal	31.9	20.3	28.7	25.2
	PC	55.9	73.7	61.0	62.6
	NDP	11.4	5.5	9.5	7.8
	BQ	0.9	0.5	0.8	4.4

Note: Cells contain main party mentions by party, as a percentage of all articles mentioning at least one party.

time. Consider, for instance, the Liberals, who consistently trended upward in all regional papers from 1993 to 2000, and then trended downward in all papers from 2004 to the present. It is no small coincidence, we suggest, that the pattern of Liberal media attention in all regional papers follows the trajectory of Liberal Party power in Canadian politics over the past fifteen years. Conservative coverage tells a similar story (see Figure 8.1).

FIGURE 8.1

Main party election coverage of the Liberal and PC/Conservative Parties
in regional newspapers

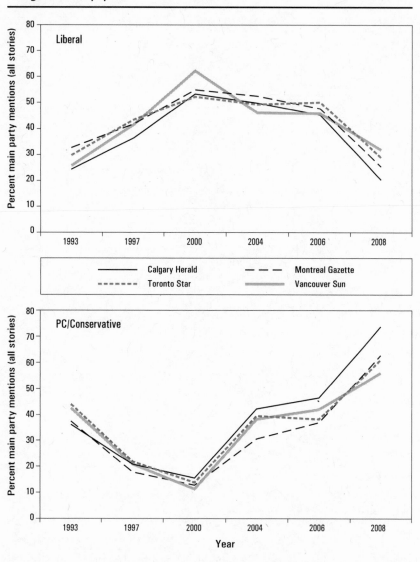

Note, however, that consistency in the ebb and flow of party prominence
does not mean that party visibility was always identical in these papers.
Relative to other regional papers, the *Calgary Herald* has focused more on
parties of the right since 1993. Similarly, the *Vancouver Sun* has tended to

print more coverage focused on the NDP than others during the same time period. The key point is that while regional differences are apparent in these papers, there has been virtually no sign that regional variance has been increasing (or decreasing) since 1993. Any changes in party prominence that occurred since 1993 have, for the most part, co-occurred in all papers and in the same direction.

The major caveat in our argument pertains to coverage of the Bloc Québécois. It is clear from Table 8.4 that English-language media have increasingly relegated the BQ to the sidelines of Canadian election coverage. Even the *Montreal Gazette* has dramatically reduced the attention paid to the BQ over the past fifteen years. In 1993-97, about one in five election stories published by the *Gazette* focused on the Bloc, compared with less than one in twenty stories by 2008. This decline is both striking and somewhat prescient, considering that the BQ's electoral success had, until its dramatic collapse in 2011, been the most consistent of any party in Canadian federal politics since 1993. We should also stress that the BQ's salience in French-language media has not declined significantly in recent years (see Andrew et al. 2006, 2008; Goodyear-Grant et al. 2004).

In short, and with the important caveat regarding Bloc Québécois coverage in mind, our results point to a clear conclusion with respect to regionalization. It is true that those who read the *Herald, Star, Sun,* or *Gazette* during the past fifteen years were exposed to a unique dose of coverage about the major parties, but it is also true that changes in party visibility tended to occur simultaneously across the various geographic regions of Canada. Save for coverage of the Bloc Québécois, our data do not support the hypothesis that regionalization of party coverage has been growing since 1993.

As an introduction to the polarization analysis, Table 8.5 provides an overview of issue salience in election campaigns since 1980. It reports the mean number of topic keywords per article. A score of 1 indicates that a word relating to that topic appears once in every election article on average, 0.5 indicates that a word relating to that topic appears in one of every two articles, and so on. Trends in issue salience are important to the polarization story, because they indicate whether issue ownership in media coverage might have translated into electoral advantages. It is worth reiterating that issue ownership, as we conceive of it in campaign media, may not necessarily produce electoral benefit for parties or leaders. That depends on a host of other factors, including the credibility of the party on the issue, the importance voters place on the issue, and the priority of the issue on the

TABLE 8.5
Issue coverage in different newspapers, by election

Issue	1980[a]	1984[a]	1988[a]	1993	1997	2000	2004	2006	2008
Agriculture/ forestry/fishing	0.08	0.10	0.11	0.05	0.05	0.05	0.06	0.04	0.05
Civil rights	0.10	0.12	0.11	0.12	0.12	0.12	0.21	0.18	0.08
Crime and justice	0.17	0.22	0.25	0.24	0.33	0.34	0.28	0.49	0.31
Economy	0.50	0.36	0.40	0.44	0.37	0.36	0.34	0.30	0.43
Education	0.11	0.08	0.10	0.16	0.15	0.16	0.14	0.15	0.15
Employment/ labour	0.12	0.22	0.15	0.32	0.25	0.11	0.09	0.09	0.14
Energy	0.49	0.07	0.10	0.03	0.03	0.05	0.09	0.07	0.15
Environment	0.03	0.01	0.10	0.03	0.03	0.05	0.04	0.04	0.07
Finance/ commerce	0.15	0.17	0.24	0.16	0.12	0.15	0.11	0.11	0.23
Foreign affairs/ defence	0.76	0.67	0.73	0.61	0.65	0.54	0.67	0.70	0.69
Health	0.04	0.04	0.05	0.12	0.17	0.26	0.28	0.17	0.10
Immigration	0.02	0.01	0.02	0.04	0.02	0.03	0.02	0.03	0.03
Social welfare	0.08	0.07	0.07	0.12	0.11	0.11	0.12	0.12	0.12
Trade (international)	0.12	0.10	0.41	0.13	0.08	0.07	0.08	0.09	0.07
Transportation	0.07	0.06	0.04	0.04	0.03	0.03	0.04	0.03	0.05

Note: Cells contain the mean number of topic keywords per article.
a *Globe and Mail* only.

party's agenda. What we document below is but one piece of a bigger puzzle, but it is nevertheless a piece of the puzzle about which little is known, and one that likely matters for how both voters and parties prioritize issues in the first place.

Note, first of all, that there are several particular elections in which a specific issue played a larger than normal role. For example, the volume of keywords related to international trade spiked during the free trade election campaign of 1988. Similarly, energy played a key role in the 1980 campaign, as did employment during the mid-1990s. To anyone familiar with Canadian politics over this period, many of the spikes in salience are highly intuitive given the context of political discourse leading up to each campaign.

What is perhaps less predictable about issue coverage over time is that there is little evidence of any consistent trends in issue salience. No issue represented in this table has consistently grown in prominence over time, just as no issue has consistently faded from election discourse. There have been ebbs and flows over the course of two or three campaigns, but in no case has there been a consistent pattern. Indeed, from the perspective of this aggregate snapshot, it is clear that no issue, and certainly no set of issues (left or right), has systematically risen (or fallen) in salience from 1993 onward.

Our tests of issue ownership at the party level are included in Tables 8.6 to 8.9. Recall that the conventional wisdom is that parties became not only more regionally entrenched in 1993 but also more ideological in nature. If parties are truly increasingly differentiating themselves along ideological fault lines, then party ownership of specific issues should show signs of strengthening over the span of our study. We address the polarization debate here by looking at whether the occurrences of issue keywords in election media content have indeed become more (or less) associated with the various parties over time.

Tables 8.6 to 8.9 present data on within-sentence co-occurrence of party/ leader names and issue keywords. To be clear: the tables show the average number of topic keywords co-occurring in sentences with party/leader names within each article. A value of 1 would suggest that, on average, articles include at least one topic keyword in the same sentence as, for instance, a Liberal Party/leader mention. Values can of course be much higher – in an article focusing on the NDP and health care, there may be 25 health care words appearing in sentences that also include the NDP party or leader name. Averages across all articles tend to produce much smaller values, since articles cover a wide range of topics. So, for instance, the top-left cell in Table 8.6 indicates the average number of health care keywords in sentences that also mention the Liberals, across all articles mentioning the Liberals in the 1980 campaign: 0.025, which means 0.025 health care keywords in all sentences mentioning the Liberals, or roughly 1 keyword in sentences mentioning the Liberals for every 40 articles. (That's not a lot of health care coverage.)

Note that these statistics capture in part the varying volume of coverage of the different parties – if a party is mentioned more, then there are a greater number of sentences in which issues may be mentioned. That prominence is included here intentionally – the data should reflect the prominence of co-occurring party and issue mentions. Note also that these statistics are not entirely independent of any shift over time in the volume of horserace coverage (Soroka and Andrew 2010). If horserace-oriented coverage increases (or decreases) consistently for parties/leaders, and mentions of any party/leader in that frame tend to occur in sentences where policy mentions are minimal, then our data will show diminishing (or rising) figures for issue/party co-occurrences. Again, this is intentional – our data should reflect the prominence of co-occurring party and issue mentions.

We focus in these tables on four prominent issues in Canadian politics: health care, foreign affairs/defence, crime/justice, and the economy. These are also issues that vary from election to election in terms of salience, as shown in Table 8.5. Broadly speaking, our expectation is that issue ownership will show signs of strengthening over time. For instance, we expect gaps between the parties most and least associated with a given topic to widen over the period of the study. This would indicate, from a news media vantage point at least, that parties have become increasingly polarized.

For health care, as shown in Table 8.6, there is no evidence that differences between parties have increased over time. The gap between the parties most and least associated with health care in 1980 (NDP versus Liberals) is quite similar to the gap in 2008 between the Conservatives and the BQ. Although there is some indication that health care ownership was occurring between 1997 and 2004 for the Liberals, differences between parties in terms of association with this issue have almost completely faded in the two most recent campaigns.

TABLE 8.6

Health care coverage in different newspapers, by party

Election	Liberal	PC/Conservative	Reform/CA	NDP	BQ
1980[a]	0.025	0.026	–	0.010	–
1984[a]	0.035	0.023	–	0.012	–
1988[a]	0.043	0.041	–	0.033	–
1993	0.040	0.057	0.073	0.037	0.004
1997	0.183	0.088	0.080	0.054	0.017
2000	0.289	0.071	0.196	0.092	0.013
2004	0.380	0.238	–	0.079	0.010
2006	0.125	0.134	–	0.091	0.004
2008	0.059	0.062	–	0.046	0.001

Note: Cells contain the mean number of topic keywords in sentences that also mention party/leader names.
a *Globe and Mail* only.

The story is similar for foreign affairs/defence, crime/justice, and the economy, as shown in Tables 8.7 to 8.9. There is no indication that the major shakeup in the party system that occurred in 1993 coincided with a trend towards issue ownership in any of these domains. Simply consider the trajectory of ownership in these areas for the Liberals and Conservatives. Since 1980, neither party could claim to have clearly seized control of any issue represented here. Indeed, although both parties have, at one point or another, laid claim to each of these issues, there is relatively little evidence for enduring ownership, or increasing ownership, in any area by either the

TABLE 8.7
Foreign affairs/defence coverage in different newspapers, by party

Election	Liberal	PC/Conservative	Reform/CA	NDP	BQ
1980[a]	0.775	0.701	–	0.221	–
1984[a]	1.001	0.766	–	0.191	–
1988[a]	0.872	0.850	–	0.336	–
1993	0.494	0.622	0.296	0.155	0.125
1997	0.598	0.475	0.487	0.188	0.186
2000	0.629	0.242	0.323	0.107	0.065
2004	0.829	0.835	–	0.228	0.067
2006	0.777	0.777	–	0.192	0.071
2008	0.480	0.814	–	0.138	0.037

Note: Cells contain the mean number of topic keywords in sentences that also mention party/leader names.
a *Globe and Mail* only.

TABLE 8.8
Crime/justice coverage in different newspapers, by party

Election	Liberal	PC/Conservative	Reform/CA	NDP	BQ
1980[a]	0.117	0.130	–	0.029	–
1984[a]	0.271	0.166	–	0.045	–
1988[a]	0.161	0.174	–	0.059	–
1993	0.095	0.138	0.097	0.036	0.028
1997	0.235	0.193	0.193	0.033	0.036
2000	0.277	0.126	0.215	0.036	0.043
2004	0.197	0.301	–	0.043	0.018
2006	0.425	0.363	–	0.099	0.021
2008	0.158	0.364	–	0.045	0.015

Note: Cells contain the mean number of topic keywords in sentences that also mention party/leader names.
a *Globe and Mail* only.

TABLE 8.9
Coverage of the economy in different newspapers, by party

Election	Liberal	PC/Conservative	Reform/CA	NDP	BQ
1980[a]	0.479	0.550	–	0.135	–
1984[a]	0.352	0.398	–	0.135	–
1988[a]	0.357	0.416	–	0.177	–
1993	0.373	0.335	0.165	0.052	0.037
1997	0.403	0.330	0.240	0.101	0.048
2000	0.441	0.131	0.247	0.084	0.013
2004	0.460	0.447	–	0.015	0.013
2006	0.316	0.370	–	0.083	0.014
2008	0.474	0.626	–	0.130	0.020

Note: Cells contain the mean number of topic keywords in sentences that also mention party/leader names.
a *Globe and Mail* only.

Liberals or Conservatives. Ultimately, parties tend not to be clearly associated with issues at all, and ideological polarization is simply not a reality, at least not in terms of media coverage.

There is evidence of Conservative strength in the 2008 election, to be sure. During that election, the incumbent governing party surged ahead in terms of association with foreign affairs/defence, crime/justice, and the economy. Liberals showed no advantage (indeed, a slight disadvantage) in the one "left" issue investigated here, health care. The 2008 Conservative campaign appears to have worked where media content is concerned, but this was not part of a long-term trend that began years before, and it is too soon to tell whether it is a shift that will last well into the future.

Conclusion

This chapter began by making the argument that we might learn something useful about party politics and electoral competition in Canada by looking at campaign-period media coverage. The analyses here have covered the past nine federal elections before the most recent one, in 2011, and have, we believe, confirmed this hypothesis. Content analysis of media data – particularly automated analyses of large bodies of media data – offer an opportunity to examine a number of critical questions with somewhat more detail, or at least different detail, than the more traditional data sources permit.

The critical questions we have explored here focus on regionalization and connections between parties and issues. Changes in the number of parties make it difficult to directly compare the levels of regionalization that existed in the third and the fourth party systems, but regionalization does not appear to have increased in the six elections since 1993. To be clear: there are certainly differences in party coverage across regions, but those differences are no greater now than they were twenty years ago. Issue/party linkages are somewhat similar; linkages between parties and issues vary over time, but there is little evidence of increasing (or increasingly divergent) issue ownership by parties in the recent past. If issue/party connections are an indication of polarization, then on this front there are no striking differences between the current system and the one it replaced.

Overall, then, our results point to a story of continuity rather than change in media coverage of the party system. Our findings are at odds with some previous work (and work in this volume) finding evidence of more profound changes in the distribution and sources of electoral support for Canadian parties. They also conflict with current, popularized accounts of an increasingly ideologically divided political process.

What accounts for this difference in results? One possibility is that the more common view – focusing on profound change in the early 2000s – is simply incorrect. There has been change in the Canadian party system, but that change has generally been overstated. We have shifted to a party system that combines features of the party system both pre- and post-1993: essentially, a united right but with the addition of one strongly regional party in Quebec. This changes the nature of party competition, to be sure, as is readily apparent in other chapters in this volume, but the basic structure of politics in Canada has actually changed somewhat less than is commonly believed.

There are of course different possibilities. Others may be wrong, but we may be as well. It is possible that that media content has not accurately reflected the dynamics of the party system in Canada. So perhaps politics is increasingly regionalized and divisive, but media coverage (1) is not being drawn in the same direction, or (2) was always regionalized and divisive. Intuitively, the latter seems the more likely possibility. We are not inclined to believe either option, however. Past work shows that media coverage tends to capture the state of public affairs rather well (e.g., issue attentiveness, party support, and the state of the economy). We expect that it does here also.

That said, there are some weaknesses in the way we have used media data to capture the nature of party competition. We do not deal with the tone of media content here, just frequencies of coverage. Shifts in regionalization may be more apparent when we consider both the frequency and the tone of party/leader mentions. So too might polarization. When references to issues are identical in quantity across parties (as was the case with foreign affairs in 2006, for instance), perhaps one party is discussed in a more positive light than another. In fact, an American study argued that parties' issue reputations influence the favourability of news treatments: candidates are covered more positively when reports focus on their own issues rather than their opponents' issues (Hayes 2008). We intend to examine this more closely in forthcoming work. We also want to consider coding that captures the possibility that attention to an issue remains roughly equal across parties but that parties have increasingly divergent positions on the issue.

Accurately capturing tone and party positions in media content is of course no easy matter, and for the time being we are satisfied with the simpler but more reliable measures used here. These measures suggest that Canadian party politics is in some critical ways not fundamentally different now from the 1980s. The Conservatives seem to have been particularly dominant on several "right" issues in 2008. This may well be the beginning of a new party system; it is too soon to tell. But it is *not* part of a general trend over the past thirty years. The media's recent portrait of party competition in Canada is markedly similar to that of the past two or three decades.

Notes

1 There is of course a body of work that focuses on links between party and electoral politics and the structure of mass media. Innis's work (1951) was among the first (and most profound) linking the structure of politics to the structure of communication. See also Abramson et al. (1988) on the parallel evolution of mass media and party politics in the United States.
2 The Conservatives were not immune, losing almost a fifth of their coverage during the same period.
3 This timing coincides with the end of the party's stint as Her Majesty's Loyal Opposition.

References

Abramson, Jeffrey B., F. Christopher Arterton, and Gary R. Orren. 1988. *The Electronic Commonwealth: The Impact of New Media Technologies on Democratic Politics.* New York: Basic Books.

Andrew, Blake C., Antonia Maioni, and Stuart Soroka. 2006. "Just When You Thought It Was Out, Policy Is Pulled Back In." *Policy Options* 27 (3): 74-79.

Andrew, Blake, Lori Young, and Stuart Soroka. 2008. "Back to the Future: Press Coverage of the 2008 Canadian Election Campaign Strikes Both Familiar and Unfamiliar Notes." *Policy Options* 29 (10): 79-84.

Bélanger, Éric. 2003. "Issue Ownership by Canadian Political Parties 1953-2001." *Canadian Journal of Political Science* 36 (3): 539-58.

Blais, André, Elisabeth Gidengil, Richard Nadeau, and Neil Nevitte. 2002. *Anatomy of a Liberal Victory: Making Sense of the Vote in the 2000 Canadian Election.* Peterborough, ON: Broadview Press.

Budge, Ian, and Dennis J. Farlie. 1983. *Explaining and Predicting Elections: Issue Effects and Party Strategies in Twenty-Three Democracies.* London: Allen and Unwin.

Carty, R. Kenneth. 1988. "Three Canadian Party Systems: An Interpretation of the Development of National Politics." In *Party Democracy in Canada: The Politics of National Party Conventions,* edited by George C. Perlin, 15-30. Scarborough, ON: Prentice Hall.

Carty, R. Kenneth, Lisa Young, and William P. Cross. 2000. *Rebuilding Canadian Party Politics.* Vancouver: UBC Press.

Cross, William. 2004. *Political Parties.* Vancouver: UBC Press.

Dalton, Russell. 1996. "Political Cleavages, Issues, and Electoral Change." In *Comparing Democracies: Elections and Voting in Global Perspectives,* edited by Lawrence LeDuc, Richard G. Niemi, and Pippa Norris, 319-42. Thousand Oaks, CA: Sage.

Gidengil, Elisabeth, André Blais, Joanna Everitt, Patrick Fournier, and Neil Nevitte. 2012. *Dominance and Decline: Making Sense of Recent Canadian Elections.* Toronto: University of Toronto Press.

Gidengil, Elisabeth, André Blais, Richard Nadeau, and Neil Nevitte. 1999. "Making Sense of Regional Voting in the 1997 Canadian Federal Election: Liberal and Reform Support outside Quebec." *Canadian Journal of Political Science* 32 (2): 247-72.

Gidengil, Elisabeth, André Blais, Neil Nevitte, and Richard Nadeau. 2004. *Citizens.* Vancouver: UBC Press.

Goodyear-Grant, Elizabeth, Stuart Soroka, and Antonia Maioni. 2004. "The Role of the Media: A Campaign Saved by a Horserace." *Policy Options* 25 (8): 86-91.

Graber, Doris A. 2001. *Processing Politics: Learning from Television in the Internet Age.* Chicago: University of Chicago Press.

Hayes, Danny. 2008. "Party Reputations, Journalistic Expectations: How Issue Ownership Influences Election News." *Political Communication* 25 (4): 377-400.

Innis, Harold A. 1951. *The Bias of Communication.* Toronto: University of Toronto Press.

Iyengar, Shanto, and Donald R. Kinder. 1987. *News that Matters: Television and American Opinion.* Chicago: University of Chicago Press.

Iyengar, Shanto, Helmut Norpoth, and Kyu S. Hahn. 2004. "Consumer Demand for Election News: The Horserace Sells." *Journal of Politics* 66 (1): 157-75.

Johnston, Richard, André Blais, Henry E. Brady, and Jean Crête. 1992. *Letting the People Decide: Dynamics of a Canadian Election*. Montreal and Kingston: McGill-Queen's University Press.

Martindale, Colin. 1975. *Romantic Progression: The Psychology of Literary History*. Washington, DC: Hemisphere.

–. 1990. *The Clockwork Muse: The Predictability of Artistic Change*. New York: Basic Books.

McCombs, Maxwell E., and Donald L. Shaw. 1972. "The Agenda-Setting Function of Mass Media." *Public Opinion Quarterly* 36 (2): 176-87.

Miller, George A., Richard Beckwith, Christiane Fellbaum, Derek Gross, and Katherine Miller. 1990. "Introduction to WordNet: An On-line Lexical Database." *International Journal of Lexicography* 3 (4): 235-312.

Namenwirth, J. Zvi, and Robert Philip Weber. 1987. *Dynamics of Culture*. Boston: Allen and Unwin.

Nevitte, Neil, André Blais, Elisabeth Gidengil, and Richard Nadeau. 2000. *Unsteady State: The 1997 Canadian Federal Election*. Don Mills, ON: Oxford University Press.

Petrocik, John R. 1996. "Issue Ownership in Presidential Elections, with a 1980 Case Study." *American Journal of Political Science* 40 (3): 825-50.

Soroka, Stuart N. 2002. *Agenda-Setting Dynamics in Canada*. Vancouver: UBC Press.

Soroka, Stuart, and Blake Andrew. 2010. "Reporting Canadian National Elections." In *Mediating Canadian Politics*, edited by Linda Trimble and Shannon Sampert, 113-28. Toronto: Pearson.

Stone, Philip J., Dexter C. Dunphy, Marshall S. Smith, and Daniel M. Ogilvie. 1966. *The General Inquirer: A Computer Approach to Content Analysis*. Cambridge, MA: MIT Press.

9

Parties, Politics, and Redistribution

The Constitutional and Practical Challenges of Politicized Apportionment

RUSSELL ALAN WILLIAMS

A cornerstone principle of democracy is that each vote should carry equal weight to the extent possible. With that in mind, in the last election we committed to restoring the principle of representation by population, which had fallen behind for the faster growing provinces of Ontario, Alberta and British Columbia.

— PETER VAN LOAN, GOVERNMENT HOUSE LEADER AND
MINISTER RESPONSIBLE FOR DEMOCRATIC REFORM[1]

If the Fathers of Confederation from New Brunswick and Nova Scotia could see what is happening now, I can tell you they would join Joseph Howe and a few others and say, "No, we're not joining this charade."

— DONALD SAVOIE, UNIVERSITÉ DE MONCTON[2]

The Harper government's proposals in Bills C-56 (2007) and C-12 (2010) for an overhaul of the redistribution formula contained in section 51 of the *Constitution Act, 1867*[3] rekindled debate about the malapportionment of Canada's electoral map and what might be done to address the problem. The proposals highlighted the fact that the absence of clear criteria for allocating representation across provinces creates considerable scope for partisan, regional, and party/political considerations to influence the weight of representation allocated to individual Canadian voters. Parliamentarians, responding to both the concerns of provinces with relatively declining populations and their own local partisan calculations, have resisted the trend towards the more "automatic" formulary systems of redistribution based on population used in most democracies. The fullest expression of this, the Mulroney-era *Representation Act, 1985*,[4] based on the "279 formula" led to sharply increasing levels of malapportionment, particularly in British Columbia, Alberta, and Ontario, where population growth did not translate into increased representation.

Despite the government's efforts to change the system and undo some of the problems created by the 279 formula, legal and political obstacles to reform (particularly during the recent period of minority parliaments) have been considerable. In Parliament, parties perceive strategic advantage in either the status quo (the Bloc Québécois, Liberals, and New Democrats from Quebec and Atlantic Canada) or a more decisive return to representation by population (the Harper Conservatives). This, in combination with the evolving jurisprudence of representation, made Harper reform efforts difficult – indeed three successive bills died on the Order Paper before the newly elected Conservative majority government was able to finally force passage of Bill C-20 (the *Fair Representation Act*[5]) in December 2011. Indeed, both the substance of the *Fair Representation Act* and the process that led to its passage highlight the extent to which parties and provincial governments have sought partisan advantage in the reform process at the expense of some clearer principle regarding representation. While the new formula itself is probably a more equitable compromise among some very conflicting goals than sticking with the existing 279 formula, how we got to this compromise has only further illustrated the extent to which majorities in Parliament have been granted considerable freedom to produce a representation formula that serves their own political goals.

The Current System of Redistribution

Section 52 of the *Constitution Act, 1867* implied a guarantee that provinces' representation would be "proportionate" to their populations. In light of the ineffectiveness of the Senate as a regionally representative institution, however, pressure built steadily after Confederation for special representational guarantees for some provinces in the House of Commons. In 1915, following persistent challenges from Prince Edward Island, which was experiencing a rapid relative decline in its population, section 51A was added to the

Constitution Act, 1867. This provision guarantees that no province will have fewer seats in the House of Commons than in the Senate, the "senatorial floor." As Sancton (2010) notes, the senatorial floor really only protects the number of House seats in Prince Edward Island and New Brunswick. Regardless, the senatorial floor turned out to be the thin end of the wedge, as over time provincial governments and MPs from regions with relatively declining populations have sought to expand on this principle and devalue the importance of population in allocating representation.

Importantly, aside from the senatorial floor, which was entrenched in the *Constitution Act, 1982,*[6] changes to the redistribution formula contained in section 51 of the *Constitution Act, 1867* do not *normally* require the consent of provinces through the general amending formula. Parliament has the constitutional right to adjust the formulas for redistribution, provided that the changes do not disturb any provisions in the Constitution. In essence, there is considerable scope for regional and partisan concerns in Parliament to influence the distribution of representation in Canada (Carty 1985), scope that Parliament aggressively took advantage of in the 1980s.

The *Representation Act, 1985*

Following the 1981 Census, Canada's chief electoral officer applied the then existing "amalgam formula" to the regularly scheduled redistribution. Under this formula, the House would have expanded to 309 seats, with British Columbia and Ontario gaining the majority of new seats. When the appointed boundary commissions presented their final reports to Parliament, MPs halted the process, refusing to accept the new distribution. The 1984 election was therefore fought on the outdated boundaries drawn up after the 1971 Census (see Sancton 1990 for an extended discussion). The major complaint levelled against the exceedingly complex amalgam formula was that the House of Commons was forced to increase in size because the formula tried to award new representation based on population growth while also guaranteeing that no province would ever have fewer seats than it did in 1974 (the "grandfather clause").[7] The addition of so many seats would also require more drastic revision of individual riding boundaries (a prospect almost all incumbent MPs dislike). These consequences angered MPs and provincial officials from regions with relatively declining populations, as they realized that the amalgam formula's emphasis on representation by population would quickly reduce the relative weight of their representation, given the country's emerging demographics. Quebec, for example, argued that it should be entitled to 25 percent of the seats in the House, regardless of population changes. While the amalgam formula was "fair" from the perspective of representation by population (a principle thought to be enshrined in the Constitution), MPs chose to abandon it.

Following the 1984 election, the new Conservative government of Brian Mulroney drafted a *White Paper on Redistribution*. Influenced by Parliament's increasing disregard for population as the standard for allocating representation, the *White Paper* argued that increasing the size of the House was too expensive, that 309 members would not "fit" in the House, and that "a sense of collegiality may be lost" (Hnatyshyn 1985, 3-4). The *White Paper* suggested a new formula that would keep the grandfather clause and restrict the growth of the House.

Backed by a large majority in the House consisting of many rookie MPs from Quebec and Atlantic Canada, the Mulroney government replaced the amalgam formula with the new 279 formula. The formula adopted a fixed divisor for calculating each province's representation. Canada's population (minus the territories) was to be divided by 279, producing an electoral quotient – the population standard for each constituency. The chief electoral officer was then to divide the population of each province by the electoral quotient to calculate how many seats each province should get. Effectively, these 279 seats were initially allocated based on representation by population. However, the 279 formula also guaranteed that no province would ever have fewer MPs than it had in 1974, meaning that any province that lost a seat as a result of the 279 formula would get a replacement "grandfather" or "bonus" seat. As additional bonus seats were required, the House of Commons would grow, albeit at a much slower rate than under the amalgam formula.

The new formula moved decisively away from population as a standard for allocating representation. As can be seen in the Appendix, the formula has entrenched fixed levels of representation for the seven provinces that have relatively declining populations, while at the same time restricting the number of new seats available to the three fastest-growing provinces to respond to real population changes. Differences in average constituency populations among provinces have grown sharply – if the required post-2011 redistribution were conducted in accordance with the 279 formula, the average constituency populations of Newfoundland and Labrador, New Brunswick, and Saskatchewan would likely be almost half of those in Ontario, Alberta, and British Columbia, steadily diminishing the relative value, or weight, of an individual's vote in those more populous provinces.

Not surprisingly, the main complaint levied against the current formula is that it is simply anti-democratic. For example, Mendelsohn (2010) has argued that it does not live up to "internationally accepted democratic standards," as the principle of representation by population is more widely violated in Canada than in any comparable democracy. "Unless Canadian laws are changed," he argues, "the inequality of the current system will worsen and the voting power of citizens will increasingly depend on which province they live in" (1). Indeed, Mendelsohn argues that deviation from representation by population in Canada is already ten times greater than in the United States and will continue to grow.[8] Mellon (2009) also notes that the current system is inconsistent with basic parliamentary principles, in which the House of Commons, as a lower house, would be the "people's house," not a house of the provinces.[9] More to the point, if the system of redistribution is not subject to clear principles – if Parliament has the unilateral right to redistribute seats however it chooses – there exists considerable scope for partisan calculation to trump the creation of a fair electoral map.

Canadian Malapportionment and Partisan Bias?

Malapportionment produces partisan bias only if the pattern of party competition varies across regions in such a way that one party gains advantage due to electoral strength in an over-represented region. There has been little evidence that Canadian malapportionment in the 1990s favoured one party over others, as partisan advantage due to malapportionment was not exacerbated by the pattern of regional electoral competition.[10] Given, however, that one of the principal effects of the 279 formula was to artificially increase the share of representation of Quebec and Atlantic Canada, and that the Conservatives have fared poorly in those regions in recent elections, existing malapportionment appears to hurt the Conservatives.

It is exceedingly difficult to accurately measure the level of partisan bias due to malapportionment, as the distortion effects of single-member plurality (SMP) electoral systems (the concentration of parties' support in certain constituencies, differences in turnout, etc.) interact with both malapportionment effects and gerrymandering effects from the process of districting (Grofman et al. 1997). Furthermore, since malapportionment effects in lower houses using SMP tend to be quite low, this simply has not been an interesting research question. The few studies that have tried to disentangle the effects of malapportionment from other forms of distortion have done so mostly in two-party competition environments where it is possible to clearly identify the distorting effect of malapportionment. Johnston and colleagues (1999), for example, use this approach to estimate the net partisan seat effect of British malapportionment. Through this method, they confirmed the "common sense" view that prior to Britain's most recent redistribution, Labour enjoyed an inherent "Celtic advantage" over the Conservative Party because of the over-representation of Scotland and Wales (where the Tories were uncompetitive). These methods are conceptually problematic in Canada's fragmented party system, but there is reason to believe that, similar to the "common sense" view in the United Kingdom, there could be a partisan bias built into the Canadian system of representation under the 279 formula.

As noted, the existing 279 formula in each decennial redistribution will increase the size of the House of Commons, as bonus seats are required for those provinces that lose seats as a result of the application of the formula. These bonus seats have the potential to distort electoral outcomes in relation to popular vote shares. As the number of bonus seats grows with each redistribution, so does the level of malapportionment. Table 9.1 illustrates the potential bias by documenting the growing number of bonus seats in the House of Commons in each redistribution under the 279 formula – both the absolute number and the proportion are likely to grow. When this

TABLE 9.1
Growth in the number of bonus seats in the House of Commons if the 279 formula is used for redistribution

	1981	1991	2001	2011	2021	2031
"Bonus" seats awarded to provinces with relatively declining populations[1]	12	20	28	32	36	41
% of total	4.07	6.64	9.09	10.19	11.32	12.73
Conservative success in seven provinces receiving bonus seats (2006 and 2008 elections)[2]			30.0%			
Conservative success in the three provinces not receiving bonus seats (2006 and 2008 elections)[2]			54.4%			

1 As the application of the 279 formula transfers representation to faster-growing provinces, additional bonus seats are required to ensure that provinces with relatively declining populations do not have fewer MPs than they had in the 1970s. All provinces except for BC, Alberta, and Ontario receive "bonus seats."

2 Based on the percentage of total seats won in those provinces in the 2006 and 2008 general elections.

is combined with a measure of how successful the Conservatives have been in winning seats in provinces that receive bonus seats, one can see why the potential bias is a problem from a Conservative partisan perspective.

The current system appeared to tilt against a Conservative government hoping to win majorities in the House of Commons, given the relatively poor performance of the Conservatives in recent elections in the seven provinces receiving bonus seats. For example, in the 2006 and 2008 elections the Conservatives won only 30 percent of the seats in these provinces, and only 17 percent of seats east of the Ottawa River, where most of the bonus seats accrue. This result is striking when compared with Conservative success in the three provinces *not* receiving bonus seats: in British Columbia, Alberta, and Ontario, the Conservatives won 54.4 percent of the seats. Because the Conservatives tend to lose most of these bonus seats, the more bonus seats there are, the larger the Conservatives' perceived electoral "deficit" will be. Crucially, this deficit was likely to get worse under the 279 formula unless the Conservatives reversed their electoral fortunes east of the Ottawa River *or* successfully changed the formula to more rapidly increase the number of seats west of the Ottawa River.

Although the Conservatives were able to break through any built-in bias in the 2011 election, the system itself remained problematic from the point of view of that party's electoral fortunes. John Wright, senior vice president of Ipsos, framed the issue in a provocative way in an August 2010 interview after an Ipsos Reid poll suggested (ironically) that no party was in a position to win a majority government. Emphasizing the electoral dominance of the Bloc Québécois in an over-represented Quebec, Wright argued that *no* party could form a majority until more seats were added in BC, Alberta, and Ontario (Taber 2010). Indeed, his advice to the Conservatives was to "give up" on trying to make inroads in Quebec, as in his view the Conservatives had no chance of forming a majority government until their redistribution proposals were passed.[11] Leaving aside the recent majority victory, Conservative strategists see the issue of redistribution in this light: changing the system to bring it more in line with representation by population in time for the post-2011 redistribution would likely be to their partisan benefit.

Legal and Constitutional Constraints to Reforming the System of Redistribution

The dramatic increases in interprovincial malapportionment under the 279 formula have led a number of observers to suggest that the courts could be called upon to place limits on Parliament's right to manipulate the redistribution system. Indeed, Sancton (2010, 1) suggests that the current distributions might not survive a court challenge:

> The last time the courts heard concerns about the distribution of seats between the provinces they found that the deviations were acceptable. However, those deviations were significantly lower than they are today and were a challenge to be brought anew, courts would have to grapple with widespread violations of the constitutional commitment to rep-by-pop that are unprecedented in Canadian history.

Past court cases attempting to find "toeholds" in the Constitution that can protect the principle of representation by population have been met by a judiciary largely unwilling to interfere with the status quo. Whether out of a sense of analytical and interpretive appropriateness or a desire to keep the judiciary out of a partisan policy field that could easily bring the bench's legitimacy under attack for activism, courts have generally not been defenders of representation by population. In fact, judicial interpretations have not only justified malapportionment as being consistent with the Constitution but have likely complicated, *and might even prevent,* the adoption of a system based on representation by population, if that system were to depart too sharply from the status quo.

Representation by Population and Section 52

In 1987, then mayor of Vancouver Gordon Campbell and Ian Waddell (a federal MP whose Vancouver seat was to be eliminated as a result of the new *Representation Act, 1985*) challenged the 279 formula in the province's Supreme Court. Campbell challenged the constitutional validity of the unilateral process by which Parliament had amended the existing system when it adopted the 279 formula, pointing out that while Parliament had the authority to increase the size of the House of Commons, it could not unilaterally amend the "principle of proportionate representation" contained in section 52 without using the general amending formula requiring the consent of the provinces.

The crux of the trial court judge's decision in *Campbell v. Canada (Attorney General)* (hereafter *Campbell*),[12] which was confirmed in a 1988 appeal court decision (hereafter *Campbell II*),[13] was his finding on the correct interpretation of section 52. The court was clearly unimpressed by Campbell's argument that Parliament lacked the authority to unilaterally adopt the 279 formula. The judge found that the principle of "proportionate representation" must not be equated with representation by population alone. Instead, the principle "has always recognized derogation from perfect mathematical proportionality for the purposes of maintaining floors of representation for provinces with declining populations" (*Campbell*, para. 39). This point was repeated when the judge, referring to the many changes over the decades to the redistribution formula in section 51, which protected provinces' floor levels of representation (e.g., territorial over-representation, the senatorial floor rule, etc.), boldly declared that mathematical representation has *never* been prescribed by the Constitution (para. 44), pointing out that Canada's constitutional history of redistribution has also been guided by the objective of cushioning provinces with declining populations against the loss of representation in the House. This way of characterizing the significance of the constitutional principle of proportionate representation implies that any marked *under*-representation of provinces with growing populations in the House of Commons does not necessarily violate a constitutional norm of proportionate representation.

It is worth noting that the trial judge did not deny that, at some point (undefined in the decision), a formula for redistributing seats in the House might run afoul of the principle of proportionate representation because the variations across ridings in different provinces would be simply too large. Nonetheless, in the absence of some sense as to where that standard might lie, the decision in the *Campbell* case might actually undermine any attempt to change the system. For example, if Parliament were now to unilaterally adopt a formula based purely on representation by population, particularly one that did away with the grandfather clause guaranteeing minimum seat totals to over-represented provinces, this would likely violate the court's interpretation of section 52, and therefore the Constitution. After all, the trial judge and the appeal court agreed that the core purpose of the principle of proportionate representation in the Constitution "is to make appropriate adjustments to protect the representation of the lesser populated provinces" (*Campbell II*, para. 50).

The *Charter* and Representation by Population

Following the *Campbell* decision, the Supreme Court of Canada was asked to decide what impact the "right to vote" under the *Canadian Charter of Rights and Freedoms*[14] might have on electoral boundaries. Reminiscent of the BC courts' decisions in *Campbell*, the Supreme Court went to considerable lengths to defend the notion that the right to vote identified in section 3 of the *Charter* does not derive from the principle of representation by population alone; factors other than voter parity, including geographic considerations and the presence of communities of interest or identity, must also be taken into account.

In the 1991 *Reference re Prov. Electoral Boundaries (Sask.)*, or *Carter* case[15] the Supreme Court was asked to determine the constitutional validity of the 1989 legislation implementing the electoral map created in Saskatchewan after the 1981 census. In arriving at the conclusion that wide population variations in that province's districts did not violate the *Charter*, the Supreme Court majority undertook an extensive analysis of Canada's constitutional history and philosophy. The majority opinion suggested that equating the right to vote with the principle of representation by population in the context of redistribution would be a *radical departure* from the more evolutionary and pluralistic notion of the right to vote that the Supreme Court said was actually captured by the *Charter.* The majority found that the purpose of the right to vote is to facilitate "effective representation" rather than representation by population, and that deviations from the principle of representation by population "may be justified on the grounds of practical impossibility or the provision of more effective representation" (para. 4). Indeed, in part drawing on an earlier British Columbia case, *Dixon v. British Columbia (Attorney General)*, the majority decision in *Carter* concluded that "only such deviations from the ideal of equal representation as are capable of justification on the basis of some other valid factor may be admitted" (para. 17),[16] but that these other valid factors included those that "contribute to better government of the populace as a whole, giving due weight to regional issues within the populace and geographical factors within the territory governed" (para. 17). Having set this constitutional standard, vague though it might be, the court also took care to offer reminders that in determining the amount of population variation that is constitutionally permissible under the *Charter* right to vote, the courts should exercise caution in interfering with the difficult legislative task of balancing conflicting policy considerations (paras. 38-39).

In short, judicial interpretation of the *Charter* right to vote illustrates that the courts are unlikely to require changes to the current system to bring it into line with representation by population. Indeed, a subsequent court decision on the validity of malapportioned districts, which referred to principles outlined in the *Electoral Boundaries Readjustment Act*[17] (passed at the same time as the *Representation Act, 1985*) to justify variations in populations across districts,[18] went out of its way to encourage parliamentarians and boundary commissioners to devalue population as a standard in drawing the electoral map.

When combined, the decisions in the *Campbell* case and the various *Charter* cases on redistribution suggested that it was unlikely that those unhappy with the 279 system would be able to use the courts to force a return to representation by population – placing the onus for reform solely on Parliament. Moreover, having interpreted the right to vote in such a way that *failing* to take into consideration the rights of regional communities of interest or identity could actually violate both the principle of "proportionate representation" in section 52 of the *Constitution Act, 1867,* the courts may have expanded the ability of those regions or groups hurt by a return to redistribution based on population to challenge changes to the existing system. This certainly seems to suggest that any move to get rid of the grandfather clause created by the amalgam formula, and expanded by the 279 formula, might require the use of the general amending formula. In short, big changes to the system appear unlikely and the government has little choice but to legislatively "tinker" with the formula contained in section 51, which requires only that a majority of MPs agree to the government's proposals. Until the new Conservative majority government was formed, this seemed to be even less likely than court-led reform.

The Political Obstacles to Reform

The Harper government's proposals to change the formula before the next redistribution illustrate both the extent to which apportionment has been politicized and, as a result, the difficulty the government faces in changing the system. The combination of (1) a minority, regionally fractured parliament and (2) increasing "positive returns" for those parties and provinces that would otherwise have lost a greater share of seats, meant that the government was unlikely to be able to alter the system, no matter how much it may be disadvantaged by it.

The Harper Proposals

During the 2006 election campaign, the Conservatives promised to address the growing under-representation of British Columbia and Alberta. In May 2007, the government introduced Bill C-56, which proposed changes to the redistribution formula. In introducing the legislation, the minister for democratic reform, Peter Van Loan, argued that the purpose of the government's bill was to increase the number of MPs for British Columbia, Alberta, and Ontario, while keeping the "grandfather" floor guarantees of no fewer seats than 1974 levels. Bill C-56 proposed that instead of using 279 as the divisor for allocating seats to provinces, the next redistribution would be based on the total number of provincial seats in the House of Commons in 1985 (which was 298, not 279). In subsequent redistributions, the divisor would be the total number of seats in the House as determined by the redistribution thirty years earlier (which would make the divisor 301 after 2021 and 308 after 2031).

In practice, the new formula would accelerate the overall growth of the House, which in turn would increase the number of seats available for redistribution to the provinces with faster-growing populations. For example, based on census projections, under the bill Ontario would likely receive 116 seats (10 more than the 106 it received in the last redistribution, and 8 more than it would receive if the redistribution went ahead under the existing 279 formula). While the formula tried to strike a balance between the principle of representation by population and traditional guarantees against seat loss, it also tried to reduce increases in the size of the House by using an electoral divisor that lagged behind real population growth. As a result, the bill would not move decisively towards representation by population. In effect, a vote in Ontario would still be worth 10 percent less than a vote in Quebec and 40-50 percent less than a vote in Saskatchewan or New Brunswick (see Appendix). The formula was in essence a moderate compromise, acting only to dampen the rate of growth of malapportionment in the 279 formula.

Partisan manoeuvring undermined the Conservatives' proposals from the start, however. Putting the appearance of moderation aside, the Conservatives' primary goal appeared to be to add considerably more seats in British Columbia and Alberta, considering their electoral success in those provinces. The bill, as described in the Library of Parliament's Legislative Summary, contained an additional provision, rule 3, which appeared to guarantee that British Columbia and Alberta would never have higher average constituency populations than Ontario.[19] This provision was a relatively innocuous but needlessly politically provocative gesture towards Ontario, in that unless there were some radical or unexpected changes in population growth, Ontario, British Columbia, and Alberta would all likely receive the same electoral quotient. As it was *actually published* in the Order Paper, however, rule 3 was substantially different: it fundamentally altered the entire formula, as it guaranteed that British Columbia and Alberta would receive the same electoral quotient as Quebec, while Ontario would not.[20] As can be seen in the Appendix, regardless of how it came to replace the earlier formula, the impact of the new rule 3 appeared politically desirable to the Conservatives. Rule 3 doubled the number of additional seats BC and Alberta would receive in the next redistribution. Put another way, despite the fact that population growth in Ontario was likely to be almost double that of BC and Alberta combined, the two western provinces would gain more seats than Ontario. Furthermore, by permanently tying BC and Alberta to Quebec, rule 3 would ensure that Ontario remained the lone province not to receive special treatment in allocating seats. Perhaps most provocatively, although unnoticed at the time, the bill would have resulted in Quebec's being under-represented relative to western Canada.[21] Not surprisingly, the Conservatives' communications strategy in relation to the bill neglected to mention the impact of rule 3. Van Loan stressed to the media that the purpose of the bill was to bring the average constituency populations of BC, Alberta, and Ontario closer to that of Quebec.[22]

The response to the Harper proposals contained in Bill C-56 and its identical successor, Bill C-22, was predictable.[23] In Parliament, the bills were condemned by the Bloc Québécois, echoing a motion passed in Quebec's National Assembly. While there was a committee debate on the proposals, in Question Period the Bloc attacked the bill as antithetical to the Conservatives' recent recognition of Quebec's special status in Canada and argued that changes that reduced the relative weight of Quebec's MPs in the House were unacceptable. Under the formula, Quebec's proportion of seats would have fallen from 24 percent (which was likely under the 279 formula) to 23 percent. It would seem that the Bloc, in focusing on this issue, did not fully understand the extent to which the bill, ostensibly motivated by a desire for representation by population, would actually shift the benefits of malapportionment in favour of western Canada. Manitoba also expressed opposition to the proposals – indeed, many political figures in the seven over-represented provinces argued that the Harper proposals were unacceptable in light of existing principles regarding representation.

The most virulent opposition came from Ontario, however, and it was largely Ontario's reaction to the proposed formulas that dominated discussion of the bills. Despite the fact that Ontario would gain eight more seats under the Harper proposals than it would get if the legislation failed and the scheduled redistribution were conducted under the existing 279 formula, Premier Dalton McGuinty repeatedly attacked the bills, arguing that the Harper proposals "will weaken democratic representation for

Canadians living in Ontario by granting us fewer seats than we are entitled to in the House of Commons. It will undermine some of our most cherished democratic rights: representation by population; one person, one vote; equality under the law and effective representation."[24] Van Loan repeatedly dismissed McGuinty's concerns as "purely partisan" (in one case suggesting that McGuinty was the "small man of Confederation") and defended the proposals by arguing that the government had to balance representation by population against the need to guarantee traditional levels of representation for other provinces; he also argued that Ontario already had a large number of MPs.

Mendelsohn (2010) and Sancton (2010) echo the concerns of the Ontario government, arguing that the Harper proposals represented a further debasement of representation by population. It is likely, however, that even under rule 3 the Harper redistribution formula would approach representation by population more closely than the status quo following the next redistribution (see Appendix). The larger point is that the Harper government was attempting to enact a formula to maximize political advantage in redistribution at the lowest cost. Effectively, Atlantic Canada's "floor" level of representation is entrenched in the Constitution; by contrast, Quebec, Saskatchewan, and Manitoba could all lose seats if the government were to abandon the grandfather clause in the 279 formula. Given the political considerations of singling out those provinces, and legal concerns (as noted above, the *Campbell* decision may mean that the existing grandfather provisions in the *Representation Act, 1985* are now also constitutionally protected), the government chose to keep the grandfather provisions and simply expand the size of the House. At the same time, there is little public appetite for rapidly increasing the number of MPs – the prime minister himself was once a very public opponent of a larger (and more expensive) House of Commons (Sanction 2010, 13). Likewise, provinces with declining populations want to protect both their absolute number of MPs and their *proportion of representation,* so there is considerable pressure not to increase the number of seats too drastically. Given these conflicting pressures, the government chose to reward Conservative seat-rich BC and Alberta with more seats and to control for growth by short-changing Ontario.

In any event, the Conservatives simply did not have the votes to pass their bill. Indeed, their efforts were decidedly half-hearted, as they knew the bill would not pass (Mellon 2009). The problem for the government was that the Liberal caucus, particularly members from Ontario, also opposed the bill, echoing McGuinty's concerns about the unfair treatment of Ontario.[25]

There was little chance of success given the opposition of both the Bloc and the Liberals.

Bill C-12

In April 2010, the Harper government tabled a new bill, C-12, with a re-worked formula. After the failure of Bill C-22, Harper and McGuinty met personally to discuss Ontario's complaints and devise a system that would accommodate the province's rapidly growing population. In explaining the changes to the Harper proposals contained in Bill C-12, the new minister of state for democratic reform, Steven Fletcher, simply said that Ontario had "a good point. The government listened to what was said and we're pleased to have brought forward a formula where the Ontario government now supports this Bill as do Alberta and British Columbia."[26]

Under the new Harper proposal each province's population would be divided by an "electoral divisor" (or national electoral quotient) to calculate how many seats that province would receive. After the 2011 census, the divisor would be 108,000. Subsequent redistributions would be based on a floating divisor, which would increase in size quite quickly.[27] Because this divisor is much lower than the national quotient used in both the 279 formula (the 279 formula would likely produce an electoral quotient of over 120,000 after 2011) and the previous Harper formula (in which the divisor would probably have been over 114,000), the new proposal would allow provinces with faster-growing populations to accumulate seats more quickly. The new formula would also maintain the existing grandfather clause. Based on census projections for 2011, the formula would likely result in Ontario's gaining sixteen seats, while Alberta would likely gain seven and BC six. Because of the larger increase in the size of the House relative to that produced by the 279 formula (the House would grow by thirty-one members instead of six), average constituency populations would be much lower, with fewer bonus seats needed to compensate provinces with relatively declining populations, and the level of malapportionment would be reduced.

From a partisan perspective, Bill C-12 ensured that BC and Alberta would still get the number of seats they were promised under the previous Harper proposal, but Ontario would now receive the same benefit, at least for the pending post-2011 redistribution. However, since the three provinces' electoral quotients are not tied to Quebec in the new proposal, and the electoral divisor grows with each redistribution, variation in the relative weight of an individual's vote in different provinces would likely begin to increase again over time (see Appendix). Nonetheless, the outcome for the next redistribution would be something more closely approximating representation by population, and would produce many new seats in suburban BC, Alberta, and Ontario, where the Conservatives are more electorally competitive.

Initially, the prognosis for the new bill was unclear. It had more support than the previous proposal. Not only did Ontario support the changes, but in a parliamentary debate over a Bloc motion to condemn the bill it was also apparent that many Liberals were willing to treat the bill as a serious possibility.[28] That said, given its partisan implications, the bill was always unlikely to pass. Despite the fact that Bill C-12 was a relatively balanced, moderate compromise, it appeared to provoke an even harsher response from some corners of the country. For example, in his vehement condemnation of the proposal, Donald Savoie argued, in a manner fully supported by governments in Atlantic Canada, that Confederation and the Constitution somehow guaranteed the Atlantic provinces a fixed share of the total representation in the House. Where floor guarantees were once offered as protection against losing MPs, since 1985 these guarantees have morphed into something far more insidious to the principle of representation by population. Steadily growing over-representation has led many politicians from regions and parties benefiting from the system to believe that redistribution need not have anything at all to do with population. On increased representation for the other provinces, Savoie suggested that "as a Maritimer, I'm deeply offended ... If we keep going down this road, I'm worried about the future of my country." This criticism reflected similar Bloc Québécois opposition to the bill.[29]

Essentially, the response to the Bill C-12 proposals fully revealed the legacy of the *Representation Act, 1985*. It has not simply increased malapportionment by guaranteeing minimum numbers of MPs for provinces with relatively declining populations. Rather, by restricting the growth of the House of Commons over the last thirty years, the *Representation Act, 1985* has fed the notion that provinces are entitled to a certain *proportion* of total representation, regardless of demographic changes in the country. "Redistribution" has come to mean something very different from what was intended.

Bill C-20

The proposals contained in Bill C-12 were ultimately moot as the 2011 election suspended further debate. Instead, fresh from winning their long sought after majority, the Conservatives have moved quickly to pass a new proposal, contained in Bill C-20, the *Fair Representation Act*. The new formula accomplishes many of the same things as the proposed formula in Bill C-12. The allocation of seats is based on dividing a province's population by an electoral quotient that is significantly lower than the one provided by the 279 formula, resulting in more new seats for Ontario, Alberta, and BC – perhaps as many as twenty-five for the next election. The act also includes the traditional grandfather clause that no province can have fewer seats than it did before the *Representation Act, 1985* – which means it would probably pass any potential court challenge that is based on the idea that the new formula is a big departure from the constitutional principles surrounding representation (and therefore should be subject to the general amending formula). Along these lines, the only major change was that the Conservatives also included a mechanism by which Quebec could potentially gain as many as three seats in the upcoming redistribution – a provision that was thought to be key in making the bill more politically palatable (as it seemed to suggest that reform of the system would also act to ensure a traditional level of representation for Quebec, something the Conservatives highlighted in their communication strategies supporting the bill).

In fact, adding seats for Quebec turned out to be one of the biggest problems with the bill in that Conservative backbenchers threatened to revolt over the issue, forcing a special caucus meeting where the government had to sell its new formula to its own members (Ibbitson 2011a). Although it is not clear how the Conservative backbench was assuaged over the issue, it is hard not to notice that the special provisions regarding Quebec in the bill were oversold in any event. While government and opposition press releases and the media all referred to the legislation as granting Quebec "three new seats," this was based on speculations drawn from now out-of-date census projections. Under the act, the new rules 3 and 4 (through some complex math) essentially create a provision by which Quebec *might* be entitled to additional representation depending on actual population trends. In reality, it is likely that Quebec will receive only two additional seats and perhaps as few as one if the lower-than-expected population growth revealed in the early analysis of the 2011 census turns out to be correct. In any event, the obscure math behind rules 3 and 4 will probably only ever apply in the next redistribution (as we transition from the 279 formula to the new formula), and unless there are major changes in population trends, Quebec will quickly lose any additional seats in subsequent redistributions (see Appendix for seat projections based on census population projections). In the end, although much of the public discussion focused on the new seats for Quebec, over the long term the new act does what earlier Conservative proposals sought to do: provide a more rapid expansion in the number of seats for BC, Alberta, and Ontario. Indeed, likely outcomes in seat totals are very similar from both the Bill C-12 proposals and those recently passed in the *Fair Representation Act,* and the complex math of the new formula masks Quebec's likely treatment under the system.

Conclusion

Proposals to address the increasing malapportionment of the 279 formula have been all too numerous, but without a majority government that would actually benefit from revising the existing system, the prognosis for all of them had been poor. Despite all the partisan manoeuvring of the Harper government, the unsuccessful Bill C-12 was actually far more consistent with traditional thinking about representation by population in Canada than the 279 formula – it was a reasonable proposal, but the response was overwhelmingly unfavourable. While the absence of clear constitutional limitations on Parliament's ability to determine the level of representation of each province allowed Parliament to create the 279 formula in the first place, it has also opened the door to an increased politicization of the redistribution formula, which the Harper government has now clearly illustrated in its manoeuvring for a new formula for allocating seats in the House.

Indeed, armed with a majority at last, the government pushed the *Fair Representation Act* through Parliament with considerable speed, in contrast to the drawn-out discussions and failures of the previous proposals. Bill C-20 was passed in the House of Commons in six weeks, despite a relatively raucous debate at third reading in the Commons. It passed in the Senate in only three days, including the time taken to send the bill to committee for a report. In the process, both the New Democrats and the Liberals proposed alternative systems. Particularly interesting in the debate was the alternative Liberal "lose-lose" scenario, in which they proposed capping the House of Commons at current levels and jettisoning the existing grandfather clause so that seats from Quebec, Saskatchewan, Manitoba, Newfoundland and Labrador, and Nova Scotia could all be redistributed to the faster-growing provinces, until such time that those provinces also hit the constitutionally entrenched "senatorial floor" (along with New Brunswick and Prince Edward Island, which are already at the floor) – a set of proposals particularly injurious to Quebec. While the Liberals played up arguments that keeping Parliament small would save a great deal of money, it is hard to see what representation principle underlay the proposal, and unlike the New Democrats' more single-minded focus on a guarantee of 25 percent of Commons seats for Quebec, it is hard to see the partisan advantage in the Liberals' ideas. In any event, the Harper majority ensured that the Conservatives' proposals would win the day.

Although the now-defunct 279 formula may not have been consistent with "internationally accepted democratic standards," the new system is not based on representation by population either. There will still be large variations in the relative weights of individual Canadians' votes, much like under the 279 formula, and those differences will likely grow over time. This reality is the product of the constitutional and legal difficulties of proposing more substantial reform. The new system does accomplish two things, however. First, it moves Canada's House of Commons somewhat closer to representation by population. Second, and more cynically, as John Ibbitson was quick to point out in his analysis in the *Globe and Mail*, it is a "political windfall" for the Tories as almost all of the new seats in BC, Alberta, and Ontario are likely to be added in the fast-growing suburban areas around major cities, all areas of Conservative electoral strength (Ibbitson 2011b). The new formula may be a fair or necessary compromise, but one thing seems certain: it is good politics for Conservative strategists.

APPENDIX: Changes in Representation – The 279 and Harper Formulas

TABLE 9.2

Province and census year	Population[1]	The "279 Formula" Representation Act (1985)				Bills C-22 and C-56 (2007)			Bill C-12 (2010)			Bill C-20 Fair Representation Act (2011)		
		Formulary apportionment	"Bonus" seats	Total, including "bonus seats"	Relative vote weight	Formulary apportionment[2]	Total, including "bonus seats"	Relative vote weight	Formulary apportionment	Total, including "bonus seats"[3]	Relative vote weight	Formulary apportionment	Total, including "bonus seats"[3]	Relative vote weight
Newfoundland														
1981	567,681	6.52		7	1.01									
1991	568,474	5.83	1	7	1.11									
2001	512,930	4.78	2	7	1.33									
2011	511,800	4.19	3	7	1.48	4.48	7	1.41	4.74	7	1.37	4.60	7	1.39
2021	511,900	3.76	3	7	1.63	4.06	7	1.53	4.25	7	1.51	4.24	7	1.51
2031	514,600	3.45	4	7	1.76	3.81	7	1.62	3.90	7	1.63	3.98	7	1.61
Prince Edward Island														
1981	122,506	1.41	3	4	2.69									
1991	129,765	1.33	3	4	2.79									
2001	135,294	1.26	3	4	2.88									
2011	142,700	1.17	3	4	3.04	1.25	4	2.88	1.32	4	2.82	1.28	4	2.85
2021	155,400	1.14	3	4	3.07	1.23	4	2.88	1.29	4	2.84	1.29	4	2.84
2031	168,000	1.13	3	4	3.08	1.24	4	2.83	1.27	4	2.86	1.30	4	2.82
Nova Scotia														
1981	847,442	9.74	1	11	1.07									

1991	899,942	9.23	2	1.11								
2001	908,007	8.47	3	1.18								
2011	940,300	7.70	3	1.27	8.23	*11*	1.20	8.71	*11*	1.18	8.46	*11*	1.19
2021	991,100	7.28	4	1.33	7.85	*11*	1.24	8.23	*11*	1.23	8.21	*11*	1.23
2031	1,038,400	6.96	4	1.37	7.69	*11*	1.26	7.87	*11*	1.27	8.02	*11*	1.26

New Brunswick

1981	696,403	8.00	2	1.18								
1991	723,900	7.42	3	1.25								
2001	729,498	6.80	3	1.34								
2011	752,000	6.16	4	1.44	6.58	*10*	1.37	6.96	*10*	1.34	6.76	*10*	1.35
2021	787,700	5.79	4	1.52	6.24	*10*	1.42	6.54	*10*	1.40	6.53	*10*	1.40
2031	811,300	5.44	5	1.59	6.00	*10*	1.47	6.15	*10*	1.48	6.27	*10*	1.46

Quebec

1981	6,438,403	74.00	1	0.96								
1991	6,895,963	70.70	4	0.98								
2001	7,237,479	67.50	8	1.01								
2011	7,900,400	64.73	10	1.03	69.14	*75*	0.98	73.15	*75*	0.95	71.07	*77*	0.99
2021	8,508,500	62.50	12	1.05	67.43	*75*	0.99	70.64	*75*	0.97	70.52	*75*	0.97
2031	9,021,500	60.48	15	1.07	66.77	*75*	0.99	68.35	*75*	1.00	69.71	*75*	0.99

Ontario

1981	8,625,107	99.13	*99*	0.94								
1991	10,084,885	103.40	*103*	0.92								
2001	11,410,046	106.42	*106*	0.91								
2011	13,209,600	108.23	*108*	0.89	115.60	*116*	0.90	122.31	*123*	0.94	118.83	*119*	0.92
2021	15,000,100	110.19	*110*	0.88	118.88	*119*	0.89	124.53	*125*	0.92	124.32	*125*	0.92
2031	16,743,800	112.25	*112*	0.86	123.92	*124*	0.88	126.86	*127*	0.91	129.37	*130*	0.92

▼ TABLE 9.2

Province and census year	Population[1]	The "279 Formula" Representation Act (1985)				Bills C-22 and C-56 (2007)			Bill C-12 (2010)			Bill C-20 Fair Representation Act (2011)		
		Formulary apportionment	"Bonus" seats	Total, including "bonus seats"	Relative vote weight	Formulary apportionment[2]	Total, including "bonus seats"	Relative vote weight	Formulary apportionment	Total, including "bonus seats"[3]	Relative vote weight	Formulary apportionment	Total, including "bonus seats"[3]	Relative vote weight
Manitoba														
1981	1,026,241	11.80	2	14	1.12									
1991	1,091,942	11.20	3	14	1.16									
2001	1,119,583	10.44	4	14	1.22									
2011	1,239,100	10.15	4	14	1.23	10.84	14	1.16	11.47	14	1.13	11.15	14	1.15
2021	1,367,300	10.04	4	14	1.22	10.84	14	1.15	11.35	14	1.13	11.33	14	1.13
2031	1,501,100	10.06	4	14	1.21	11.11	14	1.11	11.37	14	1.12	11.60	14	1.11
Saskatchewan														
1981	968,313	11.13	3	14	1.19									
1991	988,928	10.14	4	14	1.28									
2001	978,933	9.13	5	14	1.39									
2011	1,047,400	8.58	5	14	1.45	9.17	14	1.38	9.70	14	1.34	9.42	14	1.36
2021	1,101,600	8.09	6	14	1.52	8.73	14	1.42	9.15	14	1.40	9.13	14	1.40
2031	1,168,200	7.83	6	14	1.55	8.65	14	1.42	8.85	14	1.44	9.03	14	1.42
Alberta														
1981	2,237,724	25.72	26		0.96									

Year	Population	Quotient	Seats	Ratio	Quotient	Seats	Ratio	Quotient	Seats	Ratio	Quotient	Seats	Ratio
1991	2,545,553	26.10	26	0.92									
2001	2,974,807	27.74	28	0.92									
2011	3,781,200	30.98	31	0.89	35.90	35	0.95	35.01	36	0.96	34.01	35	0.94
2021	4,242,700	31.17	31	0.87	37.40	36	0.95	35.22	36	0.94	35.16	36	0.94
2031	4,703,000	31.53	32	0.88	39.10	39	0.99	35.63	36	0.92	36.34	37	0.93

British Columbia

Year	Population	Quotient	Seats	Ratio	Quotient	Seats	Ratio	Quotient	Seats	Ratio	Quotient	Seats	Ratio
1981	2,744,467	31.54	32	0.96									
1991	3,282,061	33.65	34	0.94									
2001	3,907,738	36.45	36	0.90									
2011	4,528,800	37.10	37	0.89	42.99	42	0.95	41.93	42	0.93	40.74	41	0.92
2021	5,313,800	39.03	39	0.88	46.84	46	0.97	44.11	45	0.93	44.04	45	0.93
2031	5,946,900	39.87	40	0.87	49.44	49	0.98	45.06	46	0.93	45.95	46	0.92

Territories

	Seats		Seats		Seats		Seats
Territories	3		3		3		3

Total

Year	Population				
1981	24,274,287	12	295		
1991	27,211,413	20	301		
2001	30,007,094	28	308		
2011	34,053,300	32	314	331	339	335
2021	37,980,100	36	318	339	344	344
2031	41,616,800	41	322	350	347	351

1 Estimated provincial populations come from Statistics Canada 2010. The estimates for 2011 are from the "short term scenario." The estimates for 2021-31 are from the "medium growth (M1) scenario."

2 Under the formula in Bills C-22 and C-56, the allocation of seats of BC and Alberta was treated separately from that of Ontario, producing a different minimum number of seats for those provinces than would be arrived at through normal formulary apportionment and rounding.

3 The redistribution formulas of both the failed Bill C-12 and the *Fair Representation Act* change the rules regarding rounding. In both cases, unlike earlier representation formulas, when calculating the number of seats that should be allocated to any province through the application of the formula, *any* remainder is to be rounded up. While this does little to impact the overall number of seats allocated to provinces, on paper it does drastically reduce the number of "bonus seats" as many of the slower-growing provinces, which are at their representation floors, receive more formulary-allocated seats under the new method for calculating remainders.

Notes

1 Quoted from *Hansard* 39: 1 (14 May 2007). Van Loan was speaking in defence of Bill C-56, the Conservatives' proposal to amend section 51 of the *Constitution Act, 1867* (Democratic Representation).

2 Savoie was speaking in response to the tabling of Bill C-12, one of a series of redistribution reform bills proposed by the Harper Government. See Maher 2010.

3 *The Constitution Act, 1867* (U.K.), 30 & 31 Vict., c. 3.

4 *Representation Act, 1985,* S.C. 1986, c. 8.

5 *Fair Representation Act,* S.C. 2011, c. 26.

6 *Constitution Act, 1982,* being Schedule B to the *Canada Act 1982* (U.K.), 1982, c. 11.

7 Had the amalgam formula not been subsequently abandoned, the House of Commons would have had over 370 members following redistribution after the 2001 Census.

8 While Samuels and Snyder's comparative study (2001) suggested that malapportionment tends to be higher in "new democracies" (principally in Latin America, eastern Europe, and the Caribbean), it is interesting to note that, based on data collected before the full impact of the 279 formula was felt in Canadian redistribution, they found that Canada had one of the highest rates of malapportionment among established democracies.

9 Other studies have suggested the system does not do what the framers of both the 279 formula and the *Electoral Boundaries Readjustment Act,* with their more "nuanced" views of representation, intended. If deviations from a population standard are acceptable in order to represent special communities of "interest" or "identity," it is hard not to notice that one major impact of the system is that visible-minority Canadians living in major urban centres are systematically under-represented (Pal and Chowdhry 2007). Likewise, because independent boundary commissions have been unwilling to deviate as widely from population in the process of districting as Parliament wants them to, far from protecting the representation of rural Canadians in geographically huge northern districts, the 279 formula reduces rural representation in BC, Alberta, and Ontario in favour of rural and urban voters in the other seven provinces (Williams 2005). In short, the system does not really "work"; it simply supports a particularly parochial and venal approach to representation.

10 This does not mean that malapportionment was not in some way "politically significant," just that it had little impact on partisan seat totals.

11 Without elaborating, he went so far as to say (presumably in light of some sense that there is a "ceiling" on popular support for the Conservatives) that if the Conservatives were to form a majority government, change would come not from "opinion structure" but the "structure of the House of Commons."

12 1987 CanLII 2547 (BC SC) [*Campbell*]

13 *Campbell v. Canada (Attorney General),* 1988 CanLII 3043 (BC CA) 1987 CanLII 2547 (BC SC) [*Campbell II*]

14 Canadian Charter of Rights and Freedoms, Part 1 of the Constitution Act, 1982, being Schedule B to the Canada Act 1982 (U.K.), 1982, c. 11, s. 6.

15 *Reference re Prov. Electoral Boundaries (Sask.),* [1991] 2 S.C.R. 158 [*Carter*]. Roger Carter argued the case for the critics of Saskatchewan's *Electoral Boundaries*

Commission Act, S.S. 1986-87-88, c. E-6.1, ss. 14, 20, before the Supreme Court of Canada.

16 Significant portions of the *Carter* decision were drawn from the decision in the *Dixon* case, an earlier BC decision that was penned by the same judge who wrote the majority decision for the Supreme Court. See *Dixon v. British Columbia (Attorney General)* (1989), 59 D.L.R. (4th) 247, [1989] 4 W.W.R. 393 (QuickLaw) [*Dixon*].

17 *Electoral Boundaries Readjustment Act,* R.S.C. 1985, c. E-3.

18 See *Raîche v. Canada (Attorney General),* 2004 FC 679, [2005] 1 F.C.R. 93.

19 See Barnes (2007). While the provision was ambiguous, it appeared to guarantee that if either BC or Alberta did not gain a seat, and their real electoral quotient was higher than Ontario's, they would be given an "extra" seat. The provision precluded Ontario from receiving the same treatment in reverse.

20 Rule 3 in the bill actually states: "If the number of members assigned to a province is not increased by the application of rule 2 [the grandfather clause] or section 51A [the Senatorial guarantee] and its population is less than that of the most populous province whose number of members is increased thereby, there should be added to the number of members assigned to that province such number of members as will cause its electoral quotient – obtained by dividing the population of the province by the number of members assigned to it – to be as close as possible to the electoral quotient of that more populous province without being below it."

21 Under the proposed formula, on top of the eight "bonus seats" Saskatchewan and Manitoba were likely to receive after the next redistribution, BC and Alberta would now also collectively gain four "bonus seats." Bill C-56 would have given western Canada twelve "undeserved" seats, making it "over-represented" relative to both Ontario and Quebec.

22 For his comments, see CBC News 2007.

23 Bill C-56 received little serious attention before the session ended and it died on the Order Paper. However, the Conservatives reintroduced the legislation in the fall of 2007 as Bill C-22 (the formulas in the two bills were identical).

24 See, for example, Ontario 2007.

25 *Hansard* 39: 2, 31 March 2008.

26 Quoted from Vongdouangchanh (2010).

27 In effect, the formula would mean that the divisor would increase by about 10,000 in each subsequent redistribution.

28 For an example of the range of opinions offered by MPs, go to http://openparliament.ca/debates/2010/4/20/?page=7.

29 For Savoie's complete comments, see Coyne (2010).

References

Barnes, Andre. 2007. *Legislative Summary – Bill C-56: An Act to amend the Constitution Act, 1867 (Democratic Representation).* Ottawa: Library of Parliament.

Carty, R.K. 1985. "The Electoral Boundary Revolution in Canada." *American Review of Canadian Studies* 15 (3): 273-87.

CBC News. 2007. "Tory Plan Would Create 22 New Ridings, but Nobody Knows Just Where." CBC News, 14 November. http://www.cbc.ca/.

Coyne, Andrew. 2010. "It's Like Putting a Puzzle Together." Macleans.ca, 9 April. http://www2.macleans.ca/.

Grofman, Bernard, William Koetzle, and Thomas Brunell. 1997. "An Integrated Perspective on the Three Potential Sources of Partisan Bias: Malapportionment, Turnout Differences, and the Geographic Distribution of Party Vote Shares." *Electoral Studies* 16 (4): 457-70.

Hnatyshyn, Ray. 1985. *White Paper on Redistribution*. Ottawa: Parliament of Canada.

Ibbiston, John. 2011a. "Harper Quells Unrest in Tory Ranks to Juggle Seats in House." *Globe and Mail*, 27 October.

–. 2011b. "Adding Seats to House of Commons a Political Windfall for Tories." *Globe and Mail*, 15 December.

Johnston, Ron, David Rossiter, and Charles Pattie. 1999. "Integrating and Decomposing the Sources of Partisan Bias: Brookes' Method and the Impact of Redistricting in Great Britain." *Electoral Studies* 18: 367-78.

Maher, Stephen. 2010. "Region's Voice Weakening; New Legislation Would Give 30 More Commons Seats to Larger Provinces." Halifax *Chronicle Herald*, 3 April.

Mellon, Hugh. 2009. "The Harper Government and Apportioning Seats in the House of Commons." Paper presented to the Atlantic Provinces' Political Science Association, Acadia University, Wolfville, NS, 2-3 October.

Mendelsohn, Matthew. 2010. "Some Are More Equal than Others: Canadian Representation in Comparative Context." *Mowat Note*. Toronto: Mowat Centre for Policy Innovation.

Ontario. Office of the Premier. 2007. "McGuinty Seeks Fairness for Ontario." Press release, 14 November.

Pal, Michael, and Sujit Chowdhry. 2007. "Is Every Ballot Equal? Visible-Minority Vote Dilution in Canada." *IRPP Choices* 13 (1).

Samuels, David, and Richard Snyder. 2001. "The Value of a Vote: Malapportionment in Comparative Perspective." *British Journal of Political Science* 31: 651-71.

Sancton, Andrew. 1990. "Eroding Representation by Population in the Canadian House of Commons: The Representation Act, 1985." *Canadian Journal of Political Science* 23: 442-43.

–. 2010. *The Principle of Representation by Population in Canadian Federal Politics*. Toronto: Mowat Centre for Policy Innovation.

Statistics Canada. 2010. *Population Projections for Canada, Provinces and Territories (2009-2036)*. Statistics Canada, no. 91-520-X. Ottawa: Statistics Canada. http://www.statcan.gc.ca/.

Taber, Jane. 2010. "Electoral Math: Should Tories, Liberals and New Democrats Just Give Up on Quebec?" *Globe and Mail*, 16 August.

Vongdouangchanh, Bea. 2010. "House Seats Bill Could Affect 19 Tory, 10 Grit Ridings, and One NDP Riding." *Hill Times*, 12 April.

Williams, Russell. 2005. "Canada's System of Representation in Crisis: The '279 Formula' and Federal Electoral Redistributions." *American Review of Canadian Studies* (Spring): 99-134.

10

Too Little, Too Soon

State Funding and Electoral District Associations in the Green Party of Canada

HAROLD J. JANSEN AND L.A. (LISA) LAMBERT

[In the Green Party, we] were doing the exact opposite of the spirit of the legislation. C-24 was meant to centralize parties and here we are using it to further decentralize ours.

— ANONYMOUS CENTRAL GREEN PARTY OF CANADA OFFICIAL, 2006

C-24 causes parties to not need people.

— GRAHAM FOX, *RETHINKING POLITICAL PARTIES* (2005)

The Canadian political landscape has been substantially altered over the last twenty years, as we have seen the emergence of new parties and the disappearance and recombination of old parties. The Green Party of Canada, which has existed since the early 1980s, has become much more prominent in recent years. Indeed, the party's leader, Elizabeth May, even had a seat at the debating table during the 2008 campaign, thus highlighting the "seriousness" of her party as a competitor in the election. In this chapter, we examine the Green Party of Canada in the context of changes to federal electoral finance laws in 2004. We argue that institutional changes (increased state subsidies to parties) have had an important impact on the organizational capacities and choices of political parties, affecting the nature of party organization for newly emerging parties differently from the past.

We ground our analysis in the context of the debate among both academics and policy makers about the effects of state subventions on political competition and party organization. One of the central criticisms of subsidies is that they lead parties to centralize and professionalize their operations, causing them to neglect the development of party membership and mass organization and participation (Katz and Mair 1995). In this chapter, we assess this argument through a case study of the Green Party of Canada (GPC) after the introduction of generous state subsidies in 2004. Drawing on Elections Canada financial data and interviews with party officials conducted between 2005 and 2010, we show that while the Canadian Greens remain largely dependent on state funding to finance their operations, they have used a portion of their state subvention to attempt to develop their membership and local party organization along the lines of a mass party model due to beliefs that members of the party hold about the value of decentralization.

Our data suggest that although we have seen substantial changes in recent years in party organization, the Green Party's efforts to build local party strength have been only partially successful, raising questions about the viability of this form of organization in emerging, state-dependent parties. The future of the Canadian political landscape is uncertain, and although the Green Party's sudden prominence is clearly linked to party· finance laws, its ability to remain competitive in federal politics will depend on more than the size of party coffers. Whether the Green Party will be a permanent fixture in federal elections, or whether its standing in recent elections reflects short-term flux before the electoral landscape is restored to previous norms (following historical patterns of volatility and restoration as identified in Chapter 13), remains to be seen.

State Subventions and Party Organization
There is a lively debate among political scientists about the effects of state subventions on the organizational and electoral behaviour of political parties (e.g., Fisher 2011; Jenson 1991; Katz and Mair 1995, 1996, 2002; Nassmacher 1993; Williams 2000; Young 1998). Some have argued that the granting of direct subsidies to parties constitutes recognition of the special role that they play in organizing a country's democratic life, whereas others have argued that direct state subsidies to parties fundamentally alters interactions between parties, the state, and civil society. Katz and Mair (1995) identified the most serious effect of state subventions to parties as the emergence of the cartel party. The cartel party, with its characteristic weak

membership, professionalized core, and centralized structure, provides evidence of the weakening of these parties' ties to civil society (see Pierre et al. 2000, and van Biezen 2004).

Although Katz and Mair (1995) identify many reasons for cartelization, the provision of direct state subsidies to political parties is a central cause (15). The cartel party disengages from its members and supporters because, as the party receives an increasing proportion of its income from the state, its need for contributions from supporters is reduced. As parties are rewarded for engagement with the state rather than engagement with the electorate, their ties to civil society wither. The cartel party is also more concerned with maintaining its relationship with the state than its relationship with civil society. Party members become disillusioned and parties become unresponsive, as they no longer require subscription fees and donations to contest elections. As a result, the party system becomes less competitive as parties come to collude with one another in order to maintain and enhance the system of state funding on which they have become dependent.

This marginalization of party members means that they are less involved in campaign activities; instead, parties increasingly turn to professional staff to develop and implement professional advertising campaigns (Webb and Kolodny 2006). The cartel party, then, becomes professionalized. Cartel parties also tend to centralize their operations as the grassroots become less involved in elections. The electoral campaign becomes a professionally managed affair directed by a small core of staff in the central office. The nature of party politics changes with cartelization because parties are no longer the product of a group of like-minded individuals but have become a specialist organization in order to maximize votes and maintain state subsidies.

The extent to which parties succumb to the pressures that come with significant amounts of state funding can vary. One important predictor of the extent to which parties become dependent on state funding is the party's ideology and ties to civil society. As Nassmacher (2006, 449) notes:

> Among parties, there is an increasing dependence on public subsidies. However, this differs by country (due to the overall financial regimes) and by party (due to their political legacies). Workers' parties are less dependent on public financing (mainly because of income from dues and unions), while bourgeois parties (in France and Sweden) and Green parties (in all European countries) receive more than 80 per cent of their income from

state funds. Conservative parties, which in former times depended on large donations, now have problems getting along without public subsidies because their traditional source of funds is questioned publicly.

Another factor influencing the susceptibility of a party to the temptations associated with public subsidies may be the party's relative age. Although subventions may strain any party's ties to civil society, these effects may be particularly pronounced in situations where the party is emerging and has yet to form vibrant ties with society. As van Biezen (2004, 711) notes, "early financial dependence on the state appears to have removed one of the key incentives to establish a more structural relationship with society." In the case of new or emerging parties, state subsidies might not just prevent parties from maintaining ties with civil society but also prevent those ties from becoming established in the first place.

These developments have coincided with a noticeable shift in the public's expectations of political parties from the time they were created (see van Biezen 2004). Parties were initially seen, at best, as voluntary and private institutions that could play a role in public institutions of democracy. Now, parties are seen to be essential to the healthy functioning of a democracy; the parties themselves have become public institutions. While public subsidies to parties have arguably made it more possible for parties to participate in the political life of a country, they have also entrenched the political party as a democratic necessity.

Although much of the literature on the effects of state subventions on party organization has focused on ties between parties and civil society, another concern is the effect of state subventions on the relationship more specifically between local party organizations and the central party. Katz and Mair (2002) note that in the modern era, the party on the ground (the membership and local organization) has generally outlived its usefulness, but persists largely due to "the legacy of the past and the inheritance of earlier models" (127). Further, "the emphasis of maintaining a party on the ground, and, indeed, the sheer existence of a substantial party membership, is therefore most likely to characterize parties which have progressed through a long history of organizational development, in which the legacy of the mass party model continues to weigh upon contemporary conceptions of organizational change and legitimacy" (128). Contrary to Katz and Mair's predictions, and without a legacy of local party organization or strong membership, the Green Party of Canada chose to emphasize building a party on the ground because of ideological beliefs about the value of decentralization and a general sense that building a national party meant building a network of local ones too.

Canada's Changing Party Finance Laws

Before 2004, Canada provided some public financing to political parties through tax credits and reimbursements of election expenses, but in 2004 both of these elements of the party finance regime were enriched. In addition, the 2004 reforms established a quarterly allowance; parties that garnered more than 2 percent of the national vote share (or 5 percent in the ridings the party contested) were eligible for a per-vote subsidy paid quarterly to the national party. The 2004 reforms banned corporate and union donations to the national party and placed a cap on individual donations. The 2006 *Federal Accountability Act*[1] banned all corporate and union donations and further limited the maximum individual donation. The quarterly allowance was designed to compensate parties for this lost income.

The quarterly allowance has been controversial. Cross (2004, 156), for example, was troubled by the amount of subsidy provided to parties in Canada, and noted that "parties are no longer dependent on raising funds from their supporters" and are in danger of becoming "wards of the state." Evaluating the extent to which the reforms have contributed to cartelization has been difficult, however, because of political circumstances that coincided with the 2004 reforms. Successive minority governments and frequent elections have put the parties in a permanent campaign mode. The need for constant campaign readiness has not liberated parties from the need to raise substantial funds from individuals. Young and colleagues (2007) conclude that intense competition between Canada's parties had limited the extent to which they could cartelize, but also noted that the reforms had done little to encourage parties to connect with civil society. Katz (2011) finds some evidence for cartelization in the post-2004 period but argues that Canada is not particularly fertile ground for cartel parties.

More specifically, the Canadian debate over the effect of greater state funding on parties has been shaped in part by concern over its effect on the national/local balance within Canada's political parties. Central to any discussion of this balance is Carty's franchise party model, whereby the local party organization accepts the national party's control over policy and party discipline in return for autonomy in choosing candidates and running the local campaign (Carty 2002; Carty and Cross 2006). Two features of the 2004 financing reforms in particular would seem to affect this national/local balance.

First, the bulk of the new public financing goes to the national party organization, not to the local party. The concern is that this will increase the size and power of the national party as opposed to the local party organization (Carty and Eagles 2005, 178). Coletto and colleagues (2011) find that the period since 2004 has seen a noticeable increase in the relative share of party income raised by the national party relative to the local party. This, they argue, is partly due to the quarterly allowance, but is also partly due to the increased importance of telephone, Internet, and direct mail fundraising, which require the kinds of resources typically available only to national party organizations.

Second, the 2004 reforms increased the financial reporting requirements for all parts of the party organizations, but particularly for the parties' electoral district associations (EDAs), which previously had been essentially unregulated. Just as in the case of local party nominees, EDAs must be certified by the leader, giving the national party a degree of control over the local organization. The national party can ask Elections Canada to deregister an EDA if it no longer enjoys the party's confidence. In addition, parties can be deregistered for failing to comply with the reporting requirements of Elections Canada.

Together, these two features of the 2004 reforms suggest that the national/local balance has been tilted towards the national party. Carty and Eagles (2005, 178) note that although the reforms institutionalize the local party organization, they do so in a way that could compromise their autonomy. Carty (2006, 6) argues that the net effect is something similar to cartelization:

> Parties are being transformed from popular organizations through which active citizens can control the state, into centralized institutions, independent of their supporters and dependent on parliamentarians' willingness to give them access to the state's purse ... [The registration requirement of EDAs] tilts the balance of power within the parties, to the considerable advantage of the leader, and threatens partisans' longstanding autonomy and authority within their own local associations.

The Green Party of Canada as a Case Study

The Green Party of Canada presents an excellent opportunity to study the effects of state subventions on political party growth and development. Although the party has been registered since 1983, most of its growth and development has occurred since 2004. Prior to that year, the party had

FIGURE 10.1
Proportion of political parties' revenue derived from quarterly allowance, 2004-11

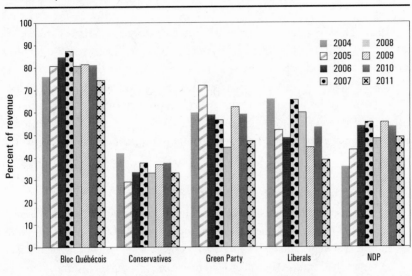

Note: Income includes transfers from loans and other units of the party.

Sources: Calculated from Elections Canada financial data (annual reports for 2004-10, quarterly reports for 2011).

never earned more than 1 percent of the vote in a national election, had never raised more than $100,000 in donations, and had never managed to nominate candidates in more than a third of the country's electoral districts in any federal election.

Former Green Party leader Jim Harris understood the incentives contained in the new party finance legislation and concluded that the party could qualify for the quarterly allowance. Harris determined that the best way to do so was to try to meet the 2-percent national vote threshold rather than the 5-percent threshold in contested districts. To maximize the chances of achieving this threshold, the party sought to nominate candidates in all 308 districts. It garnered 4.3 percent of the national vote in the 2004 election and thus qualified for a quarterly allowance of nearly $1 million per year. The party increased its absolute vote totals in 2006 and 2008, thereby qualifying for an even larger quarterly allowance.

This state funding provided a significant additional source of income for the Green Party. Figure 10.1 shows the proportion of party income (excluding transfers from other entities in the party and the election expenses reimbursement) derived from the quarterly allowance. It demonstrates that the Bloc Québécois is significantly more dependent on the quarterly allowance than the other parties. The Conservatives, meanwhile, are the least dependent. The Liberals, NDP, and Green Party fall between these two extremes.

Although the Green Party appears to be broadly similar to the Liberals and the NDP in the extent to which they are dependent on the quarterly allowance, they differ from the two older parties in one important respect. The latter have more established traditions and patterns of party organization. Unlike these parties, which developed party structures without significant state support, the Green Party's most significant organizational development has occurred in an environment characterized by significant state regulation and subsidy.

Professionalization in the Green Party of Canada

All parties had to adapt to the changes brought about by the influx of public money under the 2004 reforms, but arguably no party has seen as much of a windfall and experienced so much unexpected growth as the Green Party of Canada. The Green Party has benefited proportionately more from the increased state support than any other party in Canada. Its organizational capacity has improved, membership has increased, and fundraising has been promising. Before the 2004 election, its membership was estimated to be below eight hundred, according to a Central Party official of the Green Party.[2] By May 2007, however, this number had ballooned to over 10,000 (Green Party of Canada 2007). Fundraising, too, increased significantly, as illustrated in Figure 10.2.

After the Green Party qualified for the quarterly allowance, it began to organize itself differently. Whereas it had once relied on volunteers to do the bulk of the administrative work in their basements,[3] the party now began hiring numerous staff to work in a central Ottawa office. It invested in computers and a larger office space, and hired its first executive director. The Federal Council, a board that is ultimately responsible for the party, went from being a working board to being a governance board, which reduced the volunteer hours of council members from fifty hours a month to five.[4] The party hired provincial organizers to recruit candidates and to help form EDAs. It also began paying its national leader so that the position became a full-time one.[5] The money from state subventions enabled the party to borrow money for election campaigning and to repay these loans within eighteen months of the election. Whereas the party had always focused its media efforts on trying to get attention, the tables were turned in 2006

FIGURE 10.2
Individual fundraising by the Green Party of Canada, 1995-2011
(constant 2011 dollars)

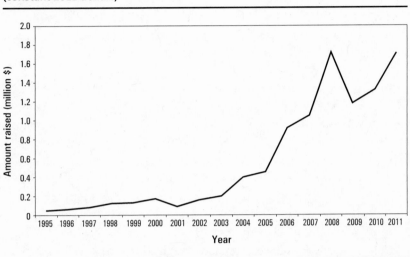

Sources: Calculated from Elections Canada financial data (annual reports for 2004-10, quarterly reports for 2011).

when it had to hire people to respond to the many interview requests from the media. The party's organization was centralized and professionalized in the Ottawa office and staff.

Professionalization in the Green Party was therefore fast-tracked as a result of state subventions. What has typically taken place over many years in other parties took place in a year within the Green Party. The pace of change put a great strain on the internal resources of the party. This was evident for most of 2005, when a series of crises nearly led to its implosion.[6] The crises were all within the Federal Council and involved the hiring and firing of staff and the firing of volunteer council members. At the heart of much of the crisis that year, though, was the party's rapid professionalization and centralization. "Professionalization loses the grassroots, but a lot of members want the professionalizing," noted one senior party member.[7] Another recalled that older members were sometimes suspicious of staff: "There was a minority of old Greenies who called for the entire staff to be fired and replaced by volunteers as they would not have the hidden agendas of staff members."[8] Many of those who were suspicious of staff agendas left the party between 2004 and 2006. Eventually, in 2006, the party's internal affairs were calmed and the party was able to elect a new leader and gain unprecedented public attention. In August 2006, it successfully held its largest-ever convention, with over 400 delegates, at the Congress Centre in Ottawa. "We had no green outtakes at the meeting," explained a relieved senior party organizer after the event.[9] The party's professionalization had become the norm and few of the members could remember the party any other way.

Centralization in the Green Party

While the evidence for professionalization is unambiguous, the same cannot be said of the centralization of party organization since 2004. Although there may be certain organizational and bureaucratic imperatives driving the party towards centralization, decentralization is a central principle of Green ideology (Green Party of Canada 2006, 21). Greens see decentralization as one of the main ways to organize in a community. One of the forms decentralization has taken in the Green Party is the building of the local party apparatus.

This commitment to decentralization coincided with a desire to build a large membership. Consistent with the franchise party model, the locus for this membership activity and organization would be the party's constituency associations (or electoral district associations – EDAs). In the words of one Green activist, "If you don't have a strong membership you won't win. Fifty people in an EDA is ridiculous. We need a thousand in an EDA and 250,000 across the country."[10]

Before 2004, the Green Party had EDAs in nearly a third of the ridings in Canada. Given that the party membership before 2004 was less than eight hundred, this is a remarkable feat, but the fact that a small membership base was spread out over so many associations raises questions regarding the vitality of the pre-2004 local organizations. Shortly after qualifying for the quarterly allowance, the party identified the creation of EDAs as an important priority, describing them as "the building blocks" of the party: "We want to build EDAs and we want to share the national database of supporters with those EDAs," David Scrymgeour, organizational consultant to the Green Party for the 2006 election, said at a workshop on voter identification and getting out the vote on 25 August 2006. Critical to achieving this was a revenue-sharing agreement adopted by the party in 2005.

During the run-up to the 2004 election, Green Party leader Jim Harris travelled the country asking EDAs to help the party reach the 2 percent vote share threshold needed to secure quarterly state subventions. His request came with a promise: help the party reach 2 percent and we will share the state subvention with the EDAs. It was an easy promise to make, but a tougher one to keep when the party did finally secure funding. The EDAs had been given a promise, however, and many of the original members of the party held strongly to the notion of decentralization.

Nevertheless, some party elites were opposed to the idea of spreading out the state subvention to hundreds of EDAs. Their fear was that this would weaken the party's ability to develop and run professionalized media-intensive campaigns. In order to resolve the issue, a committee was struck at the 2004 annual general meeting held at Bragg Creek, Alberta. The committee, chaired by political scientist and long-time Green Andy Shadrack, was charged with reviewing all the possible revenue-sharing suggestions and recommending one for a vote by the membership. The committee eventually recommended a revenue-sharing agreement (RSA) that divided the quarterly allowance between the central office, provincial divisions, and EDAs. Most of those opposed to the RSA pointed to the practical benefits of having a strong, well-funded Central Party (Manley 2005), whereas those in favour of the RSA appreciated that it was developed "with the core values of the Green Party in mind" (White 2005, 1). The RSA was narrowly accepted in a vote by eligible members – those who resided in a riding with an established EDA – in August 2005.[11]

In effect, the RSA was designed to decentralize the party. One member noted with some delight that the Greens were "doing the exact opposite of the spirit of the legislation. C-24 was meant to centralize parties and here we are using it to further decentralize ours."[12] The RSA decentralized the money that was to come from the state subvention because just one-third of the money was to remain with the central office.

The controversy over the RSA raised many issues. Those in favour of the agreement saw it as a way of developing EDAs because the formula for the money that flowed to associations was determined on the basis of (1) a flat rate for any registered association, (2) vote share in the riding during the last election, and (3) the last quarter's local membership. The RSA formula appeared to provide an incentive for associations to build membership and maximize the vote. One Green Party member noted that it was the local organizations and local organizers that had enabled the party to meet the threshold for funding in 2004, so the local organizations should be rewarded for their organizational depth and breadth:

People who want the (C-24) money in central office fundamentally mis-understand something. Who helped raise this money we got from the government anyhow? Central party did a bit but the people who organized the campaign here were the ones that got out the votes. It was the EDAs that did the groundwork for the money ... they deserve a portion of it. The agreement also provides two incentives to EDAs. One is to be organized and the other is to be developing membership.[13]

For those opposed to the RSA, the idea of sharing money meant for central parties was simply counterproductive. They argued that giving money to an EDA was a handout that would "remove the imperative for EDAs to fundraise" (Manley 2005, 2). One official who opposed the RSA did not oppose the sharing of other revenue sources: "It would be healthier for the organization if the Revenue Sharing was for fundraising. In other words if we raise a buck in your EDA we'll send you a quarter. Instead we went with Revenue Sharing on C-24 money."[14]

The RSA is one of the ways in which the Green Party has deviated from the path of creeping centralization. The party centralized substantially between 2003 and 2005, when there were few resources in EDAs and the Central Party was responsible for most operations. Once the RSA was in place, however, the party's tendency to centralize decelerated. The money sent to EDAs was relatively meagre. In December 2005, the Green Party issued a press release when it sent the first quarterly cheques to EDAs. The release announced that $70,175.54 had been transferred to 118 registered EDAs and three Provincial Divisions (PD). On average, each association received $386.29; the exact amounts were based on a formula that rewarded EDAs for membership and fundraising success. Over the course of the year, this amounted to around $1,500 for each association. Kate Storey, former national party chair and current chief executive officer of an EDA, argued that the amount, though small, was nevertheless significant:

The dollar amount per EDA is small but it does help new EDAs get started. It also provides incentive for those EDAs to establish proper financial procedures so that they can receive the share. However, once an EDA has established its own fundraising program, it can easily raise its own revenue, outgrowing its dependence on the RSA. The RSA creates a large amount of paperwork and uses significant staff time. The organizational benefit would occur with or without the RSA because it is in any political party's national interest to build EDAs. With or without the RSA, the National office of a growing party would invest money into the creation of EDAs to expand its base.[15]

FIGURE 10.3
Registered Green Party electoral district associations (EDAs),
January 2004 to December 2011

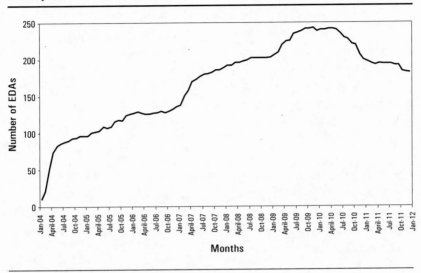

Sources: Calculated from Elections Canada financial data.

Assessing the extent to which the Green Party has been successful in establishing EDAs across Canada is difficult. One crude indication of this is the absolute number of registered EDAs nationwide. Figure 10.3 demonstrates a steady increase in the number of EDAs between the June 2004 election and late 2009. The number has peaked, however, and has declined significantly in the last year. Many of the previously established EDAs have proven to be unsustainable and cannot meet the reporting requirements of Elections Canada, leading to deregistration.

Further evidence that the Green Party has had difficulty in sustaining EDAs can be seen in the number of EDA deregistrations it has experienced compared with the other major parties. Between January 2004 and December 2011, the Greens have had three times as many EDA deregistrations (100) as all of the other major parties combined (34) (Elections Canada).

The RSA itself may have contributed to the decline in the number of EDAs. The establishment of an EDA means less money for the national party office; consequently, there is no financial incentive for the national party to establish EDAs and a direct financial reward for deregistering one. One party official observed this phenomenon:

I sometimes wonder if the presence of the RSA isn't acting as a detriment to the formation of new EDAs in locations around the country where there are presently none. Our party hasn't aggressively pursued local organizing as a priority in the last couple of years (certainly not since I joined the Party in 2007), and has instead relied on organic organizational practices, which often would benefit from Central Party guidance. Could it be that the Central Party is reluctant to create too many EDAs, given that this would lead to more money leaving Central Party coffers? Given our recent budgetary deficit, it's possible that this was at least in the back of our Federal Council's minds when organizational staff were let go this past January.[16]

Perversely, the glee of some Green Party members in creating structures that appeared to contradict the centralizing tendencies of the quarterly allowance may have been premature; that very program may reduce the incentive for the national party to encourage the growth of local party organizations.

Another criticism of the RSA is that it weakened EDAs by reducing incentives for them to engage in their own fundraising activities. Fundraising is a crucial function of Canadian constituency associations (Carty 1991, 60). One member of the Green Party Federal Council who also sat on an association executive explained that the RSA money to EDAs played an important role: "You can see the money rolling in quarterly for really not doing anything, so that means that there is money sitting there to be had, to be used at election time without having to sort of divert ourselves to fundraising."[17] A CEO of another EDA agreed with this assessment: "Sometimes knowing that the money is going to be available through the RSA means that an EDA is less likely to engage in fundraising activities locally. That's been my experience with my EDA, and I suspect others have experienced this outcome as well. Learning how to raise money, and getting in the habit of doing so, is somewhat compromised by the RSA."[18]

There is evidence to support the conclusion that local Green Party fundraising has not kept pace with the fundraising done by the national party and that the growth in the size of transfers to the local level has not corresponded with an increase in local fundraising. Following the work of Coletto and colleagues (2011), Table 10.1 compares a number of measures of the centralization of party income for the Green Party with corresponding figures for the other national parties. The first column reports the ratios of

TABLE 10.1

Income centralization in the Green Party of Canada compared with other parties

	Fundraising national/local ratio	Total income national/local ratio	Transfers down as % of total raised locally
Green Party, 2004	0.61	1.53	9
Green Party, 2005	2.00	7.20	−5
Green Party, 2006	1.40	3.42	35
Green Party, 2007	2.56	5.88	60
Green Party, 2008	1.53	2.75	78
Green Party, 2009	3.57	9.48	138
Green Party, 2010	4.20	10.31	222
Conservative Party, 2004-07	1.29	2.55	31
Liberal Party, 2004-07	0.88	2.25	23
New Democratic Party, 2004-07	1.20	2.76	49
Bloc Québécois, 2004-07	0.64	4.23	80

Sources: Calculated from Elections Canada data for Green Party; Coletto et al. (2011) for other parties.

the value of donations from individual donors to the national party versus the local party (EDAs and candidates). The Green Party is considerably more centralized than the other parties when it comes to "private" income. The second column reports that same ratio, but includes the quarterly allowance as revenue for the national party. As with all parties and as predicted by political scientists, the quarterly allowance has exacerbated the bias in favour of the national party, particularly in non-election years, when candidates do not do fundraising. Finally, and most relevant for the Green Party, is the third column. Compared with the income they raise on their own, the local entities of the party are heavily dependent on transfers for revenue. In 2010, EDAs received twice as much money in transfers from the national party as they raised through their own efforts. The fact that this proportion has increased every year since the adoption of the revenue-sharing agreement suggests that the RSA has done little to increase the financial independence of the local party organizations.

A third concern is that this financial dependence increases the ability of the national party to impose conditions on local party organization, compromising their autonomy. One Federal Council member expressed it this way: "I find Central has a tendency to use it (the RSA money) too much as a tool of power and influence rather than a tool to grow the party ... we just passed the second attempt to use it as a leverage point, 'you shall do what we tell you or else we won't give you your money.'"[19]

Given its ambiguous results, it is not surprising that the RSA has recently undergone some changes. In August 2010, the Green Party's biennial general meeting passed changes to the RSA that would see more money stay within the control of the Central Party but be designated for organizing and building EDAs. The changes to the RSA grew from two main concerns. One was that the presence of the RSA money in small EDAs sometimes had the effect of limiting local fundraising efforts. The second issue was that the Central Party was broke and had to suspend the RSA payments to EDAs in the first quarter of 2010 in order to pay back election loans from 2008. A party official worried that the RSA "leaves the National level with too little money to get anything done ... I have to wonder if it has given some EDAs more power before they were ready, i.e., organized."[20]

To some extent the debate over revenue sharing pits those Greens with an ideological commitment to decentralization against those who could be considered to have an "electoral-professional" orientation. The RSA appeared to be a triumph for the former group, but the extension of small amounts of funding to the local party may have inhibited the development of a vibrant local party organization in some areas. The RSA provided small amounts of money to all EDAs – no matter how vibrant – even if it was not enough to deliver real party organization, fundraising capacity, or volunteers for election campaigns. It appears that this was too little money provided to local organizations at too early a stage in their development, reducing the need for these local organizations to develop membership and volunteers.

Ultimately, the 2011 national election determined the fate of the revenue-sharing agreement. On the one hand, the election was a success for the party in that it achieved a crucial milestone in its evolution, electing leader Elizabeth May to the House of Commons. At the same time, the party's overall vote share dropped, leading to a decrease in public funding in the short term. The Conservative government's subsequent move to phase out the quarterly allowance before the next federal election will decrease the total amount of money available to the national party. It will also mark the end of the formal revenue-sharing agreement within the party, since there will no longer be a quarterly allowance to be shared. Local party organizations will be forced to raise money for their own activities, and the party will likely financially prioritize transfers only to those districts that will pay off electorally. Arguably, this move was already occurring with the party's emphasis on transferring money to Saanich–Gulf Islands, the district represented by May. This significant change will likely accelerate the trend towards a more organic development of local party organization within the Green Party of Canada.

Conclusion

The Green Party of Canada now appears to be a permanent fixture in the Canadian political scene. We have demonstrated how the possibility of public funding spurred the Greens to organize in the constituencies in order to gain access to state funds and, once these funds had been secured, to professionalize their organization. The result has been a more professional and more competitive Green Party. As a result, we suggest that state subvention in Canada has been the key source of a significant alteration to Canada's party system following the 2004 national election.

The case of the Green Party also shows that state subvention creates considerable pressure for parties to professionalize and to centralize. As we have seen, the influx of massive amounts of public money (at least by Green Party standards) has led the party to professionalize its operations. Paid staff now do what volunteers and party members previously did. A certain degree of professionalization was inevitable as the party became more and more successful electorally, but public funding has hastened the movement in this direction.

The record on the centralizing tendencies of the quarterly subsidy is far more complex. Although the Green Party was particularly well placed to develop along centralized lines, it initially chose to endorse a policy of sharing the quarterly money among the three constituent parts of the party. This was motivated both by Green ideals of decentralization and by the conviction that the mass party was a desirable organizational model. The party's revenue-sharing agreement was meant to build a mass organization through the sharing of seed money from the quarterly state subvention, but the infusion of small amounts of money into nascent electoral district associations did not necessarily make them stronger. As a result, deregistration of EDAs is much higher in the Green Party of Canada than in all the other major parties combined, and income centralization is also higher than in the other parties. There is little evidence to suggest that the party has succeeded in building vibrant organizations at the local level.

More broadly, the case of the Green Party of Canada confirms Katz and Mair's point (2002) about the important historical legacy of earlier forms of party development in the evolution of parties. The mass party model of organization developed as a way of financing parties through subscriptions and required a broad membership to maintain itself. The new environment of public financing may render such a party model obsolete. Furthermore, it appears to be very difficult to re-create from the top down what emerged organically in the more established Canadian parties: a system of local party organizations. The Green Party's attempt to develop local party organizations by providing seed money for this purpose has not been effective. An attempt to jump-start an organizational process by providing small amounts of funding met with limited success and suggests that strong local party organizations are more than just a healthy bank account. The Green Party may find, instead, that providing training and support to a few key individuals would be more productive than providing them with money.

Acknowledgments
The authors gratefully acknowledge the research assistance of Ashley Haughton and the helpful advice of Royce Koop, Leslie Seidle, Munroe Eagles, and Melanee Thomas on earlier versions of this chapter.

Notes
1 *Federal Accountability Act,* S.C. 2006, c. 9.
2 Anonymous interview, 13 April 2006.
3 Anonymous interview with former Central Party official, 10 April 2006.
4 Ibid., 11 April 2006.
5 Throughout the 2004 election, former leader Jim Harris maintained his full-time work as a consultant on top of his unpaid work as leader of the Green Party.
6 Anonymous interview with Central Party official, 11 April 2006.
7 Anonymous interview, 10 April 2006.
8 Anonymous interview with Central Party official, 11 April 2006.
9 Anonymous interview, 12 September 2006.
10 Anonymous interview with an EDA president, 26 October 2005.
11 Party rules required that the vote be 60 percent in favour to pass. The RSA received 61 percent.
12 Anonymous interview with Central Party official, 12 September 2006.
13 Anonymous interview with an EDA official, 7 October 2006.
14 Anonymous interview with Central Party official, 13 April 2006.
15 Interview with Kate Storey, former Green Party of Canada chair, 4 October 2010.
16 Anonymous interview with an EDA official, 7 October 2010.
17 Interview with Susan Stratton, Alberta Representative to the Green Party of Canada Federal Council, 8 October 2010.
18 Anonymous interview with an EDA official, 7 October 2010.

19 Interview with Mark Taylor, Saskatchewan Representative to the Green Party Federal Council, 11 October 2010.
20 Anonymous interview with Central Party official, 6 October 2010.

References

Carty, R. Kenneth. 1991. *Canadian Political Parties in the Constituencies.* Toronto: Dundurn Press.

–. 2002. "The Politics of Tecumseh Corners: Canadian Political Parties as Franchise Organizations." *Canadian Journal of Political Science* 35: 723-45.

–. 2006. "The Shifting Place of Political Parties in Canadian Public Life." *IRPP Choices* 12 (4): 3-13.

Carty, R. Kenneth, and William Cross. 2006. "Can Stratarchically Organized Parties Be Democratic? The Canadian Case." *Journal of Elections, Public Opinion and Parties* 16: 93-114.

Carty, R. Kenneth, and Munroe Eagles. 2005. *Politics Is Local: National Politics at the Grassroots.* Toronto: Oxford University Press.

Coletto, David, Harold J. Jansen, and Lisa Young. 2011. "Stratarchical Party Organization and Party Finance in Canada." *Canadian Journal of Political Science* 44: 111-36.

Cross, William. 2004. *Political Parties.* Vancouver: UBC Press.

Fisher, Justin. 2011. "State Funding of Political Parties: Truths, Myths and Legends." In *Money, Politics and Democracy: Canada's Party Finance Reform,* edited by Lisa Young and Harold J. Jansen, 19-36. Vancouver: UBC Press.

Fox, Graham. 2005. *Rethinking Political Parties.* Ottawa: Public Policy Forum, and Crossing Boundaries National Council. http://www.ppforum.ca/.

Green Party of Canada. 2006. "Election Platform 2006." http://web.greenparty.ca/.

–. 2007. Newsletter – May. http://www.greenparty.ca/.

Jenson, Jane. 1991. "Innovation and Equity: The Impact of Public Funding." In *Comparative Issues in Party and Election Finance,* edited by F. Leslie Seidle, 111-77. Toronto: Dundurn Press.

Katz, Richard S. 2011. "Finance Reform and the Cartel Party Model in Canada." In *Money, Politics and Democracy: Canada's Party Finance Reform,* edited by Lisa Young and Harold J. Jansen, 60-81. Vancouver: UBC Press.

Katz, Richard S., and Peter Mair. 1995. "Changing Models of Party Organization and Party Democracy." *Party Politics* 1: 5-28.

–. 1996. "Cadre, Catch-All or Cartel? A Rejoinder." *Party Politics* 2 (4): 525-34.

–. 2002. "The Ascendancy of the Party on Politics: Party Organizational Change in Twentieth-Century Democracies." In *Political Parties: Old Concepts and New Challenges,* edited by Richard Gunther, Jose Ramaon-Montero, and Juan J. Linz, 113-35. New York: Oxford University Press.

Manley, Tom. 2005. "Revenue Sharing Disagree." Letter to Green Party members.

Nassmacher, Karl-Heinz. 1993. "Comparing Party and Campaign Finance in Western Democracies." In *Campaign and Party Finance in North America and*

Western Europe, edited by Arthur B. Gunlicks, 233-67. Boulder, CO: Westview Press.

–. 2006. "Regulation of Party Finance." In *Handbook of Party Politics,* edited by Richard S. Katz and William Crotty, 446-55. London: Sage.

Pierre, Jon, Lars Svåsand, and Anders Widfeldt. 2000. "State Subsidies to Political Parties: Confronting Rhetoric with Reality." *West European Politics* 23: 1-24.

van Biezen, Ingrid. 2004. "Political Parties as Public Utilities." *Party Politics* 10 (6): 701-22.

Webb, Paul, and Robin Kolodny. 2006. "Professional Staff in Political Parties." In *Handbook of Party Politics,* edited by Richard S. Katz and William Crotty, 337-47. London: Sage.

White, Gareth McNeil. 2005. "Revenue Sharing Agree." Letter to Green Party members.

Williams, Robert. 2000. "Aspects of Party Finance and Political Corruption." In *Party Finance and Political Corruption,* edited by Robert Williams, 1-14. Houndsmills, UK: Macmillan.

Young, Lisa. 1998. "Party, State and Political Competition in Canada: The Cartel Model Reconsidered." *Canadian Journal of Political Science* 31 (2): 339-58.

Young, Lisa, Anthony Sayers, and Harold Jansen. 2007. "Altering the Political Landscape: State Funding and Party Finance." In *Canadian Parties in Transition,* 3rd ed., edited by Alain-G. Gagnon and A. Brian Tanguay, 335-54. Peterborough, ON: Broadview Press.

11

When Partisans Are Attacked

Motivated Reasoning and the New
Party System

J. SCOTT MATTHEWS

It is not always easy to be a partisan, that is, to sustain the affective commitment involved in party identification. In a competitive democracy, holding fast to one's partisan convictions necessarily implies exposing oneself to the threat of disagreement – with opposition partisans and with those who reject partisan attachment altogether. Canadian political history, for example, abounds with moments of intense partisan disagreement. Indeed, in his early study of Canadian politics, André Siegfried remarked that "there can be few countries in the world in which elections arouse more fury and enthusiasm than in Canada" (1906, quoted in Carty 2006, 7). The ensuing history of party politics would supply countless examples to support Siegfried's early conjecture. A fractious debate over conscription during the First World War would ultimately lead the Liberals, in 1925, to assert that the election of a Conservative government would lead to the outbreak of war (Cairns 1968, 65). In 1988, Liberal leader John Turner asserted that the Tory prime minister, Brian Mulroney, had "sold us out" in his pursuit of a Canada-US free trade agreement (Johnston et al. 1992, 27). Recent national elections have featured some of the most heated partisan rhetoric in memory: from the Liberals in 2006, a suggestion that the Conservatives harboured (presumably nefarious) plans to increase the presence of the military in Canadian cities (Rose 2006); and, from the Conservatives in 2008, the assertion that Liberal leader Stéphane Dion was, in fact, "not a leader" and "not worth the risk" (McLean 2008). The Liberals' major narrative in the 2011 election – that the Conservatives had abused the country's democratic institutions – was easily as aggressively partisan as any in memory (Norquay 2011).

This sort of intense partisan disagreement is not costless. Such disagreement may engender political withdrawal and a cynical orientation towards government and politicians on the part of citizens (cf. Ansolabehere and Iyengar 1997; Mutz and Reeves 2005). Yet the hidden and largely unrecognized cost of disagreement over partisan matters is the potential threat to the partisan's self-concept: *if you disagree with me, then what does this say about me as a person?*

The focus of this chapter is an examination of partisan responses to "attacks" on the competence and integrity of the parties with which they identify. An attack, in this sense, is simply a message with obvious and intensely negative evaluative implications with respect to some object. For the purposes of this research, therefore, the focus is on "partisan attacks" – *messages that imply obvious and strongly negative evaluations of political parties.*

The systematic study of partisans' responses to partisan attacks offers two principal benefits to scholars of Canadian politics. First, a focus on such responses advances our understanding of partisanship as a feature of political cognition. Indeed, as this chapter will argue, such attacks provide a unique opportunity to adjudicate between contending views of partisan political cognition. In particular, the analysis supplies new evidence with regard to the role of political knowledge in sustaining partisan divisions. This has been an important theme in recent work on partisan effects on political attitudes and perception (Blais et al. 2010; Gaines et al. 2007). This chapter builds on this work by uncovering support for a specific interpretation of the relationship between knowledge and partisan political cognition: the theory of motivated political reasoning (Taber and Lodge 2006). In the process, the analysis raises questions about the dominant model of "polarization effects" in political science, John Zaller's RAS model (1992).

Second, analysis of responses to partisan attacks offers a revealing view of the nature of Canadian partisanship. In an important sense, responses to partisan attacks represent the "high-water mark" of partisan cognition, compared with partisan responses to other political objects (such as issues) that have more equivocal partisan implications. Moreover, the data analyzed here – the 2004, 2006, and 2008 Canadian Election Study (CES) datasets – cover a critical time of change in the party system, which permits an investigation of the party system's impact on partisanship. As others have noted (see Chapters 3 and 6 in this volume), Canadian electoral politics have, among other things, become more adversarial in recent years in the wake of the merger of two right-of-centre parties and a string of minority governments. Has the nature of Canadian partisan cognition registered the effects of these political developments? This chapter theorizes the possibilities and evaluates the evidence.

At the most general level, the chapter speaks to continuities in the nature of Canadian partisanship, in spite of the paroxysms of the party system in recent years. The influence of partisan identities on political perceptions and attitudes is robust; that is, Canada remains "a party country" (Carty et al. 2000, 14), especially in the minds of its partisans.

Partisan Cognition: The Motivated Reasoning Account

That partisan commitment shapes responses to political messages, such as partisan attacks, is a long-standing claim in political science (see Berelson et al. 1954; Lazarsfeld et al. 1948). The view of Campbell and colleagues on the centrality of partisanship in perceptual and evaluative processes is neatly summarized in their famous assertion that party identification "raises a perceptual screen through which the individual tends to see what is favorable to his [sic] partisan orientation" (1960, 133). Although the conclusions of the "Michigan School" have been challenged from time to time (e.g., Bullock 2009; Gerber and Green 1999), theirs remains the standing view of partisanship's role in political cognition (Bartels 2002; Gerber et al. 2010). In this regard, critical evidence has lately been supplied by scholarship informed by the late social psychologist Ziva Kunda's theory of motivated reasoning (1990). The theory stands out as a distillation of the distinctive implications of psychological models that assume biased, as opposed to rational or "even-handed," processing of information.

The core of the motivated reasoning theory is, naturally, the assumption that all perception is subject to motivation. In other words, the theory holds that, in forming representations of the external world, social perceivers seek to satisfy various goals, albeit to different degrees across individuals and situations. The first important goal is to perceive the world accurately, at least to an approximation, given finite cognitive resources (Kunda 1990, 481). In addition to accuracy goals, however, the motivated reasoner is also influenced by "directional goals," or preferences for particular perceptual outcomes, regardless of the accuracy of such conclusions. Importantly, the theory is fairly open-ended as to the content of such directional goals.

Indeed, Kunda (1990) notes diverse sources of directional goals, such as self-esteem needs, a desire to sustain positive expectations with regard to one's performance in a given domain, and the desire to avoid cognitive dissonance. Whatever their source, the upshot is that preferences over the direction of a given conclusion condition relevant reasoning processes and, ultimately, the conclusion at which one arrives.

It is the emphasis on "process" that distinguishes motivated reasoning theory from prior approaches to biased perception, such as Festinger's theory of cognitive dissonance (1957). Kunda (1990) suggests that decisive evidence for the role of motivation in social perception is to be found *not* in the nature of beliefs and attitudes but in the nature of the *cognitive operations the social perceiver undertakes* in the course of forming beliefs and attitudes. The motivated reasoner, in this view, relies on a "biased set of cognitive processes: strategies for accessing, constructing and evaluating beliefs" (Kunda 1990, 480). At the same time, however, Kunda suggests important limits on the magnitude of such processing biases: "People motivated to arrive at a particular conclusion attempt to be rational and to construct a justification of their desired conclusion that would persuade a dispassionate observer. They draw the desired conclusion *only if they can muster up the evidence necessary to support it*" (Kunda 1990, 482-83, emphasis added).

The need to "muster up evidence" in support of desired conclusions highlights the role of effortful cognitive processes in Kunda's account of biased perception. One can imagine, for instance, an account of biased perception whereby information that challenges one's directional goals is simply ignored (e.g., Zaller 1992; see discussion below). Obviously, this sort of "bullheaded" approach to realizing preferred conclusions would not leave the residues of biased memory retrieval and belief construction that are characteristically highlighted as evidence for the motivated reasoning theory. The focus on the need to "muster up evidence" for favoured conclusions also points to the importance of domain-relevant knowledge in motivated reasoning processes. The ability to "persuade a dispassionate observer" that one's justification for her preferred conclusion is sound clearly may depend on one's available store of relevant information and argumentation.

Evidence of motivated reasoning in political settings is robust (Gaines et al. 2007; Lau and Redlawsk 2006; Lodge and Taber 2000; Redlawsk 2002; Redlawsk et al. 2010; Rudolph 2006; Taber and Lodge 2006; Taber et al. 2009). Indeed, in their influential account of "motivated political reasoning," Taber and Lodge argue that politics is a highly likely domain in which to observe processes of motivated reasoning, reflecting the fact that, as a sphere of social perception, the political world is peculiarly "affectively-charged" (2006, 756). Following Kunda (1990), Taber and Lodge suggest that in addition to accuracy goals, individuals are motivated by "partisan goals" – that is, a desire to "apply their reasoning power in defense of a prior, specific conclusion" (2006, 756). With regard to mechanisms of biased processing, these scholars emphasize asymmetrical treatment of pro- and counter-attitudinal arguments and information. In particular, whereas pro-attitudinal messages are more or less accepted uncritically, counter-attitudinal information is likely to be subject to vigorous scrutiny and to lead to the generation of counter-arguments (757). Further, given the chance, Taber and Lodge (2006) suggest, individuals will "seek out" pro-attitudinal information.

The role of domain-relevant (i.e., political) knowledge and attitude strength in conditioning motivated political reasoning is also highlighted by Taber and Lodge (2006). The "politically knowledgeable," they write, "because they possess greater ammunition with which to counterargue in-congruent facts, figures, and arguments, will be more susceptible to motiv-ated bias than will unsophisticates" (757). Likewise, strength of pre-existing judgments will index individuals' motivation to make the "effort" to engage in selective counter-arguing, information seeking, and the other cognitive operations that underwrite perceptual bias (757).

Canadian research on motivated political reasoning is fledgling at best, a conclusion that applies generally to work on partisan effects in political judgment in Canada (Merolla et al. 2008, 674).[1] Blais and colleagues' recent study (2010) of Canadian reactions to the "sponsorship scandal," which en-gulfed national politics and featured prominently in the federal elections of 2004 and 2006,[2] constitutes the sole Canada-focused evaluation of the theory of motivated political reasoning. Notably, the findings of Blais and colleagues contradict motivated reasoning theory's expectations, particu-larly regarding the role of domain-relevant knowledge, which they find to be insignificant. That said, while the study is trailblazing for Canadian stu-dents of partisanship, there are reasons to suspect that its conclusions are limited in their generalizability. As Blais and colleagues note, the proceed-ings of the commission of inquiry with regard to the scandal were "intense-ly covered by the media" in 2004-05 and "produced startling testimonies that left no doubt that there had been corruption" (2010, 4). Further, cover-age of the 2004 and 2006 election campaigns was mostly dominated by scandal-related issues of government accountability and corruption (Andrew

et al. 2006; Goodyear-Grant et al. 2004). Consequently, partisans' capacity
to "muster up evidence" (per Kunda 1990) to support their desired conclusions about the affair may have been constrained by an atypically intense
informational environment: besides being plentiful, information was both
relatively credible (i.e., dignified by an official public inquiry) and relatively
engaging (i.e., featured "startling testimonies").[3] In keeping with this logic,
the impact of the issue – at least in the 2004 election – was simply massive
at the level of the individual voter, and views on the sponsorship scandal
were "clearly a major factor in helping the Conservatives deny the Liberals
another majority" (Gidengil et al. 2006, 15). The informational context of
the sponsorship affair also clarifies the non-impact of political knowledge
on the relationship between party identification and judgments relevant to
the scandal; that is, given the intense media attention concerning the affair,
its partisan implications were likely apparent to even the least knowledgeable identifiers.[4]

Partisan Cognition When Partisans Are "Under Attack": Diverging Predictions

For the most part, evidence in favour of motivated reasoning – in politics
and in psychology generally – is experimental (e.g., Lau and Redlawsk 2001,
2006; Taber and Lodge 2006). This approach has obvious virtues with regard to measurement and internal validity. The trade-off, of course, is
external validity. An alternative, survey-based approach relies on motivated reasoning theory's prediction that biased memory retrieval and belief
construction processes are conditioned by domain-relevant knowledge
(e.g., Blais et al. 2010; Gaines et al. 2007). The implication is that, given certain informational and motivational assumptions (on this point, see discussion below), partisan effects on political perceptions will increase with
political knowledge, all other things being equal.

An obvious problem with this approach, however, is that motivated political reasoning theory is not alone in anticipating knowledge-partisanship
interactions with respect to political perceptions. Indeed, much simpler
processes, such as cue taking, are compatible with this expectation. In particular, the most prominent alternative[5] to the motivated reasoning account
of partisan perception, Zaller's "receive-accept-sample" (RAS) model (1992),
also implies that partisan differences in political perception should generally increase with political knowledge – subject to the constraint that
the "contextual information" required to connect partisanship to relevant
messages is sufficiently "obscure" (see note 4; see also Berinsky 2007). The

logic is expressed in the second major premise of the RAS model, the "resistance axiom" (Zaller 1992, 44).

Unlike motivated reasoning, however, the RAS model rests on passive acceptance and rejection of messages in light of partisan cues, rather than on biased evaluation of arguments or active generation of counter-arguments. As Zaller explains, "this postulate [i.e., the "resistance axiom"] makes no allowance for citizens to think, reason or deliberate about politics: If citizens are well informed, they react mechanically to political ideas on the basis of external cues about their partisan implications, and if they are too poorly informed to be aware of these cues, they tend to uncritically accept whatever ideas they encounter" (1992, 45). Importantly, this "mechanical" or "bull-headed" interpretation of political cognition implies a critical divergence across the predictions of the RAS and motivated reasoning theories: *in those settings where awareness of partisan cues is uniform, the theory of motivated reasoning predicts an interaction with political knowledge – as the knowledgeable are better able to generate pro-attitudinal arguments – while the RAS model does not.*

It is in the evaluation of the above prediction that responses to partisan attacks – messages that imply obvious and strongly negative evaluations of political parties – are uniquely useful. Decoding the partisan implications of such messages does not require significant political knowledge. Indeed, if the message is received, then so should be its partisan implications. Consider, for example, the following partisan attacks:

The Conservative Party is a threat to Canada's social programs.
The Liberal Party's Green Shift would really hurt the Canadian economy.
The only reason the Liberals are cutting taxes is to buy votes.
An NDP government would really hurt the Canadian economy.
The NDP is out of touch with the times.

Arguably, for the typical Canadian, the partisan implications of these messages should be very clear. The party that is "a threat" to valued entitlements, for example, is clearly not the best party with which to identify oneself. Accordingly, the partisans of that party implicated in a given attack should find it easy to recognize the cues and reject such messages; that is, recognition should not be conditional on prior political knowledge. Likewise, other partisans – those whose party is not targeted in a given attack – should be much more likely to passively accept the message, regardless of one's pre-existing store of political knowledge.

Therefore, if the RAS model fully describes the psychological under-pinnings of partisan bias in political perception, then political knowledge *should not* condition the relationship between party identification and responses to partisan attacks. If, on the other hand, motivated reasoning processes are operating instead of, or even alongside, the more mechanical RAS dynamics, then political knowledge *should* condition partisans' reactions to rhetorical attacks on parties. Assuming that the latter proposition holds yields the following hypothesis:

> H1. The magnitude of partisan effects on responses to partisan attacks increases with political knowledge.

Motivated Political Reasoning across the Party System

While H1 should generally hold, two assumptions implicit in the account of motivated political reasoning developed above bear noting. Importantly, the assumptions imply that features of the party system may condition motivated reasoning processes regarding partisan attacks.

The first assumption is that information conducive to biased evaluation of arguments or generation of counter-arguments in response to partisan attacks is relatively scarce. Clearly, this assumption may be violated under certain conditions – for instance, when the attack involves a particularly salient aspect of party conflict. Under these conditions, "evidence" supporting motivated reasoning processes may be relatively easy to "muster up," making political knowledge a less discriminating variable.[6]

The second assumption is that, strength of partisanship aside, partisans are uniformly motivated to "bolster" (Taber and Lodge 2006) partisan attacks directed at other parties. In a two-party system (such as in the United States), this assumption should generally hold; in a multi-party system with plurality elections and highly variable electoral geography – that is, in Canada – the assumption seems problematic. The latter combination of circumstances implies, in general, important variation in the intensity of interparty conflict, as reflected in competitive conditions (Johnston 2008). Consequently, the degree to which positive evaluations of one party logically imply negative outcomes for another (and vice versa) also varies. Assuming that the perception of such contingencies underlies partisan processing goals, the motivation to bolster attacks directed at parties other than one's own should, accordingly, partially reflect the pattern of competition existing between the parties.

What does this logic imply with regard to partisanship in the Canadian party system between 2004 and 2008? For one thing, the electoral progress of the Conservatives should supply significant variation in the informational environment. A straightforward possibility is simple quantitative change. If we assume that the level of information about a party roughly tracks the party's relative dominance in the system,[7] the availability of information relevant to the Conservative Party of Canada (CPC) should have increased steadily from 2004, when the party entered the system electorally, to 2008, when the party sought re-election as the government. Consequently, biased generation of arguments and counter-arguments regarding attacks on Conservatives should have become easier over time. This implies (1) *growing* partisan differences *within* levels of knowledge (as relevant information is more plentiful), and (2) *shrinking* differences *across* levels of knowledge (as information is easier to find).[8] The hypotheses, therefore, are:

H2. Controlling for political knowledge, the magnitude of partisan effects on responses to partisan attacks on Conservatives increases over time.

H3. The effect of political knowledge on the magnitude of partisan effects on responses to partisan attacks on Conservatives decreases over time.

For reasons developed in the following paragraphs, H2 and H3 can be evaluated for the major parties only (see, especially, the concluding paragraph of this section).

Apart from dynamics in informational context, the party system provides variation in the competitive foundations of motivated reasoning. An obvious distinction is between major and minor parties. Apart from their unique place in the national-level competition for government, the pattern of riding-level competition between the Liberals and Conservatives sets them apart from both the NDP and the Bloc Québécois. An examination of the over-time dynamics of riding-level competition between the parties indicates that the major parties' major competition has consistently been the other major party (whether Liberal or Conservative), while the major competition for the minor parties (NDP and BQ) was also the major parties. At the same time, the relative position of the Liberal and Conservative Parties as major competitors in relation to the NDP and the BQ changed significantly over time.[9]

This distinction – between the *consistency* of competitive relations between the major parties and the *variation* in minor/major party competitive relations – should imply differences in the extent of motivated reasoning across major and minor parties. As the focus of the analysis to come is responses to attacks on the major parties, expectations are confined to this domain. In short, the motivation to bolster major-party attacks should be greater among major-party than minor-party partisans, inasmuch as Liberals and Conservatives have consistently been each other's major electoral foes, whereas competitive relations have been more variable between the major parties and either the BQ or NDP. This implies, among major-party partisans, (1) relatively larger partisan differences *within* levels of knowledge (as the motivation to bolster is greater), and (2) relatively larger differences *across* levels of knowledge (as the informational returns to motivation are greater). Specifically:

> H4. Controlling for political knowledge, the magnitude of partisan effects on responses to major-party partisan attacks is greater among major-party than among minor-party partisans.
>
> H5. The effect of political knowledge on the magnitude of partisan effects on responses to partisan attacks is greater among major-party than among minor-party partisans.

Note, finally, that over-time variation in the competitive and informational foundations of motivated reasoning is confounded for the NDP and the BQ, which is the reason that H2 and H3 are assessed among major-party partisans only. Specifically, dramatic over-time shifts in the profiles of the leading contenders faced by minor-party candidates[10] imply dynamics that should offset the influence of changes in the informational environment – that is, increased bolstering of Conservative attacks among BQ and NDP partisans after 2004 should coincide with improvements in the informational context conducive to such bolstering.

Data and Methodology

Data from the Canadian Election Studies (CES) allow an evaluation of these propositions concerning partisan responses to rhetorical attacks on parties. Indeed, it turns out that the CES investigators have been "attacking" Canadian partisans for years! More specifically, the CES has queried reactions to each of the five attack statements quoted earlier during as many as three separate elections. These data provide a unique opportunity to consider the theory of motivated political reasoning in an observational setting. The analysis incorporates data from the 2004, 2006, and 2008 CES datasets. Only items from the telephone waves (the pre- and post-election surveys) are utilized. This yields 3,116, 3,107, and 2,426 cases for 2004, 2006, and 2008, respectively.[11]

It should be noted that the partisan attacks in these studies are, in one important regard, rather unlike the typical rhetorical attack encountered by partisans in real-world settings: the CES partisan attacks originate from a (presumably) credible source. Partisans in this context are (more or less) denied one of the easier means of counter-arguing or resisting rhetorical attacks: denigrating the source of the attack. Importantly, this dynamic should tend to inflate the impact of political knowledge on motivated reasoning, as knowledgeable partisans will be relatively more advantaged in the generation of counter-arguments than in real-world settings.[12]

As noted above, five items over the past three iterations of the CES satisfy this chapter's conceptualization of partisan attack. In the present analysis, just the first two of the attacks listed above are examined – referred to henceforth as the *CPC threat* and the *Liberals' Green Shift* attacks. The former is the only one of the five items that can be examined for all years under consideration; it is selected because it permits analysis of over-time change. Selection of the *Liberals' Green Shift* item adds a partisan attack concerning the other major party in the system. This item is substantively similar to the *CPC threat* attack, in that both items focus on policy commitments. Responses to the *Liberals' Green Shift* attack can be examined for 2008 only, however, as the item reflects a pledge made in that year's election campaign.[13] In all years, attack statements were followed by the query "Do you strongly agree, somewhat agree, somewhat disagree, or strongly disagree?" Each variable was recoded to the (0, 1) interval. Canadians were, on average, evenly divided on both attacks, whatever the year, and the measures have high variances.[14]

The principal individual-level independent variables in the analysis are party identification and political knowledge. The former is measured using the standard indicators of direction and strength of partisanship: "In federal politics, do you usually think of yourself as a: Liberal, Conservative, N.D.P, Bloc Quebecois, or none of these?" and, for partisans, the follow-up query "How strongly [party] do you feel: very strongly, fairly strongly, or not very strongly?" In the statistical models, dummies for strong and weak identifiers within each partisan group are included, where strong corresponds to those who feel "very strongly" and weak includes all other identifiers.

Political knowledge also relies on standard measurement techniques: correct responses to a battery of office recall measures are summed and then rescaled to the (0, 1) interval.[15] Each model includes the eight dummies for combinations of party identification and attitude strength (4 parties × 2 attitude strengths), along with interactions between these variables and political knowledge.

The models also include a wide range of controls. The logic behind these terms is to control for other influences on responses to partisan attacks that may also be conditioned by political knowledge, particularly policy attitudes, political values, and various demographic terms.[16] All models include controls for income taxation preferences (corporate, personal), political values relevant to the role of the government in the economy and society (regarding the role of the private sector in job creation and attributions of personal success/failure in the market), economic perceptions, age, income, and region (dummies for the West, Quebec, and Atlantic regions). The *CPC threat* models add controls for various social program spending attitudes (welfare, health, education, social housing[17]) and evaluation of the importance of social programs as an election issue. Similarly, the *Liberals' Green Shift* model adds to the baseline set of controls measures of attitudes towards program spending on the environment and evaluation of the importance of the environment as an election issue.[18] In addition – and critically – all models also include interactions between all control variables and political knowledge. (Coefficient estimates for the controls are not reported.)

Results

The implications of the empirical results can be stated simply: there is *significant* evidence of motivated political reasoning in Canadians' responses to partisan attacks. There are large partisan effects on reactions to all of the partisan attacks examined. Moreover, political knowledge is an important moderator of the magnitude of these effects. This pattern of results is robust to the inclusion of diverse controls. At the same time, there is notable variation in the nature and magnitude of partisanship-knowledge interactions. Some of the pattern makes sense in light of features of the party system, whereas other results are more difficult to interpret.

Partisan Responses to Partisan Attacks: "Bull-Headed" or Motivated Reasoning?

Table 11.1 reports ordinary least-squares estimates for four regression models, one for each dependent variable. Predicted values based on these

TABLE 11.1

Party identification, political knowledge, and responses to "partisan attacks"

	CPC threat to social programs (2004)		CPC threat to social programs (2006)		CPC threat to social programs (2008)		Liberal Green Shift will hurt economy (2008)	
Strong Liberal	0.0905*	(0.0492)	0.0350	(0.0392)	0.0624	(0.0517)	-0.0425	(0.0514)
Weak Liberal	0.0331	(0.0257)	0.0122	(0.0270)	-0.0207	(0.0320)	0.0220	(0.0318)
Strong CPC	-0.234***	(0.0538)	-0.249***	(0.0412)	-0.123***	(0.0461)	0.0738	(0.0457)
Weak CPC	-0.106***	(0.0316)	-0.180***	(0.0295)	-0.0986***	(0.0319)	0.0825***	(0.0318)
Strong NDP	0.112*	(0.0634)	0.150**	(0.0640)	0.165***	(0.0525)	0.0806	(0.0519)
Weak NDP	0.0735	(0.0471)	0.126***	(0.0451)	0.0796*	(0.0472)	0.114**	(0.0468)
Strong BQ	-0.0967	(0.0983)	0.114*	(0.0605)	0.149	(0.0907)	0.00214	(0.0903)
Weak BQ	0.0577	(0.0461)	-0.00369	(0.0396)	-0.0161	(0.0554)	0.0745	(0.0550)
Strong Liberal × PK	0.129	(0.0826)	0.202***	(0.0602)	0.187*	(0.0779)	-0.146*	(0.0776)
Weak Liberal × PK	0.0711	(0.046)	0.0805**	(0.0409)	0.148***	(0.0535)	-0.126**	(0.0531)
Strong CPC × PK	-0.0733	(0.0866)	-0.0821	(0.0613)	-0.219***	(0.0752)	0.187**	(0.0749)
Weak CPC × PK	-0.115*	(0.0559)	-0.0133	(0.0451)	-0.0788	(0.0565)	0.0760	(0.0563)
Strong NDP × PK	0.216*	(0.111)	0.0508	(0.0935)	0.0542	(0.0955)	-0.111	(0.0944)
Weak NDP × PK	0.152*	(0.084)	-0.00185	(0.0654)	0.0447	(0.0837)	-0.264***	(0.0829)
Strong BQ × PK	0.348*	(0.186)	0.0833	(0.0995)	0.130	(0.138)	-0.0954	(0.137)
Weak BQ × PK	0.0239	(0.0905)	0.102	(0.0632)	0.201*	(0.0918)	-0.139	(0.0909)
Political knowledge	0.00292	(0.122)	0.0368	(0.100)	0.0175	(0.135)	-0.104	(0.119)
Constant	0.534***	(0.069)	0.420***	(0.0652)	0.498***	(0.0804)	0.778***	(0.0658)
N	3,116		3,107		2,426		2,426	
R^2	.24		.281		.258		.197	

Notes: Coefficient (standard error). Estimates for controls not reported. PK = political knowledge.
* $p < .1$, ** $p < .05$, *** $p < .01$

Sources: Canadian Election Studies for 2004, 2006, and 2008.

FIGURE 11.1

The influence of political knowledge and strength of party identification on partisan responses to the statement "The Conservative Party is a threat to Canada's social programs," in three different national elections

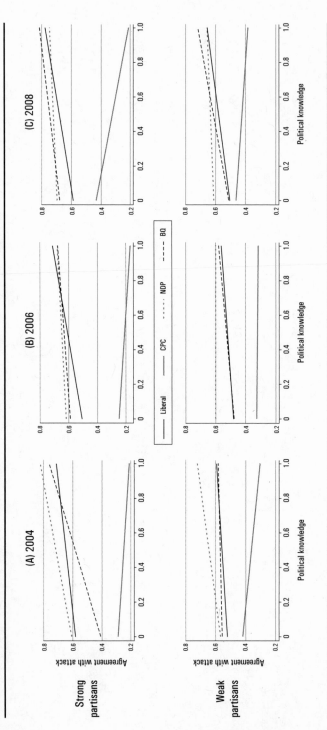

FIGURE 11.2

The influence of political knowledge and strength of party identification on partisan responses to the statement "The Liberal Party's Green Shift/carbon tax would really hurt the Canadian economy," in the 2008 national election

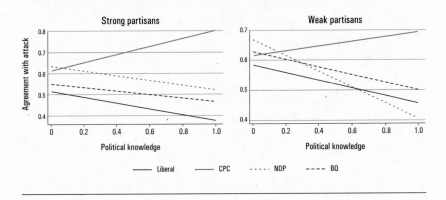

estimates are plotted in Figures 11.1 and 11.2, which indicate, for each dependent variable, the impact of partisanship by political knowledge for all partisan groups. For a given attack, the left panel indicates effects among strong partisans, while the right panel depicts effects among weak partisans.

As one would expect, the estimates imply stark differences across partisans in levels of agreement with the partisan attacks. Disagreement between Liberals and Conservatives is especially obvious: the two groups of partisans are far apart in their responses to the partisan attacks. And while differences among strong, major-party partisans are consistently larger than those among weak partisans, partisan effects are substantively large regardless of attitude strength. Differences between Conservative and minor-party partisans are also consistently large, in some cases even larger than those between Liberals and Conservatives. Between Liberal and minor-party partisans, however, differences are fairly modest. For the *CPC threat* models, this is intuitive: all non-Conservative partisans should respond affirmatively to the attack on the Conservatives. For the *Liberals' Green Shift* model, on the other hand, the pattern is more puzzling; we will come back to this point in the discussion below.

Overall partisan differences aside, the moderation of these differences by political knowledge is key to assessing the motivated reasoning account of partisan perception (H1). In this regard, thirty-two of the coefficients are of interest: the estimates for the eight partisanship-knowledge inter-actions in each model. Nearly two-thirds of the thirty-two partisanship-knowledge interactions are in the direction predicted by H1 and of sufficient magnitude to be reliably distinguished from zero.[19] Despite the obvious partisan implications of the *CPC threat* and the *Liberals' Green Shift* at-tacks, political knowledge has important moderating effects.

To convey the substantive thrust of the results, consider panel (C) in Figure 11.1, which plots the estimated partisan effects for the 2008 *CPC threat* model. At all levels of knowledge and attitude strength, Conservatives are much less inclined to agree that their party is a threat to Canada's social programs. At the same time, the gap between Conservatives and other par-tisans clearly grows as political knowledge increases (between strong Liberals and Conservatives, for example, the gap grows from less than 0.2 to 0.6 units). Between Liberals and Conservatives, furthermore, the polar-ization is highly symmetrical: as knowledge increases, strong Liberals grow in their approval of the *CPC threat* attack at roughly the same rate as strong Conservatives grow in their disapproval of the attack. In the language of Taber and Lodge (2006), strong Liberals *bolster* to the same degree that strong Conservatives *counter-argue* the sentiment. New Democrats and Bloquistes also appear to increasingly bolster the attack on the Conservatives as knowledge increases, but the effects are not statistically significant.

Among weak partisans, a congruent pattern of effects is observed. In-deed, if anything, the effect of knowledge is somewhat more pronounced. Polarization between Liberals and Conservatives increases by about five times across the range of knowledge: the difference grows from about 0.05 to 0.25. Note also that, again, the polarization is roughly symmetrical among Liberals and Conservatives. Knowledge also has a powerful effect on differ-ences between weak Conservatives and Bloquistes: the distance between these groups increases about sixfold across the range of knowledge.

The relatively larger impact of knowledge among weak partisans com-pared with strong partisans may reflect unanticipated floor and ceiling effects. For instance, the Liberal-Conservative gap in response to the *CPC threat* attack in 2008 is tripled among strong partisans but quintupled among weak partisans. At the same time, among strong partisans, initial partisan differences between Liberals and Conservatives are four times as large as those among weak partisans. This implies, among other things, less room for detectable growth in partisan polarization.

The overall pattern fits the motivated reasoning theory. These results, furthermore, are fairly typical of the findings across the models, as depicted in Figures 11.1 and 11.2. Importantly, the pattern is generic across both the *CPC threat* and *Liberals' Green Shift* attacks – at least among Liberal and Conservative partisans. Indeed, the left panel of Figure 11.2 indicates that, among strong partisans, it is with regard to this attack that the greatest increase in polarization between Liberals and Conservatives is observed: the difference between the groups grows from 0.10 to over 0.40 units across the knowledge scale – a 400 percent increase! The relationship between Liberal-Conservative polarization and political knowledge is, again, even sharper among weak partisans: the difference between these groups increases roughly sixfold (from approximately 0.04 to approximately 0.25 units) across the range of knowledge.

Among partisans of the minor parties – the NDP and BQ – the pattern of responses to the *Liberals' Green Shift* attack does not fit expectations nearly so neatly. For both strong and weak minor-party partisans, knowledge effects are trivial and, worse, incorrectly signed: statistical significance aside, these partisans appear to *resist* rather than *bolster* the attack on the Liberals. And, as noted, differences between Liberals and minor-party partisans are modest overall. The pattern is sharpened among weak New Democrats: rather than polarizing against the Liberals (as these groups polarized against the Conservatives in the *CPC threat* models), these partisans polarize against the Conservatives. Whereas the least knowledgeable of the weak NDPers accept the attack on the Liberals quite readily – more readily, in fact, than the least knowledgeable Conservatives – the most knowledgeable weak New Democrats reject the attack even more categorically (0.40) than knowledgeable, weak Liberals (approximately 0.45)![20]

The inconsistency of effects across major and minor parties in the *Liberals' Green Shift* model highlights a more general feature of the results: while roughly two in three of the estimates of the partisanship-knowledge interactions provide reliable support for H1, one in three estimates do not – either because the coefficients are too imprecisely estimated to warrant serious consideration or because they are incorrectly signed. This suggests that motivated reasoning processes may be moderated in significant ways by variables other than knowledge and strength of partisan affiliation. In keeping with earlier discussion, the obvious candidate is the party system.

The Impact of the Party System

H2 and H3 reflect the theorized effects of an informational environment increasingly propitious to motivated reasoning about the Conservatives.

H2 implies that, controlling for political knowledge, partisan differences in responses to the *CPC threat* attack should be larger in 2006 and 2008 than in 2004. H3 implies that the effect of knowledge on partisan differences should shrink over the same period.

Put simply, neither hypothesis is supported by the data. Contrary to H2, overall differences between major-party partisans appear to shrink, rather than grow, between 2004 and 2008. Indeed, at lower levels of political knowledge, partisan differences (between Liberals and Tories) are roughly one-third smaller in 2008 than in either 2004 or 2006. The general pattern holds, moreover, for both strong and weak major-party partisans, at least to an approximation. That said, in the top rank of political knowledge, partisan differences are at least as large at the end of the period as at the beginning.

Turning to H3, the results, again, do not accord with expectations. If anything, knowledge effects are, on the whole, larger in 2008 than in either of the previous years, regardless of attitude strength. The most dramatic, and curious, disconfirmation of the hypothesis is among strong Conservatives: knowledge effects in this group grow threefold between 2004 and 2008. The implication, from a motivated reasoning perspective, is that the Conservative Party's electoral success made it *more*, not *less*, difficult for the party's partisans to counter-argue partisan attacks. An interpretation of this unexpected result is offered in the conclusion.

Whereas the first two party-system-level hypotheses fail, the remaining two hypotheses fare much better. Pursuant to H4, differences between major-party partisans in response to attacks on the major parties are, on average, larger than differences between minor-party and the relevant group of major-party partisans.[21] There are significant differences between Liberals and Conservatives in responses to *all* of the partisan attacks, but differences between minor-party partisans and the relevant group of major-party partisans are unstable. The indicative case has already been noted: Figure 11.2 depicts the trivial differences between Liberals, on the one hand, and New Democrats and Bloquistes, on the other, in response to the *Liberals' Green Shift* attack. Presumably, the shifting competitive landscape, particularly the relative decline of the Liberals as leading contenders in viable BQ and NDP ridings (see note 9), had diminished the intensity of associated partisan conflicts by 2008.

Regarding the moderation of partisan effects by political knowledge, as predicted in H5, the effect of knowledge is greater among major-party than minor-party partisans, as evidenced by the strength and statistical significance of coefficients in Table 11.1 and the steeper slopes of major-party lines in Figures 11.1 and 11.2.[22]

Thus, the findings on the impact of the party system are perfectly mixed. Notably, those predictions concerning the motivational consequences of the party system (H4 and H5) fare better than those relating to the informational consequences of party system change (H2 and H3). Of course, firm conclusions about the influence of the party system must await analysis involving more party-system-level cases. More generally, it is significant that attention to features of the party system appears to resolve some of the inconsistency in the results as they pertain to H1. If we restrict the analysis of H1 to partisans of the major parties, then the supportive evidence for the motivated reasoning theory is impressive indeed.

Conclusion

Rhetorical attacks on parties – and, by extension, on their partisans – are a common feature of democratic politics that offers an uncommon opportunity to explore the cognitive dimension of partisanship. It is precisely the familiarity and simplicity of such verbal assaults in politics that makes them a useful instrument for uncovering evidence of deeper, more involving features of political reasoning in Canada.

Within the largest partisan groups, the Liberals and Conservatives, analysis of responses to partisan attacks suggests an image of the Canadian partisan as a motivated political reasoner – as an "intuitive lawyer" acting in cognitive defence of her pre-existing partisan commitments. For these major-party partisans, responses to messages that imply obvious and strongly negative evaluations of their political parties are conditioned by political knowledge, such that partisans implicated in a given attack are more likely to reject – and other partisans more likely to accept – the attack with increased political knowledge. Although such partisanship-knowledge interactions are consistent with Zaller's RAS model in certain contexts, the present set of results – assuming uniform awareness of the partisan implications of partisan attacks – is uniquely predicted by the motivated reasoning theory. This makes a notable contrast with the one previous analysis of motivated reasoning among Canadian partisans (Blais et al. 2010).

An important caveat, however, concerns the apparent moderating influence of the party system. As indicated, the best evidence of motivated reasoning is found among major-party partisans. Among minor-party partisans, on the other hand, the evidence is mixed. The consistent influence of partisanship and its interaction with political knowledge among

Liberals and Tories contrasts with uneven effects among Bloquistes and New Democrats. This pattern, of course, is sensible in light of the differing qualities of competitive relations involving the major parties compared with those involving the minor parties.

Other features of the party system do not seem to have such sensible effects. Most striking is the apparent over-time growth in knowledge effects regarding attacks on the Conservatives – a finding that extends even to Conservative partisans. It seems unlikely that the key informational premise underlying the expected decline in knowledge effects is faulty: we have good evidence that media coverage of the Conservatives did indeed grow after 2004 (see Daku et al. 2009). It is conceivable, however, that the theoretical logic is too crude. A more complex dynamic combines quantitative *and* qualitative change in information about the Conservatives. In this regard, the critical fact would be the Tories' 2006 election win: at this point, the party switched from opposition to government status, in the process becoming a likelier target of negative political rhetoric. This should have made it more difficult for Conservative partisans to resist rhetorical attacks on their party.[23]

A second unexpected result concerns weak New Democrat partisans, who, in response to the attack on the *Liberals' Green Shift*, polarized against – rather than with – the Conservatives, at least beyond the lowest levels of political knowledge. A similar effect among weak BQ partisans approaches the 0.10 threshold ($p = 0.126$). In broad terms, the inconsistency fits theoretical expectations: given their more variable competitive relations with the major parties, minor parties' partisans should have less motivation than their major-party counterparts to bolster major-party attacks. But this leaves unexplained the intriguing tendency, especially among weak New Democrats, to seemingly counter-argue the attack on the Liberals. One possible interpretation is that, at very low levels of knowledge, weak New Democrats (and perhaps Bloquistes) react much as Conservatives do, in that they accept (and perhaps bolster) the attack on the Liberals, as a straightforward interpretation of interparty relationships would imply. At higher levels of knowledge, however, these partisans recognize various deeper implications of the attack on the Liberals' environmental policy commitments, including implications for the environmental platforms of their own parties. Consequently, such sophisticated New Democrats and Bloquistes may conclude that the attack on the Liberals is simultaneously an attack on their parties, and react accordingly. This is highly speculative, but it does indicate the complexities of motivated reasoning regarding partisan attacks in a multi-party system.

Finally, an unexpected but sensible pattern is seen in the existence of apparent floor and ceiling effects. That is, counter-arguing and bolstering processes appear to exert greater effects when initial differences between partisan groups are smallest (and therefore when there is the greatest scope for increasing attitude extremity). This dynamic appears in comparisons of strong and weak partisans in three of the four statistical models. How to explain this finding? A mundane possibility is that they are a measurement artifact: with a limited number of response categories, the dependent variables may place constraints on the degree of attitude extremity that can be observed (Taber and Lodge 2006, 757). A more substantive interpretation is that strong partisans, even at low levels of knowledge, engage in significant motivated reasoning that, given cognitive bounds, creates limited room for further cognitive reinforcement.[24]

What are this chapter's broader implications? First, it adds to our picture of the Canadian partisan. Party identification in Canada is sometimes thought to be a rather inert affair – unusually flexible and lightly held, quite unlike the fiery partisanship of our Republican and Democratic neighbours to the south (for a recent statement of this view, see Bélanger and Stephenson 2010). Presumably, the turmoil in the party system in recent years – particularly the transformations among programmatic conservatives – strengthens the case for this view. A generally unstated but rather natural implication of this "flexible" view of party identification is that Canadian partisans are unlikely to engage in the defensive cognitive gymnastics that characterize the motivated reasoner. Indeed, why would a "flexible partisan" be so "inflexible" in her views? Inasmuch as this chapter lends support to a motivated reasoning view of Canadian partisanship, it also troubles (even though it does not dispose of) the image of the fickle Canadian partisan.

Second, this chapter generates a clear forecast regarding the quality of partisan reasoning over the life of the new Parliament and, most importantly, during the next election. The signal political development resulting from the 2011 election was the profound change in the competitive situation among the parties, particularly the rise of the NDP to the status of Official Opposition and the collapse of the Liberal Party. On the theoretical logic developed in this chapter, these developments imply, among Conservatives and New Democrats, an intensification of motivated reasoning processes in relation to each other's parties, candidates, and partisans. To be sure, Conservative/NDP competition had begun to intensify at the riding-level prior to 2011 (see note 9), yet the novel national-level competitive dynamics appear likely to provide these partisan groups with new motivation for biased cognition. Conversely, Conservatives and Liberals may exhibit somewhat less evidence of motivated reasoning processes in relation to each other's parties and partisans – although, of course, riding-level competition between these parties is likely to be fierce in certain parts of the country, such as southern Ontario.

Finally, the findings described here have implications for party strategy. As the analysis reveals, immunity to partisan attacks – at least those coming from a reasonably credible source (e.g., the academic survey interviewer) – depends greatly on political knowledge, *even for the strongest partisans.* This result provides important counsel to strategists of party political communication: it may be important to respond to an attack directed at your party in order to supply less knowledgeable identifiers with the cognitive ammunition they need to resist the attack's evaluative implications. Of course, for any given partisan attack, the source may be insufficiently credible or the volume of the attack insufficiently loud to have much effect on the least knowledgeable partisan. But when both of these conditions are absent, it is critical not to leave emotionally committed but cognitively disengaged partisans defenceless.

Acknowledgments
The author thanks Amanda Bittner and Royce Koop for organizing the workshop that gave rise to this book and for their detailed feedback on an earlier draft of this chapter. Thanks also to Marc-Andre Bodet for supplying riding-level electoral data.

Notes
1 Merolla and colleagues' review (2008) of work on partisanship is focused on research that explicitly conceptualizes partisanship as an "information shortcut" or "heuristic." Even so, their review encompasses most of the important work on partisan effects in political attitudes and perceptions in Canada.
2 Blais et al. (2010, 3-4) provides a concise review of the details of the scandal.
3 The possibility that perceptual bias is constrained under certain informational conditions fits with a range of studies that conclude that motivated perception hinges on informational ambiguity (e.g., Berelson et al. 1954; Festinger 1957; Lord et al. 1979; Redlawsk et al. 2010).
4 This follows Zaller's claim that the impact of political awareness (which Zaller measures using indicators of factual knowledge) on partisan selectivity in information

processing is limited to those cases "in which the contextual information necessary to evaluate an issue in light of one's predispositions is, for one reason or another, obscure" (1992, 47-48). See also discussion below under "Motivated Political Reasoning across the Party System."

5 On this point, see discussion of the theory's citations and accolades in Dobrzynska and Blais (2008, 261n1).

6 Consider, in this regard, Blais and colleagues' findings (2010) regarding partisan effects on judgments concerning the sponsorship scandal, discussed above.

7 Evidence in support of this proposition is supplied by analysis of the nature of media coverage of the parties in elections since 1993 reported in Daku et al. (2009, see especially Table 3). In a similar vein, see Nevitte and colleagues' analysis (2000) of awareness of the NDP in the 1997 federal general election.

8 Conversely, biased generation of arguments and counter-arguments regarding the Liberals should have become more difficult. The hypotheses, therefore, would be reversed in relation to responses to attacks on the Liberal Party. Data limitations prevent the evaluation of these hypotheses in relation to the Liberal Party, and I therefore focus on Conservative attacks only.

9 These conclusions derive from analysis (not shown) of the partisan distribution of each party's leading competitors at the riding level within ridings where a given party was viable – that is, placed either first or second on election day. Both Liberals and Conservatives faced leading competitors from the other major party in at least 50 percent of their viable ridings in each of the three elections. On the other hand, both New Democrats and Bloquistes were far more (less) likely to face Conservative (Liberal) leading competitors in 2008 than in 2004. Data for this analysis was provided by Marc-Andre Bodet.

10 See note 9 above.

11 The data were obtained from the Canadian Opinion Research Archive (CORA) at Queen's University at Kingston (http://www.queensu.ca/cora). Further methodological details can be obtained through the CORA website.

12 An alternative interpretation has parallel implications. It could be that knowledgeable partisans may be more aware than others of the "real" sources of the CES team's partisan attacks – that is, the parties themselves – insofar as the CES items draw on common features of the discourse of the party system. If this is so, then the knowledgeable will be in a relatively better position to engage in source denigration processes (perhaps even prior to the survey interview).

13 It should be noted that the "Green Shift" attack was actually presented in two different ways. Random halves of the CES sample were asked their reactions to (1) the statement presented above or (2) this statement: "The Liberal Party's Carbon Tax would really hurt the Canadian economy." For the purposes of this chapter, item (2) is treated as conceptually equivalent to item (1), and so discussion throughout the chapter is in terms of the "Green Shift" phrasing only.

14 Data not shown.

15 Details of these questions are available upon request.

16 Evidence of cognitive heterogeneity of this sort is legion. The classic citation is Sniderman et al. (1991). For Canadian results, see Bittner (2007) and Roy (2009).

17 The 2008 model does not include the social housing spending attitude, as it is not measured in that year of the survey.

18 Except for age, which is measured in years, all variables are scaled to the (0, 1) interval. Details of all question wordings and coding decisions are available upon request.

19 Of these thirty-two estimates, thirteen are statistically significant at the .10 level or better, four at the .15 level, and three at the .20 level. In all, fully twenty-seven coefficients are correctly signed. Just 2 coefficients are incorrectly signed and significant at the .20 level.

20 It bears emphasizing that this result is robust to controls for various indicators of policy preferences relevant to the environment. It is difficult, therefore, to attribute these effects to unmeasured policy differences between the Conservatives and the other non-Liberal parties.

21 The relevant groups are Conservative and Liberal partisans for the *CPC threat* and *Liberals' Green Shift* attacks, respectively.

22 All sixteen of the relevant coefficient estimates applying to major-party partisans (the partisanship/knowledge interactions) are correctly signed, with nine of these statistically significant at the .10 level and five at the .20 level. Among minor-party partisans, just nine of the relevant interactions are correctly signed, with five of these significant at the .10 level and two significant at the .20 level. Importantly, two of the minor-party partisanship/knowledge interactions at or approaching conventional significance thresholds are incorrectly signed: those applying to strong NDP and weak BQ partisans in the *Liberals' Green Shift* model.

23 Of course, this would have simultaneously made it easier for opposition partisans to bolster anti-Conservative claims, and there is little indication of this in the results.

24 Matthews's analysis (2010) of the impact of election campaigns on partisan bias in economic perception has parallel implications; see especially p. 234.

References

Andrew, Blake C., Antonia Maioni, and Stuart Soroka. 2006. "Just When You Thought It Was Out, Policy Is Pulled Back In." *Policy Options* 27 (3): 74-79.

Ansolabehere, Stephen, and Shanto Iyengar. 1997. *Going Negative: How Political Advertisements Shrink and Polarize the Electorate.* New York: Free Press.

Bartels, Larry M. 2002. "Beyond the Running Tally: Partisan Bias in Political Perceptions." *Political Behavior* 24 (2): 117-50.

Bélanger, Éric, and Laura B. Stephenson. 2010. "Parties and Partisans: The Influence of Ideology and Brokerage on the Durability of Partisanship in Canada." In *Voting Behaviour in Canada,* edited by Cameron D. Anderson and Laura B. Stephenson, 107-38. Vancouver: UBC Press.

Berelson, Bernard, Paul Lazarsfeld, and William McPhee. 1954. *Voting.* Cambridge, MA: Harvard University Press.

Berinsky, Adam. 2007. "Assuming the Costs of War: Events, Elites, and American Public Support for Military Conflict." *Journal of Politics* 69 (4): 975-97.

Bittner, Amanda. 2007. "The Effects of Information and Social Cleavages: Explaining Issue Attitudes and Vote Choice in Canada." *Canadian Journal of Political Science* 40: 935-68.

Blais, André, Elisabeth Gidengil, Patrick Fournier, Neil Nevitte, Joanna Everitt, and Jiyoon Kim. 2010. "Political Judgments, Perceptions of Facts, and Partisan Effects." *Electoral Studies* 29 (1): 1-12.

Bullock, John G. 2009. "Partisan Bias and the Bayesian Ideal in the Study of Public Opinion." *Journal of Politics* 71: 1109-24.

Cairns, Alan. 1968. "The Electoral System and the Party System in Canada, 1921-1965." *Canadian Journal of Political Science* 1 (1): 55-80.

Campbell, Angus, Philip Converse, Warren E. Miller, and Donald E. Stokes. 1960. *The American Voter.* New York: John Wiley and Sons.

Carty, R.K. 2006. "The Shifting Place of Political Parties in Canadian Public Life." *IRPP Choices* 12 (4): 5-13.

Carty, R.K., William Cross, and Lisa Young. 2000. *Rebuilding Canadian Party Politics.* Vancouver: UBC Press.

Daku, Mark, Adam Mahon, Stuart Soroka, and Lori Young. 2009. "Media Content and Election Campaigns: 2008 in Comparative Context." Paper prepared for presentation at the annual meeting of the Canadian Political Science Association, Ottawa, May.

Dobrzynska, Agnieszka, and André Blais. 2008. "Testing Zaller's Reception and Acceptance Model in an Intense Election Campaign." *Political Behavior* 30: 259-75.

Festinger, Leon. 1957. *A Theory of Cognitive Dissonance.* Evanston, IL: Row, Peterson.

Gaines, Brian J., James H. Kuklinski, Paul J. Quirk, Buddy Peyton, and Jay Verkuilen. 2007. "Same Facts, Different Interpretations: Partisan Motivation and Opinion on Iraq." *Journal of Politics* 69 (4): 957-74.

Gerber, Alan S., and Donald P. Green. 1999. "Misperceptions about Perceptual Bias." *Annual Review of Political Science* 2: 189-210.

Gerber, Alan S., Gregory A. Huber, and Ebonya Washington. 2010. "Party Affiliation, Partisanship, and Political Beliefs: A Field Experiment." *American Political Science Review* 104 (4 November): 720-44.

Gidengil, Elisabeth, André Blais, Joanna Everitt, Patrick Fournier, and Neil Nevitte. 2006. "Back to the Future? Making Sense of the 2004 Canadian Election outside Quebec." *Canadian Journal of Political Science* 39: 1-25.

Goodyear-Grant, Elizabeth, Stuart Soroka, and Antonia Maioni. 2004. "The Role of the Media: A Campaign Saved by a Horserace." *Policy Options* 25 (8): 86-91.

Johnston, Richard. 2008. "Polarized Pluralism in the Canadian Party System: Presidential Address to the Canadian Political Science Association, June 5, 2008." *Canadian Journal of Political Science* 41 (4): 815-34.

Johnston, Richard, André Blais, Henry Brady, and Jean Crête. 1992. *Letting the People Decide: Dynamics of a Canadian Election.* Montreal and Kingston: McGill-Queen's University Press.

Kunda, Ziva. 1990. "The Case for Motivated Reasoning." *Psychological Bulletin* 108 (3): 480-98.

Lau, Richard R., and David P. Redlawsk. 2001. "Advantages and Disadvantages of Cognitive Heuristics in Political Decision Making." *American Journal of Political Science* 45 (4): 951-71.

–. 2006. *How Voters Decide: Information Processing during Election Campaigns.* New York: Cambridge University Press.

Lazarsfeld, Paul, Bernard Berelson, and Hazel Gaudet. 1948. *The People's Choice.* New York: Columbia University Press.

Lodge, Milton, and Charles Taber. 2000. "Three Steps toward a Theory of Motivated Political Reasoning." In *Elements of Reason: Cognition, Choice, and the Bounds of Rationality,* edited by Arthur Lupia, Matthew McCubbins, and Samuel Popkin, 183-213. London: Cambridge University Press.

Lord, Charles, Marc Ross, and Mark Lepper. 1979. "Biased Assimilation and Attitude Polarization: The Effects of Prior Theories on Subsequently Considered Evidence." *Journal of Personality and Social Psychology* 37 (11): 2098-2109.

Matthews, J. Scott. 2010. "Enlightenment, Equalization or What? Campaign Learning and the Economy in Canadian Elections." In *Voting Behaviour in Canada,* edited by Cameron D. Anderson and Laura B. Stephenson, 211-41. Vancouver: UBC Press.

McLean, James. 2008. "The Messenger Is the Message." *Policy Options* 29 (10): 12-17.

Merolla, Jennifer, Laura Stephenson, and Elizabeth Zechmeister. 2008. "Can Canadians Take a Hint? The (In)Effectiveness of the (In)Effectiveness of Party Labels as Information Shortcuts in Canada." *Canadian Journal of Political Science* 41 (3): 673-96.

Mutz, Diana, and Byron Reeves. 2005. "The New Videomalaise: Effects of Televised Incivility on Political Trust." *American Political Science Review* 99 (1): 1-15.

Nevitte, Neil, André Blais, Elisabeth Gidengil, and Richard Nadeau. 2000. *Unsteady State: The 1997 Canadian Federal Election.* Toronto: Oxford University Press.

Norquay, Geoff. 2011. "The 'Ballot Question' in the 2011 Election: Two Wins, Two Losses." *Policy Options* 32 (6): 47-51.

Redlawsk, David. 2002. "Hot Cognition or Cool Consideration: Testing the Effects of Motivated Reasoning on Political Decision Making." *Journal of Politics* 64 (4): 1021-44.

Redlawsk, David, Andrew Civettini, and Karen Emmerson. 2010. "The Affective Tipping Point: Do Motivated Reasoners ever 'Get It'?" *Political Psychology* 31 (4): 563-93.

Rose, Jonathan. 2006. "The Liberals Reap What They Sow: Why Their Negative Ads Failed." *Policy Options* (June-July): 50-54.

Roy, Jason. 2009. "Voter Heterogeneity: Information Differences and Voting." *Canadian Journal of Political Science* 42: 117-37.

Rudolph, T.J. 2006. "Triangulating Political Responsibility: The Motivated Formation of Responsibility Judgments." *Political Psychology* 27 (1): 99-122.

Siegfried, André. [1906] 1966. *The Race Question in Canada.* Toronto: McClelland and Stewart.

Sniderman, Paul M., Richard A. Brody, and Philip E. Tetlock. 1991. *Reasoning and Choice: Explorations in Political Psychology.* Cambridge: Cambridge University Press.

Taber, C.S., and M. Lodge. 2006. "Motivated Skepticism in the Evaluation of Political Beliefs." *American Journal of Political Science* 50 (3): 755-69.

Taber, Charles S., Damon Cann, and Simona Kucsova. 2009. "The Motivated Processing of Political Arguments." *Political Behavior* 31: 137-55.

Zaller, John. 1992. *The Nature and Origins of Mass Opinion.* New York: Cambridge University Press.

12

Coping with Political Flux

———— The Impact of Information on Voters'
Perceptions of the Political Landscape,
1988-2011

AMANDA BITTNER

Since the earliest election studies, scholars have shown repeatedly that
voters are not very interested in or knowledgeable about politics, and that
those who are more informed perceive the political world and make decisions differently from those who are less informed (Berelson et al. 1954;
Campbell et al. 1960; Converse 1964). In response to these findings about
the general lack of knowledge in society, scholars have made substantial
inroads into understanding how individuals overcome their information
deficits. Some have suggested that in the absence of detailed information,
voters are able to use tools around them in order to come to a decision (Lupia
and McCubbins 1998), while others have argued that, cognitively, we do not
need to have detailed information about things like party platforms or issue
stances in order to make decisions because our brains process information
in such a way that we use shortcuts or heuristics to make our political decisions anyway (Brady and Sniderman 1985; Sniderman et al. 1991).

Most studies examining the nature of "uninformed" decision making
tend to focus on understanding the attitudes, opinions, and vote choices of
those voters who are less politically "sophisticated" overall, compared with
those who are more politically sophisticated (Bartels 1996; Bittner 2007;
Cutler 2002). Scholars have also conducted experiments in which they test
the decision-making processes of voters under conditions of greater or
lesser amounts of political information (Rahn 1993), and have found that,
generally speaking, even when they have more information, voters will con-

tinue to use stereotypes and shortcuts in order to formulate impressions and opinions. The study described here attempts to combine the two methods in order to understand the decision-making processes of voters according to their levels of political sophistication, while at the same time examining the vote calculus among voters during periods of electoral "flux," where the information about political "tools" and "cues" – such as parties and leaders – might be lacking.

This chapter examines the role of political information during a particularly tumultuous period in Canadian politics. The period from 1988 to 2011 saw the emergence of new parties, the near-collapse of old parties, the merger of old and new parties, and a number of leadership changes in each of these parties. Arguably, this presents voters with a political landscape that is more challenging to navigate than one in which the choices they have are more stable, where they have had more of an opportunity to become acclimatized and accustomed to the political options available. Therefore, this era provides an excellent opportunity to examine the decision-making processes of voters, and the nature of their choices in circumstances where lower than normal amounts of information are available. It will also be possible to shed additional light on the role of the party system in shaping the nature of our political decisions, as well as gain a better understanding of how Canadians have dealt with and responded to the incredible changes that have taken place in federal politics over the last twenty years.

Using data from the Canadian Election Studies from 1988 to 2011, this chapter catalogues voters' assessments of parties and leaders over time, to assess the extent to which changes in the political landscape had an impact on voters' ability to engage with the choices available. First, this chapter assesses voters' abilities to provide evaluations of parties and leaders in the first place. Second, it examines the impact of these evaluations on vote choice and, importantly, the impact of not being able to provide an evaluation – do those who say they don't know how they feel about leaders make different decisions at the ballot box from those who do provide a leader rating? Finally, what is the role of political sophistication? Are those who are more politically sophisticated better able to navigate the political landscape than those who are less sophisticated? Taken together, answers to these questions will provide us with substantial insight into the decision-making processes of voters, and, in particular, with a better sense of the impact of the electoral flux that has characterized Canadian federal politics over the last twenty years.

Informed Voters?

In one of the earliest studies of voting behaviour, Campbell and colleagues noted the general lack of knowledge of and interest in politics among the bulk of voters (1960, 25). Converse (1964) confirmed these findings a few years later, finding that voters had little understanding of basic political concepts, and that the political ideas that they did possess were not linked together logically or cohesively. Since these early studies, scholars have consistently uncovered similar patterns, pointing to the indisputable lack of information and knowledge about politics on the part of the general public.

Canadian voters are no different from voters south of the border. Scholars have repeatedly noted that they are not very informed (Fournier 2002; Roy 2007), and have made substantial efforts to determine how it is that Canadian voters make decisions, even without a high level of political knowledge (Bittner 2007; Blais et al. 2000; Cutler 2002). Scholars have also looked at whether or not voters "learn" during campaigns, to determine whether even uninformed voters may become enlightened over the course of an election (Johnston et al. 1996; Matthews 2006). The bulk of recent research suggests that campaigns matter (see, for example, Johnston et al. 2004), and that, in particular, voters' uncertainty about the political landscape has important implications for the decisions they make at the ballot box (Alvarez 1997; Glasgow and Alvarez 2000; Sanders 2001).

Glasgow and Alvarez (2000) note that as information costs increase, voters' levels of uncertainty increase. They suggest that those who are less politically sophisticated or knowledgeable are more likely to admit being uncertain about their feelings and perceptions, but they also note that, in general, voters possess higher levels of uncertainty about challengers than incumbents. This fits with Alvarez's earlier work (1997), in which he demonstrates that with more information, uncertainty decreases; voter familiarity with a candidate should decrease uncertainty, and we ought to expect that the longer a leader has been around, the more certain voters are about their feelings towards him or her. Based on these findings, we would expect that in the Canadian context (where over the last twenty years the number of incumbent party leaders has fluctuated substantially from election to election, and where the political landscape has shifted dramatically), uncertainty should be a major factor in voters' perceptions, and it should shape the types of decisions they make at the ballot box. Not only has uncertainty about candidates been found to affect voter turnout (Sanders 2001), but as uncertainty about a candidate increases, support for that candidate decreases (Alvarez 1997). Uncertainty has a direct influence on the things voters do.

Data and Analysis

In order to assess the influence of party system flux on the nature of voter decision-making processes, this chapter examines data from the Canadian Election Studies for 1988 to 2011. A large pooled dataset was built in order to assess the influence of this system flux on the way voters perceive parties and leaders, and, importantly, how this affected their vote choice. Variables examined and incorporated into the dataset include party and leader evaluations in both pre- and post-election waves, partisanship, media exposure, vote intention, vote choice, political sophistication, and basic demographics.

During this twenty-year period, seven federal elections took place and, with very few exceptions, voters were faced with new parties and new party leaders in each election. Carty and colleagues (2000) point to the emergence of a fourth party system in the 1990s, and arguably, with the merger of the Canadian Alliance and the Progressive Conservative Party, the political landscape shifted substantially once more in 2003. Table 12.1 lists the parties and party leaders competing for votes in each election since 1988.

As Table 12.1 makes clear, over a twenty-year period, the Conservative Party has had five different leaders;[1] the Liberal Party has had five separate leaders competing in elections (and is now preparing to choose its sixth leader); the New Democratic Party (NDP) has had four leaders (and has just chosen its fifth); the Bloc Québécois (BQ) emerged as a new party and has had two leaders before Gilles Duceppe lost his seat in the most recent election; both the Reform Party and the Canadian Alliance emerged and had two different leaders each; and the Green Party has emerged more recently, with a new leader on the scene for voters to take note of. Perhaps more importantly, in only two elections over this twenty-year period were voters faced with the exact same "menu" of options – in terms of both parties and leaders – as in the previous election: 1988, when the election was fought between Brian Mulroney, John Turner, and Ed Broadbent, and 2006, when the election was fought between Stephen Harper, Paul Martin, Jack Layton, and Gilles Duceppe. In all other elections, different parties and/or different leaders competed for votes.

Figure 12.1 tracks the proportion of respondents who indicated that they did not know how they felt when asked to rate each of the parties competing in the election, over time. Alvarez (1997, 81) notes that non-response can be assumed to demonstrate that an individual is "maximally uncertain" about candidates' issue placements; arguably the point applies not only to issue placements but also to general perceptions of candidates. Thus, this

TABLE 12.1
Canadian political party leaders, 1988-2011

Election	Conservative	Liberal	NDP	BQ	Reform/CA	Green
1988	Brian Mulroney	John Turner	Ed Broadbent			
1993	Kim Campbell	Jean Chrétien	Audrey McLaughlin	Lucien Bouchard	Preston Manning	
1997	Jean Charest	Jean Chrétien	Alexa McDonough	Gilles Duceppe	Preston Manning	
2000	Joe Clark	Jean Chrétien	Alexa McDonough	Gilles Duceppe	Stockwell Day	
2004	Stephen Harper	Paul Martin	Jack Layton	Gilles Duceppe		
2006	Stephen Harper	Paul Martin	Jack Layton	Gilles Duceppe		
2008	Stephen Harper	Stéphane Dion	Jack Layton	Gilles Duceppe		Elizabeth May
2011	Stephen Harper	Michael Ignatieff	Jack Layton	Gilles Duceppe		Elizabeth May

FIGURE 12.1

Percentage of respondents answering "don't know" when asked about their feelings towards political parties, by sophistication level

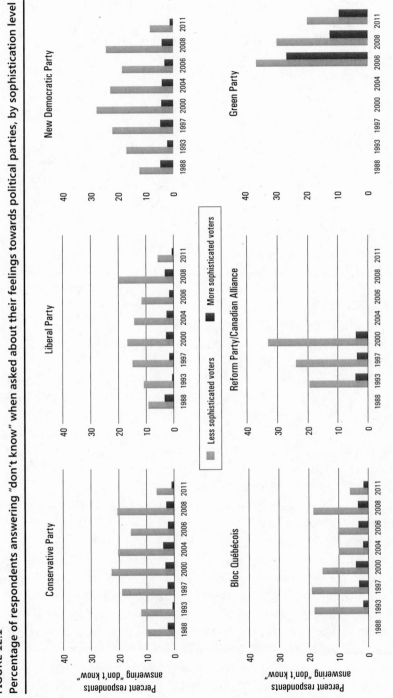

measure provides an excellent indicator of voter uncertainty. Figure 12.1 depicts the level of non-response by level of political sophistication, comparing the bottom third of respondents (those with the lowest levels of political sophistication) with the top third of respondents (those with the highest levels of political sophistication).

Figure 12.1 demonstrates that in every election, less sophisticated voters are more likely to say they don't know when asked how they feel about the various parties competing. This is not surprising, as we would expect voters with higher levels of political knowledge in general to also be more knowledgeable about parties, and therefore more comfortable providing a rating when prompted. Voters who are less sophisticated might be less familiar with the parties, as they are likely to pay less attention to the media and be less aware of political and campaign events. Figure 12.1 also demonstrates that in election years where there is more stability (1988 and 2006), the proportion of voters saying that they don't know is lower than in other years, confirming past research demonstrating that there are higher levels of certainty when voters are evaluating incumbents than when they are evaluating challengers (Glasgow and Alvarez 2000). Ratings of the Green Party in 2006 constitute an exception, as this party was quite new on the scene and voters had less time to become knowledgeable about and comfortable with the party.

In election years where there are new parties on the scene, voters are more likely to say they don't know how they feel about those new parties compared with the older, pre-existing parties. In 1993, for example, among the least informed, non-response in relation to the Liberal Party hovers around 10 percent, whereas non-response in relation to the BQ and the Reform Party hovers closer to 20 percent. The data suggest that as the less politically sophisticated become more familiar with the parties, their willingness to provide a rating goes up. Table 12.2 provides additional support for the role of familiarity. This table tracks the proportion of respondents (overall, not simply by sophistication level) providing a "don't know" answer when asked for their feelings about parties over time.

Besides tracking overall non-response to party thermometers from one election to the next, Table 12.2 also tracks non-response in pre- and post-election studies. In all but one case (ratings of the BQ in 1993), the proportion of respondents giving a "don't know" response decreased from the campaign period wave to the post-election wave of the panel. In many cases, the proportion of respondents providing a "don't know" response decreased by half or more. Although the proportions of those saying "don't know" do

TABLE 12.2

Percentage of all respondents answering "don't know" when asked about their feelings towards different political parties, over time

Election	Conservative		Liberal		NDP		BQ		Reform/CA		Green	
	Pre	Post	Pre	Post	Pre	Post	Pre	Post	Pre	Post	Pre	Post
1988	6.07	2.53	5.88	2.53	8.07	3.49	–	–	–	–	–	–
1993	3.77	2.45	3.80	1.97	6.71	5.00	5.56	6.59	8.60	7.19	–	–
1997	9.98	5.30	7.39	3.82	12.46	7.7	11.02	7.26	12.33	6.25	–	–
2000	11.09	6.86	8.29	3.56	14.90	9.14	9.23	5.21	15.69	7.97	–	–
2004	11.10	4.70	7.66	3.09	13.44	5.83	6.58	3.01	–	–	–	–
2006	6.19	3.54	4.56	2.92	7.79	4.74	5.82	3.67	–	–	30.11	28.18
2008	8.41	–	8.78	–	10.87	–	7.61	–	–	–	20.56	–
2011	4.74	–	5.02	–	6.47	–	4.37	–	–	–	18.00	–

Note: Pre = pre-election study; Post = post-election study.

vary substantially from election to election, the influence of familiarity and
attention can be seen fairly clearly in the drop in non-response between
campaign period waves. It is likely that because of the heightened media
coverage of parties and leaders during election campaigns, voters who had
previously not been terribly aware of parties become more knowledgeable
and consequently more comfortable with providing their assessments in an
interview setting.[2]

More sophisticated voters are more likely than less sophisticated voters
to provide ratings of parties as well as party leaders. Figure 12.2 replicates
Figure 12.1, but this time tracking non-response regarding party leaders
rather than parties. The less sophisticated are substantially more likely than
the more sophisticated to provide a "don't know" answer when asked how
they feel about party leaders. Furthermore, in years when there is substantial flux involving new leaders, we see a substantial jump in the proportion
of respondents who opt not to provide a rating. For example, in 2000, when
two of the five leaders were new and the Canadian Alliance competed under
this new name for the first time, the proportion of "don't know" responses
regarding the leaders of the Progressive Conservative Party (Joe Clark) and
the Reform Party/Canadian Alliance (Stockwell Day) were substantially
higher than in the previous election. In 2004, when Stephen Harper first
competed at the helm of the Conservative Party of Canada, non-response
was substantially higher than in the subsequent two elections, in which he
continued to lead the party. In 2004, after Paul Martin took over as leader
of the Liberal Party, and again in 2008, when Stéphane Dion led the party
in the election, the proportion of "don't know" responses was higher than
in previous years, when there was greater leadership stability. In 2008, when
Elizabeth May contested the election under the Green Party banner for the
first time, the proportion of respondents providing a "don't know" response
when asked how they felt about her was quite high.[3]

Again, the data suggest that when voters are faced with uncertain or new
situations – whether new parties or new leaders – they are less likely to
know how they feel about them. Table 12.3 confirms the influence of familiarity, as it tracks non-responses to leader thermometers from the campaign-period wave of the election to the post-election wave. With very few
exceptions, the proportion of respondents indicating that they don't know
how they feel decreases from one wave to the next.

Indeed, when we look more closely at the factors that influence a "don't
know" response to either leader ratings or party ratings, the importance of
information and familiarity is even clearer. Table 12.4 presents the results

FIGURE 12.2

Percentage of respondents answering "don't know" when asked about their feelings towards party leaders, by sophistication level

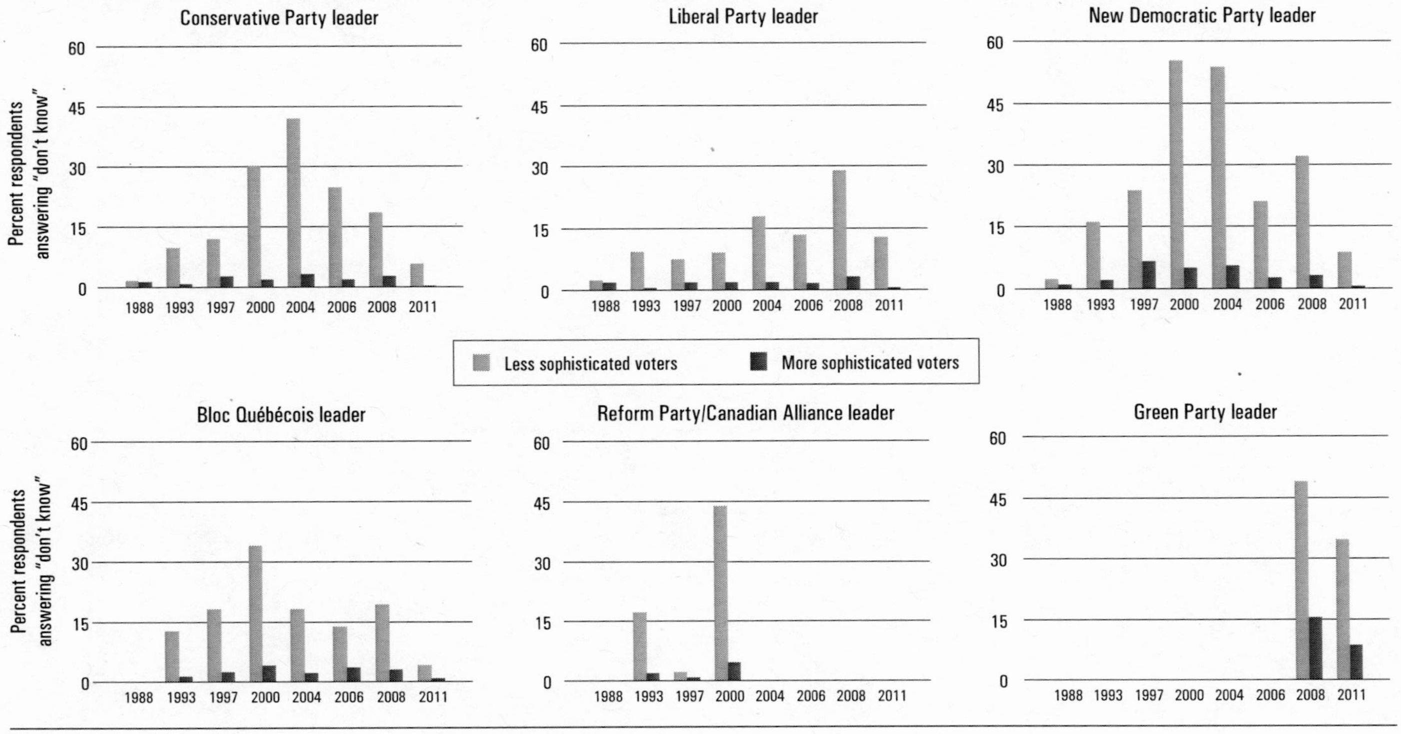

TABLE 12.3

Percentage of all respondents answering "don't know" when asked about their feelings towards different party leaders, over time

Election	Conservative Pre	Conservative Post	Liberal Pre	Liberal Post	NDP Pre	NDP Post	BQ Pre	BQ Post	Reform/CA Pre	Reform/CA Post	Green Pre	Green Post
1988	1.56	1.25	1.96	1.33	8.07	3.49	–	–	–	–	–	–
1993	3.01	1.17	2.95	1.03	6.71	5.00	3.86	4.32	5.75	3.21	–	–
1997	6.22	9.91	3.98	4.13	12.46	7.7	8.87	6.49	1.20	8.23	–	–
2000	11.91	6.93	5.1	2.01	14.90	9.14	16.52	8.72	18.98	11.65	–	–
2004	21.01	8.74	9.11	3.93	13.44	5.83	10.63	3.72	–	–	–	–
2006	8.60	4.65	5.05	3.60	7.79	4.74	7.01	4.28	–	–	–	–
2008	7.49	–	11.24	–	10.87	–	8.07	–	–	–	30.27	–
2011	3.90	–	7.36	–	6.44	–	5.11	–	–	–	26.56	–

Note: Pre = pre-election study; Post = post-election study.

TABLE 12.4

Factors influencing the likelihood of a "don't know" response to leader and party thermometers

Factor	Leader thermometer	Party thermometer
High sophistication	0.253***	0.560***
	(0.0166)	(0.0314)
Liberal partisan	0.771***	0.731***
	(0.0454)	(0.0423)
Conservative partisan	0.702***	0.677***
	(0.0434)	(0.0419)
NDP partisan	0.672***	0.629***
	(0.0551)	(0.0523)
Newspaper + TV exposure	0.135***	0.327***
	(0.0125)	(0.0292)
University graduate	0.722***	0.662***
	(0.0353)	(0.0325)
Woman	1.721***	1.828***
	(0.0809)	(0.0868)
Atlantic	1.048	1.109
	(0.0689)	(0.0737)
Prairies	0.942	0.962
	(0.0552)	(0.0564)
BC	0.975	0.899
	(0.0641)	(0.0597)
Constant	0.495***	0.521***
	(0.0343)	(0.0473)
N	17,216	16,426

Notes: Odds ratios from logistic regression analyses are presented; standard errors are in parentheses. Fixed effects for each election year are included in the model, but results are not shown. The analysis was performed outside of Quebec only.
* $p < .1$, ** $p < .05$, *** $p < .01$

of two logistical regression analyses, assessing the influence of a number of partisan and socio-demographic factors on the likelihood of providing a "don't know" response. The table confirms the patterns found in Figures 12.1 and 12.2: political sophistication is an important determinant of whether respondents will opt to provide a rating of both leaders and parties or say that they "don't know." Those who are more politically sophisticated are less likely to provide a "don't know" response (with odds ratios less than 1). Furthermore, partisans of all parties are less likely to provide a "don't know" response on both leader and party thermometers. This is also not surprising, given scholars' past findings about the strong links between partisanship and higher levels of political knowledge and interest (Campbell et al. 1960; Green et al. 2002). The influence of media exposure is also not a surprise, in that those who read newspapers and watch the news on TV are less likely to provide a "don't know" response. Those who are more educated are also less likely to provide such a response, while women are more likely to say they don't know how they feel about both leaders and parties. These relationships all support earlier findings about item non-response, which point to the non-randomness of providing a "don't know" answer (Berinsky 2004). The findings suggest that in general, those who are more informed, more involved in politics (with stronger partisan attachments), and more educated, and who have greater levels of exposure to the media, are less likely to say they don't know when asked how they feel about parties and leaders.

The impact of political sophistication on the propensity to say "don't know" extends beyond party and leader thermometers. As Figure 12.3 indicates, when asked during the campaign about their vote intention, a relatively high proportion of respondents indicated that they didn't know whom they would be voting for come election day. The difference between the most sophisticated third of the sample and the least sophisticated third is substantial; not surprisingly, those who are more sophisticated are more likely to know whom they will vote for.

In addition to the notable differences according to voters' levels of political sophistication, there is also variation across election years. In the two election years when the options were least different from the previous election (1988 and 2006), the proportion of respondents indicating that they didn't know whom they were going to vote for was lowest.[4] In contrast, in the 2000 election, when there were two new leaders as well as a renamed and revamped Canadian Alliance party, the proportion of voters who didn't know what they would do come election day was highest. The 2004 election, which saw brand-new leaders for three out of four parties, as well as an amalgamated, new Conservative Party of Canada, the proportion of voters who were not sure about their vote choice was also quite high. Both 1997 and 2008, which had three out of five and two out of five new leaders, respectively (as well as the emergence of the Green Party on the national scene in 2008), also reflected relatively high levels of uncertainty among the electorate.

FIGURE 12.3
Percentage of respondents indicating they "don't know" which party
they will vote for, by sophistication level

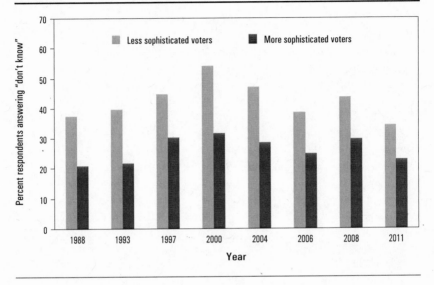

The data suggest that when there is substantial "newness," voters are less certain how they feel about both parties and leaders. The data also suggest that the uncertainty about parties and leaders contributes to the uncertainty regarding vote choice. Voters who indicate that they don't know how they feel about parties and leaders are less likely to know which party they will vote for on election day. Table 12.5 presents the results of a logistic regression analysis that examines the factors influencing those voters who are undecided during the campaign-period wave of the survey.

The independent variables included in the model are the same as those included in Table 12.4, which examined the factors influencing a "don't know" response. In this model, however, "don't know" responses to party and leader thermometers have been flipped to the other side of the equation and are included as independent variables; rather than a dummy variable to reflect those in the "high sophistication" group, a political sophistication variable was included and each independent variable was interacted with this sophistication variable.[5] The value of the linear combination of parameters was then computed, in order to obtain the odds ratios for fully informed preferences. The odds ratios and standard errors for the uninformed preferences (for example, woman) were combined with the odds ratios and

TABLE 12.5
Factors influencing the "undecided" vote intention

Factor	Fully informed preferences	Uninformed preferences	Information effect (difference)
Don't know how feel about a leader	1.743 (0.248)***	1.140 (0.130)	1.529* (0.343)
Don't know how feel about a party	1.424 (0.166)***	1.518*** (0.179)	0.938 (0.189)
Liberal partisan	0.553 (0.05)***	0.394*** (0.0444)	1.403* (0.248)
Conservative partisan	0.292 (0.030)***	0.409*** (0.0497)	0.715* (0.142)
NDP partisan	0.364 (0.05)***	0.335*** (0.0539)	1.088 (0.280)
Media exposure	0.648 (0.093)**	0.900 (0.157)	0.720 (0.200)
University graduate	1.053 (0.08)	0.982 (0.0955)	1.072 (0.163)
Woman	1.191 (0.09)**	1.332*** (0.125)	0.894 (0.133)
Atlantic	1.142 (0.125)	1.304** (0.164)	0.876 (0.180)
Prairies	0.690 (0.067)***	1.503*** (0.174)	0.459*** (0.0861)
BC	0.891 (0.091)	1.215 (0.160)	0.734 (0.150)
Constant	0.642 (0.103)**	0.491*** (0.0913)	1.307 (0.392)

Notes: Odds ratios from logistic regression analyses are presented; standard errors are in parentheses. Fixed effects for each election year are included in the model, but results are not shown. The analysis was performed outside of Quebec only. $N = 14,045$.
* $p < .1$, ** $p < .05$, *** $p < .01$

standard errors of the interacted information effect (woman × knowledge) to illustrate the impact of the independent variables for "fully informed" voters. The first two columns of Table 12.5 therefore demonstrate the comparative impact of each of the independent variables among politically sophisticated voters and among less sophisticated voters.

Partisanship has a fairly clear and not unexpected influence: partisans of the three major parties are less likely to say they don't know whom they will vote for than partisans of "other" parties – whether Reform Party/Canadian Alliance, Green, or something else. Women are more likely than men to be undecided, and this effect is even more pronounced among less sophisticated women. The effect of region is not universal, although less sophisticated voters from Atlantic Canada and the Prairies are more likely to be undecided than less sophisticated voters from Ontario (the reference group).

Not knowing how they felt about parties and leaders led voters to have a higher likelihood of being undecided about their vote choice before election day. This effect was amplified among the more sophisticated respondents: highly sophisticated voters who did not know how they felt about one of the party leaders were 1.7 times more likely to be undecided than those who were confident in giving a rating, while the effect was not statistically significant among less sophisticated voters. Both highly sophisticated and less sophisticated voters were more likely to be undecided if they were not able to provide a rating of one of the parties (odds ratios of 1.4 and 1.5, respectively). The data suggest, therefore, that generally speaking, uncertainty about parties and leaders contributed to uncertainty about vote choice before the election took place.

The next question is whether or not pre-election uncertainty also has an influence on vote choice itself. Table 12.6 displays the results of a series of regression analyses, examining the impact of saying "don't know" in response to a leader thermometer question on vote choice for the four major parties outside of Quebec.[6] Remaining independent variables include partisanship, political sophistication, media exposure, education, sex, and region (as well as dummy variables as controls for each election year); this set-up is similar to that presented in Table 12.4.[7]

As Table 12.6 illustrates, the influence of not knowing how one feels about the leaders does not have a clear pattern across parties. Not knowing was a statistically significant influence on vote choice for only two parties: the Conservatives and the NDP. Voters who did not know how they felt about the Conservative leader were less likely to vote for the Conservative Party, and those who did not know how they felt about the NDP leader were more likely to vote Conservative and less likely to vote NDP.

Of the independent variables included in the model, partisanship had the largest influence on vote choice, for all parties. Partisans were most likely to vote for their own parties, and less likely to vote for the others.

TABLE 12.6

Effects on vote choice of saying "don't know" about leader thermometer ratings

Factor	Vote choice			
	Liberal	Conservative	NDP	Reform/CA
DK: Liberal leader thermometer	0.918 (0.168)	0.924 (0.169)	1.354 (0.276)	2.109 (1.331)
DK: Conservative leader thermometer	1.021 (0.175)	0.694** (0.125)	1.309 (0.262)	0.876 (0.398)
DK: NDP leader thermometer	1.107 (0.141)	1.531*** (0.198)	0.553*** (0.0919)	0.842 (0.222)
DK: Reform/CA leader thermometer	– –	– –	– –	0.600 (0.212)
Liberal partisan	7.721*** (0.472)	0.279*** (0.0198)	0.490*** (0.0374)	0.194*** (0.0307)
Conservative partisan	0.198*** (0.0172)	11.49*** (0.777)	0.154*** (0.0158)	0.953 (0.135)
NDP partisan	0.364*** (0.0365)	0.117*** (0.0138)	18.18*** (1.569)	0.0581*** (0.0206)
Reform/CA partisan	– –	– –	– –	15.06*** (3.245)
Highly sophisticated	1.063 (0.0613)	0.926 (0.0557)	0.853** (0.0579)	0.967 (0.120)
Media exposure	1.211* (0.124)	1.199* (0.128)	0.817* (0.0974)	1.146 (0.248)
University degree	1.024 (0.0552)	0.906* (0.0502)	1.062 (0.0673)	0.817* (0.0965)
Woman	1.041 (0.0546)	0.926 (0.0502)	1.286*** (0.0794)	0.736*** (0.0864)
Atlantic	1.210*** (0.0893)	0.981 (0.0782)	1.240** (0.113)	0.346*** (0.0728)
Prairies	0.524*** (0.0359)	1.159** (0.0792)	1.072 (0.0864)	1.885*** (0.262)
BC	0.477*** (0.0354)	1.045 (0.0791)	1.613*** (0.131)	2.086*** (0.327)
Constant	0.239*** (0.0291)	0.327*** (0.0295)	0.179*** (0.0183)	0.568*** (0.109)
Observations	11,370	11,370	11,370	2,410

Notes: Odds ratios from logistic regression analyses are presented; standard errors are in parentheses. Fixed effects for each election year are included in the model, but results are not shown. The analysis was performed outside of Quebec only.

* $p < .1$, ** $p < .05$, *** $p < .01$

Partisanship appears to have mattered most for the NDP and the Reform Party/Canadian Alliance: partisans of these two parties were most likely to vote for their respective parties. While partisanship for the Liberal and Conservative parties also had a large influence on voting for those parties, the odds ratios were not quite as large.

Interestingly, the effects of partisanship were stronger when those who said they did not know how they felt were included in the model than when they were excluded. Table 12.7 replicates the analysis in Table 12.6, but instead of focusing on the impact of leader thermometer non-response on vote choice, it excludes those who did not know how they felt about the leaders and examines the impact of leader ratings on vote choice.

As can be clearly seen in Table 12.7, feelings towards leaders can have a substantial impact on vote choice. The table demonstrates the "maximal" impact of party leaders, as it reflects a change from the least positive rating of a leader possible (0) to the most positive rating of a leader possible (1). Obviously, these two extremes are rare, and we should interpret the influence of leaders in real life to be more moderate. Having said that, it is clear that voters' feelings about leaders do influence vote choice; thus, to some extent, parties are penalized when voters do not know how they feel about their leaders. When voters perceive a party leader in a positive light, they are more likely to vote for the party.

The effects of partisanship are also important, although notably the impact of partisanship when leader thermometers are included in the model is smaller than when "non-response" is included instead. Because the models presented in Table 12.7 exclude those individuals who did not know how they felt about leaders (those individuals *are* present in Table 12.6), the data suggest that partisanship matters more among those who are uncertain about party leaders. This remains true when non-response to party thermometers is included in the model in addition to thermometer ratings[8] – voters who are uncertain about parties and leaders are more likely than those who do have opinions to base their vote choice on partisanship. This suggests that theoretically, in times of flux, "old" parties may benefit from the uncertainty surrounding new parties and leaders, parties for which voters may not yet have had an opportunity to develop a partisan affiliation. Even if a new party "succeeds" in a given election (as seen, for example, in the Reform Party's electoral success relative to its newness in the 1993 election), they may not do as well as they might if voters were more familiar with the party or the leader.

TABLE 12.7
Effects of leader thermometer ratings on vote choice

Factor	Vote choice			
	Liberal	Conservative	NDP	Reform/CA
Liberal leader thermometer	74.56***	0.0696***	0.283***	0.0705***
	(11.96)	(0.0107)	(0.0430)	(0.0258)
Conservative leader thermometer	0.107***	275.5***	0.172***	0.221***
	(0.0142)	(49.05)	(0.0240)	(0.0819)
NDP leader thermometer	0.330***	0.147***	41.16***	0.176***
	(0.0493)	(0.0239)	(7.472)	(0.0683)
Reform/CA leader thermometer	–	–	–	1,046***
	–	–	–	(452.8)
Liberal partisan	5.101***	0.435***	0.525***	0.345***
	(0.360)	(0.0379)	(0.0466)	(0.0689)
Conservative partisan	0.342***	4.796***	0.260***	0.988
	(0.0340)	(0.392)	(0.0303)	(0.187)
NDP partisan	0.329***	0.170***	10.27***	0.122***
	(0.0385)	(0.0241)	(0.990)	(0.0516)
Reform/CA partisan	–	–	–	2.935***
	–	–	–	(0.740)
Highly sophisticated	0.897*	1.042	0.745***	0.950
	(0.0579)	(0.0744)	(0.0554)	(0.142)
Media exposure	1.134	0.953	0.763**	0.820
	(0.133)	(0.123)	(0.100)	(0.226)
University degree	1.055	0.997	0.966	0.997
	(0.0648)	(0.0659)	(0.0677)	(0.148)
Woman	1.004	0.977	1.233***	0.746**
	(0.0595)	(0.0629)	(0.0833)	(0.109)
Atlantic	1.079	1.244**	1.236**	0.444***
	(0.0906)	(0.117)	(0.125)	(0.113)
Prairies	0.509***	1.061	1.200**	1.611***
	(0.0395)	(0.0864)	(0.107)	(0.279)
BC	0.419***	0.995	1.730***	2.179***
	(0.0353)	(0.0912)	(0.155)	(0.428)
Constant	0.230***	0.152***	0.108***	0.259***
	(0.0298)	(0.0214)	(0.0164)	(0.0837)
N	10,281	10,281	10,281	2,166

Notes: Odds ratios from logistic regression analyses are presented; standard errors are in parentheses. Fixed effects for each election year are included in the model, but results are not shown. The analysis was performed outside of Quebec only.
* $p < .1$, ** $p < .05$, *** $p < .01$

Indeed, among voters in the 1993 election, Conservative partisans who were able to provide an evaluation of Preston Manning had a 22 percent chance of voting for the Conservative Party. Conservative partisans who responded with "don't know" to the Reform leader thermometer had a 47 percent chance of voting for the Conservative Party.[9]

In examining vote choice in the 2004 election, the role of uncertainty about the leaders becomes even more apparent. Conservative partisans who were willing or able to evaluate Stephen Harper had a 50 percent likelihood of voting for the Conservative Party. Conservative partisans who responded "don't know" to the leader thermometer for Stephen Harper had a 40 percent likelihood of voting for the Conservative Party. Harper lost votes from his own partisans because he was a new leader. Jack Layton had a similar problem in the same election: he was newly installed as the NDP leader, and NDP partisans who rated Layton on the thermometer had a 54 percent likelihood of voting for the NDP. In contrast, among those who did not know how they felt about Layton, the likelihood of voting NDP was much lower, at 41 percent.[10] Parties did better among their own partisans if those partisans were able to evaluate their leaders.

Other variables had an impact on vote choice. Women were more likely to vote for the NDP and less likely to vote for the Reform Party. Voters west of Ontario were more likely to vote for the NDP and the Reform Party/ Canadian Alliance, and less likely to vote Liberal. Atlantic Canadians were slightly more likely to vote Conservative and less likely to vote for the Reform Party. Media exposure had an impact only on the NDP vote: those who had the largest amount of media exposure were less likely to vote for the NDP than those who paid the least amount of attention to newspapers and TV news.[11] All of these patterns of behaviour follow what we expect based on past research on Canadian voters and elections.

Conclusion

Studies of Canadian voting behaviour have provided us with a substantial amount of insight into the decision-making processes of voters. We know that women tend to hold opinions and make vote choices that put them further to the left than men (Gidengil et al. 2003). We know that religion plays an important role in the calculus of Canadian voters (Blais 2005; Irvine 1974; Johnston 1985). Partisanship has been shown to play a crucial role in the minds of voters over the years, although there has been substantial debate over how to measure this variable and what exactly it means to be a partisan (Clarke et al. 1979; Johnston 1992, 2006; LeDuc 1985; LeDuc et al. 1984). We know that leaders are important to vote choice (Bittner 2011; Blais et al. 2000, 2002; Brown et al. 1988; Cutler 2002; Gidengil et al. 2000, 2006; Johnston 2002), and we know that both the media and political sophistication have an influence over the types of considerations that voters make when heading to the ballot box (Bittner 2007; Blais and Boyer 1996; Cutler 2002; Everitt 2003; Fournier 2002; Gidengil and Everitt 2003; Johnston et al. 1996; Mendelsohn 1993, 1994, 1996; Mendelsohn and Nadeau 1999). Furthermore, studies of political parties in Canada over the past few decades have pointed to the important changes that have occurred over time, including changes in party systems, party organization, party finance, and electioneering more generally (Carty 2004; Carty and Eagles 2005; Carty et al. 2000; Koop 2010; Sayers 1999).

The last two decades in Canadian federal politics have seen substantial flux, including the emergence of new parties and new leaders, the disappearance of traditional parties, and more recently the "domination" of Parliament by minority governments. The extent to which this flux has influenced the nature of the vote calculus among Canadians has not really been examined to date. Are Canadians able to cope with the emergence of new parties and new leaders, or are they confused? What happens to the nature of their decisions when voters are uncertain about the menu of options available? This chapter has begun to answer these questions.

In the eight elections between 1988 and 2011, only two were fought by the exact same parties and leaders as in the previous election. In the other six elections, we saw the emergence of brand-new parties, the virtual collapse of a traditional party, the merger of old and new, and a plethora of new leaders at the helm of all parties, both old and new. Analysis of data from the Canadian Election Studies over this period suggests that indeed voters experienced higher levels of uncertainty in election years when change was substantial. Voters were more likely to say that they did not know how they felt about both parties and leaders in years when parties and leaders were new, and they were also less likely to be certain about whom they would vote for during these elections. Furthermore, the uncertainty they felt about parties and leaders had an influence on their vote choice: partisans were more likely to rely upon partisanship in situations of uncertainty, and were also less likely to support their own party if they were uncertain about its leader.

Gradually, over the last four elections, the party system appears to be heading towards a new equilibrium. This view was borne out in the 2011 national election, when national politics appeared to enter a new party system featuring a return to a majority government and the decline of parties from four to three. Whether the NDP's recent success can be maintained in the long term remains to be seen, and it seems fairly clear that the next couple of elections may again be characterized by flux. Certainly Jack Layton's passing will be felt in future elections, and these data suggest that the NDP may be penalized in the next election unless the party can ensure that voters become familiar and comfortable with its new leader. The breakthrough of the Green Party with its first seat may further contribute to the new state of flux, and only time will tell how influential this party will be in parliaments to come. It was clear in the 2008 election that voters did not quite know what to make of either the Green Party or its leader, and the data suggest that until voters become more comfortable evaluating it, the party is likely to be penalized by voters' affiliation with other, already existing parties.

Throughout the last twenty years, voters who were more politically sophisticated appear to have been better able to cope with flux. They were more likely than less sophisticated voters to provide an evaluation of both parties and leaders; they were more likely to know how they felt about them. Furthermore, voters' comfort levels with providing an opinion about the leaders and parties had a direct influence on party fortunes. The data suggest that the changes visible on the surface of Canadian electoral competition over the last two decades have been difficult for voters to deal with, and that, more importantly, they have had a negative impact on the success of the parties themselves. Change leads to confusion and uncertainty, and uncertainty leads voters to penalize the parties and leaders they are uncertain about. These findings indicate that until Canadian federal elections are able to provide voters with a more stable menu of options, voters are going to continue to have difficulty orienting themselves in the political landscape. The question is whether the new menu presented in the 2011 national election will be long-standing, aiding voters as they participate in national politics. Only time will tell.

Notes

1 Note that I have listed the newly merged "Conservative Party" in the same column as the old "Progressive Conservative Party."
2 Note that regardless of respondents' comfort level with the political landscape, the rate of non-response is expected to decrease somewhat from one wave to the next,

as those who are most likely to say that they don't know how they feel about a question are also most likely not to be re-interviewed in subsequent waves of election studies (Berinsky 2004).

3 Note that in 2011 the proportion of respondents providing a "don't know" response decreased dramatically for all parties and leaders. Only the Liberal Party had a new leader on the scene, and while respondents were more comfortable providing an evaluation of Michael Ignatieff than they had been in the previous election with Stéphane Dion, it is important to note that the highest level of leader non-response occurred with both Elizabeth May and Michael Ignatieff, the two newest leaders on the federal scene.

4 Note again that the 2011 election marks a lower level of non-response than others: voters were comfortable evaluating leaders and parties in this election, and they were also more certain of their voting intention. This is not surprising, given the stability of most of the parties and leaders since the 2004 election. With the exception of the Liberal Party, no changes in leadership occurred since 2004, and it is likely that the place of the other parties was becoming more and more crystallized in the minds of voters.

5 See Bittner 2007 for an identical set-up, based on Bartels's methodology (1996).

6 I opted to omit the influence of party thermometers because of the proximity of party thermometers to vote choice. Indeed, when the models were rerun with "don't know" responses to party thermometers included, the coefficients for party thermometers were usually not statistically significant, and the size of the remaining coefficients did not change substantially.

7 The interacted model was also run, but did not increase the explanatory power of the model. For the sake of simplicity, I opted to present this (simpler) model.

8 Results are not shown.

9 Results were obtained using CLARIFY in Stata. All other independent variables were held at their means.

10 Results were obtained using CLARIFY in Stata. All other independent variables were held at their means.

11 Given that the intention of the analyses presented in Tables 12.6 and 12.7 was to determine the impact of uncertainty on vote choice rather than to provide a fully specified model, I do not wish to place too much stock in the relative influence of the remaining control variables. These were chosen over others for inclusion so as to maximize the number of respondents in the model, rather than to maximize the accuracy of the impact of socio-demographic variables. Studies of voting have repeatedly demonstrated the importance of other variables, including ideology, issue attitudes, and socio-demographics (age, income, union membership, and religion, among others). When these variables are all included in the model, the number of respondents decreases substantially, so a more minimalist model was chosen. When the other variables are included in the statistical model, the coefficients of those variables presented in the tables do not change substantially.

References

Alvarez, R. Michael. 1997. *Information and Elections.* Ann Arbor: University of Michigan Press.

Bartels, Larry M. 1996. "Uninformed Votes: Information Effects in Presidential Elections." *American Journal of Political Science* 40 (1): 194-230.

Berelson, Bernard, Paul Lazarsfeld, and William McPhee. 1954. *Voting.* Cambridge, MA: Harvard University Press.

Berinsky, Adam J. 2004. *Silent Voices: Public Opinion and Political Participation in America.* Princeton, NJ: Princeton University Press.

Bittner, Amanda. 2007. "The Effects of Information and Social Cleavages: Explaining Issue Attitudes and Vote Choice in Canada." *Canadian Journal of Political Science* 40 (4): 935-68.

–. 2011. *Platform or Personality? The Role of Party Leaders in Elections.* Oxford: Oxford University Press.

Blais, André. 2005. "Accounting for the Electoral Success of the Liberal Party in Canada: Presidential Address to the Canadian Political Science Association London, Ontario, June 3, 2005." *Canadian Journal of Political Science* 38 (4): 821-40.

Blais, André, and M. Martin Boyer. 1996. "Assessing the Impact of Televised Debates: The Case of the 1988 Canadian Election." *British Journal of Political Science* 26 (2): 143-64.

Blais, André, Elisabeth Gidengil, Richard Nadeau, and Neil Nevitte. 2002. *Anatomy of a Liberal Victory: Making Sense of the Vote in the 2000 Canadian Election.* Toronto: Broadview Press.

Blais, André, Neil Nevitte, Elisabeth Gidengil, and Richard Nadeau. 2000. "Do People Have Feelings Toward Leaders about Whom They Say They Know Nothing?" *Public Opinion Quarterly* 64 (4): 452-63.

Brady, Henry, and Paul Sniderman. 1985. "Attitude Attribution: A Group Basis for Political Reasoning." *American Political Science Review* 79: 1061-78.

Brown, Steven D., Ronald D. Lambert, Barry J. Kay, and James E. Curtis. 1988. "In the Eye of the Beholder: Leader Images in Canada." *Canadian Journal of Political Science* 21: 729-55.

Campbell, Angus, Philip E. Converse, Warren E. Miller, and Donald E. Stokes. 1960. *The American Voter.* Chicago: John Wiley and Sons.

Carty, R. Kenneth. 2004. "Parties as Franchise Systems: The Stratarchical Organizational Imperative." *Party Politics* 10 (1): 35-45.

Carty, R. Kenneth, and Munroe Eagles. 2005. *Politics Is Local: National Politics at the Grassroots.* Oxford: Oxford University Press.

Carty, R. Kenneth, William Cross, and Lisa Young. 2000. *Rebuilding Canadian Party Politics.* Vancouver: UBC Press.

Clarke, Harold, Lawrence LeDuc, Jane Jenson, and Jon Pammet. 1979. *Political Choice in Canada.* Toronto: McGraw-Hill Ryerson.

Converse, Philip E. 1964. "The Nature of Belief Systems in Mass Publics." In *Ideology and Discontent,* edited by David E. Apter, 206-61. New York: Free Press.

Cutler, Fred. 2002. "The Simplest Shortcut of All: Sociodemographic Characteristics and Electoral Choice." *Journal of Politics* 64 (2): 466-90.

Everitt, Joanna. 2003. "Media in the Maritimes: Do Female Candidates Face a Bias?" *Atlantis* 27 (2): 90-98.

Fournier, Patrick. 2002. "The Uninformed Canadian Voter." In *Citizen Politics: Research and Theory in Canadian Political Behaviour,* edited by Joanna Everitt and Brenda O'Neill, 92-109. New York: Oxford University Press.

Gidengil, Elisabeth, André Blais, Richard Nadeau, and Neil Nevitte. 2000. "Are Party Leaders Becoming More Important to Vote Choice in Canada?" Paper presented at the annual meeting of the American Political Science Association, Marriott Wardman Park, Washington DC.

Gidengil, Elisabeth, André Blais, Richard Nadeau, and Neil Nevitte. 2003. "Women to the Left? Gender Differences in Political Beliefs and Policy Preferences." In *Women and Electoral Politics in Canada,* edited by Manon Tremblay and Linda Trimble, 140-59. Oxford: Oxford University Press.

Gidengil, Elisabeth, and Joanna Everitt. 2003. "Conventional Coverage/Unconventional Politicians: Gender and Media Coverage of Canadian Leaders' Debates, 1993, 1997, 2000." *Canadian Journal of Political Science* 36 (3): 559-77.

Gidengil, Elisabeth, Joanna Everitt, and Susan A. Banducci. 2006. "Gender and Perceptions of Leader Traits: Evidence from the 1993 Canadian and 1999 New Zealand Elections." Paper presented at the Conference on Women and Leadership, University of Toronto.

Glasgow, Garrett, and R. Michael Alvarez. 2000. "Uncertainty and Candidate Personality Traits." *American Politics Quarterly* 28 (1): 26-49.

Green, Donald, Bradley Palmquist, and Eric Schickler. 2002. *Partisan Hearts and Minds: Political Parties and the Social Identities of Voters.* New Haven, CT: Yale University Press.

Irvine, William P. 1974. "Explaining the Religious Basis of the Canadian Partisan Identity: Success on the Third Try." *Canadian Journal of Political Science* 7: 560-63.

Johnston, Richard. 1985. "The Reproduction of the Religious Cleavage in Canadian Elections." *Canadian Journal of Political Science* 18 (1): 99-113.

–. 1992. "Party Identification Measures in the Anglo-American Democracies: A National Survey Experiment." *American Journal of Political Science* 36 (2): 542-59.

–. 2002. "Prime Ministerial Contenders in Canada." In *Leaders' Personalities and the Outcomes of Democratic Elections,* edited by Anthony King, 158-83. Oxford: Oxford University Press.

–. 2006. "Party Identification: Unmoved Mover or Sum of Preferences?" *Annual Review of Political Science* 9: 329-51.

Johnston, Richard, André Blais, Elisabeth Gidengil, and Neil Nevitte. 1996. *The Challenge of Direct Democracy.* Montreal and Kingston: McGill-Queen's University Press.

Johnston, Richard, Michael G. Hagen, and Kathleen Hall Jamieson. 2004. *The 2000 Presidential Election and the Foundations of Party Politics.* Cambridge: Cambridge University Press.

Koop, Royce. 2010. "Professionalism, Sociability, and the Liberal Party in the Constituencies." *Canadian Journal of Political Science* 43 (4): 893-913.

LeDuc, Lawrence. 1985. "Partisan Change and Dealignment in Canada, Great Britain, and the United States." *Comparative Politics* 17 (4): 379-98.

LeDuc, Lawrence, Harold Clarke, Jane Jenson, and Jon Pammet. 1984. "Partisan Instability in Canada: Evidence from a New Panel Study." *American Political Science Review* 78 (2): 470-84.

Lupia, Arthur, and Matthew McCubbins. 1998. *The Democratic Dilemma.* Cambridge: Cambridge University Press.

Matthews, J. Scott. 2006. "The Campaign Dynamics of Economic Voting." PhD dissertation, University of British Columbia.

Mendelsohn, Matthew. 1993. "Television's Frames in the 1988 Canadian Election." *Canadian Journal of Communication* 19 (2): 149-71.

–. 1994. "The Media's Persuasive Effects: The Priming of Leadership in the 1988 Canadian Election." *Canadian Journal of Political Science* 27: 81-97.

–. 1996. "The Media and Interpersonal Communications: The Priming of Issues, Leaders, and Party Identification." *Journal of Politics* 58 (1): 112-25.

Mendelsohn, Matthew, and Richard Nadeau. 1999. "The Rise and Fall of Candidates in Canadian Election Campaigns." *International Journal of Press* 4 (2): 63-76.

Rahn, Wendy M. 1993. "The Role of Partisan Stereotypes in Information Processing about Political Candidates." *American Journal of Political Science* 37 (2): 472-96.

Roy, Jason. 2007. "When Less Is More: No Information versus Low Information and the Application of Heuristics in Canadian Context." Paper presented at the annual meeting of the Canadian Political Science Association, Saskatoon.

Sanders, Mitchell S. 2001. "Uncertainty and Turnout." *Political Analysis* 9 (1): 45-57.

Sayers, Anthony M. 1999. *Parties, Candidates, and Constituency Campaigns in Canadian Elections.* Vancouver: UBC Press.

Sniderman, Paul, Richard Brody, and Philip Tetlock. 1991. *Reasoning and Choice: Explorations in Political Psychology.* New York: Cambridge University Press.

13

Situating the Canadian Case

RICHARD JOHNSTON

The 2011 national election may have changed the foundations of Canadian elections for all time. At a minimum, it created the preconditions for such change, particularly by denying the Liberal Party control of its fate. Marginalization of the Liberals would undermine the traditional Canadian pattern of "brokerage" politics, an eventuality flagged by R. Kenneth Carty in Chapter 1.

This chapter explores the electoral correlates of Canada's brokerage politics. These include domination of the system by the broker, based in turn on that party's command of the political centre. This domination coexisted with a distinctively Canadian pattern of volatility – indeed, was responsible for it. Volatility was facilitated by a multipartism that sat uneasily with brokerage but was itself also partly a reaction to brokerage. Although the connection is not drawn explicitly, the evidence strongly suggests that the old system contained the seeds of its own destruction.

I explore these points with comparative evidence from other long-standing Westminster systems. This holds key institutional features constant, thereby allowing Canada's peculiarities to reveal their full power. But first we must identify the dramatis personae.

The Players and the Stakes

This section names most of the relevant parties in Canadian history, sorts them into categories that are unfamiliar in Canadian usage, and describes key trends and patterns. Three points emerge from this synoptic overview. First, the system was dominated for more than a century by the Liberal Party, but on a steadily eroding popular base. Second, the erosion of the Liberal base was accompanied *not* by progressive strengthening of the chief alternative party, the Conservatives, but by overall fractionalization of the system. Third, fractionalization widened the scope for electoral flux and for asymmetries in that flux. The coexistence of these three patterns reflects a fourth key feature that I will outline later, the fact that the dominant party of the twentieth century commanded the ideological centre.

To make sense of this, it is helpful to classify Canadian parties as either pro-system or anti-system, a distinction that originates with Giovanni Sartori.[1] The "anti-system" parties category overlaps that of "niche" parties (Meguid 2008). In the Canadian context, "pro-system" means willing to work with the Westminster model: a majoritarian electoral formula, disciplined parliamentary parties, and (usually) single-party government. A pro-system party contests seats everywhere, or nearly so, signalling that it is serious about seeking power. "Anti-system" originally denoted parties that were outright anti-democratic, basically Nazi, Fascist, and Communist formations. Capoccia (2002) argues that the concept should be stretched to include parties of repudiation whose preferred alternative is nonetheless democratic as well as parties that are so ideologically distant from the others that they are not plausible coalition partners. The "niche" category refers to parties that are committed to a single policy dimension and thus reject the bundling of considerations that would be necessary to expand their base. Often, the single dimension can be styled as ethno-regional defence. Behaviourally, both categories point to limited contestation and a lack of interest in gaining power.[2]

This classification puts me at odds with the Canadian literature, which commonly treats all parties other than the Liberals and Conservatives simply as minor parties. To be sure, the Westminster context does make small parties seem like anomalies requiring explanation. A key feature of the Westminster model is a "strong" electoral system, one that punishes coordination failure. This in turn should focus competition on the two most viable parties; others should fall by the wayside (Chhibber and Kollman 2004; Cox 1997; Duverger 1963). At a minimum, given that small parties are excluded from office, they should specialize in something other than assembling a large electoral coalition. So it is not unreasonable to see big parties as ideologically amorphous, as "catch-all" parties (Kirchheimer 1966) or even as "brokers" (Chapter 1), and small ones as driven by issues or as representing specific social groups. But dividing the Canadian parties this way leads to misclassification of the New Democratic Party (NDP), a misclassification that blocks the explanation – indeed, the very identification – of Canada's peculiarities.

Pro-System Parties

This category obviously includes the Liberals and Conservatives, the only parties that have ever governed in Canada. But I argue that it should also include the NDP, notwithstanding its historically small size. The NDP's objective is not to change the Westminster system's fundamental character but to displace one of the major partisan alternatives, most plausibly the Liberals. Admittedly, before 1961 the party's situation was ambiguous. At its founding, the NDP's precursor, the Co-operative Commonwealth Federation (CCF), was officially committed to overturning capitalism. More to the point, the CCF declined to contest about half of all seats and presented something of a western Canada insurgent face. Even then, however, the party was influenced by reformist advocates, often with Social Gospel backgrounds (Allen 1971), and much of its intelligentsia was based in Central Canada (Young 1969). In any case, once the CCF was transformed into the NDP and a link with organized labour was made explicit, the party moved quickly to nominate candidates everywhere (Johnston and Cutler 2009). That many of these candidates were sacrificial lambs is immaterial to my argument; the key is that the party sought to create at least the appearance of credibility in all regions.

The pro-system vote has been fractionalizing for decades, although asymmetrically between parties. The evidence is in the top left panel (Votes) of Figure 13.1. The most dramatic shifts involve the Conservatives, who plunged in 1921 and in a sense never recovered. Although their post-1921 series features a handful of dramatic surges, these gains were never sustained. Since 1935, only once (1988) did they return a share in the garden-variety 40 percent range; instead the pattern has been boom or bust, mainly bust. Notwithstanding the 1990s (on which more below), however, the party is no worse off now than in 1921. If the Conservative pattern is visually arresting, the Liberal pattern is simpler but arguably more dire: the party's share has been eroding since 1911. No single setback is as great as several of those suffered by the Conservatives, but neither did any Liberal recovery restore all the lost ground. Since 1935, the complement to the Liberal share has been that of the CCF/NDP. The 1990s were a setback for the NDP, but otherwise its pattern is of a slow upward trend.

Asymmetry characterizes more than just the parties' general trajectories. It also characterizes their vulnerability to short-term forces. The standard deviation in the Conservatives' series (11.2) is nearly twice that for the Liberals (6.5). Much of this gap captures the permanent downshift in Conservative shares in 1921. But even if we focus on the years since 1921, the Conservative share is half again as variable as the Liberal one. By implication, the Conservatives often trade votes with parties outside the pro-system core.

Seat-share evidence, in the bottom left panel of Figure 13.1, confirms the mechanical effect (Duverger 1963) of Canada's first-past-the-post (FPTP) electoral system. This appears in two ways. Short-term flux is massively exaggerated: standard deviations in seat shares are roughly double those for vote shares. And the gap between Conservative and Liberal seat shares, on the one hand, and those for the CCF/NDP, on the other, is roughly twice as great as the gap in votes.[3] Swings for the Conservatives have been especially dramatic. Their majorities in 1958 and 1984 are the largest in Canadian history, but from 1935 to 1957 they constituted an exceptionally weak Official Opposition and in the 1990s they truly hit bottom.

Thanks to the electoral system, Liberal decline was masked by the party's continuing ability to form governments, usually with seat majorities. The fact that the Liberal vote was smaller after 1930 than before 1911 did not prevent the party from returning four massive majorities between 1935 and 1957. Its majorities after 1960 were never on the 1935-57 scale, but were comfortable, especially in the 1990s. But those 1990s returns masked the fact that the Liberal vote had deteriorated relative to the 1963-84 period, and elections since 2004 have torn the cover off Liberal weakness.

Anti-System or Niche Parties
The most direct avenue into this category is through a discussion of its major examples.

The Progressives. The critical fact about this 1920s movement-cum-party is that it contested almost exclusively rural ridings engaged in commodity (mainly wheat) production for export. This meant candidacies mainly in the prairie provinces and southwestern Ontario. Substantively, Progressives contested a single dimension of politics, the conflict between land, on the one hand, and labour and capital, on the other (Morton 1950). Its more radical elements, mainly in Alberta, also challenged the very idea of Westminster politics and championed a functionalist and corporatist model (Macpherson 1953). The Progressives, however, also harboured more

FIGURE 13.1

The players and the stakes

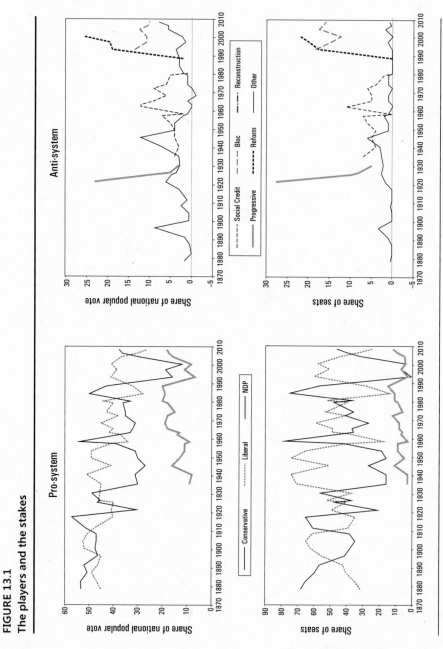

Source: Official statistics.

inclusive and programmatic elements, which were precursors of the CCF and NDP.

Social Credit in the West. This party was even more sectionally concentrated than the Progressives, starting in Alberta and later spreading to rural British Columbia. Notwithstanding superficial similarities in geography, the party appears not to have inherited much from the Progressives. Where the latter drew upon the existing leadership in the rural West and Ontario, Social Credit was led by outsiders. To the extent that the party was animated by ideology, the focus was on money and banking, an ancient agrarian and small-business theme (Irving 1959; Macpherson 1953). Smiley (1962) likened them to Pierre Poujade's Union de Défense des Commerçants et Artisans, the quintessential anti-system party of the French Fourth Republic. Eventually Social Credit morphed into a party of somewhat contentless regional defence but with a clearly conservative cast.

Social Credit in Quebec. The Ralliement Créditiste was effectively separate from the western branch of the movement and the two existed in tension, alternately breaking apart and reconfederating. Although the religious and linguistic gap between the regional variants was wide, their support bases were otherwise quite similar, as was their rhetoric.

Reform Party/Canadian Alliance. This is a truly ambiguous case, and the classification arguably should shift with time. Reform began with strong echoes of Western Social Credit, especially in its core geography. Although it ran candidates and won votes in many more places than Social Credit did, Reform was slow to enter Quebec. The party also exhibited anti-system tendencies, particularly repudiation of party discipline in favour of representation of local majority opinion. In its early years, the party reflected the conflicting objectives of its first leader, Preston Manning (Flanagan 2009), but the transformation of Reform into the Canadian Alliance signalled reconciliation with Westminster logic. In itself the shift failed, but it paved the way for the Alliance's reverse takeover of the Conservative Party. In hindsight, the party was the midwife for the reorientation of the Canadian right, originally advocated by Preston Manning's father (Manning 1967).[4]

The Bloc Québécois. Although the Bloc is a skilled parliamentary presence and presents reasonably coherent electoral platforms, it is at bottom a party of ethno-regional defence. Notwithstanding the specificity of its program, its supporters are essentially indistinguishable in ideology from the Quebec supporters of the pro-system parties (Johnston 2008, Figure 2). It does not contest ridings outside the province and its mere presence frustrates the Westminster logic in the country as a whole.

Other parties. Most other parties in the historical landscape have some kind of anti-system tendency. The 1896 election, for example, featured small-scale precursors of 1921. Candidacies by the Knights of Labour and by supporters of Dalton McCarthy, sometimes with mutual endorsements, could be seen as anticipating both agrarian and union-based politics in the next century but also spasmodic, short-term repudiation of party politics as such. *Reconstruction* in 1935 is an ambiguous case. It was the extended shadow of its leader, HH Stevens, a former and future Conservative, its program exhibited impatience with parliamentarism, and there were dalliances between it and Social Credit. But it did have a forward-looking program, and it ran candidates nationwide (Wilbur 1964).[5] The Bloc Populaire Canadien, along with a self-named "Independent Group," anticipated the later Bloc in its one appearance in 1945. The Bloc and the Group emerged from an opposition to conscription in 1942 and combined new entrants with defectors from Liberal ranks.

The count of names indicates that the West (especially the prairie West) and Quebec have been the prime sources of anti-system insurgency. With respect to these two sources, the timing of insurgency is very suggestive. The top right panel of Figure 13.1 reveals six punctuation points: 1896, 1921, 1935, 1945, 1962, and 1993. The typical instance combines economic distress with cultural tension. In 1896, a year of aborted insurgency, the country had experienced a particularly severe recession for much of the 1890s and generally poor times since the 1870s. At the same time, the Manitoba Schools Question was tearing at the party system (Crunican 1974), following intense sectarian division over schools in the Northwest (Lupul 1974) and the disposition of the Jesuits' Estates (Miller 1979). The 1921 election and the Progressive breakthrough accompanied an agricultural depression brought on by the end of the Great War. The war itself and the conscription crisis of 1917 were even more divisive than the Manitoba Schools Question had been, and the party system was staggering even before the Progressives appeared on the scene (English 1977). The 1962 election took place late in the "Eisenhower recession" but also a mere two years after the start of Quebec's "Quiet Revolution" (Pinard 1975). The 1993 election, and the advent of both the Reform Party and the Bloc Québécois, followed both the very deep recession of the early 1990s and the failure of the Meech Lake and Charlottetown Accords. The other two punctuation points appeared to have single sources. The 1945 election featured cultural tension over conscription (Behiels 1985) but no particular economic distress.[6] The 1935 election featured the opposite: the Great Depression but no projection into the federal arena of ferment inside Quebec.[7]

Interaction across the Boundary

The Canadian party system thus has an episodic dynamic. As the three pro-system parties worked within the Westminster logic to run candidates everywhere and to nationalize the vote, voters in the West and Quebec episodically pushed back. The West was the pioneer in this, as the insurgencies of 1896, 1921, and 1935 were essentially prairie provinces phenomena. Quebec assumed the mantle in 1945 and again in 1962. The distinctive thing about 1993 is that both regions went critical at the same time.

Insurgencies do tend to be beaten back, but on widely varying rhythms. The 1896 and 1945 breakthroughs were one-election wonders. The Progressive insurgency took almost a decade to subside, as did the Reform Party/Canadian Alliance breakthrough.[8] Twice, the subsidence required two decades, each time for an incarnation of Social Credit. The Conservatives under Diefenbaker absorbed Western Social Credit; the Liberals under Trudeau did the same for the Quebec branch. Sometimes, the integrating mainstream partner was the Liberal Party, as with agrarians (post-1896 and post-1921) in the West and with the 1945 and 1962 Quebec insurgencies. Sometimes the integrating partner was the Conservative Party, which soaked up much of Ontario Progressivism, Western Social Credit, and (if surrender counts as absorption) the Reform Party/Canadian Alliance.

Insurgents often cash out seats proportionally or even over-proportionally to their vote. The bottom right panel of Figure 13.1 shows that both the Progressives and the Bloc Québécois were always well represented. At their respective peaks, 1921 and 1993, each controlled the second-largest number of seats. Western Social Credit was over-represented every year before 1958, and in 1935 and 1940 returned more MPs than the CCF. The later, mainly Quebec years of Social Credit did not bring over-representation, but the party still managed to return MPs; in 1962 and 1963, Social Credit MPs outnumbered NDP ones. The Reform Party/Canadian Alliance was always well represented, although not disproportionately so. The key in every case was the geographical concentration of the insurgent vote; the FPTP electoral formula is kinder to anti-system insurgents than to small parties that seek to work within the rules (Cairns 1968).

The Duration and Size of Governments

The Conservatives and the NDP were pro-system in the sense that they usually kept their focus on the long game of gaining power. It was the Liberal Party that always seemed to win, however. Indeed, the Liberals were one of the most successful political operations of the twentieth century.

TABLE 13.1
Dominance of political parties in the twentieth century

Country	Party	Years in power	Longest period continuously out of power
Canada	Liberal	70[a]	10
United Kingdom	Conservative/Unionist	61 (65)[a, b]	16 (12)
New Zealand	Liberal/United/National	58[a, c]	17[c]
Australia	Protectionist/Nationalist/ United Australia/Liberal	66[a, d]	13

a Includes supplying the prime minister for coalition. Excludes years as subordinate partner in coalition.
b 1918-22 ambiguous case: Liberal Prime Minister but Conservative domination of postwar coalition.
c New Zealand, 1900-96 (change of electoral formula); "years" and "period" are calculated as percentage of the 97-year total.
d Reform governments of 1912-28 are not counted in Liberal/National total.

Table 13.1 shows this by comparison with other Westminster systems.[9] At first glance, the Canadian Liberals may not seem that different from their comparator. Although they did govern for more years than any other party, gaps with the Australian Liberals and the British Conservatives are not wide. The Canadian Liberals' longest period continuously out of office was only ten years, however, shorter than for any comparators. And the dominant positions of the Australian and British parties come with two qualifications. First, their genealogy is complex, reflecting party mergers and strategic changes of name. In contrast, there was never any question about the identity of the Liberals. Second, the other parties were often forced to take on coalition partners. As a governing party, the Canadian Liberals never did this.[10]

Governmental succession in Canada has not been as smooth as elsewhere. Majorities appear less often in Canada than in Britain or New Zealand, but when they do appear they are more likely to be overwhelming. For twenty-two years of the last century, one or the other Canadian party in government commanded more than two-thirds of all seats.[11] In New Zealand, this was true for only six years (fourteen, if we include the Labour governments of the late 1930s that fell just short of the two-thirds threshold). In Great Britain, overwhelming majorities appeared in only two parliaments and for nine years. The bare numbers understate the contrast: in no other country did an overwhelming majority appear after 1945; for Canada, three of five majorities came after that year (Table 13.2).

TABLE 13.2
Oversized and undersized governments in the twentieth century

Government	Canada		New Zealand		United Kingdom	
Overwhelming	1935	5	1905	3	1924	5
majorities	1940	5	1925	3	1931	4
(≥ ⅔ of all seats)	1949	4	[1935]	3		
	1958	4	[1938]	5		
	1984	4				
N (total duration)	5	22	2 [4]	6 [14]	2	9
Minority parliaments	1921	4	1911	3	1910	8
	1925	1	1922	3	1918	4
	1957	1	1928	3	1922	1
	1962	1			1923	1
	1963	2			1951	4
	1965	3				
	1972	2				
	1979	1				
N (total duration)	8	15	3	9	5	17

Note: Square brackets signify seat shares just short of the ⅔ threshold.

At the same time, Canada also has the highest frequency of hung parliaments, eight in the twentieth century, fifteen years in total (Table 13.2). Britain comes second in number although first in total duration (seventeen years). In almost every British case, however, there was at least a formal supporting party or, more often, outright coalition.[12] And as with oversized governments, so with minority ones: British and New Zealand hung parliaments are mainly pre–Second World War phenomena. In Canada, in contrast, minority parliaments were more common after the Second World War than before. Of the last fifty years of the century, Canada had either an oversized or an undersized government for twenty-three years. For Britain, the number of such years is four (a Conservative minority) and for New Zealand, none (before the Mixed Member Proportional, or MMP, system, that is).

Long-Term Fractionalization, Episodic Consolidation

Canada's alternation between oversized and undersized governments reflects two things evident in Figure 13.1: the trend towards fractionalization, and massive swings in the Conservative vote. The figure shows that breakdown first occurred among parties other than the Liberals, hence that party's massive majorities during the 1935-57 period. Then the Liberals lost ground and the opposition consolidated, giving the Liberals at best small majorities. The opposition fragmented even further in 1993, so that even modest vote shares gave the Liberals very comfortable majorities. Finally, the 2000s brought further Liberal shrinkage and some opposition reconsolidation, such that 2004 initiated seven years of minority rule. On the Conservative side, the party won two of the three landslides and formed three of the six minority governments after 1945.

For decades, electoral fragmentation seemed peculiar to Canada. An indication of this appears in Figure 13.2, which plots the "effective number of parties" (ENP), Laakso and Taagepera's measure of party system fractionalization (1979), for Canada, New Zealand, and Great Britain (once again, Australia is omitted, this time because its electoral system is unique). The index is calculated as follows:

$$ENP_t = \frac{1}{\Sigma_i p_{i,t}^2}$$

where $p_{i,t}$ is the i-th party's proportion of the national popular vote at election t. The mechanics of the index are quite intuitive and can be illustrated by example. In a party system with two equal-sized parties, p_i for each party would be 0.50, the squared values would be 0.25, and the sum of the squared values, 0.50. The reciprocal of 0.50 is 2. As the number of alternatives grows, so typically does the value returned for ENP. Also, for any given number of alternatives, the more nearly equal in size they are, the larger the value for ENP. The index systematizes the intuition that some parties count more than others and that the mere number of official alternatives does not capture the real shape of contestation for power. The intuition was expressed in Blondel's early coinage (1968) of the "two-and-a-half party system." The index is not foolproof, as it can return equivalent values for quite different system configurations, but it is not very misleading for either the Canadian case or those of its comparators. Also, it has the additional advantage of being decomposable, as will shortly become clear. For visual clarity, the plots in Figure 13.2 are smoothed.

In the early decades, the Canadian system was *not* peculiarly fragmented. In the comparator systems, however, fragmentation was not sustained. For both Britain and New Zealand, early fractionalization was one

FIGURE 13.2
Effective number of parties in Canada, New Zealand, and Great Britain, 1870-2010

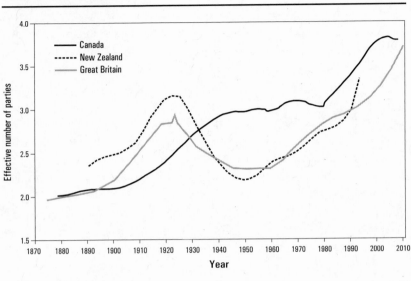

Note: Smoothed by loess; bandwidth = 0.30.

symptom of each system's transition from a pre-class basis to a class one that pits a party of organized labour against all comers. In due course, rivals to the labour party shook off their earlier differences and consolidated into a single party of the moderate right, which led to the drop in *ENP* values in the 1930s. Fragmentation came later to Canadian elections, but once the Canadian system fractionalized, it stayed that way. From the 1930s to the 1980s, the Canadian system harboured nearly one extra notional party relative to the early years.[13] Then in the 1990s, the system took on the effective equivalent of one more party, such that the *ENP* at the turn of the millennium was close to 4.[14]

Fractionalization on the Canadian scale is not supposed to happen. Duverger (1963) argues that plurality systems tend to produce two-party competition. Not only does the plurality formula operate mechanically to defractionalize the party system as votes become seats (which Figure 13.1 shows happens in Canada) but the scale of this defractionalization should induce the key actors to coordinate before votes are cast, and so consolidate the electorate itself. This describes the very process – mainly through elite manoeuvres – that reconsolidated the British and New Zealand electorates after the 1920s. When Rae (1971) wrote the first great systematic comparison of electoral system effects, this claim was largely borne out by the facts.

To account for the deviance of the Canadian case, emphasis has fallen on sectional insurgency, the appearance of small parties in some regions (Rae 1971; Riker 1976). In due course, the Canadian case provoked a theoretical reconsideration of Duverger that culminated in Cox's work (1997). Conceptually, the breakthrough was to claim that Duverger's law applies only at the local level, and that coordination across locales is a separate process. Cox (1987) supplies the mechanisms for cross-district coordination: nationalization of the issue agenda forces elites to attack the localism of MPs and reward disciplined orientation to national questions.

Canada is presented as the exception that proves Cox's rule (Chhibber and Kollman 2004). These authors accept the major premise of Cox's account (1987, 1997) but modify the minor one. In most systems, the agenda really did nationalize and local variance in outcomes was soaked up. In Canada, Chhibber and Kollman assert, the increased *de*centralization of the federal system permitted local minor parties to appear with no great detriment to the advancement of local interests. Consistent with this claim, the overall scale of sectionalist insurgency was a major theme of Figure 13.1.

This theoretical overburden bears little relationship to the rest of the case, however. This is the lesson of Figure 13.3. Because timing is now critical to my account, the *ENP* data in this figure are not smoothed. The top line is simply the undigested equivalent of the Canadian line in Figure 13.2: the effective number of parties in the electorate as a whole. It confirms, indeed dramatically sharpens, Figure 13.2's depiction of a two-stage rise in *ENP*.

The rest of the figure divides total fractionalization into its local and its extra-local components, on the model of Chhibber and Kollman (2004). Consider first the "local" component. This is the average *ENP* at the constituency level, election by election. Some constituencies obviously had fewer effective parties than this value and others had more. Where in, say, 1911 the typical local contest featured slightly fewer than two parties (reflecting the fact that many constituencies were not very competitive), after 1993 the mean local *ENP* was 2.8. Roughly speaking, local fractionalization added one whole notional party. In other words, half the total fractionalization in the Canadian system came from *local* breakdown, and by 2000 the typical riding featured three competitive parties.[15] Now consider the *extra-local* component, calculated as the difference between the total and

FIGURE 13.3
Components of electoral fractionalization

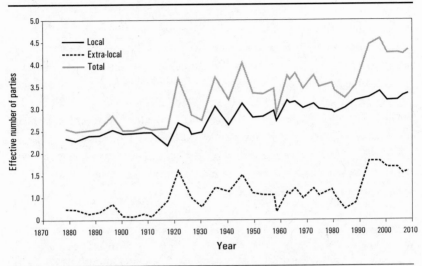

Note: "Local" is the average riding-level ENP; "extra-local" is the difference between total and local ENP.

the local *ENP*. This is the indicator of sectional breakdown. Over the twentieth century, extra-local coordination failure also added the equivalent of one party to the system. So each component contributed roughly half the total breakdown. Sectional division is clearly part of the story of national-level multipartism, but in no sense can Duverger's law be said to hold at the local level.

If the two sources of fragmentation have been roughly equal in long-term impact, they diverge markedly in their dynamics. Local fragmentation proceeded as secular change, starting in the 1930s. The secular propagation of local three-party competition reflects the likewise secular growth of the CCF/NDP.

Extra-local fragmentation, in contrast, occurred suddenly, the two upticks of 1935 and 1993, with no net gains between these dates or since 1993. It is difficult to see in the series the causal mechanism for sectional divergence posited by Chhibber and Kollman (2004). Rather than responding to a decline in the importance of the federal government, each extra-local shift occurred, as already noted, amid acute economic distress. Each period saw not indifference to the federal government but demands for it to take action. The two episodes have one other thing in common: each election terminated a Conservative government, and did so with extreme prejudice.

This is only half the extra-local story. The top line reveals equilibration that at first glance seems Duvergerian: at critical moments, *ENP* drops, that is, the system moves in the direction of bipartism. Although the system does not revert to national two-party competition, the drops are still impressive. But virtually none of this reflects consolidation where it is supposed to occur: at the local level. The consolidation action is almost all at the extra-local level. Relative to pre-1930 elections, the extra-local component was wiped out in 1930 itself, as well as in 1958, 1984, and 1988.[16] In each of these episodes, patterns converged across locales, *even as local tripartism was preserved.* Each of these years produced a Conservative majority, and (before 2011) no other year did. Just as Conservative collapses were fruitful opportunities for sectionalist minor parties, Conservative landslides compressed sectional differences.

A Peculiar Pattern of Volatility

As should be evident by now, the ebb and flow of Conservative fortunes constitutes a unique pattern, and Conservative flux inevitably leaks into the rest of the system. The uniqueness of the Canadian pattern is substantiated by Figure 13.4, which presents comparative evidence for a volatility measure popularized by Pederson (1979) and put to especially strenuous use by Bartolini and Mair (1990). The calculation identity is:

$$Volatility_t = 0.5 \, \Sigma_i \mid p_{i,t} - p_{i,t-1} \mid ,$$

where $p_{i,t}$ is defined as above for *ENP*, except that here party shares are expressed as percentages. Intuitively, the indicator is best thought of as showing the minimum percentage of the electorate that must switch parties to transform one result into the other. The indicator can identify break points in electoral history as well as capture trends, if any, in the general fixity of preferences.

Here, too, patterns pre- and post-1945 differentiate Canada from its comparators. Each of the other countries sees peaks in inter-election volatility in the 1920s and 1930s. These, of course, were the decades of system transformation, which also produced temporary fragmentation (Figure 13.2). After 1945, despite occasional upticks, volatility never remotely approaches the prewar peak. In this, the British, Australian, and New Zealand patterns are generally consistent with the European one (Bartolini and Mair 1990). The Canadian pattern, in contrast, features recurring flux, with more eye-catching swings after 1945 than before. Six episodes particularly

FIGURE 13.4

Time path of volatility in Westminster systems in the twentieth century

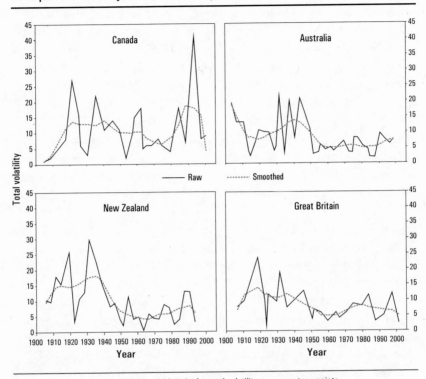

Notes: Smoothed by loess; bandwidth = 0.30. Units for total volatility are percentage points

stand out: 1921, 1935, 1958 (which should be seen as a two-election shift, also including 1957), 1962, 1984, and 1993. Two episodes, 1958 and 1984, brought overwhelming Conservative majorities. The other four brought the same party low.

Unlike the comparator cases, where the high-volatility sequence ultimately marginalized an old major party, each Canadian break point initiated a cycle of reversion. The Conservative crash in 1921, which saw the party reduced to third place in seats, was followed by a decade-long restoration, capped by a majority victory in 1930. The 1958 landslide initiated a decade of Liberal restoration. So did the Conservative landslide of 1984. The Conservative crash of 1993 took more than a decade to undo, and this restoration involved a different organizational dynamic than the others. The political pattern that emerged in 2006, however, bore many affinities to that of twenty years earlier.

Domination by the Centre

The central anomaly of the Canadian system, and the primary cause of its other peculiarities, has been its historical domination by a party of the centre. In none of the other countries is a centre party even a major player, much less the dominant one. And in each other case, the dominant party sits on the right. This is a systematic pattern: majoritarian electoral frameworks, with Westminster systems as the ideal type, elect right-wing parties with a much higher frequency than do proportional representation (PR) ones (Iversen and Soskice 2006, Table 1). The operative mechanism is not well understood, but the statistical regularity seems unimpeachable.[17] So Canada is unusual in the relative rarity of Conservative governments, but of course the Conservative Party does not yield pride of place to a party of the left. Its nemesis is the Liberal Party, resolutely a party of the centre. Liberals steal ideas from both sides and may campaign further to the left than they govern. But their starting point is between the rivals.

And this is how Canadians see matters, according to Figure 13.5. This figure is a box plot of left/right imputations from the Comparative Study of Electoral Systems (CSES; http://www.cses.org). The boxes span the interquartile range, and the vertical bar inside each box indicates the median imputation. Respondents were asked to place themselves on an eleven-point scale and then to do the same for the parties (Figure 13.5 shows party placements only, omitting individuals' self-placements).[18] For interpretive clarity, response is rescaled to the –1, +1 interval.

Canadians do indeed see the Liberals as the party of the centre, and are no more confused about its location than they are about the parties on its flanks.[19] In fact, perceptions seem more sharply focused in Canada than elsewhere. Of the four parties on the left, the NDP is furthest left. The Canadian Conservatives are seen as roughly in the same place as their British and New Zealand counterparts; the Australian Liberals seem furthest right. The gap between left and right is greater than in the other systems, mainly because of the NDP. And, most critically, in each of the other countries, the centre is effectively empty. New Zealand First is seen as very like National. In Britain, the Liberal Democrats are seen as close to Labour, or perhaps a little to Labour's left.[20] In Australia, National is close to the Liberal Party. In Canada, and uniquely in Canada, the centrist Liberals are seen as clearly distinct from the parties on their flanks, and voters' perceptions are consistent with evidence from party manifestos (Cochrane 2010).

That Canadians should be pleased to support a party of the centre comes as no surprise, given the centrism of the electorate (as measured by

FIGURE 13.5
How Canadians see the different political parties

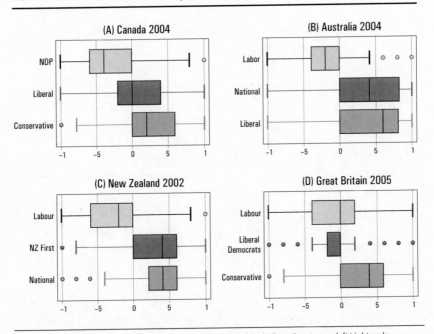

Note: Box plots show distributions of respondents' perceptions of the indicated party on a left/right scale.
Sources: Comparative Study of Electoral Systems Module 2; analyses by author.

individuals' ideological self-placements); thus, the Liberals' centrism on a left/right dimension did not hurt the party, and may even have helped it. What *is* unusual, however, is that a party so situated is seen as a viable coordination point for the mass of voters at the centre. Other electorates have a similarly centrist orientation,[21] but in those, not only is the middle party weak but it also crowds one flank or the other and the centre is effectively empty. The pattern in the three comparators is typical:

Political choice takes the form of a choice between two alternatives. A duality of parties does not always exist, but there is almost always a duality of tendencies ... This is equivalent to saying that the center does not exist in politics ... The term "center" is applied to the geometrical spot at which the moderates of opposed tendencies meet ... Every Center is divided against itself and remains separated into two halves, Left-Center and Right-Center. For the Center is nothing more than the artificial grouping of the right wing of the Left and the left wing of the Right. The fate of the Center is to be torn asunder. (Duverger 1963, 215)

In short, the strength of the Liberals and, even more, their historically dominant status require explanation.

The starting point for explanation must be the existence of a second important dimension, one on which the Liberals are not centrist but polar. Whatever its exact content, that dimension expressed itself historically in the Liberal Party's control of a bloc of seats from Quebec (Bakvis and Macpherson 1995; Johnston et al. 1992). Between 1896 and 1980, the Liberal MPs from Quebec occupied over 20 percent of the seats in the House of Commons in four of every five elections. When this happened, the Liberals won 85 percent of the time (17 of 20); when it did not, they lost 80 percent of the time (four of five). For no other similarly sized region was the pattern this crisp. This is the geographic pattern that underpins Carty's observations on the pattern and persistence of brokerage in the Liberal Party (see Chapter 1).

Not only does this factor account for Liberal longevity but it also contains the secret of Liberal decline, at least in its later stages. The 1984 election unsettled Quebec's bloc-like adhesion to the Liberals and never since have the Liberals controlled so many Quebec seats. Although this did not prevent them from governing for a further twelve-plus years, 1993-2006, their Canada-wide electoral base was weak and they benefited from opposition deconsolidation. Once the parties of the ideological right got themselves sorted, the writing may have been on the wall for the Liberals.

Looking Ahead

It would be a mistake to say that the patterns described in this chapter forecast the realignment (if it is that) of 2011. But the eventual implosion of the Liberal vote was strongly implied in the total pattern of evidence, and especially from the remarkably steady downward trend in the party's share. Also implying a change was the lesson from other countries, that the centre is very difficult to defend.

But defend it the Liberals did, and for an extended period being in the centre probably helped as much as it hurt. For years, Liberals were able to divide their opponents and so maintain their hegemony right down to the level of the local riding (Johnston and Cutler 2009). In this, the Liberals were like hegemonic parties elsewhere, in places as distinct from each other and from Canada as Mexico and Ireland (Greene 2007; Magaloni 2006;

Chapter 1). Liberal centrism was plausibly the ultimate source of other peculiarities in the Canadian field, especially Conservative boom and bust, recurring episodes of anti-system insurgency, and asymmetries among the parties in their vulnerability to flux. The weakening of the Liberals in 2011, especially if it presages even worse to come, may remove these anomalies from the rest of the system.

Critical to understanding the old system is the mere existence of Quebec. In none of the Westminster comparators is there an equivalent to Quebec as a nation within a nation. This claim needs to be made carefully, as Britain is, after all, a union of kingdoms whose components readily refer to themselves and each other as nations. New Zealand is also complex, with a Maori minority proportionally as large (by some counts) as Canada's francophone one. But as Fearon (2003) shows, Canada is an extreme case of both religious and linguistic diversity. That diversity, particularly the powerful concentration of sentiment in Quebec, is necessary in order to explain several features of the old politics, as well as its eventual unravelling. If the unravelling is permanent, then Carty's question in Chapter 1 must probably be answered in the affirmative.

Acknowledgments

Financial support for this research from the University of Pennsylvania and the Social Sciences and Humanities Research Council of Canada is gratefully acknowledged. Earlier versions of the propositions in this chapter were presented to audiences at Temple University, the University of Calgary, Princeton University, and the University of British Columbia. Captive audiences of undergraduates at Penn and UBC have kept me honest, or tried to. Research assistance from Amanda Bittner, Janine van Vliet, and John McAndrews has been critical. All errors of fact or interpretation are mine, however.

Notes

1 His most extensive exposition of the classification is found in Sartori (1976).
2 Gaining power at the centre at least. In the Canadian case, some niche parties have controlled provincial governments.
3 The strength of the mechanical effect in Canada used to be a matter of controversy. As a reflection of the succession of minority governments in the 1960s, observers (Casstevens and Morris 1972; Qualter 1968) debated whether the Canadian system was less responsive than implied in the classic cube law (Kendall and Stuart 1950). Estimations (not reported here) based on evidence over the full period indicate that the speculation was premature. By comparison with Britain and New Zealand for elections since 1935, the Canadian system is quite responsive, about the same as New Zealand's and more responsive than Britain's.

4 Most observers claim that, in a lovely twist of history, the book was written by Preston Manning himself.

5 Indeed, the party's fate – more votes than for either Social Credit or the NDP but only one seat – made it an exemplary case in Cairns (1968).

6 The 1945 election processed issues in the economic domain, in particular debate over postwar reconstruction. But this was a forward-looking discussion about the shape of a nascent welfare state, not a cry of pain over an economic downturn. Debate was spurred by CCF breakthroughs in Ontario and Saskatchewan provincial elections and in national polls. Of course, I do not see the CCF as posing an anti-system threat in the way I do the other small parties.

7 This was not for lack of such ferment: the Union Nationale (UN) emerged in 1935 as a cross-party synthesis with an initially reformist message. As an explicitly nationalist party, it anticipated aspects of the two later Blocs, but it never projected itself into federal politics (although UN operatives were prominent in the Conservatives' 1958 surge in Quebec). See Black (1977).

8 Of course, the Reform Party/Canadian Alliance did not so much subside as capture a pro-system party.

9 New Zealand used to exemplify Westminster logic better than any of the comparators (Lijphart 1999), but with the adoption of the Mixed Member Proportional system (MMP) in 1996, its electoral logic shifted. Accordingly, I use evidence only from the New Zealand system's pre-1996 incarnation.

10 Many Liberals joined the Conservative-dominated Unionist coalition in 1917, but did not supply the prime minister. Hence I do not count 1917-21 as years in government for the Liberal Party as such.

11 Australia is omitted from Table 13.2, as I am in no position to settle arguments over whether Liberal/National governments are true coalitions or merely the same party showing different faces.

12 This does not count the British wartime coalition, 1940-45, which was grafted onto an existing Conservative majority.

13 In terms of real, rather than notional, parties, Figure 13.1 reminds us that two emerged and survived across these decades, Social Credit and the CCF.

14 Again, as Figure 13.1 reveals, the system acquired not one new party but two, Reform (later the Canadian Alliance) and the Bloc Québécois.

15 For more detail on local competition, see Johnston and Cutler 2009, Figure 6.6, which shows that the third-place party is typically large enough to cover the margin between the first- and second-place finishers.

16 The value for extra-local *ENP* is always positive in those years, but this was also true before 1930. This reflects the fact that even where national competition is effectively between two parties, geographic variation dictates that many local races will be one-sided, implying local *ENP*s of less than 2. The critical thing is that in 1930, 1958, 1984, and 1988, the extra-local component was scarcely larger than in the earlier period.

17 The current explanatory contenders are Iversen and Soskice (2006), who see the majoritarian politics as a game of bluff in which the middle-income voters side with those in the top third, and Rodden (2010), who emphasizes inefficiencies in left voters' geographic distribution.

18 Canadians seem slightly less polarized than voters in the other Westminster systems, but differences among the countries are slight and Canadians are less likely to "tent" at the absolute centre than are respondents in New Zealand or Britain.

19 It is possible that variance for the Liberals is compressed by placements at the centre that are disguised "don't knows."

20 The box plot suggests that for Liberal Democrat perceptions, the median and the 75th percentile are the same value, again perhaps because of compression with de facto "don't knows."

21 In the CSES data, the four countries have means slightly to the right of centre, varying from 0.02 to 0.07 on the −1, +1 scale, but all four distributions are strongly unimodal near zero. To be sure, an element in this unimodality must be respondents offering the midpoint in lieu of a substantive opinion. It is not clear, however, that this alters that location's strategic significance.

References

Allen, Richard. 1971. *The Social Passion: Religion and Social Reform in Canada, 1914–28.* Toronto: University of Toronto Press.

Bakvis, Herman, and Laura G. Macpherson. 1995. "Quebec Block Voting and the Canadian Electoral System." *Canadian Journal of Political Science* 28: 659-92.

Bartolini, Stefano, and Peter Mair. 1990. *Identity, Competition, and Electoral Availability: The Stabilisation of European Electorates, 1885-1985.* Cambridge: Cambridge University Press.

Behiels, Michael Derek. 1985. *Prelude to Quebec's Quiet Revolution: Liberalism versus Neo-Nationalism, 1945-1960.* Montreal and Kingston: McGill-Queen's University Press.

Black, Conrad. 1977. *Maurice Duplessis.* Montreal: Éditions de l'Homme.

Blondel, Jean. 1968. "Party Systems and Patterns of Government in Western Democracies." *Canadian Journal of Political Science* 1: 180-203.

Cairns, Alan C. 1968. "The Electoral System and the Party System in Canada, 1921-1965." *Canadian Journal of Political Science* 1: 55-80.

Capoccia, Giovanni. 2002. "Anti-System Parties: A Conceptual Reassessment." *Journal of Theoretical Politics* 14: 9-35.

Casstevens, Thomas W., and William D. Morris. 1972. "The Cube Law and the Decomposed System." *Canadian Journal of Political Science* 5: 521-32.

Chhibber, Pradeep K., and Ken Kollman. 2004. *The Formation of National Party Systems: Federalism and Party Competition in Canada, Great Britain, India, and the United States.* Princeton, NJ: Princeton University Press.

Cochrane, Christopher. 2010. "Left/Right Ideology and Canadian Politics." *Canadian Journal of Political Science* 43: 583-605.

Cox, Gary W. 1987. *The Efficient Secret: The Cabinet and the Development of Political Parties in Victorian England.* Cambridge: Cambridge University Press.

−. 1997. *Making Votes Count: Strategic Coordination in the World's Electoral Systems.* Cambridge: Cambridge University Press.

Crunican, Paul. 1974. *Priests and Politicians: Manitoba Schools and the Election of 1896.* Toronto: University of Toronto Press.

Duverger, Maurice. 1963. *Political Parties: Their Organization and Activity in the Modern State.* Translated by Barbara North and Robert North. New York: Wiley.

English, John R. 1977. *The Decline of Politics: The Conservatives and the Party System.* Toronto: University of Toronto Press.

Fearon, James D. 2003. "Ethnic and Cultural Diversity by Country." *Journal of Economic Growth* 8: 195-222.

Flanagan, Tom. 2009. *Waiting for the Wave: The Reform Party and the Conservative Movement.* Montreal and Kingston: McGill-Queen's University Press.

Greene, Kenneth F. 2007. *Why Dominant Parties Lose: Mexico's Democratization in Comparative Perspective.* New York: Cambridge University Press.

Irving, John A. 1959. *The Social Credit Movement in Alberta.* Toronto: University of Toronto Press.

Iversen, Torben, and David Soskice. 2006. "Electoral Institutions and the Politics of Coalitions: Why Some Democracies Distribute More Than Others." *American Political Science Review* 100: 165-81.

Johnston, Richard. 2008. "Polarized Pluralism in the Canadian Party System." *Canadian Journal of Political Science* 41: 815-34.

Johnston, Richard, André Blais, Henry E. Brady, and Jean Crête. 1992. *Letting the People Decide: Dynamics of a Canadian Election.* Montreal and Kingston: McGill-Queen's University Press.

Johnston, Richard, and Fred Cutler. 2009. "Canada: The Puzzle of Local Three-Party Competition." In *Duverger's Law of Plurality Voting: The Logic of Party Competition in Canada, India, the United Kingdom and the United States,* edited by Bernard Grofman, André Blais, and Shaun Bowler, 83-96. New York: Springer.

Kendall, M.G., and A. Stuart. 1950. "The Law of the Cubic Proportion in Election Results." *British Journal of Sociology* 1: 183-97.

Kirchheimer, Otto. 1966. "The Transformation of the Western European Party Systems." In *Political Parties and Political Development,* edited by Joseph LaPalombara and Myron Weiner, 177-200. Princeton, NJ: Princeton University Press.

Laakso, Markku, and Rein Taagepera. 1979. "'Effective' Number of Parties: A Measure with Application to West Europe." *Comparative Political Studies* 12: 3-27.

Lijphart, Arend. 1999. *Patterns of Democracy: Government Forms and Performance in Thirty-Six Countries.* New Haven, CT: Yale University Press.

Lupul, Manoly R. 1974. *The Roman Catholic Church and the North-West School Question.* Toronto: University of Toronto Press.

Macpherson, C.B. 1953. *Democracy in Alberta: The Theory and Practice of a Quasi-Party System.* Toronto: University of Toronto Press.

Magaloni, Beatriz. 2006. *Voting for Autocracy: Hegemonic Party Survival and Its Demise in Mexico.* New York: Cambridge University Press.

Manning, E.C. 1967. *Political Realignment: A Challenge to Thoughtful Canadians.* Toronto: McClelland and Stewart.

Meguid, Bonnie. 2008. *Party Competition between Unequals: Strategies and Electoral Fortunes in Western Europe.* Cambridge: Cambridge University Press.

Miller J.R. 1979. *Equal Rights: The Jesuits' Estates Act Controversy.* Montreal and Kingston: McGill-Queen's University Press.

Morton, W.L. 1950. *The Progressive Party in Canada.* Toronto: University of Toronto Press.

Pederson, Mogens. 1979. "The Dynamics of European Party Systems: Changing Patterns of Electoral Volatility." *European Journal of Political Research* 7: 1-26.

Pinard, Maurice. 1975. *The Rise of a Third Party: A Study in Crisis Politics.* Montreal and Kingston: McGill-Queen's University Press.

Qualter, Terence H. 1968. "Seats and Votes: An Application of the Cube Law to the Canadian Electoral System." *Canadian Journal of Political Science* 1: 336-44.

Rae, Douglas W. 1971. *The Political Consequences of Electoral Laws.* 2nd ed. New Haven, CT: Yale University Press.

Riker, William H. 1976. "The Number of Political Parties: A Reexamination of Duverger's Law." *Comparative Politics* 9: 93-106.

Rodden, Jonathan. 2010. "The Geographic Distribution of Political Preferences." *Annual Review of Political Science* 13: 321-40.

Sartori, Giovanni. 1976. *Parties and Party Systems: A Framework for Analysis.* Cambridge: Cambridge University Press.

Smiley, Donald. 1962. "Canada's Poujadists: A New Look at Social Credit." *Canadian Forum* 42: 121.

Wilbur, J.R.H. 1964. "H.H. Stevens and the Reconstruction Party." *Canadian Historical Review* 45: 1-28.

Young, Walter D. 1969. *The Anatomy of a Party: The National CCF, 1932-1961.* Toronto: University of Toronto Press.

14

Parties and Elections after 2011

The Fifth Canadian Party System?

ROYCE KOOP AND AMANDA BITTNER

This book has examined Canadian federal electoral politics over the last two decades. Some chapters take an even longer view, pointing to threads of continuity that link Canada's current politics to previous periods. Chapter 1, for example, explores the extent to which a party model applied to the Liberal Party in the past can still be applied, and, in the process, refines how the model is defined; Chapter 13 examines the nature of the Canadian political system since Confederation, while Chapter 5 demonstrates how the long process of urbanization came to hold consequences for the art of cabinet making. These chapters remind us that, despite the upheavals of Canadian politics in recent years, there is much about the current politics of this country that has not changed from previous generations. Other chapters are more precise, exploring in particular the distinctive characteristics of Canadian party politics from the 1980s onward (see, for example, Chapters 8 and 12). The third group of chapters focuses on the distinctive period from 2004 to 2011, exploring, for example, the ways in which parties have approached particular groups in Canadian society (Chapters 6 and 7) and coped with minority governments (Chapters 3 and 4); the responses of voters to the challenges of this period (Chapter 11); and the seemingly unique institutional context that both parties and voters operated in (Chapters 9 and 10).

The result is a rich, detailed picture of party and electoral politics in Canada from long-, intermediate-, and short-term perspectives. We drew on the insights of all of these contributions to pen this concluding chapter, in which we situate recent electoral politics in a broader historical perspective and speculate on the future of the national party system in Canada. We first review the comparative and Canadian party system literatures, noting their distinctive characteristics and features. We then draw on original data to situate party politics in Canada from 1988 to 2011 within electoral dynamics from the 1945 election onward.

Finally, we look specifically at the 2011 election. Is this a realigning election? If so, what can be said of the period after 1988 and before 2011? We conclude by presenting our own proposal regarding this period and the 2011 Canadian party system. We stand with Carty, Cross, and Young (2000) in arguing that a fourth party system came into existence in the 1993 election; however, we also argue that the 2004 election was dealigning and marked the conclusion of this new system. Furthermore, we argue that the results of the 2011 election represent realignment into a new, distinctive party system that is fundamentally different from previous systems. While many of the contributions to this volume illuminate elements of continuity throughout Canada's recent period of instability, we point to the most important element of change: party system realignment. Although the results of the 1993 realigning election were thought to be surprising, we argue that the results of the 2011 election are much more significant and presage future patterns of party and electoral politics that will differ substantially from the patterns of the past.

Party Systems, in Canada and Elsewhere

The notion of a party system – patterns of competition between political parties in a single political system – has been a crucial innovation in the subfield of comparative politics. In part, this is because the notion of a system that exists across elections reflects the existence of long-term influences on vote choice, which lend continuity to systems over time. Nevertheless, party systems differ between democracies and become transformed in rare "sea changes" as systems dealign and realign, sometimes slowly and sometimes quickly (Key 1955; LeDuc 1985). An important question addressed by political scientists, therefore, is how these systems can be classified. Sartori (1976), for example, argues that systems should be distinguished from one another on the basis of (1) the number of relevant parties, and (2) the degree of fragmentation in the system, although how these qualities of systems can or ought to be measured is a question for debate (e.g., Blondel 1968). The result is that systems may fall into a number of categories, including two-party, multi-party, and dominant-party systems (e.g., Wolinetz 1988).

What is admirable about the party system approach is its parsimony: in the comparative literature, the emphasis is on the number and electoral strength of parties in the system. This parsimony allows for easy comparison between democracies. However, the party system approach in the Canadian politics subfield has differed from the comparative literature in two ways. First, the Canadian conception of party systems has been substantially richer than the comparative conception. Second, party systems in the Canadian politics subfield are often used as a means of understanding the historical development of the country as a whole.

In the comparative literature, the emphasis is on the number and strength of parties (see Chapter 13 for an example of this type of approach), but Canadianists have generally held to a more detailed conception of party systems. In addition to the number and strength of the parties in the system, accounts of party systems in Canada have explored the regionalization of party support over time (Carty et al. 2000, 34); party organizational styles and the nature of party appeals to Canadians (Carty 1992); the support bases of those parties (Johnston 1980); the organizational responses of parties to federalism (Koop 2011); and the role of parties in nation building (Smith 1985).

While simpler comparative accounts facilitate comparisons between democracies, the richer Canadian conception of party systems has facilitated deep knowledge of a single case. One result of this is that many contemporary studies of Canadian politics either begin with or draw upon the insights of that literature. Some political scientists disapprove of such an "introspective, insular" focus on a single state and bemoan a seeming lack of inter-state comparisons in the study of Canadian politics (e.g., White et al. 2008). While comparative research is exceedingly important, the Canadian party systems literature has the strength of demonstrating how focus on a single state can develop deep knowledge that is useful and often necessary for later inquiry.

One reason why the party system approach is foundational in the study of Canadian politics is that it has been used effectively to understand the historical development of the country. In this literature, Canadian history can be divided into systems, each characterized by long periods of majority Liberal rule interrupted by interregnums consisting of Tory government. The first system therefore began with Confederation and ended with Robert

Borden's Unionist government (1867-1917); the second lasted from 1921 to 1957 and concluded with John Diefenbaker's landslide; and the third party system commenced in 1963 and ended in 1984, with the biggest majority in Canadian history won by Brian Mulroney (see Carty 1992). Each system following the reign of John A. Macdonald had its Liberal king (Wilfrid Laurier, Mackenzie King, and Pierre Trudeau), and each interregnum its Tory usurper (Borden, Diefenbaker, and Mulroney).

Beneath these broad strokes, each national party system was characterized by different types of party appeals, party organizations, party support bases, and what Carty (1992, 583) refers to as the "dominant politics" of the system. Thus, parties in the first system used patronage as a means of state building, and the focus of parties was on winning in the constituencies. In the second party system, parties assumed the role of regional brokers as party leaders attempted to reconcile the divergent interests of the different regions of the federation. In the third system, party leaders marshalled advancements in communications technology to make direct pan-Canadian appeals for support.

The question is, what has occurred since the conclusion of the third party system? Carty and colleagues (2000) suggest that 1993 ushered in a new, fourth party system. Following the tradition of the Canadian party systems literature, they point to several characteristics of party politics in the 1990s that serve as indicators of the new system, including more competitive parties (this period saw an increase from three to five parties in the House of Commons); regional appeals by parties – the Reform Party and the Bloc Québécois (BQ) were explicitly regional in their appeals and vote shares – and very regionalized caucuses, even for the governing Liberal Party, which was centred in Ontario; and greater ideological diversity among the parties. To these authors, the nature of Canadian politics had been fundamentally altered in 1993, with old tendencies towards brokerage and national consensus replaced with explicitly ideological and regionalist parties. The fact that the Liberals formed a stable majority government and repeated this accomplishment in both the 1997 and 2000 elections confirms that Canada had entered a new system, but these new features distinguished the fourth system from its predecessors.

Despite critiques of this interpretation – notably the legitimate objection of Clarkson (2005) that the Liberal Party had not changed significantly in 1993 – it is clear that something had fundamentally shifted. But how exactly was Canadian politics different? Had Canada entered a new national party system, as suggested by Carty and colleagues (2000)? Or was the country in the midst of an extended period of protracted dealignment: a long hangover from the previous shake-up of the system (LeDuc 1985)? In the latter case, was a national system on its way?

Subsequent events and elections did little to clarify the situation. The 1997 and 2000 elections reaffirmed the strength of the Liberals and the staying power of the regional parties, although Reform had transitioned into a new party by this time. Indeed, the real drama of this period appeared to be of the intraparty variety: leadership intrigues in the Liberal Party saw the removal of Jean Chrétien as leader and his replacement with Paul Martin, and negotiations between the leaders of the Canadian Alliance and the Progressive Conservatives (PC) resulted in a merger between them, removing one party from the system. The ensuing election in 2004 gave an indication that patterns of party competition were unstable and that something substantial, perhaps party system dealignment, had just occurred. The 2006 election provided an even more substantial rebuke, as the Conservative Party of Canada (CPC) formed government for the first time in nearly twenty years.

It took two more elections for the party system to truly transform, as the 2011 election produced a result as stunning as the 1993 election. After four tries, Stephen Harper finally won a majority government. As the Progressive Conservatives had suffered in 1993, it was now time for the other ancient party, the Liberals, to experience decimation: the party declined to 34 seats. For the first time in Canadian history, the Liberal Party would form neither the government nor the Official Opposition, as the New Democratic Party (NDP) surpassed it with an astonishing 102 seats. The last vestige of Carty and colleagues' fourth party system (2000), the Bloc Québécois, won only 4 seats, as Quebec elected NDP MPs in unprecedented numbers. With perhaps significant consequences for the future, the Green Party elected its first MP, leader Elizabeth May.

1993 to 2011 in Historical Perspective

How can these dramatic events be fitted into the party system framework that has been used to such effect in the study of Canadian politics? We suggest that an examination of three key features of Canadian party systems provides important insight into the nature of the political system over the last two decades. By taking a longitudinal look at (1) the number of parties and the share of voter support the parties have obtained, as well as the regional bases of party support, (2) the regionalization of party caucuses, and (3) the ideological diversity of Canadian parties and voters, we are able to develop a better understanding of what has been happening in the last twenty years, as well as what we might expect in the future. We draw upon Carty and colleagues' insights and assessments (2000) of these three features of the party system that formed the basis of their argument that 1993 marked a break with the prior party system. However, we also employ statistical measures of these phenomena to explore the place of the last two decades in Canadian history.

Vote Shares and Seat Shares over Time

The development of Canada's historical party systems has been characterized by long periods of continuity punctuated by periods of change. While each new system appears to return to a well-established norm (long-term stable majority Liberal governments), in fact these periods have masked a long-term secular decline in popular support for the Liberal Party. By the 1990s, Chrétien's party was wholly dependent on the electoral system to parlay remarkably small vote shares into majority governments. The question is whether recent instability has produced a new party system that is quite different from previous systems, most notably in the support accorded Canada's "natural governing party."

The distorting effects of the electoral system have been identified for some time in accounts of Canadian politics (Cairns 1965), and its role in shaping the seating plan in the House of Commons over the last two decades is no different. Figure 14.1 tracks the major parties' vote shares and seat shares since the 1945 national election, based on data from Elections Canada and the House of Commons. The graphs not only track the emergence of the new parties (Reform and the Bloc Québécois) but also demonstrate the devastating effect the electoral system has had on the Progressive Conservative Party in several elections.

The electoral system has had the effect of screening out the Green Party from the House of Commons until the most recent election, as well as exacerbating the gains and losses of some of the major parties. In most years, the NDP fared worse in terms of seat share than it did in its share of votes, while in the most recent election the party's regionally concentrated success in Quebec actually helped it to achieve a share of seats that most closely reflects its share of votes over the entire time period.

Figure 14.1 tells observers of Canadian politics what they already know: Canadian politics from 1993 onward represented something new, as old parties were decimated, new parties emerged, and Quebec's seats were

FIGURE 14.1
Distribution of vote share and seat share by party, 1945-2011

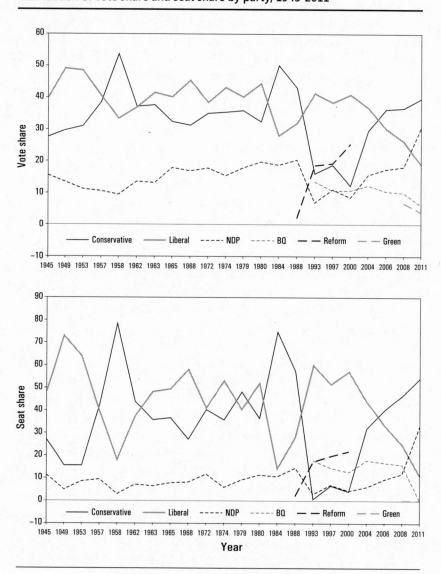

consolidated within the caucus of an avowedly separatist national party. Chapter 13 demonstrates that the effective number of parties (ENP) in Canada rose from about three in 1980 to nearly four in the 2008 election. In Figure 14.2, we expand on Figure 13.2 presented in Chapter 13, widening our scope to include the effective number of both elective and parliamentary parties for each election since 1945, which enables us to observe long-term trends in voter support as well as electoral system effects over this period.

Perhaps the most notable feature of Carty and colleagues' fourth party system (2000) was the entry of two new major parties into the system, which raised the number of competitive parties from three to five. The effective number of electoral parties reflects this spike, but the number of legislative parties does not, as the single-member plurality (SMP) electoral system punished the Progressive Conservatives and the NDP in the translation of votes to seats. Following the merger between the Canadian Alliance and the Progressive Conservatives in 2004, the system appeared to be settling into a new pattern of four-party competition, but this changed again in the 2011 election. The poor performance of both the BQ and the Liberal Party accounts for the reduction of ENP to levels that predate the 1993 election.

Does this drop signal the end of an era that began in the early 1990s and lasted only two decades? Or will Canada continue to be known for being an exception to Duverger's law of the effect of the electoral system (see Gaines

FIGURE 14.2
Effective number of parties in Canadian elections, 1945-2011, based on Laasko and Taagepera's measure of ENP (1979)

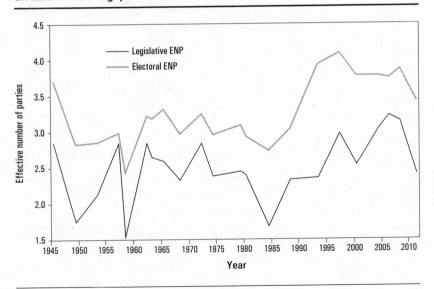

1999)? In the short term, a reduction in the number of competitive parties points to party system consolidation, suggesting that Canada is moving towards fulfilling Duverger's expectations. We return to this issue in the next section, but the 2011 election results suggest that the deck is now stacked against both the Liberal Party and especially the BQ in their attempts to rebuild and re-enter the party system as full-fledged players.

Regional Bases of Party Support and Party Caucuses
An important aspect of Carty and colleagues' argument (2000) is that beginning with the 1993 election, Canadian parties were more likely to make regionalist appeals – in sharp contrast to the regional broker role played by the major parties in the past – and to gain regionally concentrated support. These claims were, of course, based on the activities of the Reform Party and the BQ, both of which were explicitly regional parties when they entered the House of Commons in earnest in 1993. However, the Liberal Party also relied upon strong support from Ontario throughout its period of majority governments, and, as predicted by Cairns (1965), its governing priorities arguably focused on Ontario at the expense of the other regions. While we do not fully explore the extent of parties' regionalist appeals, it appears that they have declined in recent years, with the exception of the activities of the Bloc Québécois. Certainly gone are the days when leaders quarrelled over which of the parties were truly "national parties," as occurred frequently in the 1990s.

In order to get a better sense of regional patterns of support over time, we used national vote shares in each province from 1945 to 2011 to generate an index of regional variation over time for each of the three major national parties. Caramani (2004) presents a number of different formulas that have been used in the past for comparing the extent to which parties have regionalized support, as well as for assessing their strengths and weaknesses. Because of its simplicity, we opted to use the standard deviation (SD) measure of variance.

Figure 14.3 tracks the SD for the Liberal Party, the Conservative Party (PC from 1988 to 2000 and CPC from 2004 to 2011), and the New Democratic Party from 1945 to 2011. When interpreting the data presented in Figure 14.3, it is important to note that the higher the SD value, the greater the level of heterogeneity across the provinces – that is, the greater the differences between the provinces and the national average.

As Figure 14.3 illustrates, there is substantial variation in heterogeneity across provinces from year-to-year and across parties. The NDP has

FIGURE 14.3

Heterogeneity in party vote share across all regions, 1945-2011 (standard deviation measure)

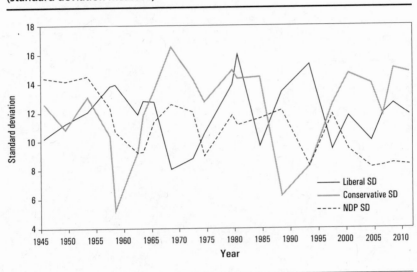

generally had more uniform support across the country, as indicated by its lower SD score. The Conservative and Liberal Parties alternate in displaying the greatest level of heterogeneity among the parties. Notable for their low scores are two election years in particular: 1958 and 1988, in which support for the Conservative Party was fairly uniform across the country. In 1968, Trudeau won the election with the most uniform level of support the Liberal Party has ever achieved, in stark contrast to the basis of support for his Liberals in 1980, when they won based on their highest level of heterogeneity. Since Mulroney's 1988 Conservative majority, we have seen a gradual upswing in the Conservative Party's SD score, indicating that support for the party is more regionally heterogeneous than in the past.

Figure 14.3 further strengthens Cairns' argument (1965) that the parties that obtain the most seats in the legislature do not necessarily do so based on "national" electoral support. The scores for the Liberal and Conservative Parties indicate that regional heterogeneity in vote shares may be here to stay, and remind us of the extent to which SMP smiles upon parties with regionally concentrated vote shares. Indeed, the vote that delivered Harper his first majority government in 2011 was very disparate across the regions, among the most heterogeneous in Canadian history. In 2011, however, the

FIGURE 14.4
Heterogeneity in party seat share across all regions, 1945-2011
(standard deviation measure)

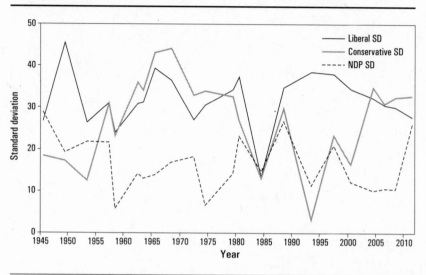

heterogeneity score for the NDP did not rise, even though much of its success occurred in Quebec. With a couple of exceptions, support for the party
in this election was relatively even across the country.

An important question is whether regionalized vote shares result in
regionalized party caucuses. Carty and colleagues (2000) argue that regionalized party caucuses were a crucial feature of the fourth party system.
Figure 14.4 places this claim in broad historical perspective by providing
the regional standard deviation of seat shares for the three major parties for
each election since 1945.

Not surprisingly given the effects of the electoral system, the seat share
SD scores are higher for all parties than their vote share SD scores.
Examining each party's trend line in more detail, it becomes clear that the
Liberal Party's decline over the past ten years has coincided with a decline
in the heterogeneity of its caucus. The party has suffered as it has lost its
ability to concentrate its vote share in particular regions over others, an af-
fliction not unlike the one that kept the Progressive Conservative Party in
the parliamentary peanut gallery throughout the 1990s despite respectable
national vote shares. This is not the case for the Conservatives or the NDP
over the same time period: the heterogeneity of the Conservative Party's

caucus has increased since 2000, and while the NDP's caucus has remained relatively homogeneous across the country over the last decade, it experienced a dramatic change in the most recent election, reflecting its incredible success in Quebec. In sharp contrast to the data presented in Figure 14.3, Figure 14.4 demonstrates that the NDP's caucus was only slightly less regionalized than those of the Conservatives and Liberals as a result of the 2011 election. While the party had a broad electoral appeal in this election, it clearly boosted its seat share through its strength in particular regions.

All of this suggests that a regionalized Parliament is inevitable as the electoral system rewards parties for regionally concentrated vote shares. This is a feature that is likely to continue into any new party system.

The Ideological Diversity of Canadian Parties

Carty and colleagues (2000) note the increase in ideological diversity of Canadian parties following the collapse of the third party system. It seems fairly self-evident that the range of ideological options opened up when the Reform Party entered the scene, given its more right-wing platforms. We wished to take a systematic look at the ideological space in Canadian elections over this two-decade period. We compiled data from the Comparative Manifestos Project (Volkens et al. 2010) and followed its coding instructions to update and extend the dataset to cover the most recent Canadian elections, coding the parties' manifestos from 2008 and 2011.

In particular, we were interested in the variable "RILE," a composite index of a number of indicators – such as party platforms – that together represent the left/right ideological placement of parties. Based on this measure, Figure 14.5 tracks the left/right placement of the major parties from 1945 to 2011.

It becomes clear immediately that the Reform Party had a major impact on the ideological space of Canadian party politics. Reform's RILE score in 1993 was twenty points more to the right than the most right-leaning party in the 1988 election, the Progressive Conservative Party. However, while this jump to the right is notable, it did not result in a widening of the gap between the right and left. The most left-leaning party also jumped to the right, by about eighteen points. Thus in 1993, rather than a widening of the ideological space between parties as a result of the new right-leaning Reform Party, we see a universal shift to the right across all parties.

The 1997 election brought about even more change. The Reform Party maintained its position, while the PCs moved to the left by about thirteen points. The Liberal Party moved slightly to the right, and the NDP moved

FIGURE 14.5

Left/right ideological placement of parties, 1945-2011

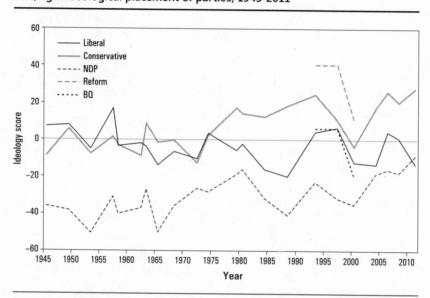

Source: Based on data from the Comparative Manifestos Project (Volkens et al. 2010).

back towards the left. This was the election in which the distance between the rightmost and the leftmost was greatest, although the distance between the two traditional governing parties, the Liberals and the PCs, was negligible – the old brokers endured, albeit in vastly different competitive situations. Both were slightly right of centre, and just five points apart. The 2000 election brought about another shift, as the Canadian Alliance moved substantially towards the centre compared with its position as the Reform Party. Indeed, all parties moved to the left in this election, and the distance between the rightmost and leftmost parties was substantially less than in the previous two elections, largely because of the shift of the Canadian Alliance.

In 2004, with the merger of the Progressive Conservative Party and the Canadian Alliance, we see a shift back to the right. Contrary to popular accounts, the new Conservative Party's platform was more right-leaning than the Alliance's platform in the previous election. The NDP also shifted towards the centre. Only the Liberal Party's platform demonstrated no real ideological movement. In 2006, all parties moved further to the right before moving slightly left in 2008. In 2011 we see yet more change. The New Democrats and Conservatives continued their rightward movement, whereas the Liberals moved back to their 2006 position. This change meant that the Liberal platform in 2011 was more left-leaning than the NDP platform.

If we look back and compare the positions of the three major parties in 2011 with those in the past, we see that the governing party and the opposition party were situated further to the right than they had ever been in Canadian political history. All three parties are more right-leaning than they were before the collapse of the third party system, with the biggest transformation taking place in the NDP platform. Over the last twenty-three years, the party has moved approximately thirty points to the right, ultimately positioning itself nearly ten points left of centre. At the same time, the Conservative Party platform indicates a rightward move also (albeit with more steep slopes and inclines), with the party positioning itself approximately eight points more to the right than in 1988. The Liberal Party is also more to the right by about eight points. Thus, since the 1988 election, the ideological space between right and left has been substantially reduced, largely as a result of the movement of the NDP: the gap was about forty points in 2011, compared with sixty points in 1988. In the most recent election, the parties were all less different and more to the right than they had been in 1988.

The RILE scores for party platforms in the 2011 election are intriguing. For the first time since 1945, the CCF/NDP's platform was more right-leaning than the Liberal platform. Perhaps not coincidentally, this was also the first election in Canadian history in which the NDP won more seats than the Liberals. While Jack Layton's embrace of the median voter appeared from popular accounts to be an innovation, 2011 in fact represents the culmination of a long-term secular movement towards the centre in how the NDP presents itself to Canadians through its platforms. Is the NDP the newest brokerage party on the scene, or just the latest example of a formerly ideological party adopting a catch-all orientation and accordingly moving to the centre in its appeals?

The same cannot be asked of the Conservatives. Since 1972, the party has increasingly presented itself as more right-wing in its platforms. Two exceptions to the trend, in 1997 and 2000 as the Progressive Conservative Party struggled to find a place for itself in the context of a hostile electoral system, came to an abrupt end in 2004 as Harper, the Reform Party's first policy director, was by then firmly in control of the party (see Flanagan

2007). If the NDP has been in pursuit of the centre, then the Conservatives have been solidifying their support on the right and shifting the terms of public debate in that direction. As Harper claimed in his address to the 2011 Conservative convention following the election, "By saying what we will do and doing what we say, one step at a time we are moving Canada in a conservative direction. And Canadians are moving with us." Harper's argument that Conservatives are pulling the terms of Canadian political debate towards them – towards the right – should be taken seriously in light of the party dynamics illustrated in Figure 14.5.

We cannot simply focus on party platforms and ignore the voters themselves. If it is the case that the menu of Canadian political parties has moved to the right, we ought to expect that diners will have moved to the right as well. It doesn't make sense that parties will move in one direction while voters move in the other. In this light, we examined voters' perceptions of their own ideological leanings, as measured in the Canadian Election Studies over the last couple of decades. We cannot extend as far back in time as the Comparative Manifestos Project, but we go further back than 1993 in order to get a better sense of what has happened during the third party system and beyond.

Figure 14.6 depicts how voters perceived themselves ideologically over time. Voters were asked to place themselves on a left/right scale, and we recoded all responses to fit within a 0-1 scale, with 1 representing the most right-leaning voters and 0 representing the most left-leaning voters. As the upward slope indicates, since 1984 voters have moved further to the right on the ideological spectrum. The average self-placement on the 0-1 scale in 1984 was just over 0.44, indicating that voters felt they were slightly to the left of centre. In the most recent election, the average self-placement was just under 0.49, suggesting that there has been an increase of nearly 0.05 points in twenty-five years. Arguably, the bulk of the drop took place somewhere between the 1984 and 1993 elections – with the end of the third party system – but the fluctuation that took place after 1993 suggests that voters were trying to sort out how they felt about politics and about the political parties. It seems that since the 2000 election, in which the Canadian Alliance made its electoral debut, the move to the right has further solidified. Thus, as parties have moved to the right, voters have too. We know that Harper was correct when he said that Canadian voters were moving to the right. What we do not know is whether the parties led the voters or whether the voters led the parties.

FIGURE 14.6
Left/right ideological self-placement of voters over time, 1984-2011

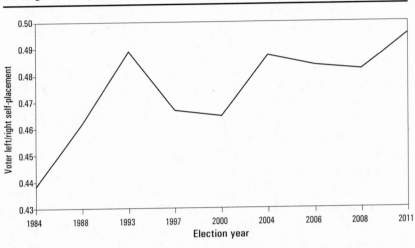

Note: The lower the self-placement value, the more left-leaning the voter.

Source: Based on data from Canadian Election Studies.

The Post-2011 Party System: A New Proposal

Canadian party systems are traditionally characterized by long periods of continuity punctuated by short periods of deviation. This is one point on which Canadian and comparative scholars of party systems agree. However, Canadians who began observing Canadian politics in the 1990s, or even in the 1980s, would find this idea strange, as, far from re-entering a new period of continuity, Canada's party system has since the 1980s changed over several times. By way of contrast, consider the second party system, in which Mackenzie King governed for no fewer than twenty-two years between 1921 and 1948.

Nevertheless, the results of the 1984 election marked the beginning of a familiar pattern: a Tory landslide followed shortly afterwards by a majority Liberal government. The Liberal government arrived on schedule two elections later, but this time brought with it two new parties, regionalist appeals, regionalized vote shares and party caucuses, and sharp ideological differences between the parties. Furthermore, the long period of Liberal government that was supposed to materialize never did; instead, the government was reduced to a minority a mere eleven years later. This curious detour from the familiar pattern of history brought with it new features that were important to the overall composition of the party system: the introduction of a new party finance system, the merger of the Canadian Alliance and the Progressive Conservative Party and an associated loss of one competitive party in the system, and the continued health of Quebec's bloc of separatist MPs.

What happened in 2004? Was this the end of Carty and colleagues' fourth party system (2000) and the country's entry into yet another deviating period? The election of Stephen Harper's Conservatives in the 2006 election suggests that this was in fact the case. Furthermore, the results of the 2011 election strongly suggest that the system has realigned and entered into a new period of stability, only this time presided over by the Tories rather than the Liberals. We wish to present this argument in the form of a modest proposal, for two reasons. First, as of this writing, the results of the 2011 election are only a few months old, and many Liberals have not yet picked up their jaws from the floor. Second, history, as the last twenty years of Canadian politics have demonstrated, is often not very instructive of what is to come.

Our new proposal is that the period from 2004 to 2011 be considered to constitute a deviating period in Canada's sequence of party systems. The 2004 election marked the conclusion of the short system of stable majority governments that had existed under Jean Chrétien and, briefly, Paul Martin. Minority governments are the first marker of instability. In addition, we suggest that the 2011 election marks a realignment of the Canadian party system into something new, enduring, and, most importantly, stable.

We think that four markers signal that the 2011 election represented such a realignment. First, in 2011, the country moved from a prolonged period of minority governments to the first majority government elected in eleven years, a movement from instability to stability. Chapter 3 captures only a small portion of the permanent campaign in which Canadian parties were engaged and to which they subjected Canadians in the minority period from 2004 to 2011. Minority governments meant the constant threat of government defeats and snap elections, which in turn led to seemingly daily hostility and brinkmanship among the parties, all reported in detail by the national media. Further, the realities of potential defeat shaped governments' legislative agendas. Whatever one thinks of Harper and his party, a majority government would appear to return Canadian politics to the days of the "peaceable kingdom."

The responses of the parties to the 2011 results appear to bear this out. The Conservative government has committed itself to fulfilling its election promises, to governing "without surprises," and to incrementally pulling Canada towards them and the right. Furthermore, the party's aversion to mega-constitutional reform, symbolized by the Conservatives' statute approach to recognizing Quebec as a distinct society and their commitment to reforming the Senate without amending the Constitution, ensures that Harper will not oversee a return to the "unquiet country" of the Trudeau and Mulroney majority governments.

The NDP, for its part, has committed to legitimizing itself as the government-in-waiting by conducting itself respectably in the House of Commons and by providing a clear policy contrast to the Conservatives. This was demonstrated in the new Official Opposition's long filibuster of the government's back-to-work legislation for Canada Post workers in 2011. The party has also turned its attention to consolidating its newfound strength in Quebec, which is necessary for maintaining its status as Quebec's new first party.

The once-great Liberal Party, for its part, appears to be convinced at long last that it no longer has the luxury of simply waiting out the Tories before it returns to government, and has turned its attention to the long, difficult task of organizational renewal. Recognizing the seriousness of the situation, the party in central office finally appeared to assert itself against the broken, emaciated party in public office, establishing a long waiting period before the vote to replace Michael Ignatieff as leader and a long list of requirements for candidates for that position, much to the consternation of some members of the caucus. Instability in the post-2011 party system will not result from the inward-looking Liberal Party, at least not in the short term.

The second marker of the new system relates to the Bloc Québécois. The 2011 election saw the virtual disappearance of the BQ, as the party was reduced to just four seats. The party's leader, Gilles Duceppe, also lost his seat. The BQ was one of two disruptive regional parties in the fourth party system. The Reform Party disappeared through its capture of the Progressive Conservative Party in 2004, its regionalist inclinations and rambunctious ideological spirit disciplined by power and the ever-present threat of defeat from 2006 to 2011. But the Bloc endured, largely as a result of a popular leader and a caucus composed of effective constituency politicians. When the party essentially ceased to exist in 2011, so too did the destabilizing regional party influences that entered the House in 1993. The result is that, while each of the three national parties have regions of strength and weakness, all of them are indeed national parties that are unlikely in the future to campaign with distinctively regionalist appeals.

Third, the institutional environment in which Canadian parties compete has lost some of the quirks that characterized it in the period between 2004 and 2011. We are thinking in particular of the system of party finance that rewarded parties for votes won, which the Conservatives promised to phase out while maintaining the ban on union and corporate contributions and limiting the amounts that individuals may contribute (see Young and Jansen 2011). While the subsidies were intended to turn the parties' attention from fundraising to more substantive matters, they instead had the unanticipated consequence of fuelling a fundraising arms race between the parties: when one party refused to rely exclusively on the subsidies and engaged in aggressive fundraising, the other parties were forced to do so as well. This was an arms race that the Conservatives, with their mass-style history of passing the KFC bucket around at small Reform Party gatherings, were bound to win, and that the Liberals, dependent for decades on the support of corporations and monied donors via celebrated party "bagmen," were destined to lose. The eradication of the system punishes the Liberal Party, which now must approach contributors cap-in-hand without even the title of "Government in Waiting" to use as leverage, and likely constitutes a death blow to the Bloc, which had become almost entirely dependent on state subsidies for funding. To the extent that the end of public subsidies will make it even more difficult for the Liberals and the Bloc to re-enter the scene as serious players, it contributes to the stability of the new post-2011 system.

Also related to institutional quirks leading up to the 2011 election was the inability of minority Conservative governments to redistribute constituency boundaries in a manner that accurately represents the changing populations of Canada's provinces (with several caveats, of course). Williams demonstrates in Chapter 9 how political opposition, particularly from the Liberals and the Bloc, contributed to the government's inability to move forward on this file. Now armed with a majority of seats in the House of Commons, Harper was able to push through legislation that was politically charged and impossible to pass during past minority governments, leading to a redistribution formula that adds seats where the Conservatives are strong.

Finally, and certainly most controversially, the 2011 election marked the beginning of a new system because, for the first time in a long while, it was clear that Canada no longer had a "natural governing party," and, if it did, it was no longer the Liberal Party of Canada. For most of the country's history, the Liberal Party was indeed the natural governing party, winning eighteen of the twenty-eight national elections held since the expansion of the franchise in 1918, and the short periods of Conservative rule that punctuated the country's political evolution did not change this fact. In recognition of this, Whitaker (1977) referred to the Liberal Party from the 1930s to 1950s as "the government party." For his part, Clarkson used the subtitle "How the Liberal Party Dominates Canadian Politics" in his 2005 account of the party.

The results of the 2011 election differed from previous Liberal debacles in two ways, however. First, it was the culmination of a substantial period of Liberal decline. Chrétien's majorities from 1993 to 2000 were manufactured by the electoral system from remarkably small percentages of the national vote. The party lost in 2006 and received its worst share of the national vote in its history in the 2008 election – that is, until 2011. Alarmingly, the party's traditional approach to maintenance of the party organization – abject neglect until disaster at the ballot box, and then serious attention to its renewal (e.g., Wearing 1981) – appeared to have been abandoned, and it was only after 2011 that the party appeared to begin addressing these tasks in earnest.

Most damagingly, the party, by virtue of having finished for the first time in Canadian history as neither the government nor the Official Opposition, has lost much of its reason to exist. More than any other Canadian party, the Liberal Party is similar to its American counterparts in being endogenous to the wishes and needs of ambitious politicians who require a reliable political vehicle in which to ride into public office (Aldrich 1995). Without its status as natural governing party, the Liberal Party cannot hope to attract the ambitious figures – Laurier, King, Trudeau, Chrétien – that enabled it to exist for so long as a successful party of the centre. This is not to say that the Liberal Party is dead, but the path back to power, or even to the benches of Her Majesty's Official Opposition, will be long and difficult. This degree of difficulty also contributes to the stability of the overall party system following the 2011 election.

In addition, Conservative pre-eminence in this new party system is enhanced by long-term trends in voter turnout. Many of the changes described in this book take place against the backdrop of another theme of continuity: declining voter turnout. From a high of roughly 70 percent at the outset of the fourth Canadian party system in 1993, turnout declined to 61 percent in the 2011 election. This last figure in fact represents a recovery of sorts from the 2008 national election, which saw the lowest turnout in Canadian history at 59 percent. It is important to keep in mind that as the politics of Canada has changed, the willingness of Canadians to fulfill their most basic democratic function has continued to decline. In one sense, a smaller electorate challenges parties to adapt, and the Conservatives have done so through targeting of their base. Low turnout tends to favour governments rather than oppositions, and it also favours parties of the right, as left-leaning parties' natural constituents are less likely to turn out to vote in the first place; accordingly, one headline following the 2011 outcome announced, "Low Voter Turnout Helps Deliver Conservative Majority" (Canadian Press 2011). Low voter turnout benefits the Conservatives and is an obstacle to both the Liberals and the NDP.

While we feel that these factors all point to party system realignment, we also consider this to be a modest proposal because there are two potential sources of party system change at play following the 2011 election.

The first sits in the last row in the far corner of the opposition benches: Green Party leader Elizabeth May. As Jansen and Lambert describe in Chapter 10, the Greens ham-handedly attempted to exploit the party finance system to break into the party system during the period examined here, and experienced some success, even gaining a seat at the table for May in the 2008 leaders' debate. SMP cruelly foiled their ambitions, however. The Greens finally learned in 2011 to work with, rather than against, the electoral system by pouring their resources into a single constituency where their leader was running. With May's election (even though the party received a lower share of the popular vote than in the 2008 election), the Greens have established a parliamentary toehold. This is a well-worn path to the breakthroughs of new parties, one travelled by, for example, Deborah Grey, the Reform Party's first MP in 1988. History therefore teaches that the Greens have a real opportunity to increase their seat share in subsequent elections, and so May represents one face of instability in post-2011 Canada. While it is difficult to imagine a large contingent of Green MPs in the House of Commons, the results of the 1993 election demonstrate how the unexpected can occur.

The second source of potential instability is Quebec and its latest *mariée*, the NDP. In 2011, many Quebec seats shifted from the Bloc to the NDP. The latter has traditionally had neither a strong provincial organization nor effective constituency associations in Quebec, and so does not normally attract strong candidates in the province. This was reflected in the post-2011 election media coverage of the NDP's new Quebec MPs, which highlighted their lack of experience and questioned their suitability for the job – it was clear that many had run as stopgap candidates and had not expected to win (see Sayers 1999).

The question is whether the NDP can consolidate those wins and build on the success of its candidates in order to construct an organization on the ground in Quebec that is capable of building on these gains in future elections. It is a tall order and it is not at all clear that the NDP will be successful. This is particularly true because of the death of party leader Jack Layton in 2011. Layton was popular in Quebec and was widely cited as the primary reason for the NDP's success there in the 2011 election. Without his leadership, the argument goes, the NDP will struggle to maintain its Quebec contingent. In the following year, one of the NDP's new Quebec MPs defected to the Liberals, claiming that her constituents had voted for Layton and that she therefore had no obligation to remain in the NDP caucus following his death. NDP failure in the next national election may lead to an entirely new crop of NDP MPs, with consequences for how we view the party system relative to previous elections. Much about the future of the Canadian party system remains to be seen.

That said, we are comfortable suggesting that Canadian party politics did not break down in 1993. It simply entered a system that brought to a close some of the consistent themes of previous Canadian party systems, such as regional brokerage on the part of the main players in the system. In retrospect, Carty and colleagues' fourth party system (2000) appears to represent the last period of Liberal majority governance, and the end of the party's status as Canada's "natural governing party." The Liberal Party's decline to minority status in 2004 closed the book on this comparably short system and brought Canadians into a period of instability that would eventually produce something new in 2011 that looks very different from previous systems. While it is risky to predict the future on the basis of a single case, we have tried to frame this argument in risk-averse terms. Nevertheless, the qualities we have ascribed to the 2011 national election accord well with both contemporary events and previous patterns of party system development in Canadian history.

And now we sit, restless and uncomfortable, waiting to see whether we are ultimately found to be correct in our prediction, or proven utterly wrong.

References

Aldrich, John. 1995. *Why Parties? The Origin and Transformation of Political Parties in America.* Chicago: University of Chicago Press.

Blondel, J. 1968. "Party Systems and Patterns of Government in Western Democracies." *Canadian Journal of Political Science* 1 (2): 180-203.

Cairns, Alan C. 1965. "The Electoral System and the Party System in Canada, 1921-65." *Canadian Journal of Political Science* 1 (1): 55-80.

Canadian Press. 2011. "Low Voter Turnout Helps Deliver Conservative Majority." CTV News British Columbia. http://www.ctvbc.ctv.ca/.

Caramani, Danièle. 2004. *The Nationalization of Politics: The Formation of National Electorates and Party Systems in Western Europe.* Cambridge: Cambridge University Press.

Carty, R.K. 1992. "Three Canadian Party Systems." In *Canadian Political Party Systems: A Reader,* edited by R.K. Carty, 563-86. Toronto: Broadview Press.

Carty, R. Kenneth, William Cross, and Lisa Young. 2000. *Rebuilding Canadian Party Politics.* Vancouver: UBC Press.

Clarkson, Stephen. 2005. *The Big Red Machine: How the Liberal Party Dominates Canadian Politics.* Vancouver: UBC Press.

Flanagan, Tom. 2007. *Harper's Team: Behind the Scenes in the Conservative Rise to Power.* Montreal and Kingston: McGill-Queen's University Press.

Gaines, Brian J. 1999. "Duverger's Law and the Meaning of Canadian Exceptionalism." *Comparative Political Studies* 32 (7): 835-61.

Johnston, Richard. 1980. "Federal and Provincial Voting: Contemporary Patterns and Historical Evolution." *Small Worlds: Provinces and Parties in Canadian Political Life,* edited by David J. Elkins and Richard Simeon, 131-78. Toronto: Methuen.

Key, V.O. 1955. "A Theory of Critical Elections." *Journal of Politics* 17 (1): 3-18.

Koop, Royce. 2011. *Grassroots Liberals: Organizing for Local and National Politics.* Vancouver: UBC Press.

Laver, Michael J., and Ian Budge, eds. 1992. *Party Policy and Government Coalitions.* New York: St. Martin's Press.

LeDuc, Lawrence. 1985. "Partisan Change and Dealignment in Canada, Great Britain, and the United States." *Comparative Politics* 17 (4): 379-98.

Sartori, Giovanni. 1976. *Parties and Party Systems: A Framework for Analysis.* Cambridge: Cambridge University Press.

Sayers, Anthony M. 1999. *Parties, Candidates, and Constituency Campaigns in Canadian Elections.* Vancouver: UBC Press.

Smith, David. 1985. "Party Government, Representation and National Integration in Canada." In *Party Government and Regional Representation in Canada,* edited by Peter Aucoin, 1-68. Toronto: University of Toronto Press.

Volkens, Andrea, Onawa Lacewell, Sven Regel, Henrike Schultze, and Annika Werner. 2010. *The Manifesto Data Collection. Manifesto Project (MRG/CMP/MARPOR).* Berlin: Wissenschaftszentrum Berlin für Sozialforschung (WZB).

Wearing, Joseph. 1981. *The L-Shaped Party: The Liberal Party of Canada, 1958-1980.* Toronto: McGraw-Hill Ryerson.

Whitaker, Reginald. 1977. *The Government Party: Organizing and Financing the Liberal Party of Canada, 1930-58.* Montreal and Kingston: McGill-Queen's University Press.

White, Linda A., Richard Simeon, Robert Vipond, and Jennifer Wallner, eds. 2008. *The Comparative Turn in Canadian Political Science.* Vancouver: UBC Press.

Wolinetz, Steven, ed. 1988. *Parties and Party Systems in Liberal Democracies.* London: Routledge.

Young, Lisa, and Harold J. Jansen, eds. 2011. *Money, Politics, and Democracy: Canada's Party Finance Reforms.* Vancouver: UBC Press.

Contributors

Blake Andrew is a Social Sciences and Humanities Research Council post-doctoral fellow in the Department of Political Science at the Université de Montréal. His research focuses on media and politics.

Amanda Bittner is an associate professor in the Department of Political Science at Memorial University of Newfoundland. She studies public opinion and voting, and her main research interests include the effects of knowledge and information on voters' decisions, as well as the institutional and structural incentives affecting voting behaviour.

Kelly Blidook is an associate professor of political science at Memorial University of Newfoundland. His research interests are in political and legislative behaviour, political representation, public opinion, and political institutions.

Matthew Byrne is a PhD student in the Department of Political Science at the University of British Columbia. His research interests are in political behaviour, public opinion, political communication, elections, and methodology.

R. Kenneth Carty is professor emeritus of political science at the University of British Columbia. His work focuses on the structure and organization of political parties in the established democracies.

William Cross is the Hon. Dick and Ruth Bell Chair for the Study of Canadian Parliamentary Democracy at Carleton University. His recent work is on intra-party democracy and organization.

Munroe Eagles is a professor of political science and director of the Canadian Studies Academic Program at the University at Buffalo–The State University of New York. His principal research interests are in the areas of Canadian political and electoral geography.

Patrick Fournier is a professor of political science at the Université de Montréal and principal investigator of the Canadian Election Study. His research interests include political psychology, elections, public opinion, citizen competence, and opinion change.

Elizabeth Goodyear-Grant is an associate professor of political science at Queen's University at Kingston. Her research focuses on Canadian and comparative politics, with particular interests in electoral politics, news media, and the political representation of women.

Allison Harell is an assistant professor in the Département de Science Politique at the Université du Québec à Montréal. Her research interests focus on diversity, public opinion, and democratic politics in Canada and other industrialized democracies.

Harold J. Jansen is an associate professor of political science at the University of Lethbridge. His research interests include political parties, party finance, and the impact of digital technologies on political communication and participation.

Richard Johnston is a professor of political science and Canada Research Chair in Public Opinion, Elections and Representation at the University of British Columbia. His central research preoccupation is with public opinion, elections, and representation, with special reference to campaign dynamics and the role of information.

Royce Koop is an assistant professor of political studies at the University of Manitoba. His research interests include political parties, representation, federalism, and municipal politics.

Lisa Lambert is a doctoral candidate at the University of Calgary. Her research interests include political parties, social movements, green parties, and women's political participation.

J. Scott Matthews is an associate professor of political science at Memorial University of Newfoundland and director of the Canadian Opinion Research Archive at Queen's University at Kingston. He studies elections, voting, and public opinion in Canada and the United States.

Anthony M. Sayers is an associate professor of political science at the University of Calgary. He is interested in the dynamics of political institutions, including political parties, electoral systems, legislatures, and federalism.

Stuart Soroka is an associate professor and William Dawson Scholar in the Department of Political Science at McGill University. His work focuses on the relationships between public opinion, public policy, and mass media.

Russell Alan Williams is an associate professor of political science at Memorial University of Newfoundland. His research focuses on Canadian public policy and political economy, with particular emphasis on the impact of globalization on the policy process.

Lisa Young is a professor of political science and dean of Graduate Studies at the University of Calgary. Her research interests include women's participation in public life, political party organization, and electoral finance.

Index

(intensification of), 120, 126, 134-35, 181, 189, 212, 238; discipline in, 66-72, 86; effective number of, 295, 314-15; evaluation of, 259, 261; finance laws, 215-17; finance system of, 324; funding, 7, 213, 217, 222, 224, 228, 278, 326, 328; identification of, 233, 236, 238, 241, 251; ideological beliefs in, 214; involvement, 32-33; leader evaluation in, 164; leaders, 14-16, 19-20, 41, 71-72, 95, 108-11, 216 275, 278, 325; in legislator, 3-5; main parties, 171, 172; major parties, 316; membership (marginalization), 213, 218; and mergers, 292; in the mind of voters, 5-6; and mobilization, 154-55; number of parties, 309, 310, 312; and party organization, 2, 10, 96, 109, 211-12, 218, 224, 226, 310, 327; platforms, 258; and professionalization, 212-13, 218-21, 227; pro-system, 285-87, 289; and redistribution, 185-210; regional support of 316-19; and strategies, 96, 252

political sophistication, 259, 261, 264, 273, 278-79

politicized apportionment, 185-210

population change, 197-201

population density, 97, 101; limitations of, 98

prime ministers, 95, 107, 109-10, 112. *See also names of individual prime ministers*

Prince Edward Island, 110, 186

Progressive Conservative Party of Canada, 2, 261, 290-91, 312-13, 315-22; candidates, 145; government, 1, 198; voters, 132, 147, 153, 189, 200, 203

Progressive Party of Canada, 287, 289-90

pro-life/choice, 69, 85, 89

proportional representation, 192-94, 198, 200, 203

Quarterly allowance, 215-8, 224, 226

Quebec, 188-89, 200-2, 289, 302-3, 313, 318-19, 324-25, 328-29

receive-accept-sample, 236-38

recruitment, 24-25, 30, 33, 39; gender differences, 30, 43; patterns in, 30-33; policies, 132

Reform Party: ideology, 319-20; merger, 289, 291, 325-26; origins, 1, 261; regionalism, 311-12, 316; support, 264, 273, 275; women, 277

regionalism, 146, 162, 172, 242, 273; and campaigns, 94, 97, 100; ministers, 108; and party caucuses, 312; regional variance, 175

regionalist parties, 311-12, 325; and appeals, 316

regionalization, 6, 108, 163-64, 169, 172, 180-81, 186, 310-11, 313, 315, 319

religion, 146, 277; and linguistic gap, 289, 303; of MPs, 76-77

Representation Act (1985), 186, 187-89, 192, 198, 200, 201; representation by population (section 52), 186-87, 192-95; section 51A, 186

reproductive technology (Bill C-13), 69, 75, 78, 88

revenue-sharing agreement (RSA), 220-22, 224-27, 249; formula for, 221

rhetorical attacks, 240-41, 249-50

ridings: characteristics and cabinet membership of, 101-8; diversity of, 113, rural, 99; urban, 99, 100, 102

right-of-centre parties, 46, 131

RILE, 319, 321; and Reform Party, 319

rural Canada, 39, 68, 78, 84-85, 94, 111-12

same-sex marriage, 69, 73-74, 89, 145

Saskatchewan, 188, 202; electoral map, 194

seat redistribution, 198-201; political obstacles to reform of, 195

self-selected candidates, 42-43

Printed and bound in Canada by Friesens

Set in Segoe and Warnock by Artegraphica Design Co. Ltd.

Copy editor: Francis Chow

Proofreader: Lana Okerlund